This study redresses the north and south imbalance of much work on economic and social history by focusing on the lives and economic impact of the building trade in the early-modern period in the context of the change from rural economy to the eve of industrialisation. The period 1450–1750 witnessed substantial changes in England: in the size of national population; the range of industry practised; the commodity structure and patterns of overseas trade; in agricultural techniques; and in the proportion of population tied to the soil. The evidence analysed in this book uses the nature of building and labouring work to consider the variations in wages and living standards allied to studies of individual towns. Using many hitherto unworked sources from local archives, the author addresses conditions of work in the building trades, levels of remuneration, the characteristics of the life-cycles of male and female workers, gender differences in work, and relationships with employers – at times running counter to the prevailing orthodoxies.

Men at work

*Cambridge Studies in Population, Economy and
Society in Past Time 26*

Series Editors

PETER LASLETT, ROGER SCHOFIELD, and E.A. WRIGLEY

ESRC Cambridge Group for the History of Population and Social Structure

Recent work in social, economic and demographic history has revealed much that was previously obscure about societal stability and change in the past. It has also suggested that crossing the conventional boundaries between these branches of history can be very rewarding.

This series exemplifies the value of interdisciplinary work of this kind, and includes books on topics such as family, kinship, and neighbourhood; welfare provision and social control; work and leisure; migration; urban growth; and legal structures and procedures, as well as more familiar matters. It demonstrates that, for example, anthropology and economics have become as close intellectual neighbours to history as have political philosophy or biography.

For a full list of titles in the series, please see end of book

Men at Work

Labourers and building craftsmen in the towns of northern England, 1450–1750

DONALD WOODWARD

University of Hull

CAMBRIDGE
UNIVERSITY PRESS

Published by the Press Syndicate of the University of Cambridge
The Pitt Building, Trumpington Street, Cambridge CB2 1RP
40 West 20th Street, New York, NY 10011–4211, USA
10 Stamford Road, Oakleigh, Melbourne 3166, Australia

First published 1995

Printed in Great Britain at the University Press, Cambridge

A catalogue record for this book is available from the British Library

Library of Congress cataloguing in publication data
Woodward, Donald.
Men at work: labourers and building craftsmen in the towns of
northern England, 1450–1750 / Donald Woodward.
p.   cm.
Cambridge studies in population, economy, and society in past time; (26)
Includes bibliographical references.
ISBN 0 521 47246 6
1. Building trades – England, Northern – Employees – History.
2. Construction workers – England, Northern – History.
3. Building trades – England, Northern – History.
4. Construction industry – England, Northern – History.
5. England, Northern – Economic conditions.
6. England, Northern – Social conditions.
7. Wages – Building trades – England, Northern – History.
8. Wages – Construction workers – England, Northern – History.
9. Cost and standard of living – England, Northern – History.
10. Cities and towns – England, Northern – History.
11. England, Northern – Population – History.
I. Title. II. Series.
HD8039.B92G78   1995
331.7′624′09427 – dc20   94–15930   CIP

ISBN 0 521 47246 6 hardback

FOR HILARY

Contents

Tables

Appendices

Preface

During the early 1980s the newly formed Economic and Social Research Council launched an initiative to support research investigating shifts in living standards since the Middle Ages under the aegis of John Hatcher. Various meetings were convened to chart the way ahead and a number of research proposals were supported: they included my own project, North Eastern Labour Markets 1550 to 1750, which was granted £28,420 and was funded for two years from February 1986. The grant was used chiefly to employ a full-time research assistant capable of coping with the intricacies of sixteenth and seventeenth-century hands. The post was filled for twenty months by Diana O'Hara and for the remaining four months by Ann Bennett. I am extremely grateful to both of them for their great diligence and accuracy. The work of collecting the data took three years: most of the work on the Hull council records was completed by Diana, who also did a great deal of work on the York records and some work at Newcastle. Ann worked mainly on the records of Beverley, Durham, and Chester. Work on the Chester records signalled that the project had begun to change shape to cover the whole of the north of England. I covered much of the new ground myself: along with my wife Hilary, who accompanied me on many research forays, I was responsible for the collection of data for Carlisle, Kendal, and Lincoln, and at various times collected a great deal of information from all of the other record offices. In particular I did most of the work on the gild records of Chester, Newcastle, and York. The project also began to move backwards in time to the middle of the fifteenth century, partly because of the discovery of the rich records of Hull Trinity House which I worked on myself. I am extremely grateful to all the archivists who serviced our many requests with such smiling efficiency, and provided so many unexpected cups of tea. I am also extremely grateful to the Elder Brethren of Hull Trinity House who allowed me access to their records and subsequently appointed me as their Honorary Archivist in 1991.

In the course of researching and writing this book I have accumulated many other debts. Writing began in the Summer term of 1990. I was granted study leave from my post at Hull which was spent at Wolfson College, Cambridge, as a visiting scholar. The warm welcome I received both there and at the ESRC Cambridge Group for the History of Population and Social Structure made writing seem like a pleasant hobby: during that period I benefited substantially from conversations with Tony Wrigley, Richard Wall, Larry Poos, and especially with Jeremy Boulton. Our stay in Cambridge was made the more rewarding by the friendship and hospitality of John Hatcher of Corpus Christi College, John Lonsdale of Trinity College, Brian Outhwaite of Gonville and Caius College, and their families. Invitations to air some of my views at research seminars have proved extremely rewarding: at Cambridge (the seminar run by Brian Outhwaite and Keith Wrightson), at Oxford (Ann Kussmaul and Richard Smith), East Anglia (Richard Wilson), and at the Catholic University of America, Washington, D.C. (Larry Poos). My colleagues at Hull have also heard a great deal about labour markets in early-modern England both in a formal seminar setting and over coffee. I am particularly indebted to David Richardson and Michael Turner, and to my great friend and mentor K.R. Andrews, who have been such willing listeners for so many years. Valuable assistance was also rendered by Eric Evans, James Foreman-Peck, Rosemary Horrox, Audrey Howes, David Palliser, Robin Pearson, Douglas Reid, Christopher Smout, John Treble, Stephen Trotter, and Simon Vicary. Additionally, I owe an enormous debt of gratitude to Richard Fisher of the Cambridge University Press, and to Roger Schofield and Tony Wrigley, the editors of the series. Their suggestions have made this a shorter and better book.

Finally, this book is dedicated to my wife, without whose support it would not have been completed.

Abbreviations

The following abbreviations have been adopted for the various record offices visited

CCORO	Cheshire County Record Office, Chester
CCRO	Chester City Record Office, Chester
CUMROC	Cumbria County Record Office, Carlisle
CUMROK	Cumbria County Record Office, Kendal
DCRO	Durham County Record Office, Durham
DFC	Five the College, Durham
DPK	Prior's Kitchen, Dean and Chapter Muniments, Durham
HCORO	Humberside County Record Office, Beverley
HCRO	Hull City Record Office, Hull
HTH	Hull Trinity House Archives, Hull
HUA	Hull University Archives, Hull
LAO	Lincolnshire Archives Office, Lincoln
LCRO	Lancashire County Record Office, Preston
NCRO	Northumberland County Record Office, Newcastle
PRO	Public Record Office, London
TWAS	Tyne and Wear Archives Service, Newcastle
YBI	Borthwick Institute of Historical Research, York
YCA	York City Archives, York
YML	York Minster Library, York

The following abbreviations have also been adopted

Acct	Account
CW	Churchwardens' accounts

1

Introduction

Two essentially different types of workmen are considered in this book, labourers and building craftsmen. Although they could often be found working side by side, their position in the labour market and the niches they occupied in urban society were markedly different. Labourers were often called in to assist their more skilled neighbours, but they frequently worked in gangs, large and small, on tasks which did not involve craftsmen: they cleansed the highways, emptied latrine barrels, scoured ditches, removed dead horses from fresh water-channels, and accomplished a thousand and one tasks which did not require specialist skills. They, and their rural counterparts, were the true wage-earners of late-medieval and early-modern England, selling their labour for cash, although it is not to be imagined that, even in the towns, they derived the whole of their incomes from wage-earning. Labourers were usually hired by the day, and provided by their employers with the tools and raw materials with which they worked.

Building craftsmen were a different breed. Strictly speaking many of them were not wage-earners in the modern sense of the term. Master craftsmen were 'small masters' or petty entrepreneurs, possessing their own tools and often supplying the raw materials for the task in hand.[1] In addition to their own labour they were often accompanied by an apprentice and one or more journeymen, who were in a state of dependency, working only for their wages and, in some cases, for their keep. But the position of some journeymen was not permanent, and they could dream of joining the ranks of the town masters or moving to a more independent position elsewhere.[2] In supplying raw materials and the labour of others early-modern building craftsmen

---

[1] Woodward 1981; Knoop & Jones 1949, 94–5.   [2] See below pp. 64–72.

1

resemble the small-scale jobbing plumbers and joiners of modern times, who make profits from their activities in addition to the 'wages' they receive for the hire of their own time, rather than the true wage-earners who toil on the shop floor. Nevertheless, in early-modern accounts building craftsmen frequently resemble wage-earners pure and simple. This is because of the nature of much building work. A shoemaker, tailor, or candle-maker could incorporate the value of his labour – and that of his assistants – in the selling price of an easily recognised and easily valued final product. Such artisans, working with their own tools in their own workshops and marketing their own products, have long been recognised as small-scale, independent producers: 'the worker is, in a sense, his own employer, making and selling his own product, and retaining for himself any surplus or "net revenue" above the cost of his own materials and his own subsistence'.[3] For building craftsmen things were not so simple. Sometimes they worked by the piece – paving at so much a square yard or casting lead at so much a stone – and sometimes they contracted to build a structure for a set price, but often this was neither possible nor desirable. More frequently, building craftsmen were paid according to the value of the inputs they made, their labour being paid for at a set rate by the day. But the receipt of such a 'wage' did not convert the early-modern building craftsman into a wage-earner in the modern sense. According to the accounts of the larger institutions of northern England, some building craftsmen were employed for weeks or months on end on the same project, and they take on the appearance of wage-earners: but when the same men worked for a day or two repairing broken pews or damaged flagstones in their parish churches they appear in their true colours as independent businessmen, providing raw materials and any extra labour needed.

When discussing building craftsmen historians think of those who set them to work as their employers. But this is to mistake the relationship. Master craftsmen were hired for a particular task by their customers. When jobs continued over long periods, and particularly when the customer provided the raw materials, the craftsman closely resembled a wage-earner, but he did not lose his basic independence. Once the project was complete the craftsman would move on to work for another customer. Of course the journeymen involved remained with their employers, the master craftsmen: such journeymen were true proletarians.

Previous attempts to discuss shifts in living standards in early-

[3] Dobb 1960, 3–4.

modern England have been based predominantly on the mass of wage and price data collected by Thorold Rogers and Beveridge, mostly for the south east. This material, digested for more widespread consumption by Phelps Brown and Sheila Hopkins in the 1950s, demonstrated that, starting from a high point in the later fifteenth century, the living standards of building workers and labourers drifted downwards for much of the sixteenth and first half of the seventeenth centuries, before recovering somewhat in the later seventeenth and early eighteenth centuries.[4] The belief that the study of the wage rates of a single segment of the labour market in relation to price movements could stand as a proxy for more general changes in the quality of life has been widely criticised. It has been argued that many workers were not so dependent on their wages as they are today and often derived only a part of their needs from the market. Moreover, we may know a great deal about wage rates, but little about annual incomes since we remain ignorant of the number of days worked each year. Additionally, some workers were cushioned against the full rigours of rising prices by being fed by those who set them to work. The prices used to construct cost-of-living indices are wholesale prices rather than the retail prices which affected ordinary consumers and which rose less steeply during inflationary periods.[5] A further problem, and one not previously confronted, is that the mass of data accumulated for the south-east of England has not been tested against material from other regions. This book will attempt to confront each of these issues through the discussion of large amounts of information derived from the wide range of accounts available for the north of England over the three centuries after 1450.

Readers of this book may wonder why building workers are being subjected to such detailed examination. Have we not heard enough about their earnings and work practices from others?[6] Why not study other groups of urban workers? One answer is that this book is not simply about building workers: there is also a great deal of discussion of labourers, who often worked independently of building craftsmen. Nevertheless, much time is devoted to building workers. This is unavoidable, since information about other kinds of workers is extremely scarce. The research on which this book is based has uncovered information relating to the payments made for many scores of thousands of man-days completed by labourers and building craftsmen, but there are only four references to the wages paid to other types of

[4] Rogers 1882–7; Beveridge 1939; Brown & Hopkins 1981.
[5] For a review of this literature, see Woodward 1981, 29–31; Rappaport 1989, 151–3.
[6] Rogers 1908; Knoop & Jones 1949; Salzman 1952; Brown & Hopkins 1981.

craftsmen: at York in 1538 a tailor helped for seven-and-a-half days making new vestments and copes for St Michael's, Spurriergate, and he was paid 6d a day, the rate the carpenters and tilers were receiving; at Hull in 1585 a fletcher was employed at 9d a day for twenty-nine days, and nearly half a century later a Newcastle fletcher received 16d for a day's work – in each case building craftsmen were being paid at the same rate; finally, 8d was paid 'to the tree-lopper for one day's work' at Hull Trinity House in 1619, which was the standard rate for labourers at the time.[7] It is impossible from such snippets of information to comment on the typicality of the levels of pay received by labourers and building craftsmen, but there seems little reason to doubt that the real wages of many other workers deteriorated during the years of inflation, and that the experiences of labourers and building craftsmen will stand proxy for other manual workers. In a period characterised by generous supplies of labour it is unlikely that most members of the labouring population would have fared significantly better than others for more than short intervals.[8] Moreover, although the evidence she used was not particularly plentiful, this was the position taken by Elizabeth Gilboy: she believed that building-trade wages in eighteenth-century London were not seriously unrepresentative of the manual trades in general.[9]

The variety of projects which involved the hire of labourers and building craftsmen was extraordinarily wide. Some projects were enormous. During the 1540s hundreds of workmen were gathered together for two major projects – the construction of Tynemouth Castle and the erection of new defences on the eastern bank of the river Hull to secure the harbour: unfortunately the detailed accounts of neither project have survived although more than £21,000 was spent at Hull in just over two years.[10] At the other extreme, labourers and building craftsmen were often employed for a day or two, or sometimes for part of a day, to make some minor repair or refurbishment. In 1666 the accountant at Hull Trinity House paid 6d 'for mortaring holes in the sail chamber where rats got in', and in 1720 the churchwardens of St Mary's paid the bricklayer, John Wiseman, 18d for 'paving over Benjamin Blaydes' grave': he got only 6d for the smaller task of 'paving over Mr Wilberforce's child's grave'.[11]

[7] YBI, PR/Y/MS/1, fo. 143v; HCRO, BRF/3/5; TWAS, 659/446; HTH, III, fo. 219r.
[8] A similar comment was made by Joel Mokyr at the conference on pre-industrial consumption patterns held at the Institute of Historical Research, London, on 2 May 1992.
[9] Gilboy 1934, 18–19.   [10] Colvin 1982, 472–7, 682–4; *VCH Hull*, 414.
[11] HTH, V; HCORO, PE/185/35, fo. 3r.

The accounts of churches, large and small, have provided a large amount of information for this project, although most new building and much of the large-scale work related to secular buildings, especially after the Reformation. The spectacular phase of church building was largely over by the later fifteenth century. The most evocative echo of an earlier age is provided by the accounts of the churchwardens for Louth which detail the erection of the church's soaring steeple in the first two decades of the sixteenth century at a cost of nearly £300.[12] But most churchwardens' accounts merely record the daily minutiae of small-scale repair work, or larger projects which could not be put off any longer: in 1657 the churchwardens of St Mary's, Chester, dutifully recorded the long process of mending the steeple and bells 'ruined by fire in the late war'. At the same church one of the most common tasks began to cause difficulty in the late sixteenth century:

Whereas 12d was paid for a 'leastall' or burial place in the church within the forms, and 16d in the aisles out of the forms, and very many desired to lie in the church because of the small charges; insomuch that great inconvenience has happened, and the church almost filled with new graves, with great danger both to infect the people with noisome smells of dead bodies too timely taken up, and likewise (which is most horrible) to crush in pieces and break asunder with spades the flesh and bones of Christian bodies before they were half rotten.

An additional problem lay in the cost of 'taking up and setting down forms, and paying for tiles and covering graves'. The church authorities took steps to husband their scarce resource by increasing the fee for those wishing to be buried in the church to 3s 4d for parishioners and to 10s for outsiders.[13] The accounts of the cathedrals of Durham, Lincoln, and York also furnish a great deal of the material. At times major jobs were in hand, such as the complete renewal of the lead covering of the roof of Lincoln Cathedral during the 1660s,[14] but as in the lesser churches much of the work involved routine day-to-day repairs.

The records of the civic authorities provide even more information. Town councils spent a great deal of money making urgent repairs to their property and, more occasionally, building new structures. At Carlisle, repairs were frequently made to the town hall, while at Kendal much of the work involved repairs to the town mill and its weir.[15] At the ports of Chester, Hull, and Newcastle large sums had to be spent repairing wharfs, jetties, and staithes. A petition from the Hull

---

[12] *Louth Accts.*   [13] CCORO, P/20/13/1.   [14] See below pp. 21, 42, 43.
[15] CUMROC, Ca/4/1–6; CUMROK, WSMB/K.

council to Elizabeth I mentioned expenditure on the jetties damaged 'through the great rage of the water of Humber', and in the mid seventeenth century blame was placed on 'the last raging wind and spring tide which broke forth at the foul south end'.[16] In April 1668 a large band of carpenters and labourers, supplemented for a day by ten soldiers, struggled to close a breach on the east bank of the river Hull. New piles were prepared, and Richard Emerson, the chief carpenter, spent six days 'fitting the gin and setting stages for driving piles'. The whole job, which was completed by the end of May, involved 328 man-days. This was just a small part of the substantial programme of work maintained by the Hull council which included expensive repairs to the town defences: in the twenty-six years after 1653/4 the council spent an annual average on such works of just under £290, ranging from the £52 spent in the first year to £726 spent in 1672/3.[17]

The most spectacular single project mounted by a town council was the rebuilding of Ouse Bridge at York after the wooden structure had been swept away in January 1565. During the hard winter of 1564/5 ice had piled up against the timbers of the old bridge and a sudden thaw on 6 January caused 'such a water that it overthrew two bows with one arch and twelve houses standing upon the same bridge, and by the fall thereof was drowned twelve persons'. Detailed accounts of the rebuilding have not survived, but the summary accounts make it plain that a temporary wooden pontoon bridge 'with ketches lying under the same' was thrown across the river at a cost of nearly £180. Just over £121 was spent for 'making one ark or case [a coffer dam] and a jetty for avoiding the water, that the masons may work Ouse Bridge that was cast down with the great flood'. The cost of the whole enterprise is not known. The new bridge had six arches and was referred to by Camden as 'a stone bridge, with the largest arch I have ever seen', and it continued to excite visitors to the city until it was replaced in the early nineteenth century.[18]

Valuable information has also been drawn from the accounts of the Trinity Houses of both Hull and Newcastle. At Newcastle the accounts do not begin until the 1620s, but they are particularly useful for the 1630s when a substantial rebuilding programme was put in hand. The Hull accounts, by contrast, begin in the 1460s and run to the end of the period in a sequence seriously broken only in the late fifteenth and

---

[16] HCRO, BRL/1397; BRF/3/20, p. 31. The 'Foul South End' was so called because rubbish was customarily heaved into the Humber at that point.
[17] HCRO, BRF/3/20.
[18] Palliser 1979, 266–7; YCA, CC5, fos. 113–20; *York Descriptions*, 8, 11, 20–1, 23, 25, 33. See also the many references in *YCR*, VI.

early sixteenth centuries. As well as maintaining the fabric of the House and other properties, a great deal was spent on the buoys and beacons which marked the Humber, and on the 'dolphin', a piled stucture in the mouth of the river Hull used to warp vessels in and out of the haven. A new dolphin, which involved the use of 'the gin to drive piles' was built in the summer of 1656 at a cost of £152 12s 10d.[19] Extensive repairs were necessary from time to time when the structure was damaged by the action of the tides or negligence of the ships' masters whose vessels collided with it.

Most of the evidence for this study is derived from the surviving records of public and private institutions, but it seems likely that the bulk of the work of both labourers and building craftsmen was for private customers whose records have not survived. Much of their time was probably spent doing small jobs which involved their moving from site to site, often working in different places during a single week, much as small jobbing building craftsmen do today. Indeed, thin though the evidence is, it must be suspected that for many 'life was a constant round of repairing doors, windows, roofs and pavements'.[20]

Any division of the country into regions is bound to be somewhat arbitrary and for the purpose of this book the north of England is taken to be the area north of a line drawn between Chester and Lincoln. This will upset those who would place Lincoln in the East Midlands, although the town is as far north as Chester, and Hull – regarded by Newcastle folk as being a long way south – is as far north as Preston. Perceptions of what is the north are bedevilled by the behaviour of the Scottish border which runs crazily in a north-north-east direction from Carlisle, leaving Lincoln some 200 miles from its eastern end, but Chester only about 130 miles from its western extremity. Within this northern region towns have not been chosen for study at random, nor for their long-term economic significance: those places which feature prominently in the account which follows appear because of the quality and quantity of their records. The major focus is on towns which were either ancient boroughs – Carlisle, Chester, Durham, Hull, Lincoln, Newcastle, and York – or, like Beverley and Kendal, were incorporated in the later sixteenth century. The bureaucracies of such towns compiled a range of accounts which are not available for towns such as Leeds, Manchester, and Sheffield, which were beginning to make a major impact on the urban hierarchy of the region by the end of the period. The only other northern town which grew to great

[19] HTH, V.   [20] Swanson 1983, 31.

significance during the period but rarely features in the following account is Liverpool: its growth came late and it was still small and overshadowed by Chester at the outbreak of the Civil War. Apart from its magnificent Town Books Liverpool does not have the type of records needed for this study.[21]

Some of the places whose records have been studied in detail were important urban centres with an influence which spread far beyond their immediate hinterlands. York was the great jewel of the medieval north, and although by the early sixteenth century it had become a shadow of its former self it was still one of the largest provincial towns in the kingdom with a population of some 8,000 in 1550. During Elizabeth's reign the city recovered and its population rose to an estimated 10,000 in 1600 and to 12,000 by 1630. Thereafter numbers stabilised until the later eighteenth century, although the city remained an important regional capital, providing the focus for the economic and social life of a broad area.[22] Both Newcastle and Hull prospered as ports from the second half of the sixteenth century. Newcastle, which gained enormously from the meteoric rise of the coal trade and the development of ancillary industries, also had important trading connections with the Baltic and its population rose from an estimated 7,500 or less in the early sixteenth century to 10,000 in 1600, and 14,000 by 1700. By the 1730s the population was approaching 30,000, perhaps four times as large as it had been in the late Middle Ages.[23] Hull was much smaller, but its merchants pursued a lively trade with the Baltic and nearby areas of western Europe. The size of the population in the sixteenth century is uncertain, but it stood at around 6,000 in the early decades of the seventeenth century and had approximately doubled by the end of the period, with much of the growth coming in the last few decades. Hull benefited from the growth of overseas trade in the later seventeenth and early eighteenth centuries, and also from its position at the entrance of an extensive river network.[24] Both Hull and Newcastle possessed excellent harbour facilities and they were both of great strategic importance, playing crucial roles in the Civil War. However, unlike Newcastle, Hull did not change hands during the conflict, holding out for parliament despite two sieges.[25] Chester, with a population of some 5,000 in the early 1560s, was an important regional capital, serving a wide hinterland,

[21] *Liverpool Town Books.*
[22] Bartlett 1959–60, 32–3; Palliser 1979, 1–22, 111–13; *VCH York*, 160–253.
[23] Howell 1967, 2–9; Palliser 1982, 351; P. Clark 1981, 16, 26; Law 1972, 25.
[24] *VCH Hull*, 157–8, 190; Davis 1964; Jackson 1972, 2; Law 1972, 26; R.W. Unwin 1971.
[25] Howell 1967; *VCH Hull*, 102–7.

and a port of modest pretensions. The population grew from nearly 6,000 in 1600 to a peak of nearly 7,500 at the Restoration, before falling back to about 6,500 in 1700.[26] But the growth of population may not have been associated with economic vitality. The city's trade developed modestly in the first four decades of the seventeenth century, although the dynamic new trade in Irish livestock was almost entirely controlled by Irish interests, and after 1660 the port was increasingly overshadowed by the rapid growth of Liverpool.[27] The five remaining towns on which this book is based – Beverley, Carlisle, Durham, Kendal, and Lincoln – were smaller for much of the period and at least three of them had been of more significance in medieval times than they were in the early-modern period. Both Beverley and Lincoln failed to recover losses sustained in the medieval period. Beverley, ranked as the tenth town in the realm in 1377, lost its cloth industry but was said to have had a population of about 5,000 in the mid sixteenth century, which may have made it larger than Hull. However, the town's economic fortunes continued to decline and by the later seventeenth century its population was no more than 3,000; modest growth thereafter may have boosted numbers to about 3,500 in 1750.[28] Lincoln, dominated like Beverley by its great medieval minster, had passed the peak of its fortunes by the sixteenth century: in 1377 it had stood fifth in the list of English towns and was one of the major national centres of the wool trade. In the sixteenth century its population was less than 5,000, perhaps considerably so, and the town remained 'a sleepy little city' into the eighteenth century when its population probably numbered no more than 3,000.[29] Durham, perhaps more than any of the other towns discussed here, was dominated both physically and economically by its massive cathedral and associated ecclesiastical administration. Like Beverley and Lincoln, the town was probably at the peak of its fortunes in the medieval period when it was the administrative headquarters of the Bishop of Durham's great estates, although it remained 'a relatively small market town throughout the Middle Ages'. Its population, which was probably between 3,000 and 4,000 in the sixteenth century had, perhaps, grown to 4,500 by the middle of the eighteenth century.[30] But Durham, no more than fifteen miles from Newcastle, shares with Beverley – which was some eight

[26] Alldridge 1986, 2, 35; Woodward 1970b.
[27] Clemens 1976; Stephens 1969; Woodward 1970c and 1973.
[28] Phythian-Adams 1979, 16; *VCH Beverley*, 80, 83, 85, 87, 105, 107–8, 118–19; Law 1972, 26.
[29] Hill places the population of sixteenth-century Lincoln at *c.* 2000 which Phythian-Adams feels is much too low: Hill 1956, 22–3; Phythian-Adams 1979, 12, 14, 16. For the eighteenth century see Hill 1966, 146.
[30] Bonney 1990, 7; Phythian-Adams 1979, 12; Law 1972, 23.

miles from Hull – the characteristic of being relatively close to a more dynamic centre of economic activity, and it will be interesting to compare the movement of wages in the two sets of towns.[31]

In the far north-west the records of Carlisle and Kendal provide substantial amounts of information relating to the labour process and shifts in levels of remuneration. Neither was large, even by contemporary standards. Carlisle probably housed around 2,000 in 1563 and no more than twice that number in the later seventeenth century. It was, perhaps, a town of 'trivial pretension' when set against the larger provincial towns, but it was 'nonetheless the dominant centre of a topographically secluded area', the regional capital of the far north-west and the traditional English bulwark of the western marches against the warlike Scots.[32] Further south, on the eastern fringes of the Lake District, Kendal, which gave its name to the local woollen cloth or 'cottons' traded throughout the country and overseas, had a population of between 2,000 and 3,000 in the later years of Elizabeth's reign and seems to have been no larger a century later. In the late seventeenth century it 'was still very much a country town', but it experienced considerable industrial development in the following century and its population had about doubled by the later 1750s.[33]

Small amounts of information can also be garnered from the fragmentary accounts of a number of sleepy little market towns in the north of England. They include Appleby and Penrith in the north-west, Louth in Lincolnshire, and Howden and Bridlington in east Yorkshire. With populations of less than 1,500 for much of the period they remained of little economic significance, serving narrow hinterlands, but the evidence derived from their records can occasionally provide a telling example in the account which follows.[34]

The period chosen for this book runs from the late medieval ages to the eve of industrialisation. Substantial changes took place in England: in the size of the national population; in the range of industries practised throughout the country; in the commodity structure and geographical patterns of overseas trade; in agricultural techniques; and in the proportion of the population permanently tied to the soil. Some of these changes affected the towns under consideration: Hull and Newcastle, in particular, developed considerably as their merchants sought to expand their activities. But in many respects pre-1750 England was a

---

[31] See below pp. 164, 202–3.
[32] Phythian-Adams 1979, 10, 15; James 1951, 137–41; Clark, Gaskin & Wilson 1989, 25–6.
[33] B.C. Jones 1960; Phillips 1981, 57–61; Marshall 1975, 189–223.
[34] Clark, Gaskin, & Wilson 1989, 27–8, 109–10, 179–80, 191–2.

society which altered slowly, and many traditional ways of life and economic organisation continued unchanged from generation to generation. Certainly it is difficult to detect any significant changes in the lifestyles of northern labourers and building craftsmen: their methods of working changed little; firms remained small to the end of the period; and the patterns of their lives altered hardly at all. It is possible to detect some waning in the strength and efficacy of the gilds; in some towns this seems to have occurred in the seventeenth century, in others in the eighteenth century. But apart from this the worlds of the labourers and building craftsmen barely changed, and the major economic and social developments, which pointed forward to the period of industrialisation, were taking place elsewhere. Historians dependent on a study of the lives of labourers and building craftsmen in the towns of northern England would not be aware that the pace of change was beginning to accelerate elsewhere.

This book is arranged in six main chapters followed by a series of appendices which lay out the statistical data on which some of the argument is based. Chapter 2 contains a discussion of the work practices and arrangements of building craftsmen: the types of work they did; the size of their businesses; their relative levels of pay; and other aspects of their patterns of work. The next chapter follows the craftsmen through their life-cycle experiences. The arrangement of the discussion – the apprentice, the journeyman, the master craftsman, and the role of the widow – seems to confirm the traditional view that most skilled men within a particular town followed the same sequence of experiences, ending up as independent masters in charge of their own businesses. But in many of the northern towns entry to the apprentice ranks was tightly controlled in order to limit the number of potential masters, and many journeymen – who had no chance of becoming master craftsmen in the town – were recruited from outside. Their period of service could last some years or just a few months, after which they moved on, either to become journeymen elsewhere or to set themselves up in business away from the regulation of the gilds. If this was the experience of skilled men in other areas of trade, the town labour forces were more fluid than the traditional approach would suggest.

In chapter 4 labourers are dealt with more briefly, since less is known of their activities: frequently they were not named in the accounts, which makes it difficult to recreate their work patterns. However, it is possible to establish the levels of pay they received, and the kinds of work they did. Moreover, we know that the great bulk of general labouring was done by men: women and children did work, but at a very low level. Chapter 5 brings the labourers and craftsmen together and discusses areas of common experience. Most labourers and building craftsmen worked away from home, although some of the craftsmen – especially the joiners, glaziers, plumbers, and black-smiths – spent at least some of their time in their workshops. Most of the workmen were paid by the day, the length of which was carefully regulated by national and local authorities: mostly they worked a day of ten to twelve hours, six days a week, when work was available. Some men worked most of the days available in a year, although work for most was highly seasonal with relatively little wage employment being offered in the winter. Two traditional buffers against privation – the acquisition of non-food perquisites and the provision of food and drink at the workplace – are examined in some detail. It is concluded that, despite some notable exceptions, non-food perquisites were not on offer to most workmen (although embezzlement may have been rife) and few workers were given their full diet at work (although small drink allowances were common). Similarly, it seems that those injured at work could expect little financial assistance from those who paid them. The chapter ends with a discussion of the extent to which labour moved from town to town, and from town to the countryside, and a brief examination of the types of supervision exercised over workmen.

In some respects chapter 6 contains the most difficult and the most tentative arguments. The first section lays out the broad changes which took place in northern wage rates over the three centuries and sets them against series for other parts of the country. The picture established for southern England by Phelps Brown and Hopkins is broadly confirmed for the north. Wage rates stagnated down to *c*.1540, but rose thereafter, although they remained at the same level, often for decades at a time, and followed sluggishly the inflation in commodity prices. Wage rates, especially for craftsmen, did not rise to the same extent in the different towns. By the later seventeenth century the northern towns had separated out into two groups: a group of towns in which rates were relatively high – Hull, York, Newcastle, and Beverley – and a group in which rates were relatively low – Carlisle, Chester, Durham, Kendal, and Lincoln. Labourers' rates varied less from town to town. As a result, the traditional ratio of 3:2 between the rates given to craftsmen and those paid to labourers altered in some places – and especially in the high-wage towns – until craftsmen received twice the rates going to the less skilled men. The second part of chapter 6 comprises a tentative examination of the factors which may have determined the timing of changes in the level of wage rates. It is argued that, although both the regulation of wages and the effect of custom played their parts, the main factor determining change was the interaction between the demand for labour and its supply. Labour was often in abundant supply in early-modern England, with demand often insufficient to mop it up. But labour did not remain passive in all situations, and the withdrawal of labour – or the threat thereof – probably helps to account for the fact that wage rates tended to move upwards during or after periods of rapid inflation, in which the living standards of wage-earners had taken a particularly severe beating.

The book concludes with a discussion of the living standards of labourers and building craftsmen in northern England. The great difficulty with traditional approaches – as exemplified by the work of Phelps Brown and Hopkins – is that we are so ignorant about changes in the number of days worked each year by the average worker. This is largely because our evidence comes from the records of the employing institutions, rather than from those of the workmen themselves. Despite this problem, the northern data broadly confirm the established position: from the early decades of the sixteenth century to the middle of the seventeenth century those at least partially dependent on wage earning for their support had to work an increasing number of days a year in order to sustain life. Some relief was gained in the later seventeenth and early eighteenth centuries when the secular trend in the price of basic foodstuffs turned downwards, and wage rates mostly stabilised, or, in some places, edged upwards. New evidence relating to the prices of fuel and housing is offered. At least at Hull – and perhaps at York also – the price of peat rose little after the middle of the sixteenth century and provided a relatively inexpensive source of fuel for the poor. Similarly, it is argued that, although it has not proved possible to establish a house-rent series, the cost of housing for the poor was not excessive. Throughout the sixteenth and seventeenth centuries small properties were available for rents which could be earned by wage-earners in just a few days. Thus, although the prices of foodstuffs rose alarmingly down to the middle of the seventeenth century, the prices of other basic necessities may have caused less concern for those languishing in the lower strata of the social hierarchy. But such conclusions remain tentative, especially since we have such a poor understanding of the sources of income open to townsfolk. It is easy to demonstrate that income could be derived from many quarters: from farming; from by-employments of bewildering variety; from leasing out property; from money lending; from the earnings of wives and children; and from doing odd jobs outside the normal working day. But it is impossible to estimate the proportion of family income which came from such sources, and to what extent such earnings changed over time. Perhaps the way ahead would be to concentrate on the history of a single town which possesses excellent records over a broad range. Indeed, recent work on Tudor and Stuart London shows how much can be learned.[35]

[35] Archer 1991; Boulton 1987a; Rappaport 1989.

2

Building craftsmen at work

The memorandum of *c*.1573 on the Statute of Artificers laid down a list of trades which could recruit their apprentices from any social group: they included bricklayers, brickmakers, tilers, slaters, tilemakers, carpenters, millwrights, sawyers, masons, plasterers, and smiths. It was explained that: 'These seem to be such trades as are for divers respects to be planted as well in country towns and villages as in cities and towns corporate, and be indeed such occupations as are most laboursome and painful, whereof some do not much differ from the trade of labourers.'[1] Indeed, there were times when those who believed themselves to possess a skill which set them above the common herd of labourers were pushed down into a lower stratum: at Coventry in 1517 it was ordered that rough masons and daubers were to be treated as mere labourers.[2] No doubt it was difficult for observers from higher social positions to perceive clearly the differences between labourers and building craftsmen, as at Durham in the 1580s when the clerk of works referred to the 'charges of wrights and other labourers at Stockton'.[3] But tedious and back-breaking though their work often was, craftsmen were more skilled than labourers and, especially in the larger towns, they strove to protect their territories of expertise through the agency of the craft gilds.[4] Craftsmen were closely identified with their particular trades, being called 'carpenter', 'tiler', or 'joiner', and in the 1690s the churchwardens of All Saints', Newcastle, went so far as to replace Christian names with the craft designation: thus we meet 'Bricklayer Johnson', 'Joiner Harrison', 'Smith Browne', 'Mason Groves', 'Carpenter Browne', and 'Plumber Hall'.[5]

[1] *TED*, I, 357–8.   [2] *Coventry Leet Book*, 653.   [3] DFC, CC/190100.
[4] Although the gilds were referred to as companies in some of the towns covered by this study, the term 'gild' will be used throughout.
[5] NCRO, MF557.

15

Building craftsmen rarely pushed their way very far up the social
ladder, even in the smaller towns; but many of them lived above the
bottom stratum of urban society which contained many journeymen,
day labourers, and shifting numbers of paupers dependent for much
of their sustenance on public and private charity. In contemporary
accounts of society skilled craftsmen were largely ignored, but not
completely:

> all artificers, [such] as tailors, shoemakers, carpenters, brick-makers, brick-
> layers, etc. These have no voice nor authority in our commonwealth and no
> account is made of them, but only to be ruled and not to rule other, and yet
> they be not altogether neglected. For in cities and corporate towns, for default
> of yeomen, inquests and juries are impanelled of such manner of people. And
> in villages they are commonly made churchwardens, aleconners, and many
> times constables.[6]

Building craftsmen could also be found occupying some of the more
lowly positions of responsibility in town hierarchies, such as bridge
keeper,[7] and occasionally they acted as churchwardens. Additionally
they ran their own affairs, under the watchful eye of the civic authorities, by acting as gild officials.

Varieties of building craftsmen

Among building craftsmen only the medieval masons have had a
scholarly book devoted to their activities: they constructed nearly a
thousand monastic establishments, collegiate churches, and hospitals,
thousands of parish churches, hundreds of royal and private castles,
together with many miles of town walls, and large numbers of municipal buildings and bridges.[8] They were a race apart. Often gathered
together from across the country in huge gangs, they lived in camps,
often for years on end, and evolved a unique form of self-protective
organisation based on the lodge. Within their ranks there was substantial differentiation between the top men, who carved the decora-
tive figures for the large churches and laid the carefully cut blocks of
stone, and the rough masons who cut the stone approximately to size
in the quarry. Although they often had substantial security of tenure
and sometimes owned farms or acted as entrepreneurs, dealing in
stone, masons 'approximated more nearly than did other medieval
artificers to modern workmen, being mere wage-earners, paid for
working on raw materials owned by their employer, and with very
little prospect of rising above this condition'.[9] This judgement, largely

[6] Laslett 1983, 31–4.   [7] YCR, V, 36–7.   [8] Knoop & Jones 1949, 2–3.
[9] Ibid., 3, 95–105.

uncontroversial in relation to medieval masons, has helped to colour attitudes to building craftsmen in general and has led historians to include all building workers among the ranks of wage-earners pure and simple.

The main phase of monastic and parish-church building was over by 1500,[10] and the Reformation caused a further severe setback to the employment of masons. York lost sixteen churches after 1547 and Lincoln a number in the 1550s, and the Dissolution of the Monasteries, by creating an enormous quarry of ready-to-use dressed stone, reduced the demand for the services of stone cutters and quarriers.[11] Much of the continued demand for masons came from country-house builders,[12] and from the crown. Urban demand for masons was at a low ebb, and there were few of them in some towns: when Ouse Bridge collapsed in the 1560s the York council had to recruit Christopher Warmsley, an outsider, to supervise the construction of the new bridge, and he returned annually for many years to oversee necessary repairs.[13] The great churches employed a small number of masons to repair the fabric, sometimes on a regular basis, but also more casually, as did some of the town councils.[14] But in many towns masons were notable by their absence. Only in the far north-west, where stone was readily available, was there much demand for the skills of masons and other workers in stone. This was especially true of Carlisle and Kendal where such craftsmen were usually called 'wallers' – which seems to imply a lower-grade occupation – rather than 'masons'. At Kendal wallers were more numerous than carpenters and joiners.[15]

Pavers also worked with stone. They were present, especially in the larger towns, in small numbers, although in many places they did not form a separate occupation: at Hull paving was often done by the bricklayers, while at York the city pavers were often referred to as 'tilers'.[16] Paving probably involved less skill than most other building operations and in late-medieval York pavers had the status of labourers, rather than craftsmen.[17]

In most towns, carpenters – or wrights as they were often known – were the most common building craftsmen.[18] Not only were they needed to repair the massive timbers which supported river banks and

---

[10] *Ibid.*, 186–7.   [11] *Ibid.*, 189; Clark & Slack 1972, 26; Woodward 1985, 180–1.
[12] Airs 1975.
[13] Palliser 1979, 172.   [14] YML, E3/52; TWAS, 543/18, fo. 123r; CCRO, MUV/3/78.
[15] Marshall 1975, 207–9.   [16] HCRO, BRF/3/15–20; YCA, CC5–20.
[17] Swanson 1983, 25–6.
[18] In some of the towns, especially Hull, carpenters were habitually called wrights, although in other places the term wright indicated a millwright. To avoid any

jetties, but they were also widely employed in the construction and repair of timber-framed buildings. As William Harrison suggested in the later sixteenth century: 'The greatest part of our building in the cities and good towns of England consisteth only of timber.'[19] This was true of sixteenth-century York and most other towns of the region.[20] Although much of their work was on a large scale, carpenters were men of considerable skill, as was demonstrated at Hull by Stephen Walker in 1656 when he spent two-and-a-half days 'making a frame for turning the arch' of a new bridge over the moat.[21] Joiners were also common, especially in the larger towns, and their work involved 'wainscotting, doors, windows, dressers, shelves, lattice work',[22] and other light work, much of which could be prefabricated in the workmen's own workshops. There are numerous references to their work: John Robson was paid 20d at Newcastle in 1598 'for trimming and squaring the table where the names of the mayors and sheriffs are to be written', and a year later at York James Dixon was paid 10s 'for making a wainscot cupboard' for the common hall.[23] Not surprisingly, there was a disputed no-man's land between the work of the carpenters and the joiners which proved difficult to police. At Hull the ordinances of the separate gilds of joiners and carpenters, drawn up in 1598, laid down that 'no carpenter, housewright, or other wright within this town, shall make any joiner work whatsoever', and that no joiner or shipwright was to do 'any work appertaining properly to the carpenter'.[24] But no attempt was made to define the different spheres, and the records of the Chester, Newcastle, and York gilds make it plain that demarcation disputes between such overlapping crafts were common. At Chester, following complaints about outsiders 'intermeddling with their trade', the joiners and carvers were separated from the carpenters in 1576, and they were joined by the turners.[25] This did not solve the problem and from time to time the joiners' gild was obliged to seek redress against those who infringed its monopoly of making joined work: as late as July 1724 the carpenters suggested that a joint committee, comprising six members elected from each gild, should meet 'for setting out and distinguishing what work belongs to the carpenters', and what therefore to the joiners.[26] Nothing further was heard of this peace conference.

confusion the term carpenter will be used throughout this study to identify the most important of the woodworking crafts.
[19] *Elizabethan England*, 113.   [20] Palliser 1979, 31.   [21] HCRO, BRF/3/20, p. 142.
[22] *Builder's Companion*, 4–5.   [23] TWAS, 543/19, fo. 91r; York, CC10, fo. 64r.
[24] *Gild Life*, 255, 260.
[25] CCRO, Joiners' miscellaneous papers, no. 1; Morris 1893, 404.
[26] CCRO, MCP/2/12–19.

The town councils themselves, theoretically the upholders of gild regulations, were not averse to breaking the rules. At Hull in 1671 five carpenters, who were often employed by the council repairing the jetties, were moved on to 'making partitions and beds for the prisoners at the house of correction', while others were employed 'repairing two prison doors being set on fire by two prisoners'.[27] Similarly, at York in the later Middle Ages, the carpenters took over much of the work of the joiners, and between 1451 and 1534 only five joiners became freemen. In 1530 the carpenters were united with the joiners and carvers 'to prevent squabbling among them', and a request for the separation of the two crafts was turned down in 1664.[28] The blurring of distinctions between crafts was probably even more common in the smaller towns: at Lincoln in the later seventeenth century £3 4s was paid 'to the joiners and carpenters for making tables and forms for Mr Mayor's house'.[29] A similar situation is suggested by the will of a Penrith man in 1746: Thomas Watson called himself a carpenter, but he bequeathed to his eldest son, 'All the work tools and implements belonging to me or made use of by me as a carpenter, joiner or wheelwright.'[30] The carpenters also overlapped with the sawyers who were always employed in pairs. They usually worked in a sawpit with the more skilled man standing on top of the timber, guiding the saw, with the less skilled 'donkey', or junior partner, down below, providing the power to rip through the timber and being deluged with sawdust. Sometimes when sawyers appear in the accounts they are both named, but often only one is named and the other called 'man'.[31] However, in some accounts sawyers are absent and it was the carpenters who 'squared timber' or sawed it into planks.

There was also considerable overlap between the work of bricklayers, tilers, and plasterers; indeed, they were often one and the same person. Brickmaking and bricklaying flourished at an early date in both Beverley and Hull, partly because of the shortage of good building stone. But even there brick was rarely used before 1600 as the sole building material for houses: it was used mostly for chimney stacks or for infilling the lower parts of timber-framed buildings.[32] Brick buildings became more common in most places during the sixteenth and seventeenth centuries, although little brick was used at Carlisle before

---

[27] HCRO, BRF/3/20, pp. 139, 268, 714.

[28] Swanson 1983, 16–17; Palliser 1972, 94; Palliser 1979, 172–3; *YCR*, III, 132; V, 99–100; YCA, B38/7.

[29] LAO, Chamberlains' Rolls 1685/6.   [30] CUMROC, Wills, P1746.

[31] At Durham in the 1530s the sawyer's assistant was called 'his marrow': DFC, CC/190066.

[32] *VCH Hull*, 77; *Hull Trinity House Building*, 153–70.

the eighteenth century.[33] Overlap and confusion between bricklayers and tilers goes back to the origin of the two crafts. In fifteenth-century accounts, the term 'tile' can mean either brick or tile in the modern sense: at the building of Tattershall Castle reference was made to 'bricks called waltile', and in Beverley bricklayers were known as 'tile-wallers'.[34] Additionally, the skills of the tiler and bricklayer were difficult to disentangle from those of the plasterer. In late-medieval York the plasterers and tilers claimed to be two distinct crafts, although in practice they were thoroughly intertwined and their gilds were amalgamated.[35] Similarly, at Hull in the later fifteenth century, Richard Bothe, one of the regular workers at the construction of Trinity House, was referred to as both tiler and plasterer, and in the accounts of the town chamberlains he was called a slater.[36] Perhaps the title changed according to the nature of the job in hand, although Salzman pointed out that it is dangerous to read too much into the wording of medieval records, since the clerks 'often liked to vary their wording more for the mere sake of variety and did not greatly worry if they used one term in several senses'.[37] In late-Tudor York some men combined the jobs of bricklayer, tiler, and plasterer, and the freemen's register for the Tudor period does not include a single plasterer.[38] Movement from one occupation to another was easy since the various tasks involved the use of lime and sand, strengthened in the case of plaster with chopped straw or hair. Often the nature of the work in hand was not stated. Thus it cannot be determined exactly what William Goeforth, a Hull bricklayer, was doing when he was paid for 'repairing the Mally tower where the prisoners broke out and other places about it where it was weak'.[39]

The term 'slater' was used as a synonym for 'tiler' in late-fifteenth-century Hull, although it seems likely that it was usually reserved for those who worked with stone, such as the workmen who 'thacked with stone' the roof of Ouse Bridge Chapel in 1550.[40] But slates could also be hung on walls to keep out the weather: the accounts of Newcastle Trinity House for 1653 refer to payments 'to the slaters for mending the house side wherein John Wilkinson dwells, the slaters finding slates, laths, nails and workmanship'.[41] The roofs of Carlisle and Kendal were covered with slates, fastened with pins on to laths and then packed with moss, 'as a ship is caulked', to make the roof

---

[33] B.C. Jones 1983, 125–6.   [34] *Tattershall Castle Accts*, 46, 57; Salzman 1952, 33.
[35] Swanson 1983, 18; 1989, 87.
[36] *Hull Trinity House Building*, 156.   [37] Salzman 1952, 317.   [38] Palliser 1979, 173.
[39] HCRO, BRF/3/20, p. 514. See also BRF/3/20, p. 958; BRF/3/21.   [40] YCR, V, 38–9.
[41] TWAS, 659/449.

weather tight. However, at the rebuilding of Whitehaven Castle in 1677 the estate steward objected to this traditional technique, and 'propounded hair and lime according to the example of Dublin'. This was 'not regarded' by the slater.[42]

The work of plumbers and glaziers was closely related and some individuals pursued both crafts. Bartholomew Gill worked at both trades for St Mary's, Hull, in the late seventeenth century, and a number of craftsmen, including John Shewsmith and his son George, had followed both callings at Lincoln Cathedral earlier in the century.[43] Such shifts were easy since both crafts involved the ability to cast and work lead. Glaziers, whose days looked numbered with the decline of church building and the catastrophe of the Dissolution, were saved from extinction by the growing popularity of domestic glazing. The use of glass spread relatively slowly in the north before the end of the sixteenth century, but then its popularity began to widen.[44] Plumbers used lead for two basic purposes – either to retain water or to keep it out. At Bishop Auckland in 1561, the Bishop of Durham's plumber was paid for mending the conduit and 'for bringing the water into all the houses of office'.[45] But most plumbers spent much of their time up on the roof, at the mercy of the elements.[46] Lead was used widely on church roofs and on some secular buildings. Jobs ranged from full-scale refurbishment to small-scale repairs: at Lincoln Cathedral during the 1660s the old lead was completely replaced, but the plumbers were also employed 'mending a hole in the roof where a pigeon built'.[47]

In his book *The Builder's Companion and Workman's General Assistant*, first published in 1758, William Pain pointed out that: 'Blacksmiths' work is done by weight; all sorts of hammered work, as chimney bars, stays, upright window bars, shutter bars, pump work, bolts, saddle bars, cramps, holdfasts, dogs, gudgeons, and all black work of the same kind ... casements, cross window bars filed ... large screw bolts and nuts ... iron doors and shutters.'[48] Strangely, he did not mention the huge variety of nails produced by smiths, although he was correct to suggest that smiths were paid by weight and that their work was crucial to the building process. A few historians have gone some way to recognising the essentially non-agricultural nature of the urban blacksmith, but only Salzman, with his encyclopaedic knowledge of the medieval building industry, recognised the true character of the

[42] *Clifton Accts*, 161; Tyson 1979, 88; 1980, 122; 1983a, 119; *Naworth Accts*, 32; CUMROC, Ca/4/1–2; CUMROK, Kendal Accts, 1659; Tyson 1984, 72.
[43] HCORO, PE/185/34; LAO, Bj/1/6–8.   [44] Crossley 1972, 424–5.
[45] DFC, CC/190086. See also TWAS, 543/19, fo. 191r.
[46] Salzman 1952, 262–6.   [47] LAO, Bj/1/7–8.   [48] *Builder's Companion*, 7.

urban smith, whom he regarded as 'an important figure in the building establishment, even apart from his work in making and repairing the workmen's tools'. Perhaps fearing that his work was running out of control, Salzman suggested that smiths' tools 'are barely within the scope of our inquiry', but he added that, 'the smithy was so much a part of the organisation of building works that we can hardly ignore them'.[49]

Among building craftsmen only painters remain to be considered, although it is by no means certain that all those who wielded a paint brush were specialists: the men employed in 'whitening the top of the town hall for a sea mark for ships' at Hull in 1657 may well have been tilers.[50] However, there were some specialists. Edward Haslam painted the arms of Hull Trinity House in 1614, using 'two books of gold', and Christopher Harrison was paid £3 5s in 1666 for applying two coats of whitening to the school walls and 'colouring in oil part of the seats which was fir to make it like wainscot'.[51] The rarity of such references suggests that little beautifying was done to early-modern civic buildings.

The position of the building trades in the urban economies

Although building craftsmen were never in a position to dominate their local communities they were not insignificant numerically in the towns of early-modern England. They comprised nearly 10 per cent of the freemen in Tudor Norwich and nearly 12 per cent in early seventeenth-century Exeter.[52] The freemen's rolls from which such statistics are derived are valuable sources and yet they are most misleading, and they have been criticised most heavily in the case of York.[53] In theory, it was necessary for everyone wishing to set up as a master craftsman to become a freeman, but subordinate workers had no need to do so. Crafts with a large number of out-workers, such as the textile

---

[49] *VCH Hull*, 151; Palliser 1979, 171; Salzman 1952, 286–317, 347.
[50] HCRO, BRF/3/20, p. 162. See also TWAS, 543/14, fo. 119v.
[51] HTH, III, fos. 145v–146r; HCRO, BRF/3/20, p. 510.
[52] Building-trade workmen were present in various towns in the following proportions: in the early sixteenth century 4 to 4½% of the freemen at Leicester and Coventry, and over 7% at Northampton; 7.6% of new freemen in seventeenth-century Norwich; 7% of the Northampton electors in 1768; nearly 12% of Exeter freemen in the early seventeenth century; in the first half of the eighteenth century 14.8% of the apprentices at Oxford were recruited to the building trades; and between 1663 and 1721 11% of Stamford craftsmen worked in stone and wood, and 7% with metal. Hoskins 1963, 80; Pound 1966, 55–6, 60, 68; MacCaffrey 1958, 163; Evans 1979, 20–1; Corfield 1982, 31; *Oxford Apprentices*, x, xii; Thirsk 1984, 313.
[53] Dobson 1973; Swanson 1983, 1989; Woodward 1970a.

trades, often had a relatively low ratio of freemen to non-freemen which means that the freemen's rolls are 'far from being an accurate guide to the strength of individual industries'.[54] This is also true for Newcastle which was dominated by the coal trade. Few of the men who loaded the coal were freemen and the coal shippers were a small elite. As a result, anyone solely dependent on information from the freemen's rolls would imagine that the coal trade formed only a small part of the town's economy.[55] Similarly, at Hull they cannot be used with any great confidence. In the sixteenth century occupations were frequently not given and throughout the period many active trades-men and craftsmen avoided the charges associated with membership of the freeman body by paying a small annual fine: 27 such fines were paid in 1634/5 and 114 in 1638/9.[56]

A further problem derives from the occupational label attached to individuals in the freemen's rolls and other records. In late-medieval towns many craftsmen and tradesmen did not restrict themselves to the occupation indicated by the official record, but followed a wide variety of alternative pursuits in the effort to boost family incomes.[57] The same was true in the early-modern period. An even more intract-able difficulty is that the freemen's rolls, by definition, relate predom-inantly to men. The efforts of women, who played a vital part in urban economies, are extremely difficult to reconstruct, although they com-prised a hidden army of labour. They worked in household service, in the businesses of fathers, neighbours, husbands, or brothers, or fre-quently ran rarely recorded side-lines of their own.[58] Women only became more fully visible after the deaths of their husbands when they can be observed continuing family businesses, sometimes for only a year or two, clearing up on-going commitments, but in other cases for considerable periods of time.[59] Historians have created further prob-lems when processing data taken from freemen's rolls by placing the various crafts in occupational groupings, since not all crafts fitted comfortably into a particular group. A classic problem involves the lowly shoemaker, whom some historians have placed in the clothing trades, alongside the tailor, whilst others have assigned him to the leather trades.[60] Similarly, some historians have put plumbers and blacksmiths into a category which embraces all the metal workers, although many of them were deeply involved in the building industry.

[54] Swanson 1983, 5.　　[55] Howell 1967, 20.　　[56] *VCH Hull*, 149.
[57] Swanson 1989.
[58] *Ibid*.
[59] For an extended discussion of the role of the widow see below pp. 84–91.
[60] Woodward 1970a, 89–90.

Table 2.1. *Admissions to the freedom at Hull*

	1620–9 %	1660–9 %	1690–9 %
Building crafts	14.6	11.0	13.4
Metal crafts	4.9	7.3	8.2
Shipping (including mariners)	23.2	16.1	10.5
Distributive (including merchants)	17.6	17.7	18.3

Source: VCH Hull, 150.

Despite all the qualifications, freemen's rolls do provide some interesting information about urban occupations. In Tudor York, 8.6 per
cent of new freemen belonged to the main-line building trades and
there were also numerous blacksmiths in the city.[61] At Newcastle the
combined figures for building and metal workers in the first six
decades of the seventeenth century amounted to between 14.5 and
20.2 per cent of admissions, whereas at Chester between 1558 and 1625
the building trades alone comprised only 5.5 per cent of new freemen.[62] For other northern towns information on the occupational
structure is either scanty, or, as in the case of Beverley and Hull, highly
unsatisfactory. At Beverley details of new burgesses are available only
for twenty-one years at the end of the sixteenth century: building
craftsmen comprised 8.7 per cent of the total and metal workers 5.7 per
cent. According to the parish registers of the early eighteenth century
5.2 per cent of townsmen worked in the building trades and 3.5 per
cent in the metal trades. Additionally 5.9 per cent were woodworkers.[63] For Hull, material is also available from both the freemen's
rolls and the parish registers. The results are disturbing and underline
yet again the problematical nature of data drawn from freemen's rolls
(see table 2.1).

The parish registers tell a rather different story. In the seventeen
months running up to the end of 1679 the father's occupation was
given at the baptism of 74 children in St Mary's, Hull: 37 fathers were
described as 'mariner' or 'master and mariner', and a further 12 followed the related occupations of waiter, boatman, shipwright, boatbuilder, and surveyor of customs. There was one representative each
from the ranks of the bricklayers, joiners, carpenters, and smiths,
amounting to 5.4 per cent of the total. In the four years ending in April

[61] Palliser 1979, 156–7, 159.   [62] Howell 1967, 353; Woodward 1968b, 67.
[63] *VCH Beverley*, 81, 114.

1715 the register gives the occupations of 158 fathers: there were 42 seafarers and 38 in other 'maritime' crafts. Building craftsmen accounted for 9.5 per cent of all fathers, but there was no mention of smiths.[64] These registers, which suggest that between a half and two-thirds of the town's labour force was engaged in trade and commerce, paint a rather different picture from that derived from the freemen's records.

Freemen were not the only ones occupied in the building trades. Apprentices and journeymen worked alongside their masters, and wives and widows, and perhaps some daughters, were drawn into the business from time to time. Additionally, the presence of an unknown number of labourers makes it impossible to calculate the total size of the labour force engaged in the building trades. Building operations were a significant element in the urban economies of early-modern England, and probably occupied between 10 and 20 per cent of the adult male labour force, but a much smaller proportion of females.

Individual businesses in the building trades

The typical business in the building trades remained small throughout the three centuries under consideration, and even after 1750 most master craftsmen worked with only one or two permanent employees, taking on unskilled labour as required,[65] in much the same way as the many thousands of jobbing bricklayers, carpenters, plumbers, and electricians still do. Even today, an industry headed by high-profile firms such as McAlpine and Tarmac, Wimpey and Barrett, still has room for a very large number of tiny operators. Many businesses in early-modern England were like that of William Goeforth, the Hull bricklayer, who worked alongside 'his man' and was paid £3 6s 2d in July 1675 'for two weeks rough casting the south side of the Trinity House'.[66] The three largest building firms discovered in the early-modern north, were those of John Chambre, a York glazier, John Westoby, a Hull carpenter, and Thomas Gill, a Chester joiner: Chambre, who became a freeman in 1415, had a workshop in 1450 where his son worked alongside four others; Westoby was frequently employed by the Hull council in the 1630s and on one occasion he was paid for his own work and 'for seven of his men'; Thomas Gill, who joined his gild in 1693 and remained a member until 1734, employed five journeymen in 1708, although over the whole period of his membership he employed less than two a year on average.[67]

[64] HCORO, PE/185/2.   [65] Cooney 1955–6, 167–9; Rule 1986, 11.   [66] HTH, V.
[67] Swanson 1983, 22–3; HCRO, BRF/3/19, fo. 59r; CCRO, G14/1.

The case of John Westoby illustrates how difficult it is to interpret the accounts on which this study is based. During 1635 and 1636 he worked at various times with a single man, or alongside three, four, five, or seven men.[68] Unfortunately we know neither the names of the other men nor their relationship to Westoby. Perhaps they were all regular employees, but it is equally possible that he hired most of them for short periods, as required, and that they were 'his men' for only a few exceptional days each year. Even where the accounts do provide names it is often impossible to determine the exact relationship between different men. It is tempting to assume that a small group of men, frequently appearing together in the accounts in the same order, were the employees of the first named. But we cannot be sure. During the 1620s, four Hull carpenters – Robert Iveson, James Brasbrick, William Penrose, and William Watherton – normally worked together, and they may well have comprised a single business unit. But perhaps not.[69] Such groupings recur frequently in the northern records, but if they did form individual businesses, they were not large. Dependency is often suggested in the accounts by differentials in levels of pay. When two workers appear repeatedly side by side, the one receiving the lower rate of pay was probably dependent on the other. But only when the relationship is explicitly stated can we be sure: thus, in 1485/6 the carpenter James Galen worked at Hull Trinity House for 6d a day, while 'his man' earned 5d a day, his 'old apprentice' 4d, and his 'young apprentice' 2d.[70] The names of the employees are not given, but the small business unit of master plus man and two apprentices is clear enough.

Institutions often hired the same small groups of craftsmen year after year. This is hardly surprising since it made a lot of sense to re-engage someone who had done a good job previously. The use of such 'trusty' workmen can be illustrated most easily from the Hull records: in 1571 – a typical year in the council accounts – three-quarters of the carpentry work was done by three small groups, and during the 1620s most of it was done by Robert Iveson and his three associates.[71] However, the practice of hiring established workers probably exaggerates the size of business units since struggling young craftsmen, working without assistance, were less likely to be hired by the larger institutions. Further insights can be gained from the records of the Chester joiners which reveal that the majority of masters employed only one journeyman at a time.[72] A similar picture emerges from a

[68] HCRO, BRF/3/19, fos. 59r–63r.   [69] HCRO, BRF/3/8–18.   [70] HTH, I, fo. 48v.
[71] HCRO, BRF/3/3,8–18.
[72] CCRO, G14/1. For a detailed discussion see below p. 68.

detailed bill of work submitted to the Hull council in 1713 by eleven master carpenters and two joiners. Each was paid at 24d a day and they were assisted by five 'men', two 'boys', and three 'sons': two of the masters each had two aides, six had a single assistant, and the remaining five were unaccompanied.[73]

The family was often the centre of economic as well as social life in early-modern England, and it has been argued that the husband and master, wife, children, journeymen, apprentices, and house servants all ate and worked together in the house and adjoining shop.[74] This may well have been the case in those branches of the building industry which were predominantly workshop based: the establishment run by John Chambre in mid-fifteenth-century York looks like the kind of family-centred business delineated by Peter Laslett. But many building craftsmen spent much of their working hours away from home, which reduced the possibility of the casual involvement of family members in the productive process. Some members of the same family did work together in the building trades. At York, in 1611, the masons Thomas Beane the elder and younger were paid £30 'for their work and pains in repairing of the staithe' and, in 1673, Marmaduke Atkinson, a Hull glazier, worked alongside his two sons, one of whom was paid 24d a day like his father, and the other 14d.[75] Some families established little dynasties of building craftsmen. At York between 1654 and 1752 there were eight Hunters in the bricklayers' gild and a large number of Harrisons; there were six members of the Goeforth family – Aaron, 'Elishey', Enoch, Joseph, Robert, and William – among the bricklayers of late-seventeenth-century Hull; at Carlisle the Railton family was similarly active towards the end of the period.[76] Elsewhere the same surnames recur quite frequently in the accounts, but family groupings did not dominate the northern building trades. Dynasties were usually short-lived and the accounts are characterised by an enormous variety of family names.

Only on very rare occasions were female members of a family paid for working alongside their menfolk: at Durham, in 1545, three male members of the Skelus family worked together walling and slating, assisted by 'Skelus daughter for bearing of gravel'.[77] The most unusual family grouping was recorded at St Mary's, Beverley, in 1713/14: William Page was paid 20d a day for pointing windows, assisted by his

[73] HCRO, BRF/6/465.   [74] Laslett 1983, 1–11.
[75] YCA, CC14, fos. 41v–42r; HCRO, BRF/3/20, p. 780. See also CCRO, TAV/1/3.
[76] YML, QQ80/2/13; CUMROC, Ca/4/11–126; B.C. Jones 1983.
[77] DPK, MC2871/5.

wife for one-and-a-half days and his daughter for half a day, who were paid 14d for their combined efforts.[78]

External controls on building craftsmen

Craftsmen and other inhabitants of early-modern towns were subject to a range of controls and obligations which affected many aspects of their working lives. Workmen were bound by national legislation which laid down conditions of work and levels of wages. National policy was enforced by the town councils, especially after the Statute of Artificers was passed in 1563. Beneath the councils were the craft gilds. They were often numerous, especially in the larger towns, and attempted to exercise close control over the lives and behaviour of their members. All townsfolk were also members of a parish, which catered for their spiritual and, occasionally, their bodily needs.

Building craftsmen were under obligations to their customers and were not free to come and go as they pleased. Once a job was begun they were expected to remain until its completion, and this was endorsed by some of the gilds.[79] Moreover, workmen were not always free to refuse work. The ordinances of the combined gild of brick-layers, tilers, wallers, plasterers, and pavers at Hull laid down that 'every inhabitant of this town upon two days warning or request ... shall have assigned unto them good and sufficient workmen to do any work they would have done more or less ... according to the laws and statutes of this land'.[80] Additionally, building craftsmen were never entirely free since they could be commandeered or pressed into royal service, sometimes a long way from home, although such impressment did not reduce them to servile status.[81]

In many towns the gild was the most important institution in the lives of craftsmen. Earlier in the present century historians saw their role as essentially economic: gilds were monopolistic and restrictive, curbing the natural development of the free market.[82] More recent research has queried such beliefs and the gilds are now viewed as more flexible, being less of a brake on economic progress.[83] Moreover, it has been argued that the nature of craft gilds changed funda-mentally in the later Middle Ages. Originally they were founded as associations for mutual support and religious expression among

[78] HCORO, PE/1/106.   [79] TWAS, 802/16; *Gild Life*, 278–9; Steinfeld 1991, 3–6.
[80] *Gild Life*, 261, 274–5.
[81] Knoop & Jones 1949, 90–4. For a discussion of Continental practice, see Small 1989, 340.
[82] See especially the work of George Unwin, 1904, 1908.   [83] Palliser 1972, 86, 111–12.

members of the same occupation, but increasingly the system came to be manipulated to serve the political and administrative purposes of the town authorities.[84] To the urban elites they were ideal mechanisms for policing the workforce, and efforts were made to breathe new life into moribund gilds or to create new ones where there were none before.[85] Gilds could not exist without the permission of the town council and their ordinances had no force until they had been given official approval. At Lincoln the mayor signalled his control by appointing auditors for each gild, and the link between town and gild was symbolised neatly at Newcastle and York where fines for infringements of gild ordinances were split equally between the gild and the council.[86] The city fathers benefited considerably from the existence of the gilds by having a carefully structured labour force with mechanisms for control and punishment.[87] Serious disputes between workers were referred to the council: in 1672 the Hull council adjudicated between the conflicting claims of the joiners and carpenters, laying down what could be done by each group, and when in 1606 the Chester carpenters objected to the employment of a foreigner they were told to appear before the mayor bringing their charter with them so that he could reach the correct decision.[88] When necessary the authorities did not shrink from taking strong measures against gild members. At York in 1552 the leaders of a strike by building craftsmen were thrown in gaol, and the officers of the Chester joiners spent four days in prison for an unspecified offence in 1605: 18s 8d was 'spent in the Northgate, being there four days when we were committed by Mr Mayor: for all our charges, our diets, garnish, for our beds and other expenses'.[89] In most towns the gilds remained entirely subservient to the town authorities, without any voice in a higher political sphere. However, in a small group of northern towns – including Carlisle, Durham, Newcastle, and York – some of the gilds helped to elect the mayor, although at York they were replaced by wards after 1632.[90]

The gilds offered a range of economic advantages to members. Within the framework of the officially approved ordinances the members were free to run their own affairs: they regulated entry to the trade, monitored the quality of work, fined miscreants, and disposed of accumulated funds. To such men the protection provided by the gild was real enough and, although they proved difficult to defend,

---

[84] Swanson 1988, 30–1, 39; 1989, 5–6, 112–13; Palliser 1972, 106; Davies 1956.
[85] See the reorganisation of the Hull gilds in 1598; *Gild Life*.
[86] Hill 1956, 31; TWAS 802/16; YML, QQ80/2/11.   [87] Phythian-Adams 1979, 117.
[88] Davies 1956; *Chester Minutes*, 30.   [89] Woodward 1980b; CCRO, G14/1, fo. 71v.
[90] Howell 1967, 42–3; Palliser 1972, 107–9; Sowler 1972, 85–6; YCR, VIII, 9–10; IX, 1–2.

craft boundaries were frequently enforced and interlopers repelled. As the York bricklayers expressed it in the early eighteenth century: 'no trade can advantageously go forwards without good and lawful orders made and pains laid for the public interest of the same'. Their complaint was against large-scale undertakers who were threatening to drive out the small jobbing builder or make him totally dependent on subcontracted work.[91]

In the old-established boroughs of Chester, Newcastle, and York gilds were numerous and, seemingly, influential. In the later Middle Ages York had over fifty different craft gilds and a number of informal trade groupings, while Chester had about twenty-five gilds, some of them catering for the needs of more than one craft.[92] There were also about twenty-five gilds in late-medieval Beverley, although a spate of amalgamations in the late sixteenth century reduced the number to seventeen principal gilds.[93] Lincoln had only about a dozen gilds in the sixteenth century, a small number for a town which had been so prominent in the medieval period.[94] Hull, a new town at the end of the thirteenth century, gradually acquired the trappings of a corporate borough in succeeding centuries: the number of gilds remained small, although new life was breathed into them with the establishment of new ordinances in 1598.[95] In the two north-western towns gilds were less important. Carlisle had no more than seven or eight gilds in the sixteenth century, while at Kendal twelve gilds were established when the town was incorporated in 1575, but they included one enormous conglomeration which covered eleven of the building crafts together with the millers and coopers.[96] The creation of the Kendal gilds supports the suggestion that, from the point of view of the town authorities, they had a significance that was political rather than economic. It is inconceivable that such a large, catch-all gild could have organised the building trades effectively.

The importance of the craft gilds to individual members is difficult to assess. At Chester, Newcastle, and York, where gild records have survived in profusion, they have an appearance of high activity. Elsewhere, the shortage of such registers and accounts gives the impression that the gilds were less active. At Hull, apart from some gild ordinances, only the order book of the bricklayers' gild has survived, which has led to the suggestion that the gilds were less strong than at

---

[91] YML, QQ80/1/11, p. 37.
[92] Swanson 1989, 111; Palliser 1972, 89; Clark & Slack 1976, 28; Groombridge 1952.
[93] *VCH Beverley*, 82.   [94] Clark & Slack 1976, 28; J.W.F. Hill 1956, 29–32
[95] *VCH Hull*, 58–9, 151–2; *Gild Life*.
[96] CUMROC, Ca/2/17; Walker 1981, 25; Phillips 1985, 31; Knoop & Jones 1949, 232.

York.[97] This was probably so, although it is somewhat dangerous to argue about the relative significance of institutions based on the survival of their records. Various references in the council minutes indicate that the Hull gilds were showing some signs of life in the seventeenth century,[98] although whether or not they were an effective force in the town is a moot point.

Even where detailed records have not survived it is often possible to learn a great deal about gild policy from the ordinances, supplemented by those registers and accounts which do exist. The ordinances, endorsed by the town councils, 'were in the main essentials remarkably alike', especially within the same town.[99] New members swore an oath to abide by the regulations: they vowed to obey their leaders; to act in a brotherly fashion towards each other at all times; to deal honestly with all men; to attend gild meetings and feasts; to pay their small dues of a few pence each quarter; to be present at the burial of brother craftsmen or their wives; to keep the rules relating to the employment of apprentices and journeymen; to refrain from the employment of non-licensed outsiders; to do work of good quality; and to keep the secrets of the gild, or aptly named 'mystery'. Failure to abide by any of the regulations would attract an appropriate fine or, in extreme cases, expulsion.[100] Each gild was headed by one or two officials, usually known as aldermen, who presided over meetings and represented the gild in its dealings with outside agencies. They were usually assisted by two stewards who took responsibility for less onerous tasks such as calling the members to meetings and keeping the accounts.[101] The officers were elected annually, often near the day of the saint connected with the particular occupation: the Newcastle bricklayers held their elections on St Mathias's day and members had to be present on that 'Head Meeting Day' by 8 a.m.[102] Most gilds also had a small number of part-time paid employees. In the early 1730s the Newcastle joiners employed a clerk and beadle for 10s and 6s 8d a quarter respectively, and 'a woman that keeps the meeting house' received 2s a quarter.[103] It is not always clear where gild meetings took place, although in post-Reformation York most were held in St Anthony's Hall, leased from the council for a small sum.[104] Meetings, which could be extremely boisterous affairs, were called at least four

---

97 *Hull Bricklayers; VCH Hull*, 151–2. For a contrary view, stressing the strength of the Hull gilds, see Gillett & MacMahon 1989, 133.

98 Davies 1956.   99 Groombridge 1952, 95.

100 E.g., *YCR*, III, 175, 179–80, 186–7; *Gild Life*, 257–82; TWAS, 802/5.

101 Groombridge 1952, 95. See also the records of the gilds of Chester, Newcastle, and York.

102 TWAS, 802/16.   103 TWAS, 648/4.   104 Palliser 1972, 96; 1979, 25.

times a year, when quarterage payments were due, and on other
occasions as required.[105] The Newcastle bricklayers met an average of
eleven times a year between 1665 and 1670, the number ranging from
five to seventeen.[106]

Before the Reformation the gilds played an important part in the
religious pageants which marked various staging posts of the
medieval year, and some gild amalgamations were to allow poorer
crafts to share the costs.[107] The pageants, and especially the great
Corpus Christi celebrations, were the most dramatic expressions of
civic ceremonial and played an important role in helping to bond gild
members together. The sense of belonging to an important body was
furthered by the liveries which the gildsmen wore on special occasions
in many of the towns.[108] In medieval Beverley 'the glovers merely
expected their brothers to wear new clothes if possible, but most gilds
ordered that their livery should be worn'. It was usually replaced
every two or three years, and gild members were forbidden to sell or
give away their current outfits, which they were to wear also at gild
feasts.[109] In the sixteenth century, the custom fell into disuse with
each gild 'divided in sundry colours within themselves'. As a result, in
1573, the council ordered that: 'Every occupation or brotherhood ...
shall within four years next coming at the furthest, clothe themselves
in new vestures, that is to say, in comely and decent gowns and every
alderman and his brethren in one only colour by themselves.' It
was anticipated that some members would have difficulty finding
the 34s 8d needed to buy four yards of broadcloth at 8s 8d a yard, so a
box was to be provided to receive weekly or quarterly contributions:
all were to be newly clad by St Mark's day 1574 at the latest. Anyone
who wished to buy more expensive cloth could do so providing that
the colour was appropriate. Any money saved was to go to the
gildsman's widow should he die.[110] The Chester bricklayers expected
members to wear their gowns at all meetings, and the gild which
included the smiths and plumbers insisted on gowns at funerals.[111]
The joiners could put on a fine display: the leaders wore tippets
trimmed with lace; the beadle carried a staff which was silvered at the
cost of 12d in 1602; and the whole body of men marched behind a
fringed banner, renewed in 1596, which together with the new socket

---

[105] Palliser 1972. See below pp. 78–81.   [106] TWAS, 802/2.

[107] Phythian-Adams 1979, 111–12; Swanson 1989, 120; YCR, II, 161–2.

[108] Swanson 1989, 119; Phythian-Adams 1979, 111. See VCH Beverley, 42–9, for an
       excellent account of gild ceremonial in the Middle Ages.

[109] Ibid., 46; Swanson 1988, 38.   [110] HCORO, BC/II/7/3, fo. 19r.

[111] CCRO, Bricklayers' Book 1583–95; G20/1.

cost 6s 10d.[112] The York bricklayers had 'one large flag and two little ones, and a buff belt with a socket belonging to it' in the early eighteenth century.[113]

As in all closed, mutual-aid societies throughout history, gild members ate and drank together on a number of occasions during the year. Election days always involved drinking, and apprentices were expected to provide a dinner for members as part of the cost of full gild membership.[114] The Chester joiners usually spent a shilling or two 'in the tavern upon the fifth day of August, being the King's holiday'. At other times they drank at the house of one of the gild officials, although in the early eighteenth century they were to be found in a number of local inns.[115] The quality of the fare provided at feasts is not stated, although in November 1620 the Chester joiners provided a dinner for twenty-nine at 9d a head: sack and strong beer cost a further 4s 10d, and 'the music' 3s 4d.[116] It seems likely that the dinners of most lowly craft gilds were relatively modest, and to avoid unnecessary expense the York bricklayers decided, in 1634, to have only one dinner a year, on St James's Day or within the next fortnight, and the carpenters did likewise.[117]

Craftsmen expected economic advantages to flow from gild membership. The ordinances, with their stress on the closed shop and the maintenance of trade exclusivity, were not pious expressions of forlorn hopes. Demarcation disputes could never be resolved to satisfy everyone, but the minutes of the building-trade gilds make it plain that members were frequently fined for 'trade offences', and that encroachments by other groups of workers were challenged strenuously. It is inconceivable that the gilds would have continued to press for the maintenance of restrictive practices had they proved to be totally ineffective over the centuries.[118] The gilds managed to control the number of apprentices; they imposed fines when one man took the work of a brother; they fought long and hard to restrain foreigners from invading their territories; they strove to maintain the quality of production; and, most particularly, they took vigorous action against fellow townsmen who strayed over a traditionally respected craft

---

[112] CCRO, G14/1, fos. 49r, 63r, 66r, 84v. The smiths also had a banner: CCRO, G20/1. See also *YCR*, II, 171.

[113] YML, QQ80/1/3.   [114] See below pp. 73–4.

[115] CCRO, G14/1, fos. 77r, 82v, 110r; G14/3.

[116] CCRO, G14/1, fo. 104r.

[117] YML, QQ80/3/2; YCA, B35/240b. See also B33/79b, B36/232b.

[118] Heather Swanson, who has queried whether or not restrictive practices could have been enforced effectively, was working in a period largely devoid of detailed gild records. Swanson 1989, 117–18.

boundary.[119] Fury relating to a demarcation dispute reached its peak
in late-fifteenth-century York. To the great annoyance of the masons, a
new tower was being built out of brick. Passions ran high, and 'divers
children of wickedness', thought to be masons, broke and stole the
bricklayers' tools. But worse was to follow. A bricklayer was murdered,
and William Hyndeley, the master mason at the Minster, and his
assistant were arrested on suspicion.[120]

Gilds insisted on members keeping brotherhood secrets, although
Salzman suggested that they were unsuitable in 'the ordinary organisation of a gild, with its ordinances open to the control of the local
authorities'.[121] But gilds did have secrets, and it is in the nature of
secrets that they are difficult to detect, especially when an oath of
silence has been taken. At Newcastle in 1672 the loose tongue of one of
the carpenters gave the game away. An order had been made among
them that they should provide 'all the windows and doors in buildings
or else they would not build the house'. Thomas Oliver told this to
Anthony White who was building a house and 'intended to employ
joiners to make the windows'. As a result of the order 'he was forced to
make use of the carpenter'. Unfortunately the story was 'spoken in the
hearing of ... John Goften, who afterwards informed the company of
joiners and also the magistrates of this town'. Oliver was fined by the
carpenters for revealing their secrets. Two years later he fitted a
casement made by a joiner, Matthew Oliver, who was promptly fined
by his gild, and it was ordered that any others 'making joining work
for carpenters' were to forfeit the price of the job. Clearly, villainy ran
in the Oliver clan. In May 1676 Henry Wallis was reported to the
joiners' gild 'on suspicion of letting his key be in Matthew Oliver's,
deceased, custody fourteen days time when they were stewards, and it
is reported that the company of carpenters that time had the ordinary
of the company of joiners all that time'. The whole idea of having a box
with more than one lock and key was to avoid such problems.[122]

The effectiveness of the gilds can be viewed from different perspectives. From the point of view of the town authorities they were a
success: the provincial towns of early-modern England were not beset
by major internal conflicts, either between various groups of craftsmen
or between the 'haves' and 'have nots'. Relations often broke down
into rancorous dispute, but only one fatality has been recorded.
Members of thriving gilds were given considerable economic and
social support. However, the gilds were generally stronger during the

[119] HCRO, BRL/1458; TWAS, 802/2, 4, 16; 817/6; YCA, B33/120, 292b.
[120] Palliser 1979, 171–2; Swanson 1989, 88–9.
[121] Salzman 1952, 40.   [122] TWAS, 648/3.

early part of the period covered by this study than in the later stages. In some towns they remained vigorous into the eighteenth century: this was probably true of Chester, Newcastle, and York, although there may have been a falling-off towards the middle of the century.[123] At Chester, gild meetings became less frequent, and the Newcastle joiners recruited a declining proportion of their apprentices from outside the city as the century progressed.[124] However, in some of the smaller towns the gild system was either weak throughout the period or declined dramatically: it is believed that the gilds of Carlisle and Lincoln collapsed in the seventeenth century.[125]

Contracts and methods of payment

Sir Christopher Wren told the Bishop of Oxford: 'There are three ways of working: by the Day, by Measure, by Great.'[126] In the northern towns all three methods of working were used by the employing institutions, although by far the most common was the hiring of labour by the day. Many institutions adopted a fourth, hybrid method of setting labour to work: key workmen were given contracts, usually for a year, and were paid a small salary as a retainer which obliged them to work whenever required, usually for the going daily rate. Finally, a few craftsmen were hired on full-time yearly contracts, almost exclusively to work on the fabric of the great churches such as York Minster or Durham Cathedral.

On the few occasions that structures were made or altered for a set price – that is, 'by great' – the first task was to obtain an estimate of the amount of work to be done and its cost. Few such documents have survived, although at Chester 'An estimate of work to be done at the Northgate' was drawn up in 1702. The job was priced at £56 19s including £11 for brick work, £20 for carpentry, and £5 for glazing. A further estimate of 'joiners' work to be done in the treasure room' was made.[127] Often it was the larger jobs which were contracted for at a set price, such as the new gildhall at Hull erected during the 1630s under contract by John Catlyn. He was the town's most prominent builder,[128] although he never appears in the council accounts of the period as a jobbing builder. Clearly he was too important for that. At Newcastle in

---

123 Walker 1981.   124 Groombridge 1952, 96; TWAS, 648/12.
125 Clark & Slack 1976, 108–9; J.W.F. Hill 1956, 31–2, 205.
126 That is day work, piece-work, and contracting to erect a building, or part of it, for a set price. Quoted by Airs 1975, 46.
127 CCRO, TAV/1/4. See also the assessment for repairing the steeple of St Mary's, Chester, in 1657: CCORO, P/20/13/1. See also LAO, Bj/1/7.
128 Gillett & MacMahon 1989, 111; Neave 1983.

the later sixteenth century, Alexander Cheesman, a mason, was regularly employed by the council both by day and 'by great' to undertake extensive repairs at the south shore and new quay: between May
and October 1594 he was paid £84 for the work.[129] Occasionally small
jobs were done 'by great': at Hull two bricklayers agreed to build 'the
fence wall of the charity hall garden' for £3 in 1662.[130] At times it must
have been difficult to estimate the price of a job sufficiently accurately
to keep all parties happy. Anthony Hedley, a late-sixteenth-century
Newcastle carpenter, was paid an extra £1 by 'command of Mr Mayor
... in consideration of his loss he sustained of his bargain for building
the south shore', while at York in 1543 an organ maker was given an
extra 3s 4d 'reward over and beside our promise, because he should be
no loser'.[131] One age-old problem with any contract was getting the
work completed on time. In February 1587 an agreement was made
between the Chester city treasurer and Howell ap Richard, a mason,
'for raising of the house of stone at Boughton ten feet high'. In May he
was contracted to dig a well, but over a week passed, and 'misliking of
Howell's deferring of the work and fearing lest thereby I should be put
to more charges than the bargain was and also to be disappointed in
the end of the prefixed time, which is Whitsunday [4 June 1587], I
brake with Howell, and agreed with Thomas Mounfort mason to do
the same work upon the same conditions with all expedition and
workmanlike'.[132]

Although most carpenters, bricklayers, tilers, and masons were paid
by the day, some types of building craftsmen were frequently paid
piece-rates. Plumbers were usually paid by weight when casting lead,
but by the day when laying it; glaziers were sometimes paid by the
square foot; pavers by the square yard.[133] According to Wren, piece-
work had much to recommend it: 'the best way in this business', he
argued, 'is to work by measure'.[134] But not everyone agreed. When a
new barn was being planned for Sir John Lowther in 1699 a marginal
note suggested that: 'The slating I would choose to have done by day
[work] for otherwise most workmen do not use to do it so well.'[135] The
relatively rare use of piece-rates in the northern towns suggests that
more customers agreed with Lowther than with Wren.

The town councils employed a small army of part-time and full-time
salaried workers – both men and women – to perform a wide variety of

[129] TWAS, 543/18; 659/448.   [130] HCRO, BRF/3/20, p. 353.
[131] TWAS, 543/19, fo. 193v; YBI, PR/Y/MS/1, fos. 181v, 187v. See also YBI, PR/Y/MG/19,
p. 215.
[132] CCRO, TAV/1/1. See also YBI, PR/Y/MG/20, fo. 58.
[133] *Builder's Companion*, 7; LAO, Bj/1/8; DPK, LB26; YBI, PR/Y/MS/2, fo. 34v.
[134] Airs 1975, 51.   [135] Tyson 1983a, 109–12.

tasks: there were clerks, market keepers, gaolers, door-men, cooks, waits, minstrels, beadles, sword-bearers, physicians, and many others. Newcastle even had a town whipper.[136] Town councils, and many churches, also paid retainers to building craftsmen. All the councils for which information is available retained pavers and masons.[137] The terms of their contracts varied, but workmen were usually paid by the day for work done and for any materials supplied. When not working for the institution they were free to ply their trades elsewhere. At Newcastle the council derived large revenues from the coal trade and the jobs of the paver and his assistant were more or less full-time. The post was held by William Benson in 1561 and he worked for the council for about 290 days a year during the 1560s: in 1567 he clocked up 294 days, losing only 19 days apart from Sundays. He remained in post until the early 1590s when he was pensioned off at £1 a quarter because of his blindness.[138] Many town councils and churches also retained plumbers and glaziers, and on occasion the same man doubled up to do both jobs.[139] A blacksmith and a carpenter were retained at Lincoln Cathedral in the seventeenth century.[140]

The stipend paid to retained craftsmen varied considerably. The lowest recorded payment was the 6d a year paid by St Martin's, Coney Street, York, in 1589 to Henry Dereham 'for upholding the bell frame yearly whilst he liveth'.[141] Many fees were for only a few shillings a quarter, but some fared much better. At Beverley, John Parsyvall was paid £6 a year for plumbing and glazing at the Minster in the mid 1570s, and in 1630 his successor as glazier received £10 a year, although this was reduced to £8 in 1637.[142] Similarly high fees were received by the pavers of Chester and York in the eighteenth century.[143] Many of the retained craftsmen kept their positions for decades, but they were not necessarily sinecures. In July 1613 William Wyan, a mason, petitioned the Chester council asking that in return for 'his pains overseeing the breaches in the walls' he should have 'either the yearly stipend of 26s 8d and be given the yearly livery coat or 15s in lieu of it'. However, as he had been discharged from that duty 'and had never

---

[136] TWAS, 543/24. At Chester a fee was paid 'for dusting the records': CCRO, TAR/2/30.

[137] E.g., *Newcastle Chamberlains' Accts*, xxiv; *VCH Hull*, 375; YCA, CC5–36; LAO, Chamberlains' rolls, Boxes 1–5; *VCH Beverley*, 224–5; *Louth Accts*, 20, 67, 90; HCRO, BRN/14b. At Beverley in 1562 the paver was given a stipend of 6s 8d and was allowed 5s for house rent: HCORO, BC/II/7/2, fo. 49r.

[138] Howell 1967, 300; TWAS, 543/14–16, 18.

[139] E.g., *Kirkby Stephen Accts*, 180; LAO, L1/7/1; YBI, PR/Y/MG/19–20; NCRO, EP/13/68, pp. 266, 271, 277.

[140] LAO, Bj/1/6–8.   [141] YBI, PR/Y/MCS/17, fo. 14v.

[142] HCORO, BC/II/6/33; 7/4, fo. 66r.

[143] YCA, CC28–36; CCRO, TAV/1/15, 29–30.

seemed to do any work' his petition was rejected. Two years earlier, when George Salt, the town plumber, asked to be paid his arrears of £3 6s 8d the council inspected his work before deciding whether or not he should keep his post.[144]

The great majority of workmen employed by the institutions of the northern towns were paid neither 'by great' nor by the piece. A few workers, especially those employed by the larger churches, were paid by the week, and sometimes their weekly pay amounted to slightly more than six times the daily rate. But such examples are extremely rare.[145] Most workmen were paid by the day at the going rate.

Little is known about the times at which workmen were paid. Accounts drawn up on a weekly basis convey the impression that payment was made at the weekend, but there can be no certainty of this since the date of payment is never specified. For those working a full six-day week, payment on the Saturday evening made a great deal of sense for the customer. At Levens, near Kendal, in the late seventeenth century, the new steward was told, 'let them be paid every Saturday night'.[146] Payments were made at the same time when the Hull Citadel was being built in the 1680s, since, it was argued, when paid on a Friday the workers were 'addicted to be debauched and absent from the works the next day'.[147] But payment was not always forthcoming at the correct time. At Doncaster several cases were presented in the early sixteenth century relating to the non-payment of wages, and at Newcastle in April 1597 two labourers were owed 18s 'for three weeks' work apiece which was behind and unpaid': two months later money was also owed to the carpenters, masons, and smiths.[148] A request was made to the Lord Mayor of York in July 1596 on behalf of the city paver who 'desireth his wages or fee . . . remaining behind unpaid . . . and so we require you will pay him accordingly, the rather because the man is willing to do well'.[149] A similar request for prompt payment was made to the Bishop of Durham in December 1691 on behalf of a glazier. He was owed 3s, and the letter ended with a postscript: 'Pray speed his payment, he is poor.'[150] In an attempt to avoid the problems of late payment, the York bricklayers forbade members from working 'where another is owed money'.[151]

During the seventeenth century most institutions increasingly adopted a more indirect method of payment by which workmen, and

[144] *Chester Minutes*, 48, 66.
[145] DFC, CC/190045, 190067, 190069, 190071–2. See also *Louth Accts*, 23–6, 35–8, 53–4.
[146] *Levens Letters*, 155. [147] Tomlinson 1973, 18.
[148] *Doncaster Records*, II, 42, 53, 67; TWAS, 543/19, fos. 25v, 33r and v.
[149] YCA, CC8, fo. 80r. [150] DPK, LB25. [151] YML, QQ80/2/11.

especially the master craftsmen, submitted bills for work done. Inevitably this system involved delays which were likely to be particularly acute when workmen agreed to do a job for a fixed price. A Kendal carpenter agreed to build a new farm house for £8 10s in 1693: he was to receive £4 'when the house shall be raised' and the balance 'when the same is finished'.[152] At Hull and elsewhere payments were not made very promptly in the later seventeenth and early eighteenth centuries.[153] Detailed evidence is rare, but fortunately a fine set of bills submitted to the Carlisle council in the first half of the eighteenth century provides some interesting insights.[154] In some cases payment was almost immediate, although the work might have been spread over some months. Thus, in 1723, Henry Thompson did work between 26 April and 27 September and received payment on the last named date. At the other extreme, George Railton waited a long time for his money. In late 1733 and in 1734 he plastered ceilings, built two 'apartments' at the Charity House, and did various other repairs which were itemised in five bills totalling £59 1s 9½d. These bills were then consolidated in an account headed 'An Account of the Several Bills Given in by George Railton for the Corporation' and he was paid £10 on an unspecified date. A further payment of £34 was made in April 1735, and on 16 June he received the final instalment of £15 1s 9½d. He had, however, been doing other work during 1734 and the consolidated bill referred to 'the new stable at King's Garth not included being yet unfinished'. The account, for £10 17s 7d, was settled on 26 March 1736. Thus George Railton had had to wait for well over a year for some of his money. Sufficient information is provided in a further twenty bills to allow a similar analysis: three were settled almost immediately, seven within a month, four within three months, two within six months, and the remaining four within a year. When the job had been stretched out over some months the workman was out of pocket for even longer than this analysis suggests.

A few similar examples exist for other towns. At Chester the mason Charles Whitehead made out a bill in February 1732, amounting to £33 6s 4d, which began with work he had done in March 1729, together with work in each of the succeeding years.[155] Any craftsman who could carry debts of that nature over many months, or even years, was a long way from the margin of subsistence. The records of other towns, although not susceptible to detailed analysis, suggest that late payment was not uncommon. However, such bills relate chiefly to the

---

152 *Levens Letters*, 189.
153 E.g., HCRO, BRF/6; CCRO, TAV/1/12–13; NCRO, EP13/69.
154 CUMROC, Ca/4/11–126.   155 CCRO, MUV/3/36.

activities of well-established craftsmen and their ability to cope with late settlement. That the elite workers of the building trades were able to survive despite repeatedly delayed payment is demonstrated by the estates of four building craftsmen from the north-west who died between 1730 and 1750: they were owed debts amounting to an average of nearly £170, which comprised some 78 per cent of their combined estates as listed in their probate inventories.[156] Lesser men, struggling to survive, would have been less fortunate.

Wage differentials among building craftsmen

As Elizabeth Gilboy remarked, 'it is almost impossible to differentiate accurately between the degrees of skill encompassed in the term "mason" or "carpenter". Master craftsmen were indicated clearly, for the most part, but varying types of journeymen helpers, etc., could not be distinguished in the bills.'[157] Sometimes the accounts refer to 'his man' or 'his boy', but more often dependency is not stated. Nevertheless, where the records are more continuous than those used by Gilboy it is sometimes possible to gain insights into the changing status of individual workers. Young men can be observed emerging from their apprenticeships and gradually working their way by a succession of increments to the full wage of the skilled craftsman.[158] Alternatively, a lack of progression or failure to receive a wage increase could suggest some deficiency of skill or strength: such men probably remained in a dependent state. At Hull during the 1660s many master carpenters received 22d a day whereas two men – William Searge, who began work in 1652, and William Fletcher, who began in 1657 – remained at 18d throughout the lengthy period of their employment.[159]

During the later fifteenth and early sixteenth centuries most skilled building craftsmen in the north were paid similar rates. In part, this was due to the influence of the statutes which laid down national maximum wage rates for various classes of labour. The Act of 1444/5 divided the building trades into two groups: free masons and master carpenters who were to take no more than $5\frac{1}{2}$d a day in summer when feeding themselves, and others who were not to exceed $4\frac{1}{2}$d a day. Fifty years later, the Act of 1495 lumped all building craftsmen together and decreed that they should not receive more than 6d a day in summer when feeding themselves: only the master carpenter in

---

[156] CUMROC, inventories of Thomas Milburn of Appleby (owed £105), Isaac Monkhouse (£322 5s) and Robert Railton (£27) of Carlisle, and Robert Wilson of Penrith (£222 15s).

[157] Gilboy 1934, 224.   [158] See below p. 61.   [159] HCRO, BRF/3/20.

charge of six or more men could receive as much as 7d. These maxima were repeated in 1514.[160] Although these rates represented an increasingly poor return for labour as commodity-price inflation began to bite from the 1510s, the statutory maxima were generally observed until the later 1530s or 1540s when steep price rises made it impossible to hold the line.[161] At Durham, where the documentation is particularly rich, most building craftsmen were paid at the same rate. There were minor variations from time to time, but there was no tendency for one type of craftsman to be paid consistently at a higher rate than the others: in particular plumbers and carpenters were paid at the same rate down to the middle of the century.[162] The Statute of Artificers of 1563 removed the old national maximum wage rates, replacing them with local maxima to be determined annually by the JPs. This change in policy allowed regional differentials in wage levels to emerge more fully than previously and also made it easier for differentials to develop between different crafts.[163]

Within particular crafts differentials were associated chiefly with different levels of skill and responsibility. This was recognised by the Act of 1495 and had been demonstrated in the building accounts of Hull Trinity House during the 1460s and 1470s: Robert Paget, the carpenter in charge of the whole job, was paid 8d a day compared with the 6d a day paid to rank-and-file craftsmen.[164] Those who took charge of a large job were usually paid more than the men beneath them. High levels of skill were also rewarded: at Durham, in 1545, Cuthbert Huson received 10d for a day's work on the bell wheel, while other skilled men got 6d, or occasionally 7d a day; just over a century later, at Carlisle, Roger Walworth was paid 10s 10d 'for three days repairing the horsemill and showing the art therein'; and at Chester in 1728 Thomas Gill was paid 15s 'for drawing several drafts for the altering of the mayor's court'. He began work at the high daily rate of 30d, but then turned the job over to three of his men, who were paid 18d or 20d a day.[165]

Differentials also emerged between different types of craftsmen, and particularly between the plumbers and the rest. Thorold Rogers dis-

---

[160] 23 Henry VI c.12; 11 Henry VII c.22; 6 Henry VIII c.3.   [161] See below pp. 171–2.
[162] See appendix 1.4 for Durham sources.
[163] 5 Elizabeth I c.4. Before 1563 the most noticeable regional difference in wage rates was the high level of wages paid in London and allowed under the act of 1515: see Rappaport 1989, 403–7. For a discussion of the effects of the statute see below pp. 184–91.
[164] *Hull Trinity House Building*, 157–63.
[165] DPK,MC2756;CUMROC,Ca/4/3;CCRO,TAV/1/21,166;LAO,Bj/1/8;PRO,E101/458/ 24; 459/5–6; 463/17–20; 483/16–17; Colvin 1975, 417.

covered that plumbers were the most highly paid building operatives in southern England during the later sixteenth and seventeenth centuries,[166] and the same was generally true in the north. The timing of their emergence as an early aristocracy of labour is not easy to chart since they did not appear in the accounts each year: at Hull in the later sixteenth century plumbers appeared in the accounts of only four years out of twenty-one, but on each occasion they were paid 12d a day, 20 per cent above the rate received by the most highly paid carpenters.[167] In the later seventeenth century the differential could be even greater: at York in the early 1660s Martin Croft was paid 30d a day while his man was getting 18d, the same rate as the masons; similarly, at Durham, William Snowden received 24d in the early 1680s, but he had moved on to 30d by the end of the decade.[168] At the Restoration a large part of the roof of Lincoln Cathedral was re-leaded.[169] When the accounts open in 1660 Philip Peach was the contract plumber working for 14d a day, while other building craftsmen received 12d. It must be assumed that the task of renewing a large part of the roof covering was beyond him since a certain 'Mr Lawes' was employed at 30d a day during 1660/1 and other plumbers were soon engaged. Two outsiders were quickly at work casting lead at 40d a day each, which presumably covered their subsistence costs. Four more plumbers were employed that year at 30d a day, including William Carter who took over from Philip Peach as the retained plumber at the cathedral. After the Civil War the northern plumbers were normally paid considerably more than other building craftsmen, but it is the contrast between their wages and those of the labourers working alongside them which is most stark. Labourers generally received between two-thirds and a half of the rate given to building craftsmen,[170] but at the extreme they might earn as little as a quarter of the rate paid to a plumber: in 1669, when Marmaduke Atkinson was earning 24d a day at Hull, the man 'heating his irons' – admittedly a job of little skill and probably less effort – earned 6d.[171] And wide differentials existed elsewhere. Lincoln labourers received 8d or 10d a day in the 1660s when the plumbers were getting 30d, and Durham labourers got 12d a day in the 1680s compared with the top rate of 30d for the plumbers.[172]

There is no immediately obvious explanation for the high rates of pay offered to many plumbers. All craftsmen were expected to follow

[166] Rogers 1887, 639.   [167] HCRO, BRF/3/2–5.
[168] YML, E3/65/1, 3. See also HCRO, BRF/3/20; DPK, LB25; CCRO, TAV/1/27–9.
[169] LAO, Bj/1/8.   [170] See below pp. 171–7.   [171] HCRO, BRF/3/20, p. 677.
[172] LAO, Bj/1/8; DPK, LB25.

an apprenticeship of at least seven years, so that the exceptionally high rates of pay were not a reward for long training in a particular branch of the industry. Plumbing was a particularly noxious activity, especially when lead was being cast or lead ashes refined, but this would not explain the high levels of pay of the seventeenth century compared with the relatively modest rates of the early sixteenth century. Perhaps the answer lies in the availability of plumbers and the demand for their work. The Dissolution of the Monasteries led to a significant reduction in the total area of leaded roofs in the country and, no doubt, the number of plumbers fell. Those who remained probably found it difficult to obtain enough work as plumbers and often doubled up as glaziers. Perhaps sudden surges in demand then led on to inflated levels of remuneration. The Lincoln case is highly instructive. Philip Peach, the local plumber, had been receiving 14d a day along with the glazier, but the rush of new work necessitated the recruitment of outside labour which seems to have been able to name its own price. Once the rate had been set at 30d it was difficult to shift it, although an adjustment was made after a large-scale enquiry into the alleged malpractices of Henry Mansford, the clerk of works.[173] The summer rate was left undisturbed at 30d a day, but a rate of 18d a day was instituted for winter working. When William Carter, the new head plumber, worked as a glazier during the winter months he was paid only 14d a day, the going rate for that craft. When he changed hats and returned to his trade of plumber his rate of pay altered correspondingly. The high wages often earned by plumbers may have been compensation for the erratic demand for their labour: high daily wage rates did not necessarily translate into high levels of income. Unfortunately, insufficient is known about the work patterns of plumbers to test such a hypothesis. However, when a plumber worked as many days as William Carter in 1661/2 he could live well: he worked for 229 days and was paid an extra £24 19s for casting lead.

Discussion of wage differentials is bedevilled by our ignorance of the demand for labour and its supply in particular towns. It has been argued that although the demand for building in stone fell from the sixteenth century, and that for building in brick rose, this 'did not affect the relative wage rates of different categories of building workers'.[174] Perhaps this was due to a significant decline in the number of masons, or to a dramatic rise in the number of bricklayers, or to the dead hand of custom which precluded radical change. Perhaps all factors were at work, but in the absence of a substantial

[173] See below pp. 141, 143–4.   [174] Knoop & Jones 1949, 204–5.

volume of evidence to support any particular explanation it is wise to remain silent. Despite the many qualifications which need to be made, it is evident that most building craftsmen in most northern towns were paid at similar rates at particular points in time. Higher wages went to those who took charge of a job, to those who possessed exceptional skills and, perhaps, to those whose skills were in particularly short supply. But the great majority were paid similar rates which changed little from year to year.

The provision of raw materials

It is agreed that the church wardens for this next year inquire where and at what rates they can provide wood and stone and other materials for building the steeple.[175]

The provision of raw materials, at least on some occasions, provided building craftsmen with the opportunity to earn profits on top of their wages. The extent to which they benefited in that way cannot be established, although the extant accounts indicate that the practice was widespread, and this is confirmed by the stocks of materials revealed by building craftsmen's probate inventories.[176] The practice varied from trade to trade, and according to the scale of the job in hand. Smiths usually supplied any new iron required, although they were sometimes asked to rework old iron and, sometimes, partly paid in it. At the other extreme, it was rare for urban masons and pavers to provide the materials they worked with.[177] Carpenters, joiners, bricklayers, tilers, plumbers, and glaziers supplied materials on some but by no means all occasions. All craftsmen were more likely to do so when the job was relatively small-scale. The situation can be illustrated many times over: at Lincoln Cathedral the glazier supplied 'coloured glass of divers colours'; Lancelot Slater laid down five graves in York, and supplied two sacks of lime and some sand; the regular plumber at Newcastle, William Golightly, supplied '56 stone of lead of his own at 12d a stone for repairing the conduits to the cloth market'; a Carlisle slater was paid for 'finding slate, moss, pins and his workmanship'; and two carpenters working on a Chester steeple supplied 'five boards for the repair'.[178] It is simply not true that 'with the exception of the

175 YBI, PR/Y/MG/19, fo. 288a.
176 Woodward 1981, 34–9. See also inventories for north-western building workers in the first half of the eighteenth century: CUMROC and CUMROK.
177 Some masons supplied the stone to construct country houses: Airs 1975, 48.
178 Lincoln 1628–9, LAO, Bj/1/7; York 1640, YBI, PR/Y/HTG/12, fo. 374; Newcastle 1667, TWAS, 543/15, fo. 278r; Carlisle 1615, CUMROC, Ca/4/1; Chester 1568/9, CCORO, P/65/8/1, fo. 43r.

glaziers, few builders supplied the materials on which they worked'.[179] Such an impression may be gained by concentrating on large-scale building projects for which building craftsmen only occasionally supplied materials. But large-scale operations were not typical of building work in general. Most building craftsmen spent the bulk of their time doing small-scale repair work of the sort illustrated by the collection of Carlisle bills: in all but three out of seventy-nine bills the head craftsman supplied the materials with which he and his gang worked. The jobs were relatively small-scale, but they covered quite a wide range. John Railton was paid 9d for half a day, plastering alongside two labourers, and he provided lime and hair valued at 2s. At the other extreme George Railton made out a bill for plastering and bricklaying amounting to £5 14s, which included payments for a substantial quantity of materials – 10 cartloads of sand, 15 of lime and 3 of slate, 2,000 bricks, 1,760 laths, and $8\frac{1}{2}$ stone of hair.[180]

Timber was needed on most building sites and carpenters occasionally contributed to supplies even on the largest projects: in 1623 John Westoby, a leading Hull carpenter, supplied 134 feet of timber for a jetty, although most of it came from other sources.[181] Imported deals and boards were usually bought in bulk from the town's merchants.[182] Heavy timber for structural purposes was mostly oak and was generally bought by the town councils and other institutions *in situ*, then cut down and transported to the site at their expense. Sometimes the purchases were large: in 1594 the Newcastle council bought 120 trees in Byker Wood for £48, and in 1583 the Hull council negotiated to buy ten score of trees from Thorganby in the East Riding for £100.[183] Carpenters were often employed to select timber in distant woods. In the summer of 1634, Thomas Bannister, the chief carpenter at Lincoln Cathedral, was paid for 'setting out the timber' and organising the felling of 'thirteen trees of great timber in the Minster wood' at Harby, near Newark, and sawing them into planks.[184] Similarly, a Hull overseer, Matthew Hardy, scoured parts of the East and West Ridings, and north Nottinghamshire for suitable timber during the 1660s and 1670s.[185] Occasionally, the towns were given timber for a particular project. In 1527 the Abbot of Fountains gave ten trees for the repair of Ouse Bridge at York, from 'our woods at Thorpe', and in 1577 the Queen gave 300 trees for the Hull defences from the West Riding, each

[179] Swanson 1989, 82.
[180] CUMROC, Ca/4/11–126. Five of the eighty-four bills are not suitable for this analysis.
[181] HCRO, BRF/3/11; Woodward 1981, 34.
[182] HCRO, BRF/3/20; HTH, III–V; Jackson 1972, 29; Salzman 1952, 247.
[183] TWAS, 543/18, fo. 94v; HCRO, BRF/3/5, BRM79.   [184] LAO, Bj/1/6/2.
[185] HCRO, BRF/3/20, pp. 345–6ff.

capable of providing timbers 16 inches square and 24 feet long.[186] Trees
were carried by river craft whenever possible, although on at least one
occasion the Humber and its tributaries must have resembled a Cana-
dian lake: in 1580 £2 10s 8d was spent on empty casks for 'fleeting of
the timber' and 6s had to be spent 'saving one piece of timber from
being carried away with the water in the west country'. Ropes to lash
the logs together cost £1 2s.[187]

At Hull, the council signed a number of agreements with bricklayers
to supply the town with lime. There was a lime kiln in the town as
early as the 1430s,[188] and in the seventeenth century it was leased out
to a succession of bricklayers, who also appear in the accounts wielding their trowels. On 20 March 1635 a lease was granted to Thomas
Tesh, who had worked for Trinity House as early as 1615 and was
warden of the bricklayers' gild in 1621, 1624, and 1633.[189] The lease was
for three lime kilns and other property alongside the Humber which
had been in the tenure of Richard Bennington, deceased, who had
supplied bricks, lime, and sand to Trinity House twenty years before.
Tesh was to hold the property for twenty-one years, at an annual rent
of £13 6s 8d, and keep it in good repair. The agreement was to be
terminated if he failed to deliver lime at 10s 8d a chaldron to townsmen
'at their houses or such other places there as they or any of them shall
appoint with such quantities as they shall desire of good and well
burned lime'. That year he supplied nearly twenty chaldrons of lime to
the council, and also worked for $5\frac{1}{2}$ days laying bricks at 14d a day. In
October he was paid 3s 'for telling over 26 thousand tiles at fort'.[190] In
1675 the kilns were leased to John Purver, and the lease specified that
they had previously been in the control of Thomas Tesh, bricklayer,
Thomas Harpham, bricklayer, William Worrell, and Mr William Robinson, all of whom had supplied the town with lime.[191] John Purver's
first lease in March 1675 was for three years and it covered two lime
kilns and outbuildings 'adjacent to the Humber and lime kiln creek'.
The annual rent was £7 13s 4d and he was given the right, almost
certainly possessed by earlier lessees, to dig for chalk at the nearby
'lime kiln cliff' at Hessle. He was to supply lime during the first year of
his tenancy at 13s 4d a chaldron, but for the second and third years the
price was set at 12s for burgesses and at 13s 4d for non-burgesses. He
was given further leases in 1677 and 1688, the latter being for thirty-

[186] *YCR*, III, 106–7; Gillett & MacMahon 1989, 152. See also HCRO, BRI/17.
[187] HCRO, BRF/3/4. See also DPK, MC/2942/2, 2987 for bulk purchases of timber, and
Laughton 1987–8, 108, for floating logs.
[188] *VCH Hull*, 57.
[189] HCRO, BRN/193; BRF/3/19; HTH, III, fo. 47; *Hull Bricklayers*, 49.
[190] HCRO, BRF/3/19.   [191] HCRO, BRN/391b; BRF/3/19–20.

one years for which he gave £100 'in hand, paid as a fine' and £10 a year.[192] Purver, who had first appeared in 1653 as an apprentice bricklayer earning 6d a day for his master, remained in the lime-burning business until at least 1709, and on occasion he also supplied bricks and worked as a jobbing bricklayer.[193]

Some gilds allowed their members to trade in raw materials, although attitudes varied from gild to gild. At Hull the joiners could 'buy wainscot, clapboards, or any other stuff belonging to their occupation', but 'such only as they shall work and no other'. However, the York carpenters were to refrain from buying before noon 'to the end that all citizens and other inhabitants of the said city may buy such timber as they shall have occasion to use for their own uses and not to sell again': the implication was that only woodworkers had the right to trade in timber.[194] This was confirmed in 1589 when the carpenters and joiners were in dispute with Thomas Gibson, a tiler, who had been handling such materials. It was resolved that the carpenters and joiners could buy timber between 10 a.m. and 2 p.m., after which others could buy, but only for their own use. However, Gibson was to be allowed to continue trading as long as he paid a fee of 3s 4d a year and made a similar payment to atone for past offences.[195] At Chester an order of 1557 laid down that the joiners were to buy only enough timber for their own use, although the situation seems to have changed by the later part of Elizabeth's reign when the gild had a protracted dog-fight with Robert Brerewood, a glover by trade, one of the town's leading citizens and a very rich man. The gild objected to his trading in timber. He had been buying up timber in Wales during the late 1570s and the council ordered him to stop. There were further complaints, but Robert Brerewood was too important and influential to be curbed effectively by the council, which he ruled over as mayor on three occasions. At his death in 1601 he possessed an enormous stock of timber, stacked all over the town, valued at more than £100, and he was owed debts of over £18 by a number of timbermen.[196]

It has been argued that the gilds had nothing to do 'with the financing, supply, and providing of raw materials' or with capital investment.[197] In many instances that was probably the case, with gilds merely providing an umbrella of regulation and protection beneath which small businesses could shelter. But two of the Newcastle gilds

[192] HCRO, BRN/391b, 446. The chaldron was stipulated at 32 Winchester bushels.
[193] HCRO, BRF/3/20–1, BRF/6/313, 349, 353, 417.
[194] *Gild Life*, 254; YML, QQ80/3/2.   [195] YCR, IX, 76–7.
[196] CCRO, A/B/1, fo. 91r, MCP/2/1–6, 8–9, 11; CCORO, P/20/13/1; Woodward 1968b, 83.
[197] Phythian-Adams 1979, 105, 108.

did more. During the seventeenth and early eighteenth centuries the joiners' gild ran a timber-purchasing scheme, the details of which are not entirely clear. According to an ordinance of 1719 the stewards were given a salary of £2 'for going about and buying timber'. Their job was to negotiate with the owners of timber for its purchase, and then offer it to the members who were free to take a share of the bargain or reject it. The gild never owned the timber, and the stewards' salary seems to have been to cover travelling expenses and to provide hospitality to lubricate deals: in 1658 6d was spent 'going to see Thomas Todd's clapboard'.[198] The bricklayers were even more deeply involved in the production of their chief raw material. In 1727 the gild made an agreement with four men who were 'to act as brickmakers and diggers of clay'. The four agreed that they 'with the rest of their servants ... shall serve the company for the year next ensuing, truly and faithfully in digging clay and making bricks; and shall make merchantable bricks'. They forswore absenteeism and agreed to use the same mould as the previous year. The top man was to get 14d a day 'when he casts bricks' and 16d 'when he makes bricks', and the others a few pence less. Two extremely detailed account books chart the progress of the business for the years 1725–9 and 1738–42: it was a large enterprise with annual receipts averaging £450.[199] It is possible that similar schemes existed elsewhere although the records of any such activity have not survived.

Craftsmen working on small-scale projects and supplying small quantities of materials were unlikely to become rich by that route, although every addition to the family income, no matter how small, was welcome to those living relatively simple lives uncomfortably close to the subsistence line. Those who were able to move beyond such narrow horizons and supply materials on a larger scale had the chance of pushing out of the lower ranks of building craftsmen. A few such men emerged in late-medieval York, including a plumber and a mason who traded in lead.[200] But virtually nothing is known about the profits which could be made from dealing in building materials, although the succession of men prepared to work the Hull lime kilns suggests that returns were adequate, despite the fact that prices were fixed by the council. During the 1570s most lime sold in the town for 9s 4d a chaldron, although prices ranged from 8s to 10s 4d. From the 1610s to the Civil War the price was fixed at 10s 8d, and at 13s 4d from the

---

[198] TWAS, 648/6, p. 27; 648/8. See also 648/3, 6, 13. See also the case of the Chester shoemakers: Woodward 1968b, 74.
[199] TWAS, 817/9; 802/7–8. [200] Swanson 1989, 134.

mid 1650s to the mid 1670s.[201] That is, the price of lime rose less than 50 per cent over the course of a century.

The provision of tools and capital equipment

Craftsmen were also set apart from common labourers by their possession of specialist tools of the trade. Tools were simple and most craftsmen had only small amounts of capital invested in them, but they did need replacing from time to time and were an essential charge on their resources.[202] When the York builders went on strike in 1552 they argued that they could not accept the low wages offered 'unless you do rate all manner of tools and tool-makers and all victuallers as you do your poor orators'.[203] Individual tools were sometimes listed and valued in probate inventories, but the price of only a single tool which changed hands is known: at Newcastle in the summer of 1592 4s 6d was laid out 'for a wright's axe which beheaded the seminary', and 'a hand axe and a cutting knife which did rip and quarter the seminary priest' cost 1s 2d.[204] Perhaps the larger axe resembled the 'broad mouthed crooked axe' bequeathed by a Cumbrian carpenter in 1644.[205]

Although they owned their own tools, craftsmen did not always bear the full cost of keeping them in good order. In particular, the edge tools of masons and pavers needed sharpening frequently and the customer or employing institution often paid the bill: at Kendal in 1592 John Becke was paid a shilling 'for sharpening picks for a year past'.[206] Unlike most other building craftsmen, masons and pavers were sometimes provided with some of their basic tools by those who set them on work. Masons' lodges usually housed a range of tools, and new tools were provided for the masons at the building of the new haven at Chester in the late 1560s. Similarly, at Newcastle during the later sixteenth century the city's paver, William Benson, was supplied with many of his tools by the council.[207] Few other workmen received such benefits, although at Hull in 1657, when a large amount of timber work was being done at a jetty, the council provided a new grindstone for the carpenters, and at Newcastle in 1594 the council paid for some 'soap to the wrights for their saws'.[208] Occasionally, when workmen

201 HCRO, BRF/3/3–20.   202 Swanson 1989, 129; Woodward 1981, 36–8.
203 Woodward 1980b, 9.
204 TWAS, 543/18, fo. 252v.
205 CUMROC, P1644, will of William Robanks of Lazonby.
206 CUMROK, WSMB/K. See also TWAS, 543/15, fo. 241r; CCRO, TAR/3/58a; DFC, CC/ 190072; Salzman 1952, 337; YCR, VI, 125.
207 Knoop & Jones 1949, 60–9; *Chester Haven*, 100, 117; TWAS, 543/14–16, 18.
208 HCRO, BRF/3/20, p. 171r; TWAS, 543/18, fo. 94r.

were required to work away from home they were paid for the cost of moving their tools. Two shillings were paid at Durham in 1545 'for carriage of instruments of plumbers' when they worked at Bedlington in Northumberland.[209] An alternative arrangement was adopted some years later when eight masons and seven labourers were sent from Durham to build a spiral staircase at Norham Castle near Berwick: they received three days' travelling expenses in each direction, and a man was sent to Berwick 'to provide and borrow work looms there'. A carpenter was employed at the site to make twelve barrows, a sled, and a barrow called 'a six men's barrow'.[210]

In addition to their hand tools, some craftsmen also possessed larger items of gear or tackle. At Newcastle in 1671 a dispute broke out between the bricklayers and the slaters. Previously the slaters had been allowed to do bricklayers' work on payment of a fine of 3s 4d, but the arrangement had fallen into abeyance. It was decided that the old scheme should be revived because the slaters were 'better fitted with ladders for that use'.[211] Other craftsmen owned ropes or other unspecified 'tackle'. In 1597 a carpenter working for the York council supplied some boards and lent 'his tackles and ropes', for 2d. At St Michael's, Spurriergate, a carpenter was paid 'for the use of his cables and pulleys', which no doubt resembled the 'large rope and pulleys' belonging to a Penrith mason who died in 1744.[212] Some jobs required scaffolding. The traditional method involved lashing wooden poles and cross-members together with ropes and then adding planks, and some craftsmen were able to supply the necessary gear. In 1667 the chief carpenter at Lincoln Cathedral submitted a bill 'for scaffolding for the free masons'.[213] But in most cases it was supplied by the employing institution. Sometimes the poles and ropes were acquired specially for the occasion: at Hull in 1675 Ann Kneebone was paid 5s 4d 'for a parcel of second hand ropes for making fast timber and for scaffolding ropes'.[214] On other occasions, poles and ropes were taken out of the storehouse and re-used.[215] Other, more expensive, items of capital equipment were also supplied by the employing institutions. At Durham in 1543 the clerk of works at the cathedral bought some 'ropes

[209] DPK, MC2781. See also YML, E3/51; TWAS, 543/16, fo. 133v.
[210] DFC, CC/190078.
[211] TWAS, 802/16.
[212] YCA, CC9, fo. 56r; YBI, PR/Y/MS/2, fos. 69r, 104v, PR/Y/MS/5; CUMROK, inventory of Hugh Law, P1744.
[213] LAO, Bj/1/8. See also HCORO, PE/1/83; YBI, PR/Y/MS/2, fo. 45r.
[214] In 1670 she had supplied 'a double and single tackle block and hooks': HCRO, BRF/3/20, pp. 683, 840. See also BRF/3/4, 10; TWAS, 543/18, fo. 116r; HCORO, PE/1/59; LAO, Bj/1/7; CCRO, TAR/3/43.
[215] HCRO, BRF/3/20, p. 243; HCORO, PE/121/37.

for the cradle for pointing', and a similar piece of equipment, called 'the plumber or glaziers' stool' was mentioned at York Minster in 1581.[216] Cranes, 'gins' or windlasses, and pile-drivers were either borrowed from other bodies or owned outright by the institutions, although some machines, like the crane made in three-and-a-half days by a Beverley carpenter in 1494, were probably not very sophisticated.[217]

Institutions also accumulated a number of tools and other items of equipment which were used by labourers and building craftsmen, or for cleaning up after them. Very occasionally a piece of specialist equipment was acquired, like the 'long small guiding rope for the plumber' bought for Lincoln Cathedral in 1624.[218] But most of the equipment was more basic: wheelbarrows, spades and shovels, brushes to clean the windows and to bring down spiders' webs, mops and brooms, chamber pots and baskets for carrying out dirt, ladders, and fire-buckets were all bought. At Beverley in 1562, 'one great chain for pulling down of houses' was acquired.[219] During the seventeenth century the Hull council owned one or two carts for essential town business, and other towns may have done likewise. But on most occasions carts were hired from local operators as needed, sometimes from the building workers themselves: at Kendal in 1639 George Fell, a prominent mill-wright, hired out his horse to help move some new mill stones.[220]

Reflections

Building craftsmen stand out more clearly than any other group of manual workers in early-modern England. The accounts of town councils, churches, and other institutions have survived in profusion and provide many thousands of references to their employment and payment. Typically they worked by the day for a set daily wage: most were paid at similar levels, although the more skilled men in charge of a project usually earned more. Additionally, after the middle of the sixteenth century the plumbers emerged as an early aristocracy of

216 DFC, CC/190072; YML, E3/58. The York stool required a rope weighing $8\frac{1}{2}$ stones.
217 HCORO, BC/II/6/15; *YCR*, I, 51–2; II, 138–9; Salzman 1952, 85–7, 323–8; Ayers 1979, 6; HCRO, BRF/3/4,8,20; *Louth Accts*, 27; *Kirkby Stephen Accts*, 173; CCRO, P/65/8/1, fo. 90v; TWAS, 543/15, fo. 259v; YBI, PR/Y/MS/2, fo. 92r.
218 LAO, Bj/1/7.
219 HCORO, BC/II/6/25. There are many dozens of references to such purchases scattered through the sources used for this study.
220 HCRO, BRF/3/20, pp. 237, 305–6, 402, 709; CUMROK, WSMB/K; CUMROC, Ca/4/11–126.

labour, earning rates substantially higher than those of other building craftsmen. But master craftsmen were not wage-earners in the modern sense: in addition to their own labour they often supplied that of a journeyman or apprentice, and, especially on the smaller jobs, they often provided at least some of the raw materials. Both accounts and gild records make it plain that firms in the building trades remained small throughout the period: few involved more than one or two men, and one-man firms were common. In part this was due to the fragmented nature of the market. On many occasions small amounts of work were required to repair damaged property: when larger projects were in hand a range of small firms would be gathered together to work under the supervision of a foreman or overseer.

In many towns building craftsmen were a sizeable group, although they did not form a cohesive whole: in the larger towns they were divided into small sub-groups, each organised by its own gild. Gild membership brought substantial benefits. Demarcation lines were stoutly defended and, in at least some of the gilds, surplus funds were distributed amongst the members at the year end. Moreover, the frequent drinkings and feastings which were such a marked feature of gild life made humdrum lives more palatable. Above all gild membership brought a sense of belonging and the opportunity for ordinary men from humble callings to rise to positions of authority and respect. Building craftsmen were unlikely to progress far up the social hierarchies of early-modern towns, but they could aspire to leadership of their craft gilds, positions which would bring them into contact with the leaders of town society.

In the next chapter the life-cycle of building craftsmen is explored. Those who became master craftsmen usually progressed through a formal apprenticeship and then endured a period as journeyman for one of the established workers. However there were others drafted into the towns from the countryside to work as journeymen. Those who did become masters were given the opportunity to prosper, although most did not live long to enjoy it: over half of them failed to survive into their fifties. As a result many firms were left without a hand on the tiller and a surprisingly large number of widows took up the challenge and tried to keep the family business going.

3

The life-cycle of building craftsmen

The apprentice

Apprenticeship was a valued institution in early-modern England. It provided training, chiefly in the manual arts and crafts, and, as contemporary observers were quick to point out, ensured that large numbers of young people were closely controlled during the years before they had acquired sufficient discretion and wisdom to govern themselves and establish their own households. Apprenticeship also regulated the flow of potential master craftsmen, thus avoiding an unacceptably high level of overstocking in the skilled labour market. Finally, it has been argued that apprenticeship provided master craftsmen with a plentiful supply of cheap labour.

Only boys were apprenticed to building craftsmen in the northern towns. No reference has been discovered to the apprenticeship of girls, although some women did participate in the building process: the ability of some women to step into their dead men's shoes suggests that they had received some informal training.[1] Young men were recruited into the building crafts both from within the various towns and from the surrounding countryside. The place of origin is known of 127 of the 286 young men apprenticed to York bricklayers between 1654 and 1752: 61 or 48 per cent were drawn from the city.[2] At Newcastle about a third of the apprentice joiners was home-grown in the later seventeenth century, although internal recruitment became more important in the early decades of the eighteenth century (see table 3.1).

[1] On the training of female workers see: B. Hill 1989, 85–102; Snell 1985, 273–98; Swanson 1989, 116.
[2] YML, QQ80/2/13.

Table 3.1   *The origin of apprentices of Newcastle joiners*

	Number	Newcastle %	Northumberland %	Co. Durham %	Other %
1650–74	75	37.3[a]	34.7	22.7	5.3
1675–99	104	33.7	40.4	15.4	10.6
1700–24	95	54.7	27.4	12.6	5.3
1725–49	68	60.3	25.0	14.7	—
Total	342	45.6	32.5	16.1	5.7

Source: TWAS, 648/13.
Note: [a] The Newcastle number for 1650–74 includes sixteen young men referred to as 'son of' which implies that they were from the city. Seven young men whose place of origin was not given are not included.

Immigrants came predominantly from Northumberland and Co. Durham, although sometimes this involved only a very short journey: twelve young men came from Gateshead, just across the Tyne, and one from neighbouring Dunston. Of those from further afield, eleven were from Yorkshire, two from Lancashire, one each from Cumberland, Westmorland, and London, and four from Scotland.[3] Many young bricklayers were also drawn from the city in the later seventeenth century: of the fifty-six whose place of origin is known forty were home grown, twelve came from Northumberland, one from Co. Durham, and three from further afield.[4] At Chester only a third of the young glaziers indentured between 1595 and 1665 came from outside the city.[5] Recruitment to the Kendal building trades in the same period was more widespread: 28 out of the 72 recruits came from the town, 19 from elsewhere in Westmorland, 17 from Lancashire, 6 from Cumberland, and 2 from the western parts of north Yorkshire.[6]

The occupation or status of the father of 293 apprentices is given in the records of the Newcastle joiners for the years 1647 to 1750. Over 200 of the fathers were said to be 'yeomen', 51 of them were from the city itself. However, in the north-east the term 'yeoman' was used to describe small landholders, and did not carry the implication of relative superiority common elsewhere: this suggests that the majority of young men were from relatively humble rural origins. The remaining

[3] At Carlisle anyone taking a Scottish boy as an apprentice was to be fined £10. *Carlisle Records*, 66.
[4] TWAS, 802/2. One came from each of Yorkshire, Scotland, and King's Lynn: the place of origin of four was not given.
[5] Alldridge 1986, 19.
[6] CUMROK, Apprentice Enrolment Book 1640–1789; Book of Indentures 1680–1736.

fathers included 20 mariners, 12 tailors, 7 smiths, 6 millers, and 19 in the building trades. A few belonged to higher social groupings: 14 were described as 'gentleman', including 2 from the city itself, and the sons of a hostman and a merchant were apprenticed in the early eighteenth century.[7] The occupation or status of the fathers of eighty apprentice bricklayers in York is known for the period 1654 to 1752. The most common parental occupation was bricklayer – 21 in total, 11 of the young men being bound to their fathers – while 12 of the fathers were called 'yeoman'. However, there were no gentlemen among the fathers and only one merchant. The remainder included eight other building craftsmen, two brickmakers, a smith, a limeman, and seven labourers.[8] Information relating to the occupations of apprentices' fathers is inadequate in various respects and cannot provide more than a very rough indication of their social origins. However, many – especially those reared in a town – came from craft-dominated households, although many of the country boys seem to have been from agricultural backgrounds.[9]

The Statute of Artificers laid down a minimum term of seven years for apprenticeships.[10] This had long been common in many English towns. At York the last ordinance to allow a shorter period was made in 1503, and by 1530 seven years was the norm.[11] The same had been established at Grimsby in 1498, at Chester in 1557, and at Lincoln in the early fifteenth century.[12] After 1563 some gilds insisted on a longer period of service. The York carpenters moved to eight years in 1586, while the bricklayers insisted on a minimum of eight years in 1590: between 1654 and 1752 only one bricklayer was apprenticed for seven years and over 90 per cent of the 286 young men indentured were bound for eight years. Similarly, some Chester gilds insisted on longer than the statutory minimum.[13] The Statute also insisted that apprenticeships should 'not expire afore such apprentice shall be of the age of four and twenty years at the least'. Such an age was widely regarded as the time at which men developed a sense of responsibility:

Until a man grow unto the age of 24 years, he (for the most part though not always) is wild, without judgement, and not of sufficient experience to govern himself, nor (many times) grown unto the full or perfect knowledge of the art

---

[7] TWAS, 648/13. For a discussion of the meaning of the term 'yeoman' in the north-east see Wrightson 1987, 189.   [8] YML, QQ80/2/13.
[9] For London the relatively humble origins of apprentices in the construction industry has been stressed: Rappaport 1989, 307–8.
[10] 5 Elizabeth I, c.4.   [11] Palliser 1972, 97–8.
[12] From information provided by E. Gillett for Grimsby; CCRO, A/B/1, fo. 91r; LAO, L1/3/1, fo. 4v.
[13] YML, QQ80/2/11, 2/13, 3/2; *Chester Minutes*, 97.

or occupation that he professeth, and therefore had more need still to remain under government, as a servant and learner, than to become a ruler, as a master or instructor.[14]

The northern authorities probably obeyed this instruction, although only one indenture insisted that the period of service should last until twenty-four.[15] Thus, young men would have been seventeen or sixteen respectively at the start of a seven or eight-year stint, and, like the apprentice carpenters of London who were over nineteen on average when indentured, 'hardly the boys of textbook fame'.[16] Although it would have been difficult to guarantee the age of recruits, the need for strength and maturity on the part of building-trade apprentices suggests that evasion of the age requirement was probably not excessive. In south Yorkshire James Fretwell was nearly sixteen when he began his training as a carpenter in July 1715, and the Alnwick Orders of 1701 for masons insisted that an apprentice should 'be able of his birth and limbs, as he ought to be'.[17] But not all remained so. William Harle, the son of Robert Harle, a yeoman of Otterburn in Northumberland, was apprenticed to the Newcastle joiner Paul Cook for seven years in January 1703, but nearly three years later, 'by reason of his bodily infirmity, not being able to serve his time, he hath by consent of his master come to the meeting house and crossed this his enrolment out of the book'.[18] Although it is never explicitly stated, it seems likely that the small number of apprentices bound for more than seven or eight years – whichever was the norm in a particular gild – began their training at a relatively young age. That was probably so in the case of William Maxwell who was apprenticed at York in 1584. He had 'put himself an apprentice to Peter Currer, joiner, with him to dwell as apprentice from this day for and during twelve years ... in respect that the said apprentice is the child of a poor decayed citizen'.[19]

Young men began their training with a period of probation of a few weeks or months before they were formally indentured.[20] No doubt this was to test the compatibility of master and servant before the die was finally cast. But the system could be abused: in 1593 the Chester joiners insisted that no brother should keep a young man unbound for more than three months, and the Newcastle bricklayers reduced the period to no more than three weeks after 1700. At Chester apprentice

---

[14] *TED*, I, 354. Memorandum of *c.* 1573 on the Statute of Artificers.
[15] TWAS, 648/13. The York glovers recommended twenty-four as the suitable age for the end of apprenticeship: Palliser 1972, 99.
[16] Rappaport 1989, 295.   [17] *Family History*, 182, 189; Knoop & Jones 1949, 276.
[18] TWAS, 648/13.
[19] *YCR*, IX, 47.   [20] Ben-Amos 1988, 50–1.

bricklayers and smiths were to be enrolled at the next meeting after they had been taken on.[21]

Little is known about the training or about the daily lives of apprentices, although it is usually assumed that they lived in the homes of their masters, receiving board, lodging, and clothing along with professional training.[22] Two Beverley indentures are more than usually revealing. Robert Johnson was apprenticed to a tiler for six years in 1572, and he was to receive, 'every of the six years, 1d and meat, drink, clothes and all other necessaries meet and convenient. And in the end of the said six years decent apparel for holy days and working days.' For his part the young man agreed 'to use himself as a true, just and obedient servant unto his said master both in deed and word in every respect during the said term'. A year later, Thomas Hall from Hedon was bound to a smith for thirteen years: he was to receive 1d a year 'for his wage', together with sufficient meat, drink, and apparel, and his master promised to teach him the art of the blacksmith 'in his best manner'.[23] At Hull the bricklayers were expected to 'bring up reverently their servants in the fear of God, and teach them good manner, so far forth as in them lieth. And every master shall bring his servant to the church upon Sundays and holy days, to hear divine service and sermon, if they be able to come and not forth of the town, or can show sufficient cause of their absence to the warden'.[24] The gild records indicate that occasionally things did not work out as planned. In 1641, Margaret Williamson, the widow of a Chester joiner, complained to the gild that her apprentice would not carry her timber, refused to go with her to church, and was altogether 'very sturdy against her'.[25] In 1719 the Newcastle joiners established a fine of 6s 8d for any apprentice who stayed out of his master's house after 9 p.m., wasted or embezzled his master's goods, or abused his master and his family.[26] At London, serious offences were punished by public humiliation and beatings, but such treatment has not been recorded in the northern building trades, although beatings were used to enforce discipline on the north-eastern coalfield.[27]

Some apprentices never finished their terms, although the haemorrhage seems to have been much less acute than in London, where only 41 per cent did so.[28] At York between 1654 and 1752 only 20 out of 286 apprentice bricklayers were recorded as not running the full course,

[21] CCRO, G14/1, fo. 5v; G20/1; TWAS, 802/16.   [22] Palliser 1972, 99; Dunlop 1912.
[23] HCRO, BC/II/7/3, fos. 65v, 69r. In neither case was it made clear why the unusual terms were laid down.
[24] *Gild Life*, 277–8.   [25] CCRO, G14/2, p. 81.   [26] TWAS, 648/6, p. 20.
[27] Rappaport 1989, 209; from information provided by John Hatcher.
[28] Rappaport 1989, 77, 233, 313–14.

although the reason for non-completion is known in only two cases: one young man simply 'went away' and another died.[29] Gild records are often tantalisingly terse: William Coats was apprenticed at York in July 1672, but the minutes simply record that he 'deserted his master's service the 21 December 1672'.[30] No explanation is given. Perhaps he was insufficiently robust for the job, or half starved by his mistress and abused by his master. Similarly we have no way of knowing why a poor boy apprenticed to a Newcastle joiner attended a meeting in September 1684 and 'crossed himself out of the book'.[31]

The training of some apprentices was disrupted when they were 'turned over' or transferred to another master, usually because of the death of the original master. In the second half of the seventeenth century, 183 young men were apprenticed to Newcastle joiners and 16 of them were transferred, 3 of them twice. On all but two occasions the turnover was caused by the master's death, although once the master had 'gone away'. On twelve occasions the apprentice was transferred to 'his dame', that is, to the widow of the dead master.[32] At York, where only 13 of the 286 bricklayers' apprentices were recorded as turnovers, the records may not be complete.[33] Some turnovers involved a substantial degree of friction between master and apprentice. At Chester in 1624 John Hey, an apprentice joiner complained to the mayor about his master. The mayor ordered the gild to meet to arrange a transfer, but the dispute was patched up and the two promised to 'agree together' in future.[34] At Newcastle a more intractable dispute broke out in 1655. Robert Cuthbertson had been apprenticed to a bricklayer in June 1652, and when his master died he was transferred to Charles Robson, early in 1655. But things did not work out and in December 1655 the gild recorded 'the general vote and consent of the company touching Robert Cuthbertson, how he shall be disposed of'. Eight members of the gild agreed that Cuthbertson had been 'fairly contracted for' by William Jameson, who, therefore, 'ought to enjoy his said servant having already paid for him'. But Cuthbertson was not happy with the new arrangement and he was put on open offer, to see 'who will give more money for him and now hath or would outbid him'. John Watson did so, although Cuthbertson, 'now in difference, being called in before the whole company and asked whether he would serve John Watson or not, gave answer that he was resolved never to serve John Watson so long as he liveth'. The final

[29] YML, QQ80/2/13; YAS PR, XI, 41.   [30] YML, QQ80/2/13.
[31] TWAS, 648/13.
[32] TWAS, 648/13.   [33] YML, QQ80/2/13.   [34] CCRO, G14/2, p. 64.

resolution was not recorded.[35] Such protracted disputes were rare and the great majority of apprentices quietly served out the remainder of their terms with their new masters. Gild records make it plain that the apprentice usually had a say in the choice of a new master. At York in 1613, Giles Dodsworth, a bricklayer's apprentice, 'made choice of William Dixon to be his master and to serve out his term in his indentures to come'.[36] But the trainees did not have a free hand. The whole process was monitored and approved by the gild: among the York bricklayers turnovers needed the agreement of the searchers and the majority of gild members.[37]

Apprenticeship was regarded as an important phase in the life-cycle as individuals passed from childhood to full adult status at the age of twenty-four and beyond. Apprentices and other young men, with their propensity to wildness and ungovernable passions, needed to be kept under firm control and, in normal circumstances, should not be allowed to marry and establish households of their own.[38] Many gilds ruled that apprentices were neither 'to commit fornication' nor to marry.[39] But some did so. In mid-sixteenth-century London, 21 out of 2,000 apprentice carpenters married, and at Newcastle an apprentice joiner and three bricklayers were each fined £2 for marrying before the end of their terms, and two of them were fined for fathering children, at the rate of £2 per child.[40] Robert Coates, who was admitted to the bricklayers' gild at the meeting of 11 August 1670, had the most expensive time and needed four years to pay. At that meeting he paid £2 for his gild membership and £2 for marrying as an apprentice, and agreed to pay a further £1 for each of the next four years, 'being in all £4 for begetting of two children during the term of his apprenticeship'. He also promised to give gloves to the members at the next meeting.[41]

It has been suggested that seven-year apprenticeships were 'scarcely necessary in any of the crafts coming under the scope of the statute of artificers', although 'they protected established workers from competition and gave the masters the benefit of cheap, tied labour'.[42] This may well have been true from the training point of view, but the system was expected to deliver more than just the transmission of skills. If few apprentices acted like the hot-blooded Robert Coates, the institution of apprenticeship was doing the job required by contemporary attitudes in ensuring that most craftsmen did not marry and

[35] TWAS, 802/1. [36] YML, QQ80/2/1. For a similar case see TWAS, 802/1.
[37] YML, QQ80/2/11, p. 19 for 1664.
[38] Ben-Amos 1988, 42; Rappaport 1989, 325–6.
[39] TWAS, 648/6, p. 7, 802/16; CCRO, G20/1, G14/1; Rappaport 1989, 236–7.
[40] *Ibid.*, 237; TWAS, 648/9, 802/1, /2. [41] TWAS, 802/2.
[42] Clarkson 1971, 169–70; Clarkson 1982, 15.

establish independent households until they were in their mid to late twenties.[43] Historians tend to assume that master craftsmen benefited from the acquisition of cheap labour, but the level of benefit cannot be established. The master's costs included the fee he paid to the gild when taking on an apprentice and the long-term expenditure on food, clothing, and lodging: benefits included whatever premium the young man brought with him and the value of his labour. Whether or not the whole exercise was conducted at a profit to the master depended on his ability to secure sufficient work for the apprentice to cover the cost of his keep.

Apprenticeship premiums were common in early-modern England, although they were often low for apprentices entering the manual occupations.[44] Direct evidence relating to premiums has not been discovered for the northern building trades, although two snippets of information suggest that such payments may have been made, albeit at a relatively modest level. In 1725, Thomas Nixon, a Carlisle bricklayer, left £10 to each of his three sons 'in order to put them to a trade', which he did not specify, while at York in 1590 two poor boys were apprenticed to joiners and each master was 'to have with him 13s 4d out of the common chamber'. In one case the payment was lower than normal, since, 'in consideration that he is a poor boy' the master was relieved of the gild dues.[45] Two fees were normally paid: a small fee for enrolling the indenture – in the seventeenth century this was 2d for the Chester joiners and 4d for the bricklayers, while the Newcastle joiners paid 2s – plus a larger fee for taking on the apprentice. The latter varied: at York it was set at 6s 8d for the carpenters in 1482, but reduced to 2s 6d in 1563; the Newcastle bricklayers paid £1 in the 1660s and £6 in the next century when the joiners were paying £3. In the seventeenth century the Newcastle joiners also paid quarterage of 1s or 2s for their apprentices.[46]

In many trades the value of an apprentice's labour could be built silently into the selling price of a finished article: but this could rarely be done in the building trades, especially where the master craftsmen and journeymen were being paid by the day. In such circumstances a 'wage' was paid in respect of the apprentice's work. This has led to some confusion. One eminent historian argued that the Statute of Artificers was misguided, since 'the preamble speaks of the wages of

[43] In London, craftsmen usually married and established households of their own two to three years after ending their apprenticeships: Rappaport 1989, 325–8.
[44] Elliott 1978, 60–1; H. Cunningham 1990, 125; Ben-Amos 1988, 44–5.
[45] CUMROC, P1725; YCR, IX, 103, 110.
[46] CCRO, G14/1, /2, p. 17; TWAS, 648/8, /13; 802/2, /16; YML, QQ80/3/2.

apprentices, who of course received none'.[47] However, wage assessments laid down the rates to be paid for the work of apprentices, and many accounts refer to their wages. Such payments, which accrued to the master and not to the apprentice, were essential if the master was to be recompensed adequately for his work. The economic relationship between an apprentice and his master was described correctly by Knoop & Jones:

> The courts have long held that an apprentice's master is entitled to what an apprentice earns, and there can be no doubt that in earlier times, too, the wage paid in respect of an employee's apprentice would have belonged to the employee, who in his turn would have been responsible for the board, lodging and clothing of his apprentice. The balance, if any, after meeting the expenses, would be the craftsman's remuneration for his trouble in looking after and teaching the apprentice.[48]

Both master and apprentice benefited from a long apprenticeship: 'The master for that he should have the longer service of his prentice which must needs turn to his great profit, for one year's service at the latter end is more worth than four at the beginning.'[49] This differential benefit was reflected in the level of payment for their work, higher rates being paid for older apprentices. At Durham in the late fifteenth century, John Bell, the chief mason at the cathedral, was authorised to train an apprentice for whom he was to receive four marks a year for the first three years, six marks during the next three years, and seven marks in the final year.[50] The same was true for James Galen, the Hull carpenter, who received different rates of pay for his two apprentices.[51] Occasionally it is possible to glimpse a young man moving up the pay scale. Thus Ebenezer Emerson worked alongside a group of Hull carpenters in the summer of 1678 at 4d a day, but he advanced to 6d at the end of April 1679, and to 8d in July.[52]

Specific references to apprentices working alongside their masters are relatively rare in the northern accounts which is somewhat perplexing since the gild records suggest that the apprenticeship system was flourishing, especially in the larger towns. There are various possible reasons for this: apprentices may have masqueraded under the title 'man', or may simply have been listed under their own names

---

47 Bindoff 1961, 68; Woodward 1981, 32.
48 Knoop & Jones 1949, 162–3. For a similar view see Rogers IV, 1882, 512.
49 *TED*, I, 356.
50 Knoop & Jones 1949, 167. Salzman 1952, p. 49, mistakenly believed that the apprentice was to receive the money: but see the document on pp. 593–4 where it is made clear that the money was paid for the apprentice, not to him. See also the evidence of wage assessments; Roberts 1981, 154.
51 See above, p. 26; see also *Louth Accts*, 26–7.
52 HCRO, BRF/3/20, pp. 928, 959–60.

in the accounts; customers may have refused to pay for them; or perhaps apprentices were sometimes employed elsewhere, apart from their masters. Independent work by apprentices was probably unusual, although the situation did arise: according to an ordinance of the York bricklayers in 1590 apprentices and servants were not to work independently of their masters unless they had been vetted by the searchers and were known to be good workmen.[53] Very occasionally such practices were recorded. Thus, at Lincoln in 1620 two apprentices of Thomas Bannister, the cathedral carpenter, worked for six days sawing wood at 10d a day each.[54] It is also possible that apprentices were occasionally allowed to work on their own account as suggested by an ordinance of the Newcastle bricklayers: any apprentice doing work above the value of 2s 6d without his master's leave was to be fined 3s 4d for each offence. This implies that an apprentice could do smaller jobs without permission.[55]

In London and other places towards the end of the period apprentices began to receive regular payments,[56] but there is very little evidence for such a change in the north. The gild records of Chester, Newcastle, and York reveal only four examples of payment to apprentices. Two young men were apprenticed to York bricklayers in 1699 and 1700: one was to receive '10s wages for the eighth year' and the other was 'to have 2s 6d for the eighth year'.[57] At Newcastle two trainee bricklayers recruited in the 1660s were to receive 10s and 13s 4d a year throughout their terms: the higher-paid apprentice was Robert Coates.[58] However, he seems to have been an exceptional character, perhaps considerably older than usual, and there is no reason to suppose that northern building-trade apprentices were normally paid.

If one of the reasons for apprenticeship was to provide master craftsmen with cheap assistance, the gilds and town councils took steps to ensure that the system was not abused. In all towns restrictions were placed on the number of apprentices each master could engage. Most gilds laid down that newly qualified masters could not take an apprentice immediately: at York the joiners set the period at three years in 1586 and later raised it to four years; the bricklayers placed a ban on recruitment for seven years, although they made an exception for the sons of freemen. Similar restrictions were imposed elsewhere.[59] Numbers were also regulated either by stipulating the maximum number of apprentices for each master, or by specifying a

---

53 YML, QQ80/2/11.   54 LAO, Bj/1/7.
55 TWAS, 802/16: probably early eighteenth century.
56 Earle 1977, 172–3; Roberts 1981, 155; Dunlop 1912, 195–6.   57 YML, QQ80/2/13.
58 TWAS, 802/2.   59 YML, QQ80/2/11, /3/2; TWAS,648/6, 802/16; *Gild Life*, 281.

minimum interval between successive apprentices. The result was the same, and masters were usually limited to two apprentices at any one time. During the first half of the sixteenth century the York authorities, anxious to boost the city's flagging economy, allowed masters to take 'as many apprentices as he shall think profitable for him', but as prosperity returned later in the century gild after gild imposed a maximum of two apprentices per master.[60] The northern accounts and gild records indicate that most masters did not employ excessive numbers of apprentices. With few exceptions, urban markets were too fragmented to encourage the emergence of large building firms. Nevertheless, some master craftsmen did flout the rules, if only at the margin. It was ordained in 1590 that a master bricklayer at York could not enrol his first apprentice until he had been a brother for seven years, although he could take a freeman's son after two years. A second apprentice could not be taken until the first had served at least six years, thus limiting a master to a maximum of two apprentices. The regulation was repeated in 1668 and made subject to a fine of £3 6s 8d, which was raised to £10 in 1674.[61] Between 1654 and 1752, 35 of the 58 master bricklayers who took 2 or more apprentices offended against these regulations on at least one occasion. Twelve offended on the maximum number of occasions open to them. The worst offender was George Stevenson who took eight apprentices between 1680 and 1704. Assuming that none of his young charges died, ran away, or were turned over to someone else – and the record is silent on this matter – he had three apprentices on four occasions for periods varying from nine to twenty-seven months, and he always took another apprentice within six years of taking the last. The level of offences against the apprenticeship regulations imposed by the York bricklayers was probably rather lower than suggested by the data since some apprentices may have died or dropped out of the system unnoticed. Nevertheless, the apparent frequency with which offences occurred suggests that infringement was commonplace and that the fines imposed in 1668 and 1674 were regarded as fees to license offences.[62]

There can be little doubt that master craftsmen benefited substantially from the apprenticeship system, otherwise it would have withered away. Although contemporary craftsmen were not able to calculate accurately the cost of training apprentices, it would soon have become apparent to a family when it was markedly worse off. When that occurred further apprentices would not be recruited, and if

[60] YCR, III, 125; Palliser 1972, 98–9; Palliser 1979, 269–70.   [61] YML, QQ80/2/11.
[62] YML, QQ80/2/13. Unfortunately it has not been possible to conduct a similar analysis for any of the other northern towns.

conditions within the family became intolerable any existing apprentice could be turned over to someone else. But such cases were
probably rare. In the early years, when the young man's inexperience
attracted only low levels of pay the master was cushioned by whatever
premium he had received. Later, the apprentice's growing strength
and expertise would help to compensate the master for early losses.
That apprentices were regarded as unexpired assets is suggested by
five remarkable probate inventories for the Sheffield region which
recorded the residual value of current apprentices.[63]

The journeyman

A journeyman is understood to be one, who has by apprenticeship or other
contract served such portion of his time ... as rendered him capable to execute
every branch or part of the trade, whereby he is at full liberty ... to set up in the
world as a master of his profession; and is only called a Journeyman while he
continues to serve under the direction of others at certain wages.

This statement, which appeared in a pamphlet supporting protests of
the London tailors in 1745, neatly summarises the usually accepted
position of journeymen, although it has been recognised that it was
often difficult for young men to establish their own independent
businesses.[64] The quotation helps to perpetuate the belief that
journeymen were part of a tightly controlled, closed system whereby,
in different towns up and down the country, boys progressed through
their apprenticeships and served some time as journeymen or hired
hands, before joining the ranks of the self-employed master craftsmen.
Most additions to the body of masters probably came via that route. As
the Newcastle joiners' gild laid down in 1719: 'No apprentice to take
work in hand after his years be expired, but shall work as a journeyman until he has made himself free with both town and company,
paying 16d yearly until he makes himself free.'[65] The intermediate
stage between apprenticeship and full master craftsman status was
specified in the case of four Newcastle apprentices: they were to serve
with their masters as 'hired man' in the year after the completion of
their terms.[66] The York locksmiths had made the condition more
general in 1572: in the year after his apprenticeship a young man was
'to be hired as the master and he can agree'.[67] Although many newly
qualified ex-apprentices did spend some time in the twilight world of
the journeyman, it will be argued at the end of this section

[63] Hey 1972, 29–30.   [64] Quoted in Rule 1986, 19. See also Laslett 1983, 7.
[65] TWAS, 648/6, p. 4.
[66] TWAS, 648/13, 802/1.   [67] YCR, VII, 54.

(pp. 68–72), largely on the basis of evidence drawn from the records of the Chester joiners, that many of those who served as journeymen were not *en route* to becoming urban master craftsmen, and that many of them were not drawn from the ranks of the town apprentices. But first it is necessary to discuss what little is known about the lives of journeymen building workers.

Young men can be observed in the accounts progressing through the ranks until they reached the status of master craftsmen, although it is rarely possible to determine exactly what position they were in at any particular time. During the late 1610s, when master carpenters were receiving 12d a day at Hull, James Brasbrick progressed from 10d a day during 1618 and the early months of 1619, to 11d on 24 April 1619, before receiving the full rate of 12d for 145 days' work in 1620. Whether or not he became an independent craftsman when his pay reached 12d is unclear.[68] Many similar instances could be quoted, but a single example will suffice: during the 1610s John Shewsmith was the chief glazier, and part-time plumber, at Lincoln Cathedral earning 12d a day. During 1619 he was joined by his son, George, who was paid at 4d a day for the next six years: his wage then moved to 6d in 1625, to 8d in 1627 and to 10d in 1630, his twelfth year of working alongside his father. George graduated in the spring of 1631 when his pay moved to 12d a day, and between late April and mid July he worked for 67 days by himself. During 1631 George Shewsmith did nearly all of the glazing at the cathedral, although in January 1632 he and his father worked together 'mending a pane in the great east window'. A year later John Shewsmith stopped working at the cathedral and George took over as the chief glazier, a post he held until the early 1670s. During the 1660s George Shewsmith's son worked alongside him for a time.[69]

Even less is known about the lives of building-craft journeymen than about those of apprentices. The extent to which they were housed and fed by their masters is unknown: no doubt some were, but any records which could help to resolve the issue have not been unearthed. According to the Statute of Artificers, journeymen were to be hired by the year, and many subsequent wage assessments laid down maximum annual payments for them. Annual hiring had been insisted on as early as 1482 by the York carpenters: workmen were not to be hired for more than fourteen days except by the year, and in 1576 the council insisted that servants should not be put away before the end of their terms.[70] However, it has been suggested that in practice

---

[68] HCRO, BRF/3/6–14.   [69] LAO, Bj/1/6/2, /1/7–9.
[70] *York Memorandum Book*, 281.

journeymen were commonly hired by the week or month,[71] and the fragmentary evidence available from the records of the Chester joiners suggests that many journeymen remained with their masters for less than a year: in 1673 nineteen journeymen were listed, but nine were recorded as 'gone' within the year. In 1683 Widow Johnson hired four journeymen, of whom two served for a full year, but two stayed for only six months or less. Some journeymen failed to serve a full year because they graduated to the ranks of the master craftsmen, but many belonged to a floating population of more or less casual labour, moving between town and country at frequent intervals. In an unusually detailed reference we learn that Richard Woodwall left without his master's permission in 1618, and the gild forbade anyone else in the brotherhood to employ him.[72]

Whatever their particular circumstances journeymen remained dependent on their employers and, although the exact nature of that dependency cannot be determined, a master's powers were much greater than even the harshest employer could dream of today. At Hull in June 1664 Robert Man was paid 1s 6d for 'beating three bushels of cement in the house of correction being there upon a misdemeanour towards John Silkwood his master'.[73] Unfortunately the nature of the problem was not revealed, and records relating to friction between masters and men are extremely rare for the early-modern north.[74] Although they were skilled, journeymen were not usually allowed to train their own apprentices: at Chester in 1739 the bricklayers refused to allow Edward Smith to join the gild since he had been bound to Peter Bowden, 'a journeyman bricklayer who had no right to take an apprentice'.[75] Although a 'country journeyman' might occasionally be accompanied by an apprentice or his man,[76] the general embargo on the practice underlined the dependent status of journeymen and reminded them that they did not belong to the elite group of master craftsmen.

In some towns journeymen formed their own organisations,[77] but no trace of such bodies has been found for northern building workers: on the contrary, the established gilds exercised a close control over journeymen and extracted quarterly payments for their work: the

[71] Walker 1981, 28.   [72] CCRO, G14/1, /2, p. 17.
[73] HCRO, BRF/3/20, p. 424.
[74] Unfortunately, English sources are nothing like as rich as those for eighteenth-century France which reveal a substantial level of conflict between masters and men: Sonenscher 1989, 3–6.
[75] CCRO, G4/1.   [76] See below p. 70.
[77] Phythian-Adams 1979, 99, 129; Swanson 1989, 115; Palliser 1972, 100. Journeyman organisations were common in eighteenth-century France: Sonenscher 1989, 77ff.

Chester joiners and bricklayers listed their names each year.[78] Masters could not engage journeymen as the whim took them, and at a meeting of the Chester joiners in 1690 Hugh Hand was fined 'for employing two journeymen without asking the consent of the Aldermen and Stewards'.[79]

A crucial question when considering the living standards of both journeymen and master craftsmen is the level of payment actually received by the journeymen. Unfortunately, a satisfactory answer cannot be given. A journeyman who lived in his master's house and ate at his table would not receive the full wage paid by the customer for his labour. Early in 1577 the Chester joiners ordered that a journeyman should not be paid more than 2s a week 'for his wages, having his diet with them' at a time when skilled men were receiving 8d or 9d a day without food and drink, that is, some 4s or 4s 6d for a full week. Those working by the piece were not to receive 'over the third part of the work in value gotten, charges considered': indeed, 'no brother shall give to the piece worker above the third part of the value of his work'.[80] In 1590 the carpenters, sawyers, and slaters were criticised for setting unskilled outsiders to work and retaining part of their wages. The men were given 'such wages they be not able to live on, and themselves [the masters] taking such excess wages as hath been a slander to the corporation'.[81] This suggests that the men were living in their own establishments, or perhaps in lodgings. The only other evidence relating to the pay of journeymen comes from the wording of the building accounts, although it would be unwise to place too much reliance on that source. Some accounts merely state the wage against each man's name without indicating any connection between individuals, but in others a formula such as the following was adopted: 'To John Anderson for working two days and a half at the south block-house, 2s 1d; To him for his man for working two days and a half there, 1s 10d.'[82] A unique formulation, used at Hull in two bills of 1708, points in the same direction. The master craftsmen received 24d a day, and rates of 12d, 18d, and 20d were paid for the work of various 'men'. The bills were signed by the master craftsmen after the statement 'received by us, each our proportions': what the men actually received is not stated.[83] Some of the most interesting entries relating to journeymen's pay come from the York council accounts for 1606. William Harrison,

---

[78] CCRO, G4/1, 14/1, 3.
[79] CCRO, G14/2, p. 242. Fourteen voted to fine him 13s 4d. He was fined a further 6s 8d for employing a turner as a joiner and 3s 4d 'for entertaining Richard Totty's apprentice without leave of his master'. The total fine of £1 3s 4d was reduced to 10s.
[80] CCRO, G14/1, fos. 3r, 11v.   [81] Unwin 1904, 66.   [82] Woodward 1981, 34.
[83] HCRO, BRF/6/408–9.

the city's contract paver, was paid for his own labour, for that of his man, and also for the hire of his horse. Entries take the following forms: 'to him for his man'; 'to him for his horse'; 'to William Harrison for his man's wage'.[84] To what extent were horse and man treated alike? Presumably the man received some cash in hand, but we do not know how much. What seems certain is that in many cases – if not in all – the wage of a dependent journeyman was given to the master who then paid a portion of it, or perhaps all of it, to the man. No doubt levels of payment reflected both the circumstances of the journeyman, including whether or not he was married and lived in his master's house, and the rapacity of the master.

Journeymen were not always paid their dues promptly. The ordinances of the Hull joiners ordered that: 'No master of the said occupation withhold his servant's wages due to him over the space of six days after the same be due.'[85] From the master's point of view such delays would seem justified if the customer delayed payment to him for work done. But it is hard to avoid the suspicion that journeymen often had the worst of it. In most cases they probably received only a portion of the wage, and they did not have access to the various sources of profit open to the master craftsmen.

The records of the Chester joiners provide valuable insights into the position of journeymen. The gild was a small one: membership grew from around fifteen in the early seventeenth century to an average of twenty-one in the 1630s and 1640s. Eight members died in the plague of 1647: membership, reduced to nine in the next four years, averaged only 13 through the 1650s. Thereafter, numbers grew steadily to reach a peak of 29 during the 1700s. Before the Civil War the number of journeymen almost matched the number of masters, the ratio being 0.95:1, but the crisis of 1647 was followed by a major change of practice. During the period 1640–59 the ratio of journeymen to masters fell to 0.38:1, and, although the number of journeymen increased in the post-1660 recovery, the ratio only stood at 0.62:1 during 1660–99, and at 0.67:1 in the first three decades of the next century. This again underlines the relatively small size of firms in the building trades.[86] There was a substantial turnover of journeymen. Half remained in their posts for a year or less during the period 1600–40, although 17 stayed for ten or more years, not always consecutively (see table 3.2).

[84] YCA, CC12.
[85] *Gild Life*, 253. They were drawn up in 1598 and confirmed in 1629.
[86] CCRO, G14/1. The numbers of journeymen are exaggerated in the above analysis, since if they appear in the records they are recorded as working during a particular year, although not all stayed for a full year.

Table 3.2. *Journeymen joiners at Chester 1600–40.*

Number of years employed	Number of journeymen	%
1 or less	121	50.4
2	50	20.8
3	24	10.0
4	10	4.2
5–9	18	7.5
10–14	4	1.7
15–19	8	3.3
20–4	3	1.3
25–9	1	0.4
30–5	1	0.4
	240	100.0

Note: The table relates to the 240 journeymen who served between 1600 and 1640 and anyone serving at the beginning or end of the period has been traced backwards or forwards to try to reconstruct fully their histories as journeymen. *Source:* CCRO, G14/1.

Most of the long-stay journeymen appeared early in the period: six of the twelve journeymen recorded in 1600 were each employed for more than ten years. Thereafter short periods of service became more common.[87]

Historians have assumed that urban craftsmen moved progressively from apprentice to journeyman and, finally, to the position of master craftsman. Some would fail to complete the course: apprentices occasionally died or ran away, and a journeyman might not be able to accumulate sufficient capital to found an independent business. But according to the orthodox assumption many would complete the metamorphosis. However, between 1600 and 1640 only 20 of the 39 recruits to the ranks of the master joiners came from the ranks of the 240 journeymen. Of the 20 who graduated to full gild membership, 4 did so within a year of ending their apprenticeships, and a further 9 did so within three years. Only three took more than five years, including Randle Adeage who joined the gild in 1603 after serving as journeyman from 1587. No doubt the records of the Chester joiners are not completely accurate, but the message is unequivocal. Some young men worked for a while as journeymen after they had completed their apprenticeships, although others seem to have passed almost immedi-

---

[87] A rapid turnover of journeymen was common in eighteenth-century France: Sonenscher 1989, 140ff, 177, 187.

ately into the ranks of the master craftsmen. But a very high proportion of the journeymen had not been apprenticed in the city. Given the
restrictions on the number of apprentices who could be enrolled with
individual craftsmen this was bound to have been so if the number of
masters and journeymen were to be in balance. In 1581 the gild
ordained that a master could not take more than two apprentices and
that the first had to serve at least two years before the second could be
taken.[88] Assuming that all masters took the maximum number of
apprentices (and, of course, they did not) they could enrol new
trainees during years 1, 3, 8, 10, 15, 17, 22, 24, and so on, during their
careers. This means that in 40 years, say 1601–40, each master could
take on 12 apprentices. During that period membership of the gild
averaged 16.4 so that members could have taken on a total of 196.8
apprentices at most, or less than 5 a year in total. Thus, even if all
masters had taken the maximum number of apprentices, and all
ex-apprentices had worked as journeymen for some time, they would
not have been sufficiently numerous to satisfy the demand for
journeymen. Unfortunately, the gild records say little about the origins
of the extra journeymen, although they do provide a number of
interesting hints. In 1609 and 1610 Thomas Kinsley of Warrington
worked as a journeyman, and in 1640 Richard Jones of Nantwich was
taken on, but later had 'gone with consent'. Some of the journeymen
were mature men like Richard Moon and Richard Manners who
worked alongside their sons in the 1630s. Similarly, Richard Wright,
first employed in 1634, was re-engaged at Candlemas 1637 alongside
his son, referred to as a 'new apprentice and sick': Wright himself soon
ailed and died. But it is Martin Goulding whose career holds the
greatest fascination. He first appeared in the ranks of journeymen
joiners in 1615 and, with only a few brief breaks, worked until 1641
before making a final appearance in 1646. Almost certainly he was a
fully trained man from outside the city and was often registered along
with 'his man', or one or more apprentices. In the early 1620s he and
his man worked for William Catterall, although in October 1630 he and
his apprentice were contracted to William Williams. In 1634 he was
registered as having two apprentices. At Whitsuntide the elder 'ran
away', although later 'he came again': one ran away in 1635. For three
years Goulding managed with a single apprentice, but in 1639 he was
back to two again.

The records of the Chester joiners suggest that the journeymen were
a highly transient group who, for the most part, did not stay long in

88 CCRO, G14/1, fo. 5r.

the city. Of the 18 journeymen hired in 1639 – including Martin Goulding and his two apprentices – five were recorded as 'gone without consent', two had 'run away', and one had 'gone with consent'. Such information is rarely provided, but in 1662 the dates of arrival were given for half of the 18 journeymen employed that year: two 'came at Midsummer', and one each on 10 May, 9 June, 26 June, 24 August, 26 September, and at Christmas, and Candlemas. Richard Palin was a frequent visitor to the city, working for at least a part of 15 years between 1610 and 1630. During at least some of his periods out of the city he did not go far away. In February 1618 he left with his master's agreement, although other members of the gild were barred from employing him. However, a month later the joiners complained to the city fathers that he had 'bought large timber in the city and sawed it into pieces' and had also 'worked much of the said timber in the country, and sold it in the city', especially a standing bed 'now in the house of Robert Fletcher, baker'.[89] No doubt there were others who tried to grub a living of dubious legality by working in an unregulated way on the fringe of the city, but others, like the journey-man who was given 3s 4d in 1626 'for a journey to London', moved further afield. Payments were also made to some who called in at the gild probably looking for work or assistance: 2s was given in 1680 to James Taylor, 'a poor joiner on his travayle [travels]'.[90] Similarly the Newcastle joiners frequently gave money to their travelling colleagues in the second half of the seventeenth century: 2s 6d went 'to a London joiner' and 6d 'to the country joiner' in 1672. The peak of activity came in 1679/80 when small sums were given to six travellers, although such payments were not made every year.[91]

Other gild records say far less about journeymen, although there are some hints that outsiders were also significant at York. In 1482 the carpenters laid down the fees which were to be paid if 'it shall happen a young man that is not cunning in work of the said occupation come into this city to learn the occupation better': if given 20s a year or more, and their food, the master was to pay 20d, but if the salary were under 20s the fine was set at 40d, which suggests that it was related to the potential profit available: the lower the wage the higher the licence fee. Thirty-five years later a weekly fine of 4d was established for those engaging 'strange carpenters', and after 1586 a special licence had to be obtained from the mayor if strangers were to be set to work.[92]

Given that all craft gilds placed restrictions on the number of

---

[89] *Chester Minutes*, 17–18.   [90] CCRO, G14/2, pp. 181, 200; G14/3 for 1739 and 1740.
[91] TWAS, 648/8–9. See Walker 1981, 34, 43 for comments on the early eighteenth century.
[92] YML, QQ80/3/2.

apprentices individual masters could enrol, and that such regulations were frequently tighter than those imposed by the Chester joiners,[93] it seems almost certain that the recruitment of 'strangers' as journeymen was commonplace. If the number of journeymen was to be maintained at anything more than a very low level the inflow from the ranks of the apprentices was simply not enough. Extra men, with no hope of advancing to the rank of master craftsman, had to be drafted in. It has been argued that journeymen could accept their lowly status because they had the chance to progress, and because their poverty was not permanent.[94] But the majority of those who laboured alongside the Chester joiners had no chance of advancement in the city. Any hope of establishing an independent business had to be pursued elsewhere, in a village or unincorporated town. If these suggestions hold true for other towns and other trades, and it is almost certain that they do, the journeyman body was more heterogeneous than usually imagined. Some were able to graduate to the ranks of the master craftsmen, but the majority moved in and out of the larger towns, gaining experience and dreaming of a less dependent existence elsewhere.

The master craftsman

In most crafts the term 'master' was applied to one who, having served his apprenticeship, had set up in business; he was a master of his craft but not necessarily an employer of others.[95]

Craftsmen came in a variety of guises. At the bottom were young men, just out of their apprenticeships, striving to establish their own businesses. In many cases business, household, and family were established at more or less the same time, when many of the young men were in their mid to late twenties.[96] Hampered by the lack of a good reputation, which could only be acquired over time, and by the cost of obtaining their freedom and joining a gild, many must have struggled in the early years. No doubt from time to time they accepted work as journeymen, but, granted a modicum of good luck, a keen eye for the market, and longevity, even humble building craftsmen could hope to carve out relatively prosperous careers for themselves.

In some of the northern towns only those who were freemen and

---

[93] At Newcastle in 1719 the joiners argued that they were so numerous as to be impoverished. They ordered that no brother should take an apprentice until he had been free for five years and then only one at a time. That would mean that, at a maximum, a master could not take his seventh apprentice until he had been in the gild for forty-one years: at most a group of twenty masters would have been able to start just over three apprentices each year. TWAS, 648/6, p. 16.

[94] Rappaport 1989, 286.   [95] Salzman 1952, 48.   [96] Rappaport 1989, 326–9.

gild members could establish their own independent businesses. Unfortunately, the relationship between gild membership and the town freedom is imperfectly understood, partly because practice varied and partly because insufficient attention has been paid to gild records. It has been suggested that at Chester gild membership was taken up after the freedom of the city had been obtained,[97] and that may well have been so in most cases. Indeed, most of the young joiners became freemen and joined the gild in the same year, although some did not join until the following year and a few delayed for up to twelve years. However, occasionally the sequence ran in the opposite direction. Additionally twelve men not listed in the freemen's rolls were gild members in the later seventeenth century.[98] Those who delayed joining their gild may have worked for a spell outside the city or as journeymen within it. Whatever the reason, delaying entry to full gild membership saved money, and some of those who took out their freedom as joiners never joined the gild.[99]

On occasion those who aspired to gild membership had to undergo a test of their skills. In 1599 the Newcastle gild of bricklayers and wallers decided that: 'There shall no man come to be agreed within the company of wallers but that he shall be tryed to be a workman.'[100] Similarly, at York in 1613 the carpenters complained of an overstocked labour market and decreed that no apprentice should be admitted to the gild until he had made 'a proof piece of work' worth 40s.[101] Potential gild members also faced a financial hurdle, the height of which varied from craft to craft. At Chester in the seventeenth century the entry fee was generally between £3 and £5, plus the provision of a dinner for existing gildsmen.[102] The joiners had set the fee at £3 as early as 1578, in addition to a dinner for members and their wives, and in October 1616 it was agreed that John Garfield and Robert Thomason should be allowed to share the cost of a twenty-shilling dinner. The entry fee was raised to £8 plus a dinner in 1662, and in 1730 members voted to raise the fee to £15 'for one that is not a brother's son' and half that amount for their own offspring.[103] The entry fees were distributed among paid-up gild members: they each received between 4s and 7s in

[97] *Chester Minutes*, xxx.

[98] CCRO, G14/1; *Chester Freemen I*. A detailed investigation of gild membership and its relationship to the freemen's records is beyond the scope of this study, but there is scope for more work in this area.

[99] Six joiners became freemen during the period 1678–90 but did not join the gild: CCRO, G14/1; *Chester Freemen I*.

[100] TWAS, 802/16.   [101] YML, QQ80/3/2; YCA, B34/6.   [102] *Chester Minutes*, 98.

[103] CCRO, G14/1, fo. 5r, 8v, G14/2, pp. 10–12, 203, G14/3. The bricklayers offered the differential rates of £6 and £3 in the eighteenth century: G4/1.

the early seventeenth century, and 10s from the £10 paid in 1684.[104]
The York carpenters established their fees at a lower level: they were
20d in 1482, and no more than 3s 4d in 1563.[105] Other building-craft
gilds set entry fines somewhere between those of the Chester joiners
and the York carpenters.[106] But even when fines were low some must
have struggled to meet the cost. In the late sixteenth century the York
council tried to control the cost of feasting, complaining of the 'great
exactions for dinners': it was ordered that gilds should not allow more
than £1 to be spent on food. Brotherhood dinners were banned altogether in 1649, at least for a while, 'having been to the prejudice of
divers young tradesmen'.[107]

Little is known about the financial circumstances of young men
fresh out of their apprenticeships, although it must be presumed that
many did not find the transition to the senior ranks easy. They also
needed capital to fund the establishment of an independent household and to tide them over the early months when expenditure was
likely to be greater than income. Occasionally the gilds offered some
assistance. At Newcastle two men were allowed to spread the payment
of their fines over some years, and a Chester joiner gained entry to the
gild in April 1619 by taking two pieces of plate to the meeting 'in pawn'
for his fee of £3, which was to be redeemed in four equal instalments.[108]

Some young men could hope to benefit from the various schemes set
up to provide struggling young businessmen with loans, at low rates
of interest or interest free. At Chester such start-up capital came from a
trust fund set up by Robert and William Offley, natives of the city, who
had prospered in London.[109] The money was to be loaned out by lot in
£25 parcels to young men for five-year periods, and in 1611 a glazier
was one of the recipients. A year later some of the money went to John
Garret, a carpenter, and William Salisbury, a joiner. But by no stretch of
the imagination could Salisbury be regarded as a young man: he had
joined the gild in 1593 and had been its alderman since 1610, which
made him a 'young man' in his mid-forties in 1612. In 1628 £25 went to
each of twenty-two young men, including two glaziers and the joiners
Richard Bolland junior, who had joined the gild in 1620, and Raph
Davies, who had joined in 1602 and was probably aged about fifty.[110]

[104] CCRO, G14/2, pp. 10, 37, 59, 203.   [105] YML, QQ80/3/2.
[106] TWAS, 802/1, /2, /4; see also 648/6, p. 7.
[107] YCA, B31/240, B33/79b, B36/232b; YML, QQ80/2/1.
[108] TWAS, 802/2; CCRO, G14/2, pp. 24, 26. Similarly Robert Thomason had given 'a
    silver salt as security' in 1616: *ibid.*, p. 10. See also p. 59.
[109] Woodward 1970b, 119–20; Rappaport 1989, 372–3.
[110] *Chester Minutes*, 51, 57–8, 82, 101–2, 148.

The career progression of individual craftsmen can be plotted from gild records. In all gilds there were positions of responsibility and leadership to be filled by vote or by nomination by the elder brethren. But only in the case of the Chester joiners are the records sufficiently detailed to permit a comprehensive analysis. The minute book covering the years 1576 to 1750 provides an annual list of the aldermen, stewards, and ordinary members. Members were listed in chronological order according to the date they joined the gild, so that the identity of an individual member is never in any doubt and the usual problems of identification associated with nominal linkage disappear. Any member who left the gild for a number of years and then returned to the fold was replaced in his old order of precedence when he reappeared.[111] Such hierarchical nicety was paralleled by the regulation of the bricklayers' gild which insisted that in meetings 'every brother is to take his place according to the time of his being admitted'.[112] Between 1591 and 1719, 91 of the 124 members of the joiners' gild acted as steward. Most were elected to the position early in their careers: two young men became steward in their first year in the gild and fifty-nine began their first term in their fourth year or earlier.[113] Experience was valued and only seventeen failed to be re-elected: sixty-four served between two and four times, five acted on five occasions, and the remaining five were steward for between six and nine years. The mean period of service as steward was 2.8 years. The highest positions were occupied by the two elected gild aldermen. Experience as steward was an essential stepping-stone to the higher office: only one alderman had not been steward, and the thirty-three who became aldermen had served nearly four years on average as steward. One man was elected alderman in his ninth year, but members waited for almost twenty years on average to become aldermen. Once chosen, re-election was the norm. Fourteen members served for less than five years, but ten were aldermen for between five and ten years, five for ten to fourteen years, and the remaining four – Thomas Bolland, William Salisbury, Thomas Hull, and Samuel Leen – served for fifteen, twenty-one, twenty-eight, and thirty-six years respectively. The dignity of the position is reflected in the reaction of Richard Walker who refused to be steward in 1616 on the ground that he had been alderman two years earlier.[114]

---

[111] CCRO, G14/1; for a discussion of the role of the gilds see above pp. 28–35.

[112] CCRO, G4/1. The smiths were also expected 'to keep their proper places': G20/1.

[113] The searchers of the York gild of bricklayers were also relatively young in the early seventeenth century: most had been in the gild for five years or less. YML, QQ80/2/1, 4–5.

[114] CCRO, G14/2, p. 9. He died in 1623.

Table 3.3. *Longevity among the Chester joiners, 1591–1719*

Period in gild	Date of death known (total 61)	Date of death unknown (total 63)	Estimated age
Years	%	%	
Less than 10	23.0	36.5	Less than 37
10–19	29.5	20.6	37–46
20–9	24.6	14.3	47–56
30–9	6.6	12.7	57–66
40–9	11.5	12.7	67–76
50–9	1.6	3.2	77–86
60–5	3.3	—	87–96

Note: Members listed in 1591 were traced back as far as possible and those present in 1719 were traced forwards; this probably results in a small measure of under-countings. Ages in the final column have been calculated by assuming that apprenticeships ended at the age of twenty-four and were followed by a few years as journeymen; in the first half of the seventeenth century the twenty young men who became masters had served for an average period of three-and-a-half years as journeymen.
Source: CCRO, G14/1.

Progress in the gild was probably dependent on a range of factors including character and business success, but longevity was probably the most important ingredient. Given that it often took twenty years, and never less than nine, to rise to the position of alderman there were many who simply did not live long enough to be eligible: the longevity of the Chester joiners is shown in table 3.3. Unfortunately, the dates of death are known for only half of the men, but some indication of longevity can be given for the others.

The men represented in the third column include some who left the gild prematurely and did not return. This is supported by the fact that 11 of the 124 took breaks from membership of the gild: they all stayed away for less than ten years except Richard Totty, who was listed from 1687 to 1699, but did not return until 1717. Although the number of men involved is small, the table indicates that the majority of the Chester joiners were gild members for less than twenty years, which suggests that they died in their mid forties or earlier. Nevertheless, about a quarter of the members survived into their late fifties and beyond. The information relating to twenty-eight York bricklayers in the mid seventeenth century paints a roughly similar picture: thirteen were gild members for less than twenty years, while seven survived to their late fifties and beyond.[115] The 1598 ordinances of the Hull carpenters listed fourteen members, twelve of whom can be traced working in the town for an average span of twenty-eight years: four were active for more than thirty-five years.[116]

A few building craftsmen emerged as experts in their chosen fields. They acted as foremen on large jobs, surveyed buildings, viewed completed work, and sometimes planned new projects. On the larger jobs the top man was usually named first in the weekly accounts and paid a few pence more each day than the other craftsmen. Occasionally, however, a particular man was specially picked out: in 1656 Matthew Rowton, a leading Hull carpenter, was referred to as 'our chief workman' at Trinity House: he was responsible for making 'the new dolphin and taking up the old one'.[117] Similarly, Edward Watson was called the 'master workman' when the river banks were being repaired in 1668. At the end of the job he received a bonus of 10s, 'given him as a gratuity for his pains and care in taking the charge and oversight of the work being allowed to others before'.[118] The work of viewing buildings and giving advice was sometimes organised by the gilds: in 1476 the searchers of the York carpenters and tilers gave evidence relating to boundaries and the ownership of gutters, and in 1727 those of the bricklayers inspected work done at the city walls.[119] But on many occasions the individual craftsmen were probably working on their own account: thus, at Newcastle in 1593, a labourer was paid 4d 'for to go and seek a mason ... to know his counsel'.[120] At Hull, house owners added a clause to their leases which permitted them to view their property at regular intervals. They were entitled, 'once every year during the said term to enter into the said messuage or tenement with two workmen, viz., a wright and a tiler to view and see what reparations shall be needful to be made and done'.[121]

The top men involved in such work were usually highly skilled leaders of their professions. They normally worked according to traditional precepts, and only used models on rare occasions: indeed, only two examples of such practice have been found for the north.[122] But the presence of highly skilled men in many of the towns did not

[115] YML, QQ80/2/1, /4–6.
[116] *Gild Life*, 259–61. The estimate of longevity based on the Hull accounts is on the low side, since the council accounts are missing for the period 1587–1618 and it is necessary to rely on the much slighter accounts of Trinity House.
[117] HTH, IV; HCRO, BRF/3/20.   [118] HCRO, BRF/3/20, p. 637.
[119] YCR, I, 7–8; YCA, CC33.
[120] TWAS, 543/18, fo. 142r. See also YBI, PR/Y/MG/20, p. 46; CCORO, P/65/8/1, fo. 85r; *Chester Minutes*, 167; Colvin 1982, 360.
[121] HCRO, WG38, BRN/132, /226, /235.
[122] Airs 1975, 75; YBI, PR/Y/MG/20, p. 49r; LAO, Dviii/3/B/41.

guarantee that all work would be of high quality. The building trades were always plagued by 'cowboys',[123] and the gilds tried to protect customers against the inadequately skilled and fined offenders. In 1572, the York plasterers and tilers ordered that no apprentice or journeyman should work 'out of his master's company unless that he be first seen by the searchers and known by them to be a good workman', and in 1551 the searchers of the carpenters and tilers had been ordered 'to make search upon the workmanship of St Saviour's Church and ... present the offenders therein to my lord mayor and his brethren'.[124] Sometimes the work was so bad that it had to be taken down. A chapel was rebuilt in Cumbria in 1663, but the roof was so badly constructed that 'if it had not been speedily taken down it had endangered the falling of the roof together with the south and east walls'.[125] Occasionally the problem was caused by an outsider who had supplied his own references. In 1677 a London mason 'well versed in bricklaying' arrived at Whitehaven from Dublin and offered to erect two chimneys. After two days the agent 'turned him off, finding him no true labourer of his hands which made me suspect all his boasts for falsities'.[126]

Some aspects of gild activity – especially the feasting and drinking and the presentation of a united front against outsiders – give the impression of a cohesiveness which was often absent. Gild ordinances required members to be loving to each other. The Chester bricklayers were not 'to call any of the brothers worse than his proper name in wrath or anger', and their Newcastle colleagues laid down a fine of 6s 8d for any 'who shall at any time scandalise, demean, vilify or otherwise abuse any other of the said company in the meeting house'. Any member of the company 'who shall in anger either strike or beat any other brother ... with his fist or any other weapon' was to be fined likewise.[127] The minute book of the Chester gild of joiners, turners, and carvers for the first half of the seventeenth century reveals a society in which relationships were often far from loving.[128] It may be imagined that friction within the gild was generated by internal demarcation disputes between the different crafts, but this seems unlikely since the gild was dominated by the joiners who comprised about three-quarters of the membership. Moreover, the frequency of disputes in other gilds suggests that the problem was more one of personality than

[123] Airs 1975, 173–4.   [124] *YCR*, VII, 57; V, 67. See also YCA, CC33; TWAS, 802/3.
[125] Tyson 1983b, 64. See also E. Hughes 1952, 26.
[126] Tyson 1984, 77–8. For a similar example see HCRO, BRL/1458.
[127] CCRO, G4/1. See also *YCR*, V, 112; TWAS, 802/16.
[128] CCRO, G14/2. The following discussion is based on this source with membership statistics taken from G14/1.

of trade. Each year between 1616 and 1626 (when there is a gap in the records until 1640) members of the Chester gild were censured and fined for falling out with each other, both verbally and physically. In December 1616 it was reported that many meetings were disorderly 'because of multiplying of many words to small effect', and brothers were exhorted to speak 'in gentle and quiet manner' with the rest of the members listening in silence. Between 1616 and 1626 no fewer than twelve of the twenty-one members of the gild were fined for 'disorderly' or 'foul and uncivil' speeches, or for brawling – most of them more than once and some of them frequently. John Garfield, who joined the gild in 1615, was a frequent offender. He exchanged foul words with Raph Davies in 1617 and in 1620 his wife cursed William Salisbury, then alderman of the gild, 'upon her knees' calling him 'an alderman of thieves'. During the following years Garfield was fined for various offences, more or less as an annual event, but his notoriety peaked in January 1626 when, in the meeting house,' in a most vehement and bitter manner [he] railed against many of the brethren now present calling them by the name of Doggs puke and hath cursed them with the pox and wished the devil to take them'. He was banned from meetings until he had paid his past fines and a new imposition of 3s 4d.

Perhaps John Garfield's behaviour was a product of personal inadequacy and inferiority since, unlike the majority of his colleagues, he never became a steward of the gild, although he remained a member for thirty-two years. Nor did his business thrive. In 1624 he was spared a fine of 6s 8d because of his poverty: the fine was for seeking to involve a stranger in making a coffin. But any suggestion that disputes between members were caused by economic and social differences is probably misplaced: of the 12 offenders, 9 rose to the rank of steward, and 7 became aldermen of the gild. Prince of offenders was Raph Davies, who worked as a journeyman during 1601 and 1602 when he joined the gild, became steward for the first of five occasions in 1604, and was alderman of the gild eight times between 1630 and 1640. Davies had an extraordinary flair for disputation. He exchanged blows and foul words with many of his colleagues between 1616 and 1626, but his chief adversary was William Salisbury who had joined the gild in 1593, filled the position of steward on four occasions, and was alderman from 1610 to 1629 inclusive and again in 1632. The two men swapped invective throughout the period, although Davies seems to have been the prime mover. It is possible that his abusive behaviour sprang from a sense of frustration with the leadership of a slightly older generation, especially as Davies could write his name whereas

Salisbury was illiterate. For whatever reason, the Chester joiners were a fractious lot and the behaviour of Raph Davies was different only in degree from that of his colleagues. The incidence of recorded offences was rather lower by the end of the seventeenth century, although passions could still run high. One member might still regard another as 'a stinking knave', and unspecified 'bad words' or 'bad language' were not uncommon. In October 1720 the case of William Millington was considered. His offence, 'of bidding the aldermen kiss his arse, out of the meeting house', looked serious, but eighteen members voted against a fine, presumably on the ground that the words were uttered beyond gild territory.

Plain speaking was also common among York craftsmen,[129] but it is the minutes of the Newcastle gilds which furnish large numbers of comparable examples. One historian has claimed that the 'numerous episodes of violence, trickery, temperamental outbursts' among craftsmen during the Civil War were indicative of 'a growing dissatisfaction with the restraints imposed by the guilds'.[130] However, such occurrences were not new and they did not subside with the coming of peace. During the 1670s Henry Wallas, a Newcastle joiner, was the chief villain of his gild, although, to be fair to him, he had had a disturbed upbringing: he had been apprenticed to Arthur Story in July 1655, but he died and Wallas was turned over to the widow.[131] In October 1672, by then probably in his mid thirties, he called John Gofton 'a witches bastard and cuckoldy fellow, struck him with a quart pot, hit him on the head, tore his band, and made a great tumult, with several members present'. Wallas continued to abuse his fellow joiners verbally through the 1670s and, occasionally, was accused of assault. His colourful insults included: 'white lugged rogue'; 'sheep driver'; 'loggerhead rogue'; 'pick-lock rogue and whoreson'; and 'copper nose fellow'. The colleague who called him an 'idle fellow, and not fit to come into civil men's company' seems to have hit the nail squarely on the head. But such cursing was commonplace among the Newcastle joiners.[132] The bricklayers were equally rough tongued. They were frequently accused of 'speaking unbrotherly words'. Their insults included: 'bastard and that he would prove him one'; 'pitiful sneaking fellow'; 'Jack of all trades and good for none'; 'a good for nothing dog'; 'only half a man'; and 'a manshit and a lubbard'.[133]

The use of such intemperate language was probably part of everyday life among the lower orders of society. The gilds sought to stamp

---

[129] YCR, VIII, 56; IX, 29.   [130] Howell 1967, 279–80.   [131] TWAS, 648/13.
[132] TWAS, 648/3.
[133] TWAS, 802/2, /4, /5.

Table 3.4. *Literacy among building workers*

	Chester joiners 1626 (total 14) %	York bricklayers 1663–1700 (total 124) %	Newcastle bricklayers	
			1663 (total 51) %	1729 (total 39) %
Using a mark	35.7	52.4	54.9	5.1
Signing	64.3	47.6	45.1	94.9

Sources: CCRO, G14/2, p. 74; YML, QQ 80/2/11; TWAS, 802/2, /4.

out such behaviour, or at least establish punitive penalties, although they often tempered punishment with great mercy and frequently reduced fines after the furore had died down. Thomas Moor, a Newcastle joiner, was treated with great leniency. By October 1737 he owed over £27, but the whole sum was abated, and in August 1739 he paid 3d, his only payment after nearly twenty years of offending.[134] But patience could be stretched beyond breaking point and a member was occasionally thrown out of his gild, although the threat of ejection was usually sufficient to ameliorate the behaviour of the unruly.

The figures presented in table 3.4 suggest that nearly half of the York and Newcastle bricklayers could sign their names by the late seventeenth century, and that literacy had advanced markedly at Newcastle by the end of the third decade of the following century: an increasing number were able to read the growing number of builders' manuals which appeared in the eighteenth century.[135] In the early seventeenth century the majority of Chester joiners were literate, although illiteracy was not a barrier to office holding: neither William Salisbury nor William Pue, the two aldermen in 1626, could sign their names.

Although many building craftsmen were illiterate, some historians have found it 'hard to imagine how they could have operated their own businesses without rudimentary skills in reading, writing, and arithmetic'.[136] But manage they did. It may be difficult for us to make the imaginative leap, but it is evident that literacy was not essential for commercial success in early-modern England: some sophisticated businesses were headed by illiterates.[137] Numeracy, and especially the

---

[134] TWAS, 648/12.   [135] See also Houston 1982.
[136] Rappaport 1983, 116. See also Airs 1975, 28; Rappaport 1989, 300.
[137] See the case of Robert Brerewood, the leading businessman in Elizabethan Chester: Woodward, 1968a; Woodward, 1968b, 103–4.

ability to reckon money, was probably more crucial for the aspiring craftsman, although historians have not yet devised a way to measure general levels of numeracy in Tudor and Stuart England.

Gild members could expect some pastoral support in times of trouble, and the clearest statement of intent comes from the ordinances of the York carpenters for 1482:

> Also it is ordained that if any of the said fraternity fall to poverty, so that they may not work, or happen to be blind, or to lose their goods by 'unhap of the world', then the foresaid brotherhood to give them 4d every week, as long as they live, by way of alms, so that he that is so fortuned have truly fulfilled the ordinances above written.
>
> Also it is ordained that what brother shall so be admitted to take alms, shall be sworn upon a book that he shall truly live upon his alms and his own goods, without waste or giving away of them, and whatsoever he leaves at his dying that belongs to himself, his debts paid and his burial reasonably done, shall remain to the said fraternity as their own proper goods.[138]

But such levels of support were beyond the means of building-craft gilds. Pastoral payments were rarely recorded in the minutes, and the relatively low levels of their incomes meant that acts of charity were bound to be sporadic. In March 1619, the Chester joiners voted to return 4d of John Fletcher's quarterage because of his poverty and long sickness. Two years later, in a rare act of charity to an outsider, the gild agreed to give 2s to a shoemaker, 'his wife having been speechless for a long time'. In 1637, the Chester smiths gave 8s 'to the widows of our company' and 1s 4d to the poor in the almshouses.[139] But at Newcastle the joiners were more anxious to distribute any surplus funds among themselves than give to the needy: in 1658 they gave 2s 2d to the poor and 3s to the widows, but £2 5s was distributed among the members. When help was given to the unfortunate, like the sixpence given to John Fairlees by every brother 'for his bedding at the almshouse', it stands out as exceptional.[140] Small sums were doled out from time to time, but support for the poor and feckless was not given a high priority. However, it is possible that through the maintenance of informal networks, which could provide job opportunities, and by encouraging casual charity from one member to another the gilds provided a safety net for the unfortunate. More formal attempts to relieve unemployment were made by some of the gilds. In 1482 the York carpenters laid down that outsiders were not to be employed if any of the brethren were out of work, and an employment officer was to be chosen so that 'he that would have a workman may have

---

[138] *York Memorandum Book*, 279–80; Rule 1987, 113; Palliser 1972, 103.
[139] CCRO, G14/1, /2, pp. 24, 40; G20/1, fo. 14r.
[140] TWAS, 648/3, /6, /8. See also 802/1, /4.

knowledge of him that is out of work'.[141] Other gilds tried to control the employment of outsiders and town councils appointed a place where the unemployed were to gather early in the morning, with their tools in their hands, and wait to be hired.[142]

Old age came early, and in 1590 the York bricklayers laid down that 'any person of the said occupation of sixty years old shall not be charged to come to their assemblies or meeting but at their own will and pleasure'.[143] One of the interesting features of the period is that, while contemporaries paid a substantial amount of attention to the level of wages to be paid to young workers, they were totally silent about those whose strength was on the wane.[144] The onset of effective old age varied from man to man, but the evidence of the long-term employment of some men and the enduring involvement in gild affairs by others suggests that at least some of them remained active into very old age. But their effectiveness and productivity must be questioned. Perhaps declining physical powers were adequately compensated for by greater skill and wisdom, so that older men would be transferred to a supervisory role, befitting their age and experience, like the mid-fourteenth-century carpenter at York Minster: 'the carpenter is an old man and cannot work at high levels. It is ordered that another young man be employed in his place, and that the other old man shall supervise defects.'[145] But the authorities were not always so generous. In 1669 the leaders of the Hull carpenters nominated five men for the town's work, but they were rejected on the grounds that they were 'old, weak and unfit'. Since the gild refused to co-operate with this exercise in ageism the council sought outside help.[146] Some building craftsmen moved into almshouses in old age, although none of their gilds seems to have owned one. At Chester in 1631, a baker was chosen to replace the joiner, John Higgen, in Vernon's almshouse: he had been a member of his gild from 1597 to 1630 and had served as alderman for seven years, starting in 1615. Similarly, Raph Davies, the combative joiner, was admitted to the same house in September 1642.[147] He remained a member of the gild until 1649, although he had probably stopped work. But such support was dependent on the general availability of charitable institutions in the towns.

Gild members expected their obsequies to be properly observed, and those who absented themselves from the funeral of a colleague or his

---

[141] YML, QQ80/3/2; *York Memorandum Book*, 280.
[142] J.W.F. Hill 1956, 78; *Norwich Records*.
[143] YML, QQ80/2/11.   [144] Roberts 1981, 133–41.   [145] Salzman 1952, 55.
[146] Davies 1956.
[147] *Chester Minutes*, 166, 211.

wife, or widow, were fined.[148] At Newcastle, however, only those selected as bearers were expected to attend the funerals of bricklayers after 1723. The joiners maintained their traditional arrangements, and in the early eighteenth century four men were fined for 'going wrong at Joseph Weldon's funeral'. Presumably they were drunk.[149] The gilds sometimes paid for the burial of an impoverished member. In 1597 the Chester joiners paid for the burial of Lawrence Wright:

Paid for a winding sheet for our brother Lawrence 2s 6d.

Paid to the vicar and the clerk for his burial 1s 4d.

Paid to John Rogerson for his 'leystall' 1s 6d.[150]

At Newcastle in the eighteenth century the bricklayers went a step further and agreed to pay 40s towards the funeral expenses of all brothers and their wives or widows.[151] Some years earlier a rather curious form of assistance was offered by the gild. Two black cloths were bought and members could borrow them 'for the burial of any friend': the 'greater cloth' could be hired for 2s and the 'lesser cloth' for 12d.[152]

Some building craftsmen prospered, but for the most part they were humble men playing out their lives within the confines of family, gild, and parish. For all but a handful, the pinnacle of power and influence was to become leader of their gild, although that could lay them open to the abuse of men like Raph Davies. As gild aldermen their prestige was at a much lower level than that of the urban elite. The only man appearing in the accounts on which this study is based who is known to have soared to greater heights is George Railton, a leading Carlisle builder of the second quarter of the eighteenth century. Between 1733 and his burial in St Mary's churchyard in January 1752, he 'served on the Corporation of Carlisle as one of the capital citizens, a position in which he could find work for his trade'.[153]

Beyond the grave: the role of the widow

Women appear in the building accounts and gild records of northern England in three main guises: they supplied some of the food and drink provided on some building sites, and this subject will be dealt with in chapter 5; women also appear from time to time as general labourers, carrying sand and water or doing other low-grade tasks,

[148] Gittings 1984, 27; CCRO, G4/1, G14/2, G20/1; TWAS, 802/1, /16.
[149] TWAS, 648/3, /12, 802/2.
[150] CCRO, G14/1, fo. 52r; TWAS, 802/3 for the burial of a bricklayer's widow.
[151] TWAS, 802/16.
[152] TWAS, 802/2. The cloths were hired out on various occasions.
[153] B.C. Jones 1983, 126–8.

and this aspect of their lives will be discussed in chapter 4; finally, small numbers of women attempted to continue the building enterprises of their late husbands, at times with great success.

Recent accounts of women in late-medieval and early-modern society have stressed their importance, not merely in the household economy – baking, brewing, and doing a thousand and one other tasks essential to the maintenance of family life – but in the wider economies of town and village.[154] But frequently they remain shadowy figures, making rare appearances in official records. Indeed, 'the evidence for female participation in the medieval urban economy is not great; but this is more a reflection of the sexual bias of the surviving data', for 'women ... tend to be invisible as far as many historical sources are concerned, rarely appearing, or doing so only fleetingly'.[155] Women tended to congregate in occupations associated with domestic labour, or in the 'casual menial end of the market': that is, in areas such as domestic service, the victualling trades, petty retailing, nursing, lace-making, and spinning.[156] Much of the problem lies in the fact that many young women did not undergo a formal apprenticeship and become enfranchised. At York only about 140 women were admitted to the freedom between 1272 and 1500, and many of them were widows eager to continue the businesses of their late husbands: in the Tudor period women comprised only 1 per cent of admissions.[157] Nevertheless, an increasing volume of literature demonstates that some women conducted businesses independently of their husbands, while others worked alongside their spouses in the family business.

In most towns a woman had the option of continuing her husband's occupation after his death. This right, which was an ancient one, was confirmed for all trades at York in 1529 and at Chester in 1606, although it was often lost when a widow remarried.[158] During her widowhood a woman became a member of her late husband's gild in her own right, although she did not enjoy equal status with the male members, and her involvement in the gild was often temporary. She paid quarterage for herself, her apprentices and journeymen, and could engage extra labour as required. But she remained a second-class

---

[154] Berg 1987; Charles & Duffin 1985; Hilton 1985; Hutton 1985; Swanson 1989; Wright 1985.

[155] Charles & Duffin 1985, 10; Hutton 1985, 96.

[156] Berg 1987, 74; Goldberg 1986, 35; Hilton 1985; Lacey 1985, 47–57; Swanson 1989; Wright 1985, 103–11.

[157] R.B. Dobson 1973, 13–14; Goldberg 1986, 32; Palliser 1972, 100. For the situation in London see Rappaport 1989, 36–7.

[158] Palliser 1972, 100; *YCR*, III, 125–6; *Chester Minutes*, xxviii. See also A. Clark 1919, 150–1, 187; Rappaport 1989, 39–41.

member and could not advance in the gild hierarchy. This was signalled most clearly in the records of the Chester joiners in which widows were listed as an afterthought beneath the name of the most junior male member.[159] In late-medieval Coventry, widows could run the family business only for as long as it took their sons to complete their apprenticeships and 'there was no question that widows might perpetuate the business by training up apprentices on their own account'.[160] This was not the case in the northern towns. While some widows continued the business for only a few months in order to tidy up existing commitments, others continued to ply their late husbands' trades for many years. Unfortunately, much of the evidence is fragmentary and only in the records of the Chester joiners can their careers be studied systematically.[161] Between 1591 and 1675 eighteen active widows were listed, but thereafter only the six who employed journeymen between 1680 and 1721 were named. There may have been others who did not employ journeymen. The widows had been married to 24 of the 136 men who were in the gild in 1591, or had joined it not later than 1719. Their husbands had all enjoyed some success in the gild: all had been steward and eleven had risen to the rank of alderman. Of the eighteen widows who appeared before 1675, four of them were listed only once, and two were recorded in adjacent years: this suggests that a third of them either ran down the business quickly or, perhaps, looked for a speedy remarriage to restore their fortunes. Five of the widows seem to have been trying to make a success of the business and were listed for three years: the career of one was ended by death, while the name of Margaret Williamson was crossed out in 1642 and the marginal note 'married' added. Four of the widows were recorded for four or five years, but only three continued to be listed for longer. They were:

Alice Bolland: widow of Richard Bolland, a member of the gild for seventeen years, steward on five occasions and alderman five times. She was listed from the year of his death in 1637 to 1646.

Margaret Kettle: widow of Thomas Kettle, a member of the gild for ten years and steward four times. She was listed from his death in 1655 to her death in 1664. In 1660 she employed two journeymen.

Alice Calcot: widow of either Richard Calcot (a member from 1637–47) or Edward Calcot (member from 1610–47), although she

---

159 In late-medieval London women were allowed to join the gilds but as second-class members: they could not participate fully in the councils or in social events. Lacey 1985, 45–6.
160 Phythian-Adams 1979, 91–2.   161 CCRO, G14/1.

was not listed until 1656. In 1664 she was said to be 'willing to leave the company', but did not do so until some time in 1668. By then John Calcot was a journeyman 'with his mother': he joined the gild that year and remained a member for fifty-eight years.

The careers of the six widows who employed journeymen after 1680 cannot be charted with such accuracy, although it is known that four of them employed journeymen in one or two years, and that two had more substantial careers. They were:

Widow Johnson: widow of Henry Johnson, a member of the gild from 1656 until his death on 29 June 1680. He was steward on four occasions and alderman twice, and his widow employed one or more journeymen in the years 1681–3, 1685, and 1687.

Widow Cross: widow of Isaac Cross, a gild member from 1669 to 1689 and steward on three occasions. She had one or more journeymen during twelve of the years between 1691 and 1707.

Thus, between 1591 and 1721 at least 24, or just over 18 per cent, of the potential widows of the 132 Chester joiners attempted to continue their late husbands' businesses for at least some time. This is a substantial proportion, since some women would have predeceased their husbands and those whose husbands died in old age were unlikely to have had much stomach for the rough-and-tumble of this male domain: of the 124 joiners whose ages can be estimated, 32, or just under a quarter, died or left the gild when they were in their late fifties or beyond.[162] Indeed, the husbands of the widows who endeavoured to maintain the family business died relatively young, having been in the gild for an average of sixteen years: two had been in the gild for over thirty years, but five for less than ten years. The majority probably died in their thirties or forties.

The relatively high level of participation by the Chester widows may have been due in part to the workshop-based nature of the trade. Widows probably featured less strongly in those trades which were practised chiefly away from home: Alice Clark suggested that 'the carpenters who often were engaged in building operations could not profit much by their wives' assistance'.[163] The northern accounts bear this out: a very rare reference to a wife assisting her husband comes from Chester in 1556 when Harry Weller, who was probably a bricklayer, was paid 8d 'for his day work' and his wife 2d 'for carrying water and sand'.[164] Only two further references to widows engaged in the building-site trades have been discovered: at Chester in the early seventeenth century 6s 8d was paid to Widow Butler's servants, 'two

[162] See table 3.3 above p. 76.   [163] A.Clark 1919, 183.   [164] CCORO, P/20/13/1.

of them for five days in amending the common hall with slates at 16d per day'; at Durham in 1724, Widow Hudson was paid for the masonry work of five men.[165] Other widows who played a similar supervisory role in one of the outdoor trades have not left any trace in the records.

In those crafts which were either predominantly or partly workshop based – those of the smiths, glaziers, plumbers, and joiners – there was probably more scope for wifely involvement. If a wife did no more than lend an occasional hand or simply pass through the workshop from time to time, she would have had the opportunity to pick up at least some rudimentary knowledge and skills which could be further developed after her husband's death. In some cases wives may have played a more central role, toiling at the work-bench alongside their spouses on a regular basis. This may have been the case with the wife of Charles Trumble, a Newcastle joiner: she offended the gild by employing house carpenters to make coffins in her husband's absence.[166] Without the development of some expertise it is difficult to see how widows could have continued the trade, although many may have been forced to rely on the support of their male employees.[167] Alice Clark told the story of a painter's widow whose apprentice had already served seven years out of nine and alleged that the widow refused to instruct him. She insisted that she had provided competent workmen to do so and that he was now able to give good service.[168]

Some widows ran blacksmithing businesses. At Chester.in 1574 five widows were named alongside thirty-five male smiths, and female smiths were found in both northern and southern England in the late-medieval period.[169] Three York women supplied nails and other ironwork, while at Hull, the appropriately named Elizabeth Smith ran a highly successful smithy for more than ten years after her husband's death in 1668.[170] Other active widows included two Newcastle women who paid quarterage for their journeymen joiners in 1658, and a York widow who was reported by the gild of painters and glaziers in 1594 for employing foreigners.[171] Similarly, Widow Buckton was employed as a plumber and glazier by the churchwardens of St Michael le Belfry, York, in 1685, as was Widow Dolby at St Mary's, Chester, during 1682–3.[172] But Ellen Pears, who had worked for the same church as a

---

[165] CCRO, TAR 2/31 for 1614–15; DPK, Audit bills, Bundle 16.
[166] TWAS, 648/3 for 1677.
[167] A. Clark 1919, 173, 189–90; Charles & Duffin 1985, 10–11; *Oxford Apprentices*, xiv–xv, 182; Hutton 1985, 89.
[168] A. Clark 1919, 188.   [169] *Ibid.*, 155; Swanson 1989, 67–8.
[170] YBI, PR/Y/HTG/12, p. 343; PR/Y/J/18 for 1708; YCA, CC36–7. Widow Roberts supplied some ironware in 1673: HCRO, BRF/3/20.
[171] TWAS, 648/8; YCA, B31/85.   [172] YBI, PR/Y/MB/34; CCORO, P/20/13/1.

plumber between 1605 and 1630, is the most interesting of the Chester widows. Her husband had worked at the church during 1604, and she also worked from time to time for the city council, where she was sometimes referred to as 'Ellen Plummer'.[173] The accounts of St Mary's are quite explicit about her role:

1605 Paid Ellen Pears and her boy for their four days' work, 5s.
1607 Paid to her for two days work for herself and man for mending many places on the leads, 3s 3d.
1609 Paid Ellen Pears for work with her boy being three several days mending leads, 3s 6d.

Ellen Pears was not simply supervising the work of others: she mounted her ladders and scrambled around on the church roof, cutting out decayed lead and replacing it with new. She also supplied solder and lead on many occasions, and in 1611 some old lead was carried 'to Ellen Pears shop' where, presumably, it was cast into new sheets. She usually worked with a single assistant, variously referred to as her 'man', 'boy', or 'son'. This was probably Peter Pears whose christian name was first recorded in 1624. His mother seems to have retired from active plumbing in 1630 when Peter had 'Ellen Pears man helping', and 'young Peter Pears' – perhaps Ellen's grandson – heating the irons. After 1630 the Pears family stopped looking after the church leads, although in 1669 a Thomas Pieres and his wife were paid for casting lead.[174] Ellen Pears probably developed her skill as a plumber during her husband's lifetime, and may well have worked alongside him on the city's roofs. As a widow she was probably unusual in not confining her activities to the workshop.

Various women – probably widows for the most part – supplied a range of materials rather than their own labour. At Hull, Mary Carter ran a timber-supply business during the 1650s and 1660s, and other women, often the widows of substantial merchants, supplied timber from time to time.[175] Widows supplied bricks at Tattershall Castle in Lincolnshire in the 1450s, and also at Lincoln over 200 years later, and at Hull in the later 1660s.[176] William Guy, the chief supplier of lime at Hull, died in June 1638 and his widow continued the business for a year or so. Other women supplied ropes and leather.[177]

A number of women followed their late husbands into the carrying trade, presumably after inheriting capital equipment in the shape of a

---

173 *Ibid.*; CCRO, TAR 2/30, /33, /37, /39. See also Laughton 1987–8, 109.
174 CCRO, TAR 3/55.
175 HCRO, BRF/3/20. For merchants' widows in late-medieval Hull see *Hull Customs*, xxiii.
176 *Tattershall Castle Accts*, xxix; J.W.F. Hill 1956, 201; LAO, Bj/1/12; HCRO, BRF/3/20.
177 HCRO, BRF/3/20; HCORO, PE/158/1; YBI, PR/Y/MG/20, fo. 105r; YCA, CC35–6.

horse and cart, or a river craft.[178] During the second half of the sixteenth century Widows Manwell, Chapman, and Thompson carried sand and ballast in their boats on the Tyne, and a female carter was employed at Louth in 1500 carrying stone for the new steeple.[179] But it is the Hull accounts for the 1660s and 1670s which indicate how important women could be in the trade.[180] During those two decades seven widows took over their husbands' businesses as common carriers and, in some cases, as scavengers. Unfortunately, it is impossible to say how long the widows remained in business, since their absence from the council records does not necessarily mean that they had retired. Two widows were recorded in only a single year, but three – including Mary Thompson – worked for four consecutive years. Ann Soulsby operated as a carrier and scavenger between 1659 and 1668, but Ann Herring was the longest serving of the Hull carrier-widows, plying her trade between 1661 and 1679. Ann Soulsby and Mary Thompson did most of the work for the council in particular years. Ann Soulsby was married to Christopher Soulsby, a leading carrier in the town during the 1650s, who was buried on 16 April 1659.[181] She quickly established herself in the trade and was the leading carrier employed by the council between 1663 and 1668: indeed, her dominance was such that she was the only carrier employed on building sites by the council during 1665–7. She did not work for the council after 1668, although she made a fleeting appearance as a carrier in the Trinity House accounts for September 1675.[182] Her place as top carrier for the council was taken over by John Thompson, who had been operating his haulage business since at least 1663 and was the chief carrier from 1669 to 1672. When he died in 1673 he was replaced by his widow Mary, who worked as the chief carrier for the council between 1673 and 1676. Like so many business enterprises in early-modern England these carriers worked on a small scale. On occasion, both Ann Soulsby and Ann Herring operated with two men and two horses, and on one occasion the wording of the accounts suggests that Ann Herring may have been leading the horse herself.

The frequency with which widows stepped forward to fill their late husbands' boots is difficult to judge. In the case of the Chester joiners the picture is clear enough, at least before 1675, but the extant accounts reveal only a minority of the male building craftsmen in a particular town, and, probably, an even smaller proportion of the active widows. The fact that some women predeceased their husbands and that some

---

[178] Cross 1987, 89.
[179] See the many references in TWAS, 543/15–16, /18; *Louth Accts*, 7.
[180] HCRO, BRF/3/20   [181] HCORO, PE/158/3.   [182] *Ibid.*

men lived to a ripe old age, meant that some wives were never given the opportunity to practise the craft in their own right. But some did, and there are sufficient examples to suggest that, even in the building trades, widows were able to maintain family businesses, although they were more likely to be successful in the workshop-based crafts.

Reflections

Those who were fortunate enough to become masters of their trades moved from the dogsbody existence of the apprentice to that of journeyman before progressing to the senior ranks. The apprentices, drawn from town and countryside, were generally from humble backgrounds and most were probably in their late teens when their indentures were signed. In order to control the number of potential masters their numbers were tightly regulated in most towns. As a result, the annual flow of apprentices finishing their training was too small to provide more than a very small number of journeymen, so that their numbers had to be augmented by those from outside the towns. Certainly that was the case at Chester and probably at some other northern towns. At Chester the great majority of journeymen joiners were outsiders who drifted in and out of the town and never had the chance of joining the ranks of the masters. This finding changes dramatically our perceptions of the usual career structure of building workers. Many ex-apprentices did graduate to the senior ranks, although the costs incurred in joining a gild, becoming a freeman, and setting up a new business could delay the progression for some years. Once he became a master a young man could begin to make profits on top of his wages and progress through the gild hierarchy, and those who lived long enough had the chance of becoming gild aldermen. Supportive though the building-craft gilds were of their members' business interests, they had a relatively poor record in terms of pastoral support: only small amounts were given to the poor and feeble. Despite the *bonhomie* apparent at the feasting there was an undercurrent of rancorous discord. In gild after gild members reviled each other on frequent occasions and were often reproved for their 'unbrotherly words'. But death was a great healer of past enmities and members were expected to turn out in force at a brother's funeral. Since many gildsmen died in mid-life or earlier they often left widows and children who needed support, and many widows sought to perpetuate the family business. They were given gild support, albeit as second-class members, and sometimes continued the business for many years. Widows were probably more likely to be successful in a workshop-based trade, although some were active in the outdoor trades.

Also present on building sites, and anywhere else in the urban economy whenever brute force was needed, were labourers. Sometimes they were gathered together in vast gangs, but on other occasions they worked in ones and twos. Although labourers were often not named in the accounts a surprisingly large amount is known about them, as will become apparent in the next chapter.

4

Labourers

According to an early-eighteenth-century dictionary, carpenters and other building craftsmen belonged to the 'mechanic arts' which 'require more of the labour of the hand and body, than of the mind'. But labourers were engaged in 'drudgery work'.[1] There were times when long association with a particular type of craftsman gave a labourer some specialist skill: at a very fractious meeting of the Newcastle bricklayers' gild in 1749 a complaint was made against William Yarrow 'for saying he had wrought at London with labourers as good workmen as any of the bricklayers in the company'.[2] Perhaps there was much truth in the accusation, but most labourers were not specialists. However, it would be a mistake to regard them as unskilled. Their methods may often have looked rough and ready to the casual observer, but even the use of a spade or shovel involves some skill. Urban labourers differed from building craftsmen in a number of respects: they did not provide the raw materials with which they worked; they did not employ labour; and they did not usually supply their own tools. Many institutions provided basic tools such as spades, shovels, and wheelbarrows which could be used by labourers and craftsmen alike.[3] As on building sites today the organisers of large projects bought tools in bulk. When the Hull defences were being repaired in 1577 the council purchased 120 spades, 120 shovels and 60 pickaxes, and the churchwardens of All Saints', Newcastle, bought six eight-penny shovels for the grave digger in 1725/6.[4] Labourers reached

---

[1] Quoted in Roberts 1985, 132–3.
[2] TWAS, 802/5. For a discussion of specialisation among rural labourers see Smith 1989, 19–26. He includes shepherds, hedgers and ditchers, and building labourers among his specialists.
[3] See above pp. 50–1.
[4] TWAS, MF557, p. 383; Gillett & MacMahon 1989, 152. See also HCRO, BRF/3/20, pp. 201, 246, 281, 323, 440.

their maximum earning potential at a relatively early age and had little to look forward to in terms of career or income progression thereafter. All wage-earners were held in low esteem,[5] although it is clear that the more specialised craftsmen were able to claim a higher social status than labourers and had higher income expectations. The lowly social position of labourers is neatly symbolised by their anonymity in many contemporary accounts which makes it extremely difficult, and often impossible, to recreate their patterns of employment. Only occasionally did labourers force themselves into public view.

Varieties of labouring work

The work of urban labourers fell into three main categories: some worked as assistants to building craftsmen; others – such as the porters of Hull and York – were specialists doing a single task; but the majority worked in gangs doing a thousand and one varied jobs, sometimes alongside craftsmen, but often not.

All building craftsmen needed the assistance of labourers from time to time. Carpenters were normally aided by trained journeymen and apprentices, and only rarely – as in the raising of a heavy timber structure – did they need an extra input of brute force. Bricklayers also instructed apprentices and worked alongside skilled journeymen, but in most cases they needed the assistance of labourers. As today, the basic tasks of mixing mortar and carrying bricks fell to a 'bricky's labourer': the ordinances of the York bricklayers specifically referred to those 'set to work ... as a labourer'.[6] In some cases the labourer was referred to as the bricklayer's 'man', which may imply a degree of dependency, although such men were usually paid at the same rate as general labourers. A reference at Newcastle indicates that some brickies' labourers possessed unusual qualities: in 1655 two of them were paid 1s 8d for 'a day counting bricks and piling them'.[7] Labourers were also taken on to work alongside other building craftsmen. During the late-medieval period masons were often assisted by labourers: at Durham in 1489 some of them were called 'barrowmen' rather than labourers.[8] At York Minster in 1579 the plumber's assistant was known interchangeably as his 'man' or his 'labourer', while at Durham during the hard winter of 1495/6 a gang of casual labourers was assembled to help the plumber with 'unfreezing the monastery aqueduct at the time

[5] Clarkson 1982, 21; Rule 1981, 118.   [6] YML, QQ80/2/11 for 1590.
[7] TWAS, 659/449.
[8] Knoop & Jones 1949, 69–72; DFC, CC/190049.

of the great frost this year'.[9] Such examples could be multiplied many times over from the northern accounts.

At three of the northern ports – Hull, Newcastle, and York – groups of labourers were maintained on a more or less permanent basis to handle goods brought to the quayside. Two groups of labourers were licensed at York: the free labourers who were employed to unload vessels at the wharf, and the porters who distributed such wares around the city. The number of porters was set at sixteen in 1495 and raised to twenty-four in 1640, and rates were laid down for carriage according to the distance covered.[10] The council protected their monopolies and in 1585 they were ordered to wear distinctive clothing to help to maintain their exclusivity: 'Labourers now appointed at staithe shall, before Wednesday come a sennett [week], provide of their own costs, for every one of them, one harden shirt with sleeves, and the porters likewise harden shirts with hoods.'[11] The free labourers were also distinguished from other labourers by enjoying the protection of their own gild, and in 1477 they were ordered to elect two searchers from their number to collect money to support the masons' pageant. Although the gild continued throughout the next two centuries it left few records and seems to have lacked the vitality of the craft gilds.[12] There was also a gild of labourers in late-medieval Beverley, although whether or not it survived into the early-modern period is not known.[13] Like the York men, the Hull porters enjoyed a degree of monopoly over the carriage of goods, although it is not known if this was formally endorsed by the council. They operated a tight closed shop. According to a contemporary observer: 'The porters carried each of them three deals at once. They will scarce suffer any other men to carry them although they be their own.'[14] Little is known about the organisation of the Newcastle porters, or about the gang of labourers who shifted ballast at 2d a ton on the south shore of the Tyne in the years around 1600, although it seems to have consisted of 'old labourers'.[15]

[9] YML, E3/56; *Durham Abbey Accts*, III, 654.
[10] Palliser 1972, 94–5; Palliser 1979, 161. See also many references in *YCR* and the York council records, accessed by an excellent card index in YCA under the headings Labourers and Porters; YML, QQ80/5/1; *YCR*, II, 122, VII, 40.
[11] *YCR*, VIII, 106.
[12] Swanson 1983, 26; Swanson 1988, 40; Swanson 1989, 96; Palliser 1979, 294–5; YML, QQ80/5/1.
[13] *VCH Beverley*, 46.
[14] *Henry Best*, 132. The rates they could charge for carriage around the town were regulated in great detail by the council.
[15] TWAS, 543/19.

But the great majority of labourers neither worked as personal assistants to building craftsmen nor belonged to specialist groups licensed by the civic authorities. Rather, they were hired by the day to perform a kaleidoscopic range of heavy tasks which required a modicum of common sense, a fair amount of brawn, but little specialised knowledge. The northern accounts give a vivid picture of the wide variety of jobs available to labourers. At Hull in 1661 Patrick Lidgerd and Richard Rodwell were paid for three days, 'digging holes for setting posts betwixt the vicarage and Mr Shoor's garden and for housing a hundred bushels of cement and for opening the sewer at Hessle gates and carrying out rubbish of the school house garden'.[16] Much of the work was heavy. Labourers were to be found 'digging and levelling ground before the paver', 'helping to take up the old bridge', and 'taking down the mud wall and trenching to lay the foundation', while 16d was paid in the summer of 1574 by Hull Trinity House 'to Blackbeard for scouring the well'.[17] At York eighteen men were needed in 1740 to raise 'my lord mayor's barge out of the river being sunk by the fury of the great flood of water and the ice'.[18] Labourers were also needed to clean out sewers and cesspits: at Hull Trinity House, on the eve of the Civil War, ten men were paid 30s 6d 'for dressing and carrying the filth away of the old wives' privy house'. Such payments were made regularly and in 1654 between twenty-six and twenty-eight loads of 'manure' were carried from the House each quarter. The town's fresh-water channel needed constant attention and, from time to time, dead horses had to be dragged out of it.[19] Shovelling snow off the roofs of churches and council buildings was a common winter activity, although the job was not always done too carefully: in 1701 the Dean and Chapter at York had to pay Robert Clark 17s 9d compensation 'for damage done his house by snow throwing off the Minster'.[20]

Some tasks were more unusual. Labourers helped to prepare for royal visits: at York, on Saturday 16 April 1603, four labourers received 2s 4d 'when the king came: for filling the dikes and making the majesty a way through the closes that day', and similar payments were made at

[16] HCRO, BRF/3/20, p. 315. See also TWAS, 659/447.
[17] HCRO, BRF/3/20, pp. 166, 353, 603.
[18] YCA, CC36, fo. 14v. See also CCRO, TAR/2/30.
[19] HTH, IV, V, for 1640, 1643, 1645, 1649, 1654, 1674, 1686; *Hull Rentals*, 103; Gillett & MacMahon 1989, 114; HCRO, BRF/3/20, pp. 28, 304. At Lincoln in 1724 Mr James Blithe – clearly not a common labourer – was paid 1s 4d 'for taking a dead horse out of the church' (St Benedict's), LAO, L1/7/2. A remarkable number of horses' heads were found at the excavation of the Bishop's Palace moat, Beverley.
[20] YCA, E4a; YML, E3/53–4, 56, 631–2; HCRO, BRF/3/20, p. 389; HCORO, PE185/34–5.

Chester, Hull, and Lincoln.[21] A group of Hull labourers catered for the opposite end of the social spectrum when they were employed to duck women on three occasions in less than ten years.[22] Finally, two tasks assigned to labourers at York and Newcastle were respectively potentially gruesome and positively horrific. At York in 1608, 4s 8d was paid 'to certain labourers for digging the garth of Uxor Jackson who was slandered to have killed her husband and buried him there'. The outcome was not recorded. At Newcastle in 1593, when the usual daily rate for a labourer was 6d, 9d was paid to 'a labourer hanging up the three quarters [*sic*] and head of the [seminary] priest'.[23]

The number of labourers in the northern towns

There are substantial difficulties in attempting to assess the number of labourers in any town. At first glance the problem does not appear too acute in the case of Beverley: labourers were admitted to the freedom and in the late sixteenth century they comprised nearly 7 per cent of new burgesses. By the early eighteenth century they amounted to just over 15 per cent of those whose occupations were recorded in the parish registers.[24] Perhaps these were the men who derived the bulk of their incomes from labouring, although in terms of the potential number of casual labourers available to urban customers such figures have little meaning. Almost anyone (man, woman, or child) capable of wheeling a barrow, carrying a basket or wielding a shovel – excluding only the very young, the ancient, the sick, and the lame – could swell the ranks as required. Numbers could also be augmented from the surrounding countryside. Obviously, some labourers were more adept than others and could provide better value for money. Experience, heavily calloused hands, and a strong back made the work easier, but they were not essential prerequisites. Labourers were born, not made. Early-modern towns contained pools of surplus labour,[25] and only on rare occasions was there likely to be a shortage of willing drudges. The problem often facing the civic authorities was how to prevent the excessive growth of the labouring population. A thorough investigation was ordered at York in 1577. As a result, sixty-five labourers were licensed to work in the city, but twenty-one immigrant labourers and their families were ejected. Most had come from neighbouring

---

[21] YCA, CC11, fo. 69g; Palliser 1979, 32,56. See also LAO, Bj/1/7; HCRO, BRF/3/20, p. 477; CCRO, TAB/1, fos. 16v–17r.
[22] HCRO, BRF/3/20, pp. 60, 227, 272.
[23] YCA, CC13, fo. 53r; TWAS, 543/18, fo. 123r.
[24] *VCH Beverley*, 81, 114.   [25] Clarkson 1982, 16; Coleman 1955–6.

villages, although three were from as far afield as Richmond, Hull, and Norwich.[26] Although most towns probably housed enough labourers to meet normal levels of demand, sudden surges of activity necessitated emergency measures. There were three basic responses: large numbers of citizens could be conscripted for particular tasks; local garrisons could lend a hand when required; and nearby villages could be tapped for extra workers.

The system of conscripting the citizenry was most highly developed at York. Jobs performed by such forced labour was known as 'common work' or 'common day work', and included 'carrying earth forth of Thursday market', 'common work under Ouse Bridge', and 'common day works at cleansing of the watering place and mending causey'. The mixed gang comprised 'the labourers, women and children at common work' in 1590, although only a single individual can be identified: in 1565 two barber-surgeons were paid 3s 4d 'for healing the finger of Elizabeth Ellerbeck, servant to Abram Harkay, which was hurt with a stone in the common works'. Her master was a weaver. The York workers were encouraged around 1600 by Edmond Archer, the drummer, often referred to in the records as 'Archer Drummer'. On one occasion he was accompanied by John Balderston on the pipe.[27] A similar system of conscription was used at Chester in the mid 1610s, although it is not clear if the townsmen were called out on other occasions. A 'great hole' had been made in the river bank at the Roodee and it was filled by making a timber frame which was stuffed with 'gorse and thorns and ... earth to fill it'. An unnamed drummer was paid 8d for drumming 'whilst servants carried muck to the breach'.[28] At Newcastle in 1593 the appropriately named John Belman, a keelman, was paid 8d 'for going about town four times to command every man for to help to weigh the ship', a French vessel which had been 'overthrown at the ballast north shore'. Belman was used to collect men for similar tasks on other occasions.[29] Communal work was also regarded as part of the townsfolk's obligations at Hull, although it is not clear how frequently the system was used. In the late fifteenth century the council decided to remove a jetty and every townsman was expected to provide labour or contribute to the cost. On other occasions householders were required to provide a volunteer for the

[26] Palliser 1979, 276.
[27] See the many references to common work in YCA, CC5–15, and *YCR*, IX, 114. For Harkay see *York Freemen*, 272.
[28] CCRO, TAR/2/31. Bridlington also had a town drum in the seventeenth century: *Bridlington Charters*, 148. For the Hull drummer see HCRO, BRF/3/19, p. 32.
[29] TWAS, 543/18, fos. 143r, 145v, 189r, 199r.

noxious task of cleansing the sewers, and in the seventeenth century they were expected to help to maintain the defences.[30]

Towns with garrisons were able to tap a ready supply of reasonably disciplined labour. In 1642 thirty soldiers worked for a day at York,[31] and such labour was particularly useful at Hull where a regular garrison was maintained after the Civil War. Between April and July 1658 groups of soldiers from various companies worked in gangs of between three and twelve pointing and driving piles at the river bank. Small numbers were also employed 'helping to land timber' and assisting with piling work.[32] Captive labour was also used occasionally, a practice which offered two obvious advantages: prisoners were kept active and out of mischief, and they were able to contribute to their own keep. At Durham in March 1557, 5s was 'given in reward' to six prisoners who carried sand and lime for twelve days.[33] No doubt prisoners were employed elsewhere, but the remaining evidence all comes from the Hull accounts for the third quarter of the seventeenth century. Prisoners in the House of Correction were employed 'beating cement' at 6d a bushel, and large amounts were produced on occasion: in August 1679 £3 12s 6d was paid for '145 bushels of cement beat up by several prisoners'.[34]

There were times when labour was needed in quantities that were beyond the resources of an individual town. The erection of new defences on the east bank of the river Hull during the early 1540s involved 300 labourers and more than 200 skilled men, many of whom were brought from outside the town, including some from York.[35] During February and March 1585 new ditches were dug on the same site in a five-week period, and the number of labourers rose from 31 in the first week to 98 and 96 in the final two weeks. Only a relatively small proportion of the labourers – between 17 and 33 per cent – came from the town.[36] The rest were drawn from the East Riding, mostly

---

30 *VCH Hull*, 76, 104, 375, 377; Speck 1989, 190.   31 YCA, CC23, fo. 27v.
32 HCRO, BRF/3/20, pp. 207–8, 360, 480–2, 602, 723.
33 DFC, CC/190082.
34 HCRO, BRF/3/20, p. 954; see also pp. 132, 237–8, 244, 263–4, 276, 769, 799, 831, 833, 919, 921.
35 Colvin 1982, 474–5; from information provided by D.M. Palliser.
36 The calculation is based on the men hired during weeks two to five of the project. There is a considerable degree of double, treble, and quadruple counting since many of the men were probably hired for more than one week, but it is impossible to say what proportion were so hired since the record only gives the places of origin and not the names of the men. Of the 330, 55 were said to be from Hull, 222 from various places in the East Riding, while the place of origin of 53 was not given. If all the unknowns were from Hull they would have amounted to 32.7 per cent of the total, but if none were from Hull townsmen would have amounted to no more than 16.7 per cent of the total. HCRO, BRF/3/5.

Table 4.1. *The place of residence of labourers hired at Hull, 1585*

Place of Settlement	Number	%
Not given	53	16.1
Hull	55	16.7
Less than 5 miles from Hull	186	56.4
Five to 10 miles from Hull	35	10.6
More than 10 miles from Hull	1	0.3

Source: HCRO, BRF/3/5.

from settlements within five miles of the town such as Willerby, Cottingham, Sutton, Marfleet, and Drypool. All but one of the rest lived less than ten miles away in Swine, Skirlaugh, Preston, Routh, and Lelley. Most of them could have walked to work each day, but this was certainly not true of the man from Bridlington, nearly thirty miles away, who worked for four days in the third week of the project (see table 4.1). All of the men – townsmen and countrymen alike – received 6d a day.

Nearly a hundred years later, large numbers of labourers were needed for the construction of the Hull Citadel. Many were drawn from the surrounding countryside, and they were roundly condemned as 'a dull lazy sort of people'. The situation was exacerbated because the military governor refused to allow the garrison soldiers to be employed as labourers and because country labour was scarce as harvest was not finished. As a result, the country men 'knowing our want of men, mutinied, and would not work under 10d a day', which was the going rate for labour at Hull in the later seventeenth century. At one stage work was abandoned because of the labour shortage. Demands for workmen were made in several market towns and country churches, and labourers had to be drawn to the town from as far away as Lancashire.[37] The assumption that countrymen were cheaper is not confirmed by the northern accounts. In most towns labourers were paid at the going rate, although there were occasional slight differences in wage levels which may have been due to a range of factors.[38] In receiving the same rate of pay as townsmen many country dwellers were getting a poorer deal since they were not paid for any additional travelling time or subsistence costs: in effect they received a lower hourly return for the period they were away from their homes.

[37] Tomlinson 1973.   [38] For a discussion of wage rates see below pp. 107–8.

Patterns of employment for labourers

The absence of labourers' names from many of the northern accounts makes it difficult to chart the careers of individual men. Most of the evidence which follows comes from the detailed Hull accounts.[39] During the 1560s and 1570s labourers were named in eight years: 1563–6, 1568, and 1571–3. The council hired a large number of men on a casual basis and a smaller number more regularly. During the 1560s 49 men were hired in the five years under observation: 38 were hired in one year only, 6 in two years, 3 in three years, 1 in four years, and 1 for the whole period. The 49 worked for an average of nineteen days a year. Employment in more than one year did not necessarily mean that more days were worked: the man employed throughout the period averaged only thirteen days a year for the council. The two most heavily employed men were Robert Woodwerd, who did not work for the council in 1565, but averaged sixty-seven days in the other four years, and Thomas Mawthe, who averaged forty-eight days a year during 1563–5. During the three years from 1563 the two men did just over a third of the general labouring required by the council, although neither man was still in the council's employment during the early 1570s. Indeed, of the 49 men hired during the 1560s only 8 were among the 27 hired during the early 1570s. Again the majority worked in only one of the years 1571–3, and only three men worked in all three years, including two who had been employed in 1568. During 1571 and 1572 none of the labourers was dominant, although in 1573 nearly three-quarters of the small amount of work required was done by just four men.

During the 1580s the accounts rarely give the names of the labourers, although in 1584 named men worked for some 200 man-days or just over half of the days worked. Of those named, William Spilsby did sixty days alongside twenty-nine other labourers who averaged less than five days each. Even if the twenty-nine had done all of the unattributed work they would still have averaged less than twelve days each. Also during 1584 gangs of between twelve and eighteen mariners helped on occasion with the heavy work of hauling some 'great trees' to the top of the defences. That was labouring work at its most casual, and the sailors were paid between $1\frac{1}{2}$d and $2\frac{1}{2}$d on each occasion, presumably for an hour or two of work. During 1584 Henry Morley worked for ten days and for the next three years he was named in the accounts, although other labourers were not. In the four years

---

[39] See the bibliography for references to the Hull accounts.

Table 4.2. *Number of days worked in single years by individual labourers at Hull, 1652–79*

Average number of days worked in a particular year	Number of Labourers
Less than 20	45
20–49	34
50–99	43
100–49	46
150–99	35
200–49	28
250–99	11

Note: This analysis relates only to general labourers and not to bricklayers' labourers. A labourer appearing in a particular year is counted as one, so that labourers appearing more than once will be counted a number of times. *Source:* HCRO, BRF/3/20.

1584–7 he worked for a total of 188 days: in 1586 the 57 days he put in amounted to nearly 39 per cent of the labouring work paid for by the council that year. Fragmentary data for York, also for 1584, suggest a similar picture of some reliance on regular labourers, although the bulk of the work was done by casuals. Thirty-three men did 272 days work, an average of just over eight days each, and the range was from half a day to the thirty-eight and forty-six days completed by Robert Johnson and Thomas Plomer respectively. Only three other men each did more than ten days work for the council that year.[40]

The policy of the Hull council of using a central core of more regular labourers, which may be seen in embryonic form during Elizabeth's reign, became much more developed in the next century, although some men continued to be hired for very short periods. The system probably developed more fully before the Civil War: between January and September 1640, 269 days work (or nearly 65 per cent of the labouring work that year) were done by four men, and the remaining 146 days by an unknown number of unnamed men. The use of some names and the omission of others suggests strongly that the council was distinguishing between a group of trusted regulars and a miscellany of irregular casuals. For the period 1652–79 the accounts are particularly detailed, and reveal what we may call the 'trusty labourer system' in full bloom. Occasionally a small gang of men did all of the work, although in most years casual labourers were employed for a

[40] YCA, CC5.

Table 4.3. *Length of service of labourers at Hull, 1653–79.*

Length of service in years	Number of labourers
1	41
2	14
3	7
5–9	10
> 10	6
Total	78

Source: HCRO, BRF/3/20.

small number of days. The structure of employment is shown in table 4.2

The total amount of labouring work fluctuated from a low point of less than 400 days in 1654 to nearly 1900 days in 1670, although it tended to rise over the period.[41] The number of labourers fluctuated from fifteen in 1655 to five in 1675, although the average number of labourers declined as the volume of work increased: numbers averaged nearly twelve in the 1650s, but less than eight in the 1670s. Despite the existence of the trusty system, most labourers worked for the council for only one or two years, as is shown in table 4.3.

The year most dominated by trusty labourers was 1677 when they worked for 1,530 days, averaging 255 days each. The gang consisted of Patrick Lidgerd, the longest serving of the trusties, three more regulars – John Wilson, Hugh Smithson, and Francis Hewardine – plus two relative newcomers, Henry Kilpin who started work for the council in 1674, and Henry Reeves who began in 1676. The following year eleven labourers were employed, the old four, who averaged 202 days each, plus Kilpin and Reeves who managed only eight and 19 days respectively. To their number were added William Mayne who did 175 days – he was a trusty in the making – and four casuals who did a total of 73 days between them. The council was actively pursuing a policy of giving the bulk of the work to a small band of trusted men who mostly worked together on the same projects. This made a great deal of sense and the council must have benefited from being able to call out such an experienced group whenever needed. Loyalty was rewarded: those who served for a larger number of years clocked up a higher average number of days of service.

Patrick Lidgerd, the longest serving of the trusties, was already

---

[41] Work available rose from an average 770 days in the 1650s to 1,300 in the 1670s.

Table 4.4. *Trusted labourers at Hull, 1652–79*

Name	Number of years served	Days served	Average p.a.
Thomas Hutton	4.25	459	108
Robert Oliver	5	558	112
John Almon	5	342	68
Christopher Almon	5	800	160
Isaac Harlam	5.25	501	95
Henry Kilpin	5.75	563	98
John Studley	6	1,057	176
Christopher Harper	8.25	585	71
John Pearson	9	1,153	128
John Waddington	9	1,112	124
Richard Rodwell	11	1,138	103
Hugh Smithson	12.75	2,360	185
Martin Nicholson	13	1,016	78
Francis Hewardine	17.75	3,281	185
John Wilson	19.75	3,166	160
Patrick Lidgerd	27	3,911	145

Note: The calculations are based on three months in 1652 and nine months in 1679, making a whole year.
Source: HCRO, BRF/3/20.

working for the council in the autumn of 1652 when the accounts re-open and he was still working in 1679, albeit at a relatively low level. Over the whole period he worked a total of 3,911 days at an annual average of nearly 145 days. During the first part of the period, from 1652 to 1664, when the system was still evolving, he averaged 87 days a year, but between 1665 and 1678 he worked less than 100 days only once and achieved an overall average of just under 200 days. He was probably close to retirement in 1679: a year earlier he had completed 227 days for the council, but in the first three quarters of 1679 he worked for only eleven days, whereas five other regulars averaged 91 days. The careers of Patrick Lidgerd and the fifteen other trusties are set out in table 4.4.

The accounts for the period 1680 to 1693 have not survived, but when they re-open in 1694 it is evident that the system of trusted labourers was still in place. The careers of only two men straddled the gap from 1679 to 1694: Christopher Slater first appeared in 1679 and worked during the years 1695–8; Hugh Smithson worked throughout the period 1667–79 and re-emerged for the years 1694–9. He had a labouring career spanning more than thirty years, and averaged 163 days in the mid 1690s. The two other important trusties in the 1690s were Richard Heward and Richard Akee both of whom worked throughout the period 1694–1701, averaging 148 and 143 days a year respectively.

The existence of the Hull gang was probably not an accident. The group was referred to variously as 'the town's labourers', 'our own men', 'our labourers', 'our own workmen', and 'our own labourers'. When the Citadel was built in the 1680s they were called 'the mayor's labourers'.[42] Whether or not they were hired as a group or as individuals, and whether or not they were given formal contracts by the council is unclear. However, the frequent re-appearance of the same men, usually listed in the same order, suggests some degree of group cohesion. Moreover, the wording of some fragmentary early-eighteenth-century accounts suggests that the gang did operate as a collective of sorts. Richard Heward seems to have emerged as the leader: in July 1709 he was paid 23s for as many days work done by 'Richard Heward labourer and partners', and similar language was used on subsequent occasions.[43] There can be little doubt that Patrick Lidgerd had been leader in the earlier period, although both he and Heward received the same daily rate as the others. A similar analysis cannot be conducted for other northern towns, although it seems highly likely that the system was used elsewhere. Town councils and other employing institutions tended to hire the same craftsmen over long periods of time and they are likely to have adopted the same procedure for labourers. Although the Hull gang did not receive higher wage rates than casual labourers they did benefit from more regular employment, and from the availability of extra earnings. They were able to supplement their earnings in three ways: they were paid 6d a week emptying the 'tubs of office' at the Town Hall; they dug out the latrines at the dungeon on a quarterly basis; and they were employed to watch the fresh-water dyke to prevent abuses.

In most towns regular part-time jobs were done under contract for a set fee. Some of the larger towns employed a small army of street-cleaners, scavengers, and others. At Beverley a cleanser of markets and pavements was appointed in 1446, and the same official was paid 6s 8d a year in the later sixteenth century.[44] The Newcastle chamberlains paid Bartram Fletcher 2s a month in 1598 for 'dighting three privies

---

[42] HCRO, BRF/3/20, pp. 404, 669, 714, 782, 808; BRF/3/21. I am grateful to Audrey Howes for allowing me to see her material on the Hull Citadel.
[43] HCRO, BRF/6/411, 417, 433A, 469.
[44] *VCH Beverley*, 225; HCORO, BC/II/6/35, BC/II/7/2–3. His successor was Henry Reed: BC/II/6/37.

about the new gate', and they entered into a variety of contracts with window cleaners in the early 1590s.[45] Very occasionally labourers were given contracts which were probably intended to keep them in full-time employment: thus at Newcastle in the mid seventeenth century the chamberlains paid £10 a year, plus a pair of boots, to Robert Haddock for repairing the town dikes.[46]

Churches habitually employed two specialists – grave-makers and sextons. They were paid a basic salary which covered a wide range of duties, plus additional wages for extra work. Their availability meant that on many occasions the churches did not need to hire outside labourers or assistants for craftsmen. At St Mary's, Hull, in the late seventeenth century Matthew Wardell was employed as gravemaker for £2 a year, plus 4d quarterly for drink, and he earned 9d a day on the odd occasion that he helped a craftsman.[47] Similarly, at All Saints', Newcastle, in the 1730s £1 was 'paid the grave digger for burying the bones all the last year', and he received small payments for additional work.[48] But most of the extra, day-to-day labouring was done by the sexton, or bellman as he was known in pre-Reformation Louth. His duties – for which he was to receive 4s 4d a year – were set out clearly:

First to keep the church or lady quire and St Peter quire clean as oft as need shall require, twice in the year to sweep the roof of the church if need require.

He shall keep always clean all the leads of church and aisles and the galleries of the steeple.

He shall bear and convey 'the Christ or Christs' as needs shall require to every place in the town where any corpse is or corpses as it shall happen.

He shall take for setting of the hearse every time he sets it 1d and no more and all other things beside this he shall do as he and other bellmen hath been accustomed afore to do.

He also received 2d for laying down a grave.[49] Further duties were specified for the sexton of St Mary's, Chester, in 1658. He was paid a basic retainer of 10s for 'his years wages for ringing five o'clock in the morning and eight in the evening and for mending bell ropes', plus 2s for sweeping the church clean and covering the graves for a year, and 4s 'for the executing of his office, that is, to whip out dogs, keep the people from sleeping and boys from playing at sermon time'.[50]

[45] TWAS, 543/18, fos. 115v, 217v, 227v, 252r; 543/19, fo. 87r.   [46] TWAS, 543/33.
[47] HCORO, PE185/34.
[48] TWAS, MF557.   [49] *Louth Accts*, 217, 224.   [50] CCORO, P/20/13/1.

Wage differentials among labourers

Most adult male labourers hired in the same town in the same year were paid the same daily wage rates. Unfortunately, when different rates were occasionally paid we are rarely told the reason. Thus, at Chester in early 1710 over a hundred labourers were paid 10d a day, although one of their number received 8d a day, and three 6d.[51] Perhaps they were young, but they might equally well have been old or feeble or, perhaps, female: there is no way of knowing. However, on a few occasions it is possible to gain some insight into wage differentials between labourers.

Some labourers may have accepted relatively low wage rates in exchange for regular employment, and an implicit contract of that nature may have operated at York Minster in the later fifteenth century. During 1484/5 William Walter worked as a labourer for 104 days at 4d, and for 22 days at 3d (total £2 0s 2d), although Robert Park, another labourer, was only paid 16d a week. But Park was paid for 52 weeks that year and earned a total of £3 9s 4d. It is tempting to believe that he accepted a relatively poor daily rate in return for guaranteed employment and payment throughout the year. Or perhaps he did not work a six-day week. This pattern, established in the 1470s, whereby labourers were paid 16d a week for a nominal 52-week year, continued at York Minster almost to the middle of the sixteenth century.[52] Sextons and other church officials were often paid relatively poor daily rates, presumably because they received quarterly or yearly retainers. At St Mary's, Chester, in 1619 the masons were assisted by a labourer at 8d a day – the usual rate for labourers in the city – whereas 'our clerk' was paid 6d a day for 'two days helping masons'.[53] Similarly at Beverley during the seventeenth century the sexton at St Mary's was paid at a rate rather lower than that prevailing in the town for other labourers.[54] However, the general similarity of the rates paid to labourers in individual towns suggests that implicit contracts, in which the promise of regular work was used to depress wage rates, were rarely used in the northern towns.

Very occasionally the degree of difficulty or unpleasantness of a particular job affected the rate of pay. At Carlisle in June 1684 labourers

---

51 CCRO, TAV/1/7. Similarly in the summer and autumn of 1751 large numbers of men were hired at 12d a day but one of them – Daniel Cannon – received 10d. Again the reason is not apparent: TAV/1/35.
52 YML, E3/26–46.   53 CCORO, P/20/13/1.
54 There is not a lot of evidence to go on but the sexton seems to have received a few pence less each day than other labourers: see the introduction to Beverley wages, appendix 1.1.

who normally received 12d a day were given 16d a day for working in water at the weir. They included Thomas Barnes who was paid 7s 4d, 'for seven days work thereof of which one day he waded, 4d more'.[55] Two labourers were paid well above the going rate at Lincoln Cathedral in the mid 1660s for refining lead ashes, which was a particularly noxious activity.[56] In similar fashion, Hull labourers were sometimes given a *douceur* when cleaning out the sewers: on one occasion 6d was 'bestowed upon them and the wright before they went into the vault of the sewer'.[57] In contrast, men set to do light or easy tasks were occasionally paid at a relatively low level. Thus at Hull in May 1669, a man received 8d a day rather than the customary 10d for spending five days 'laying wait to prevent soil throwing down at Beverley Gates and the manor side'.[58]

Some labourers were paid relatively high wages when they worked alongside craftsmen. In 1677 Francis Hewardine worked for 166 days alongside the carpenters at 12d a day, which was 2d more than he got for general labouring.[59] Likewise general labourers received 1d a day drink allowance when working alongside the bricklayers, but not otherwise.[60] Finally, Marmaduke Readman, a Beverley sexton, received 9d a day for general labouring work around the church during the 1650s, but 19d a day when he assisted the plumber.[61] However, it must be stressed that the great majority of labourers in a particular town were paid at the same level.

Female and child labourers

Women accounted for a significant proportion of the unskilled labour force in the towns of late-medieval England, although they were frequently ignored by official record keepers and consequently remain even more shadowy figures than their male counterparts.[62] The northern accounts provide many illustrations of such work, although women did a very small proportion of general labouring and building work. Some institutions were quite prepared to employ female labourers from time to time, but others, like York Minster, did so rarely, if at all: not a single reference to female labourers has been found in the Minster records.[63] Elsewhere women occasionally made an impressive

---

[55] CUMROC, Ca/4/3.   [56] LAO, Bj/1/8.   [57] HCRO, BRF/3/20, p. 365.
[58] HCRO, BRF/3/20, p. 634.
[59] HCRO, BRF/3/20, pp. 900–3, 930–2.   [60] See below p. 156.
[61] HCORO, PE/1/59–62.
[62] Swanson 1988, 40; Rule 1986, 13. See also Penn 1987, 1–7; Smith 1989, 28–30; Snell 1985, 51–7.
[63] YML, E3/24–65.

appearance. At Hull in 1635 they laboured for a total of forty-seven days, which amounted to 3.3 per cent of the general labouring work in a year of substantial activity. However, they did not feature at all during the next four years, and they accounted for only 0.9 per cent of the labouring work during the five-year period.[64]

On rare occasions women played a leading part in a particular type of work. According to Salzman, moss-gathering was usually women's work,[65] and a sizeable body of women was brought together for that purpose at Durham in 1555. The gang, which contained a handful of men, was employed for ten weeks from mid July to mid September to gather moss and carry gravel to a new weir dam. The number of women varied from 21 to 103 with an overall weekly average of 68: additionally an average of 13 children was employed.[66] Women were frequently employed on the bishopric estates to do similar tasks and to carry other materials from the later fifteenth century to the later sixteenth century when the flow of records begins to dwindle.[67] Other northern accounts fall somewhere between the extremes presented by the accounts of York Minster and those of the Durham Abbey estates, but compared with male labourers the appearances of female labourers were always spasmodic and intermittent. Women could be found doing a substantial array of tasks, although it remains true that 'in general, women were a very insignificant element in the labour force on most building sites'.[68]

Unfortunately, female labourers are even more difficult to trace than their elusive male counterparts since their names and status were rarely given in the accounts. Adequate analysis of their role is rarely possible, although there are some interesting hints about them from time to time. Women were occasionally hired as part of a family team: at Durham in 1687 John Baker and his son worked for four and a half days and 'Margaret Baker his wife' for two days 'repairing the flags in church and cloisters and carrying away the dirt' – John received 12d a day, compared with the normal 10d for a labourer, and his son and wife each got 6d a day.[69] Such examples are uncommon and only one family can be traced in the records on more than one occasion. During the summer of 1655 Anthony Gowland and his wife were employed at

[64] HCRO, BRF/3/19.   [65] Salzman 1952, 235.
[66] DPK, MC 3017/9, /14, /16; 3018/3, /5, /12, /15, /25. For moss-gathering at Chester see CCRO, TAV/1/15.
[67] DFC, CC/190047, 48, 56, 66–7, 69, 71–2, 75, 77, 82; DPK, LB25; MC 2674, 2854/5, 2878/2, 2916/2, 3028/6, 3057/2, 3308/2.
[68] Airs 1975, 155; Salzman 1952, 71.
[69] DPK, LB25. See also Brunskill 1951, 20; YCA, CC7, fo. 60v for 1590; HCORO, PE/1/51; YBI, PR/Y/MB/34; HCRO, BRF/3/20, p. 26; CUMROK, WSMB/K.

Newcastle on a number of occasions doing jobs such as 'riddling lime and sand and making up lime and filling and carrying rubbish', although their individual rates of pay were not specified. Interestingly, Eppie Gowland and her sister had been employed at the same work in 1651.[70]

The ages and status of labouring women are rarely known, although the Durham accounts which detail the large gangs of women carrying moss and gravel to the weir dam in 1555 suggest that most of them were unmarried and, perhaps, young: of the eighty-six women hired in the first week of the project only four were referred to as 'Dame' and the rest were merely named.[71] The churchwardens of St Mary's, Chester, employed women on a number of occasions. Sometimes, as in 1619 when they referred to Widow Mosse carrying water and other materials to make mortar, they specified marital status, but at other times they merely gave the woman's name which again suggests that she was unmarried.[72] But there is far too little information to allow any firm pronouncement about the ages and status of female labourers, although it is evident that – as at Stiffkey in Norfolk – women of all ages could boost the family income by labouring. The female labourers of Stiffkey included fifteen unmarried women living with their families, five widows, three wives of husbandmen or craftsmen, and thirteen wives of day labourers. They ranged from girls of less than twenty – like the 'two little wenches' hired at Kendal in 1632 – to old women, like Mother Alwick who may well have been over seventy.[73]

A substantial question mark hangs over the ability of early-modern women to manage heavy tasks. It has been suggested that when women appeared on building sites 'their duties were usually light', although in eighteenth-century agriculture they did even the heaviest tasks.[74] Certainly some women had broad, strong backs: John Locke told the story of Alice George who 'said she was able to have reaped as much in a day as any man, and had as much wages'.[75] But there can be little doubt that women in general were able to shift smaller weights than men. At first glance the northern accounts seem to suggest that women were doing some of the heaviest work: they were to be found most frequently carrying sand and lime, gravel and mortar, and engaged in that most timeless of all female occupations, carrying water.[76] In bulk all of these materials are heavy, but they share the

---

[70] TWAS, 659/448–9.   [71] DPK, MC 3017/9.   [72] CCORO, P/20/13/1.
[73] Smith 1989, 30; CUMROK, WSMB/K.
[74] Airs 1975, 154; B. Hill 1989, 70.   [75] Retold by Laslett 1983, 124.
[76] There are dozens of entries for this kind of work in the accounts of the northern towns. See for example CCRO, TAR/1/14; TWAS, 543/18, fo. 109v; 543/19, fo. 279v; 659/446–7; NCRO, M18/31 for 1690; HCRO, BRF/3/3–5, 19–20 – various; HTH, I–II,

characteristic of being capable of division into small units: buckets could vary in size – as could spades, shovels, and wheelbarrows – and, if small tools and receptacles were not available, the full-sized versions could be filled only to the half-way mark or less. The most exotic entries relating to women's work come from Chester in the 1560s. The council built a new stone quay down the river at Neston which necessitated the use of a 'great crane of iron' activated by a tread-wheel powered by women labourers. The account for August 1563 runs as follows: 'in the wheel of labouring women four, who three of them for six days and the other for five days at 3d the day'. On other occasions reference was made to 'maids in the crane' or 'four women that went in the crane for six days at 3d the piece'.[77] Without knowing the size of the blocks lifted, the dimensions of the wheel, and the nature of the gearing we cannot tell how strenuous the job was, but it was probably worth avoiding.

Women could be found doing a wide range of other jobs. They weeded gardens and helped the thatcher. Relatively little urban thatching has been recorded, although at Kendal in 1639 Myles Becke's wife helped him to thatch the town kiln, and in the countryside serving the thatcher or 'yelming' was a task commonly done by women.[78] Women were also employed as street or sewer cleaners, sometimes under contract to the town council, and some widows took on the jobs vacated at the death of their husbands.[79] At Newcastle Jenette Dunne was employed for at least the last twenty years of the sixteenth century as a street cleaner at 4d a week, plus a coat each year: in March 1592 her 'russett coat against Easter' cost 6s.[80] In the mid seventeenth century Margaret Chaber was engaged 'for looking to the town court' at 26s a quarter and on one occasion 'her maid' was given 4s 'for helping her to sweep the court for a quarter'.[81] Women were also employed to clean churches and their surroundings. At St Michael's, Chester, 'the cobbler's wife' was paid 16d for sweeping the churchyard in 1563, and similar entries were made in later years.[82] Other women were employed by the churches to wash altar cloths and surplices, and at least one woman managed to step into her late

various; YBI, PR/Y/MG/19–20; PR/Y/MCS/16; YCA, CC15, fo. 97a. See also Willan 1980, 120; Laughton 1987–8, 125; Goldberg 1986, 24–5; *Newcastle Accts*, 104.

[77] *Chester Haven*, 94, 117.
[78] *Percy Papers*, xxxii; HTH, II, fo. 66r; III, fo. 219v; HCRO, BRF/3/3 for 1570–1, 1572–3; CUMROK, WSMB/K; Roberts 1981, 164; Salzman 1952, 223–5; *Henry Best*, 144.
[79] See the many references in HCRO, BRF/3/19–20; YCA, CC5, fo. 65r, CC27, fos. 25v, 28r, CC28, fo. 10v.
[80] TWAS, 543/16, fo. 231v, 543/18–19.   [81] TWAS, 543/36.
[82] CCORO, P/65/8/1, fo. 21r. See also YBI, PR/Y/MS/2.

husband's shoes as sexton: Robert Dawson the sexton of St Mary's, Hull, was buried on 7 March 1696 and his widow Elizabeth took over his duties. She was paid a salary of £2 a year and was referred to in 1699 as Elizabeth Dawson 'who officiates the sexton's place' and also as 'Elizabeth Dawson who officiates as sexton with help of her son'. From 1698 she worked alongside Ann or Widow Wardell who kept the chimes for a salary of £1 a year.[83] Women also did cleaning jobs for other institutions. At York in 1559 'uxor Richardson, widow' was paid 16d, for an undisclosed period, 'for keeping clean the place of Ouse Bridge called the water holes and locking the door at night', while various women were employed by Hull council in the 1570s 'dressing and sweeping the castle and chambers'. A 'poor woman' was employed by the council 'for washing the school house seats' in 1665.[84] The York council employed Ann Hart from 1726 to 1730 'kindling fire in common hall and sweeping before mayor's house' for £1 a year, and she shared the job with Ann Waterhouse in 1730. Ann Waterhouse then took over the job for more than twenty years.[85]

Women hired by the day almost invariably received lower wages than those paid to men and such a differential had biblical authority: it was laid down in Leviticus that a woman should receive three-fifths of the male rate.[86] In obedience, women were paid 6d a day and the men 10d at Durham in the late seventeenth and early eighteenth centuries, and the same was true at Chester in the early eighteenth century.[87] But the practice varied from place to place, and from time to time. During the 1550s Chester women were paid 2d a day and the men 4d or 5d, while at Durham the ratio changed as the century progressed: women continued to receive 2d a day from the early sixteenth century to the 1570s, while the male rate rose from 3d or 4d a day, to 6d in the 1560s. This widening of the differentials may help to explain the popularity of female labourers at Durham during the sixteenth century.[88] One man in particular, a waller called Rauf Younger, favoured the employment of women: he engaged them frequently in the late 1580s and 1590s paying them 2d or 3d a day. The mixed gang employed by Younger is demonstrated by his bill of 6 July 1590:[89]

[83] *Louth Accts*, 12,14,29,103; YBI,PR/Y/J/18;PR/Y/MCS/18;PR/Y/MS/2;HCORO,PE185/34–5.
[84] YCA,CC5,fo. 73v; HCRO, BRF/3/3 for 1572/3, 1573/4; BRF/3/20, p. 472. See also HTH, II, fo. 66r; V.
[85] YCA, CC33–8.   [86] Tzannatos 1986/7; Leviticus 27: 3–4.
[87] See appendices 1.3 and 1.4 for Chester and Durham.
[88] See above p. 110.   [89] DPK, LB25. See also DPK, MC 3203–3323.

Working stonework, mending dam and to labourers there.

Rauf Younger 14 days at 8d	9s 4d
Matthew Newton 2 days at 7d	1s 2d
Richard Oliver 14 days at 5d	5s 10d
Christopher Armstrong 14 days at 5d	5s 10d
Margery Davyson 14 days at 3d	3s 6d
Margery Young as long as much	3s 6d

Women were paid at low levels in other northern towns: at Newcastle in 1601 six women were paid 4d a day, or half the male rate; at Lincoln in 1617 women received 4d compared with the male rate of 6d, but they got only 6d against the male rate of 10d in the 1660s; in mid-eighteenth-century Beverley a woman received 6d a day, which was half the male rate.[90]

On a few occasions women received more equal treatment. At Newcastle in 1591 two women were paid 5d a day, compared with 6d for the men. A few Kendal women managed to achieve parity with the men in the 1630s, although most got less. In August 1632 'Bateman's wife' and 'Myles Becke's wife' were paid 8d a day for haymaking, which was also the male rate, although 'Bateman's daughter', 'Cloudsley's daughter', and the 'two little wenches' only received 4d a day.[91] At Lincoln in April 1743 Robert Hudson and Martha Hall were each paid 12d a day for eleven days cleaning the library and chapter house, and Martha was paid at the same rate when she worked by herself in the September of that year.[92] In one case where men and women performed the same tasks they were invariably paid at the same rate. During the third quarter of the seventeenth century the Hull council paid for large amounts of cement to be made in the House of Correction by both male and female prisoners. The rate for 'beating a bushel of cement' was 6d which was paid equally to men, women, and boys.[93] Assuming that they were able to produce cement of a consistent quality the total amount of effort incorporated in the production of each bushel would be roughly equal, and the council recognised this fact by paying a flat piece-rate which did not discriminate by age or sex. However, no doubt some of the men could produce each bushel in less time.

But few women earned high rates of pay. For the most part they did not earn more than two-thirds of the male rate and their daily pay could fall as low as a third. Traditional explanations for such wide

[90] TWAS, 543/19, fo. 279v; LAO, Bj/1/7–8; HCORO, PE/1/114 for 1740, 1743; Charles & Duffin 1985, 18–19.
[91] TWAS, 543/18, fo. 185r; CUMROK, WSMB/K.   [92] LAO, Bj/1/13.
[93] HCRO, BRF/3/20, pp. 26, 56, 99, 307, 386, 418–19, 508, 704.

differences have tended to stress the strength factor, although it has been suggested that low rates were paid to women because they were less resourceful in dealing with unexpected situations, because they regarded wage-work as a temporary measure, and because they were not usually bread-winners. Maurice Dobb delivered the insult traditionally levelled at women's work when he spoke of them earning 'pin money'.[94] Even collectively such explanations are not completely adequate: the relatively low rates of pay offered to women reflected deeply embedded male attitudes relating to the economic and social inferiority of women which were buttressed by biblical authority.

There is a widespread belief that high levels of child labour prevailed in early-modern England, although 'there is ... evidence which points in the opposite direction, and which suggests that at any point in the period there was a large number of children for whom no work was available'. Information drawn from the accounts of northern institutions fully supports the suggestion that children found little employment in some areas of the urban economy and remained an underutilised 'little dirty infantry'.[95] There is no doubt that 'in most out-door work weight and strength are an advantage',[96] and that young boys were rarely engaged as labourers. However, there is a problem in determining the age at which 'boys' became 'men' or 'labourers' and found regular employment on building sites. According to some wage assessments male workers were not to be given the full rate of pay until they reached the age of twenty-four, and thus in theory remained boys until that age.[97] Unfortunately the northern records provide no assistance with this problem and there is no way of knowing the age at which labourers began their careers.

When they do appear in the accounts boy labourers were paid at rates substantially lower than those of the men. At Hull, boys were employed by the council in nearly half of the years between 1618 and 1640, generally at 4d a day, or half the adult male rate, although in 1620 three boys were employed at only 3d a day.[98] Similarly, at Newcastle in 1651, when adult male labourers were generally getting 12d a day, a group of six boys were each paid 6d a day for 'carrying lime, stones and rubbish and helping to make clean the chapel and court'.[99] Sometimes the exact rate of pay for a child is not clear. The churchwardens of St Michael's, Spurriergate, York, hired two tilers and their men in

---

[94] Dobb 1960, 149–50; Roberts 1981, 185; Schwarz 1989, 27–8; Wootton 1962, 62–3; Charles & Duffin 1985, 18–19.
[95] H. Cunningham 1990, 115–17, 148.
[96] *Ibid.*, 146, quoting a mid-nineteenth-century source.
[97] Roberts 1981, 133–40.   [98] HCRO, BRF/3/19.   [99] TWAS, 659/448.

1538, and paid 10d 'to two children of the tilers that served them and bore them mortar' for an unspecified period and in 1655 the Hull council bought eleven tons of sand and paid 8d 'to a boy for trimming up the sand and watching the sand until it was led away'.[100]

Reflections

Most of the casual labourers employed by the institutions of the northern towns were adult males. Women appeared from time to time – sometimes in large gangs, especially when they were getting relatively poor wage rates or when there was a sudden surge in the demand for labour – but they rarely performed more than a very small proportion of the work. Children found even less employment, although they may have featured more prominently in the large gangs of labour dragooned into service in some of the towns. The range of tasks accomplished by labourers is clear enough, although the personnel involved are often difficult to trace because many of the accountants failed to name them: this in itself is an indication of the low social standing of labourers compared with building craftsmen, who were named much more frequently. Nevertheless, labourers were named sufficiently often in some places – and especially in the Hull accounts – to permit meaningful analysis. The Hull council employed a group of regular or trusted workers: the system was fully in place by the third quarter of the seventeenth century although there are signs that it was developing in the previous century. From the fragmentary data available for other towns it seems that the system was used elsewhere, although in all towns – including Hull – there was also a long tail of labourers who worked for the institutions for only a few days each year. The niches they occupied in the urban economies and the manner in which they subsisted for the rest of the year is unknown.

The next chapter brings together labourers and building craftsmen in order to discuss those aspects of their working lives which were common to both groups. Because they often worked side by side they were usually treated in a similar fashion: thus they generally worked days of a similar length in particular towns and were equally affected by the low winter demand for their labour.

[100] YBI, PR/Y/MS/1, fo. 146v; HCRO, BRF/3/20, p. 102.

5

Conditions of work for labourers and building craftsmen

Except for those workmen who were employed on permanent contracts the jobs offered to labourers and craftsmen were essentially
casual and intermittent. In most cases they were hired to perform a
particular task and paid off once it had been completed. It was an
uncertain world in which weeks or months of regular employment
could be followed by a prolonged bout of idleness. Some workmen
were more likely to be offered work than others. As with modern
householders, there was a tendency to employ known workmen who
could be relied on to give good value for money, and in all towns there
were networks which could be used to suggest the name of a new
workman when his skills were required: relations, neighbours, drinking companions, shopkeepers, fellow gildsmen, and churchgoers were
all available for consultation. Unfortunately, the historian is rarely able
to observe the operation of such networks, although churchwardens'
accounts indicate that membership of a particular church could lead to
the offer of work.

The importance of the parish to townsmen has been stressed for
Tudor York: 'their parish churches ... had the primary claim on the
loyalties of citizens ... It was the parochial unit which gave the citizens
their strongest sense of continuity with the past ... Parochial loyalties
could retain a hold on families even after they had left the city.'[1] Parish
membership often involved workmen in the repair of the church fabric
or of some other durable possession. This can be demonstrated for two
York parishes by comparing the names of those employed by the
churchwardens with those listed in the parish register. At Holy Trinity,
Goodramgate, between 1580 and 1700, of 58 individuals who worked

---

[1] Palliser 1979, 228. See also Rappaport 1989, 215, and Alldridge 1988 who stresses other
aspects of loyalty and identity within the parish. He assumes that parishioners would
provide the labour needed to maintain the church fabric: Alldridge 1988, 91.

at the church in only a single year 24 belonged to the parish: however, 16 of the 22 who appear in the accounts of between two and four years were parishioners, and all but one of the 16 workmen who appear in five or more years were from the parish. All told, parishioners were responsible for some two-thirds of the jobs done at the church by named workmen.[2] And the fragmentary accounts for St Michael le Belfry for the period 1640–90 tell a similar story. Some families formed little dynasties, with several members working for the church on a number of occasions. Thus, at St Michael le Belfry three members of the Haggis or Haggas family were employed as masons. They were:

Thomas: his children were baptised during 1621 to 1630, and he worked at the church in the early 1640s and served as church-warden in 1657 and 1660. 'Thomas Haggis the old mason was buried 8 April 1671.'

John: he was the son of Thomas and was baptised in 1623. He laid graves in the early 1660s.

Edward: he worked at the church on many occasions between 1660 and 1690 and was buried in 1702.

Similarly, Thomas Buckton, who mended the lead roof and windows during the 1660s and 1670s was buried in 1680. He was succeeded by 'Widow Buckton' who repaired some of the windows in 1685. Not surprisingly, other parishioners were called on to supply the special-ised products of their trades: during the 1650s and 1660s the baker Robert Fowler, whose seven sons were baptised during the 1640s and 1650s, regularly supplied bread to the church.[3]

Such systematic analyses have not been conducted for other York churches, but there can be no doubt that similar practices were adopted elsewhere. The churchwardens of St Michael's, Spurriergate, regularly employed the same workmen, including Martin Croft, a glazier. On 12 May 1643 – 'after the death of Fall, late parish clerk' – Martin Croft 'was elected by majority vote to receive all the profits, dues and duties belonging to the office'. It was questioned whether or not he could continue in his position of churchwarden, to which he had been elected recently, but it was decided that he could do both jobs. He continued to be paid £4 a year as parish clerk for the next three decades and was probably still holding the post when he died in 1674. He was also frequently employed at the church as plumber and glazier, and at the nearby Minster, during the 1660s and early 1670s.[4] Similar case studies can be derived from the accounts of All Saints', North Street: Michael Acroid, who was churchwarden in 1663, paved

[2] YBI, PR/Y/HTG/12; *Goodramgate PR.*   [3] YBI, PR/Y/MB/34; *Belfry PR*, I and II.
[4] YBI, PR/Y/MS/5; YML, E3/65/1,3,17; E4a.

graves and did other work at the church between 1646 and 1671, and John Hindle, churchwarden in 1683, did unspecified paid work during the 1680s. But the most interesting case is that of George Conn, a bricklayer, who worked frequently for the city council in the later seventeenth century. He was employed at the church during 16 of the years between 1682 and 1706, and from 1705 he paid £1 a year rent for 'one house in the occupation of George Conn'. From 1709 it was paid by Widow Conn.[5]

The practice of employing workmen from the neighbourhood, and especially from the same parish, was not confined to York. Richard Dawbe was employed at St Mary's, Chester, as a glazier between the late 1540s and early 1570s, and he was chosen churchwarden in 1559.[6] When Robert Whitby, a young civic official, built a new house in the city in the early seventeenth century he favoured the employment of neighbourhood workmen: indeed, it is probable that he 'opted for craftsmen who lived in the same ward or parish as himself and that his first loyalties lay with his own particular area. Even a small and compact city like Chester thus appears to have comprised a series of urban "villages", each the focus of the allegiance and affection of its inhabitants.'[7] A similar situation existed at Hull, where the bulk of the work at St Mary's in the late seventeenth and early eighteenth centuries was done by parishioners. Most of the plumbing and glazing was the responsibility of Bartholomew and Jonathan Gill, father and son, during the years 1684–1702 and 1699–1719 respectively, whose vital events were recorded in the parish register. Similarly, Jonathan and Joseph Snaith supplied much of the ironwork, while others like Richard Roebuck, who supplied stone, and Henry Mold, a carpenter, became churchwardens.[8]

The work place

Unlike many of their fellow townsmen, building craftsmen spent much of their time away from home, constructing new buildings and repairing or modifying existing structures according to the dictates of their customers. This was particularly true of the bricklayers, carpenters, masons, plasterers, thatchers, and tilers, since these were trades in which only a limited amount of preliminary preparation could be done in the workshop. For such men the separation of work and home was a fact of life, as it was also for labourers. For the glaziers, joiners, plumbers, and smiths, work was divided between the workshop and

[5] YBI, PR/Y/ASN/10.   [6] CCORO, P/20/13/1.   [7] Laughton 1987–8, 111.
[8] HCORO, PE185/2, 34–5.

the edifice under construction or repair. Being away from home, either for all or part of their working time, made it difficult for the wife of a building craftsman to acquire enough skill to be able to maintain the family business after her husband's death: as suggested earlier, continuation was more likely in those trades which were at least partly workshop-based.[9] Joiners spent long periods in their shops making doors, window frames, other house fitments, and furniture, and the ordinances of the Newcastle joiners for the early eighteenth century indicate that such shops doubled up as work places and retail points: work gear was not to be removed from another brother's shop; goods were to be sold in the shop and not in the open market; and no brother was to call a customer from a colleague's shop.[10] Nearly half a century earlier, in 1673, a searcher of the gild had complained that Nicholas Stephenson had refused to let him view his work and had 'bid him go out of his shop, pitiful fellow, you are not able to do the like [work]'. Three years later Stephenson himself complained about a fellow joiner who had dared him to come out of his shop, and had added a further insult by calling his wife 'a barren doe'.[11] Such shops and their contents were often listed in joiners' probate inventories, and they can be illustrated from those drawn up for three members of the Chester gild of joiners.[12] They were:

Robert Sevell who joined the gild in 1599 and was steward in 1600 and 1602. His inventory is dated 20 September 1605.

William Williamson who worked as a journeyman between 1629 and 1631 and joined the gild in November 1631. He was steward in 1633 and 1638, and was elected as alderman of the gild in June 1640, but died six weeks later. His inventory is dated 24 July 1640.

Richard Hodgson who worked as a journeyman between 1628 and 1635, and joined the gild in January 1636. He was steward in 1639, and 1640, and his inventory is dated 12 February 1644.

It may be assumed that the valuation of the trade goods of the trio was accurate since in each case two of the appraisers were well-established members of the gild: of the six appraisers three were aldermen of the gild in the year the inventory was taken, one was a past alderman, and the remaining two were stewards during the year in question.[13] The three joiners were comfortably off, despite the relatively short periods they had spent as masters. They lived in well-furnished houses – although it is possible that some of the furniture they contained was

---

[9] See above pp. 87/9.　　[10] TWAS, 648/6, pp. 11, 15, 29.　　[11] TWAS, 648/3.
[12] CCORO, WS, Sevell 1606, Williamson 1641, Hodgson 1643.
[13] CCRO, G14/1. In 1640 there was one more appraiser and two more in 1605 and 1644, all non-members of the gild.

for sale rather than for personal use – and they possessed considerable supplies of timber and stocks of finished or part-finished sale items in their shops. At his death at the beginning of 1644 Richard Hodgson possessed:

In timber in the backside and abroad belonging to the decedent	£30 0s 0d
The tools and benches and all the implements in the shop valued at	£1 10s 0d
One long table, one short table, one cupboard and three high beds finished and unfinished, and one cradle and two stool frames	£5 0s 0d
More in the shop: one standing cupboard, three truckle beds, one field bed, one canopy bed, one chair, one table, one chair frame, one cradle, one close stool, one coffin, beside other loose wainscott and eight table feet with other odd stools	£3 10s 0d

The shops of the other two men contained similar items of ready-made furniture, and Robert Sevell had a lathe among his tools. Table 5.1 provides a breakdown of the goods listed in their inventories.

Although much of the work of carpenters could only be carried out on site some of them also had 'shops', which were listed in their inventories, but these seem to have been workshops rather than the combined work and retail places run by the joiners. Four out of seven carpenters from Boston and Lincoln who left inventories had workshops which housed their tools, work benches and small amounts of timber, but not finished items for sale.[14] The same was true of the 'shops' belonging to two Cumbrian carpenters in the late seventeenth and early eighteenth centuries.[15] Movement by a woodworker between workshop and building site can be glimpsed from 'an account of work and materials for mills belonging to the corporation of Carlisle' submitted by George Dixon in 1742. He claimed 16d a day for himself and his journeyman for 'days working at my house', but 18d a day when working at the mill. He claimed a flat rate of 12d for his apprentice throughout the operation.[16] Whether or not such differential rates were claimed by other craftsmen is not known.

Glaziers, plumbers, and smiths divided their time between their workshops or smithies and their customers' property. Although they

[14] LAO, Inv. 15/222, 52/132A, 68/67, 71/295, 73/293, 109/112, 296.
[15] CUMROC, P1669, P1748. The inventories of John Nicholson of Penrith and John Blamire of Carlisle.
[16] CUMROC, Ca/4/vouchers 1742.

Table 5.1. *The goods listed in the probate inventories of three Chester joiners*

Name	Household goods			Timber			Stock			Tools			Total			Debts owed to him			Debts he owed		
	£	s	d	£	s	d	£	s	d	£	s	d	£	s	d	£	s	d	£	s	d
Sevell	61	8	5	10	12	6	5	3	5	1	1	8	78	10	0	10	2	10	36	19	2
Williamson	43	11	1	47	2	8	5	19	4	1	13	4	98	6	5	63	16	3	not given		
Hodgson	53	4	8	30	0	0	8	10	0	1	10	0	93	4	8	not given			not given		

Source: CCORO, WS, Sevell 1606, Williamson 1641, Hodgson 1643.

were sometimes provided with work places by their customers, most glaziers and plumbers needed their own workshops. A Boston glazier had some lead both 'in the shop' and in the yard, and there are references in both the York and Newcastle accounts to plumbers working at home: in September 1632 some new gutters were being made for Holy Trinity, Goodramgate, York, and a shilling was 'bestowed on the plumber at his house when he cast it and when we weighed it and brought it home'.[17]

Most of the larger churches provided work places for some of the building craftsmen they employed, and especially for the masons who needed to be under cover when carving stone. Many cathedrals maintained permanent lodges, especially in the later Middle Ages, and when a new gallery was being constructed at Durham in the late 1530s a carpenter and other workmen were employed 'to make masons' lodge'.[18] Similarly, at York in 1569, carpenters were paid for 'working upon the masons' lodge', and a new lodge was made in a quarry for some masons at Newcastle in 1509.[19] At times the precincts of Lincoln Cathedral must have resembled an industrial complex: during the seventeenth and early eighteenth centuries reference was made to the masons' house and lodge; the woodhouse, wood yard, and sawpit; the glasshouse and glazing room; and the plumbhouse, plumbhouse yard, casting house, lead furnace, and melting pot.[20] During the 1660s four great cisterns, each weighing about 6 cwt, were made by refining the ashes left over when the lead from the cathedral roof was recast. Two

---

[17] LAO, Inv. 112a/293. For an extremely well-set-up glazier see Farr 1977; YBI, PR/Y/ HTG/12, p. 335; PR/Y/MS/2, fo. 34v. See TWAS, 543/19, fo. 86r for similar comments.
[18] Salzman 1952, 45–6; Swanson 1983, 5–7; Knoop & Jones 1949, 56–8; DFC, CC/190069, 190071.
[19] YML, E3/51; *Newcastle Accts*, 57.   [20] LAO, Bj/1/7–13.

were for the wood yard and the other two for the masons' yard, and
they were made 'upon the complaint of the workmen for want of
water'. They served the secondary purpose of supplying water 'if any
fire should happen in the Minster or Minster yard', and also for the
'residentiaries' who 'may thence fetch water for the necessary occasions of their houses, with which in probability these cisterns will
sufficiently furnish them, if they do not give it away to other persons
for whom it was not intended'.[21] At Beverley in 1608 James Ridsdall
was paid 5s 4d 'for making a pit in the minster to cast lead in', and it
was used on various occasions during the next century and a half by
workmen employed by the churchwardens of St Mary's.[22]

Town councils also provided store places and work stations as
required. In early-sixteenth-century Newcastle the council maintained
a place known as 'the plumber tower', and in the early 1590s, 3s was
paid 'for the use of a house where Alexander Cheesman [mason and
paver] did melt lead for the pavement at Newgate and laid his work
gear all the time of their working'. A few years later, carpenters were
supplied with timber 'from the storehouse'.[23] During an economy
drive at York during the 1560s, timber from some ruinous houses
which were being demolished was stockpiled in a council 'storehouse'.[24] In the later seventeenth century the Hull council employed a
storekeeper who looked after the town's stock of timber, tiles, and
other materials, and in the 1680s a rent of £3 a year was paid 'for the
yard where the town's timber is laid'.[25] Some materials were also
stored in the North Blockhouse although the military commander,
Colonel Gilby, was accused in 1681 of purloining some of the bricks: it
was also claimed that timber stored there had been spirited away,
partly by townsmen and partly by countrymen, and some of it used for
firewood.[26] Hull Trinity House had its own 'rafe yard' for storing
timber.[27]

The working day and week

In early-modern England, building craftsmen and labourers were
usually paid by the day, and only on a few rare occasions, when they
were working overtime, were they paid like modern workmen, by the
hour.[28] Occasionally, payments were made for half a day, or for some

[21] LAO, Bj/1/8.   [22] HCORO, BC/II/6/48; PE/1/57–8, 60, 114.
[23] *Newcastle Accts*, 237–8; TWAS, 543/18, fo. 215r;/19, fo. 83r.
[24] Palliser 1979, 265.
[25] HCRO, BRF/3/20, pp. 597, 599, 602, 630, 673–4, 679; BRF/6/239.
[26] HCRO, BRM/362.   [27] HTH, V for 1684.   [28] Knoop & Jones 1949, 116.

other portion of it, and on a few occasions, when working on river-bank maintenance or similar tasks, workmen were paid by the tide, usually getting 40 or 50 per cent of the daily rate for each tide worked.[29] Since payment was by the day, both local and national authorities were keen to regulate its length. In such circumstances it is hardly surprising that workers in the urban building trades seem to have been keen clock-watchers. This may have been in marked con-trast to the situation in the countryside since it is usually believed that in relatively primitive rural societies 'work is not regulated by the clock, but by the requirements of the task'.[30] However, it could be argued that, even in agriculture, workers hired by the day were being paid by the unit of time rather than by the task, and that both masters and men were likely to be aware of the progress of the clock. Servants hired by the year and independent agriculturalists were more likely to be task oriented.[31]

According to one fifteenth-century writer 'in cities and towns men rule them by the clock',[32] and this was explicitly accepted by the framers of labour legislation. Hours of work were first laid down in the act of 1495 which exhibited concern about the slack time-keeping of many artificers and labourers, who: 'waste much part of the day and deserve not their wages, some time in late coming unto their work, early departing therefrom, long sitting at their breakfast, at their dinner and noon meat, and long time of sleeping at afternoon, to the loss and hurt of such persons as the said artificers and labourers be retained with in service'.[33] To combat such laxness it was laid down that between mid-March and mid-September workmen should be at their posts by 5 a.m., take breaks of no more than two to two-and-a-half hours in total, and remain at work until 7 or 8 p.m. During the winter they were to be 'at their work in the springing of the day and depart not til the night of the same day'. These times were repeated in 1514 and, in most essentials, in the Statute of Artificers of 1563, which remained the final parliamentary word on the subject until the end of our period.[34] Thus, the central government attempted to fix the length of the working day at between twelve and thirteen hours in summer, and many late-medieval town councils took a similar view. But were such dictates obeyed? It has been suggested that the regularity of hours of work and of conditions of employment laid down in 1563

[29] TWAS, 543/15, fo. 247r, 543/18, fos. 2r, 82v, 85r, 89v; HCRO, BRF/3/19, fo. 139r.
[30] Thomas 1964, 52. On attitudes to time see also Whipp 1987, 210–19 and Joyce 1987, 25.
[31] See the forthcoming paper: D. Woodward, 'Hours of Work and Means of Payment in Early-modern England'.
[32] Clark & Slack 1976, 15.   [33] 11 Henry VII c.22.
[34] 6 Henry VIII c.3; 5 Elizabeth I c.4.

'was a tribute to the non-existence of that regularity', and that 'labour-ing constantly from morning to evening with regular breaks ... did not happen'.[35] Certainly it is not difficult to find contemporaries who were of like mind. Keith Thomas quoted Bishop Pilkington, who lamented the habits of clock-watching workers, as have middle- and upper-class observers through the centuries:

> The labouring man will take his rest long in the morning; a good piece of the day is spent afore he come at his work; then must he have his breakfast, though he have not earned it, at his accustomed hour, or else there is grudging and murmuring: when the clock smiteth, he will cast down his burden in the midway, and whatsoever he is in hand with, he will leave it as it is, though many times it is marred afore he come again; he may not lose his meat, what danger soever the work is in. At noon he must have his sleeping time, then his bever in the afternoon, which spendeth a great part of the day; and when his hour commeth at night, at the first strike of the clock he casteth down his tools, leaveth his work, in what need or case soever the work standeth.[36]

Similarly, in the mid seventeenth century, judges were asked to enquire whether there were workmen who 'do not continue from five of the clock in the morning til seven at night in the summer and from seven til five in the winter'.[37] Some may have worked even longer. In seventeenth-century London 'all artificers making great sound' were to cease work at 9 p.m. and not to begin again before 4 a.m. In the interest of noise abatement, men were also requested not to beat their wives or servants after 9 p.m.[38]

No doubt there were those who arrived late, took long breaks and left early, and the Act 'touching victuallers and handicraftsmen' of 1548 attempted, among other things, to nip in the bud any conspiracy among workers to regulate their hours of work.[39] But it seems unlikely that workers were able to control their own hours on a regular basis and flout all regulations when employed by well-organised institu-tions. Moreover, it is hardly credible that private customers would have been prepared to accept persistent bad time-keeping by men they were paying by the day. Foremen and overseers were engaged for large projects and it was one of their tasks, as it was also for the master mason, to ensure that workmen were kept up to the mark.[40] At Carlisle in the 1540s the authorities took the unusual step of acquiring a bell from the dissolved priory at Wetheral 'to call the workmen to work at the making of the new citadel ... and mending of the castle'.[41]

The northern accounts show that the hours laid down by parliament

---

[35] Coleman 1955–6, 291.　　[36] K. Thomas 1964, 61.　　[37] Laslett 1983, 30.

[38] Falkus 1976, 249–50.

[39] 2 & 3 Edward VI c.15.　　[40] Knoop & Jones 1949, 61.

[41] Perriam 1987, 128, 148.

were not always adhered to. In many places the summer starting time was 6 a.m., rather than the stipulated 5 a.m. or earlier. In 1576 the York authorities tried to enforce the long working day of 5 a.m. to 7 p.m., but at Newcastle some years later workmen were given extra pay for working before 6 a.m.[42] At Liverpool a bylaw of *c.* 1540 suggests a relatively late start to the day: 'The priest of St John's altar shall daily say mass between the hours of five and six o'clock in the morning to the intent that all labourers and well disposed people minded to have mass may come to the church to hear mass at the said hour.'[43] Similarly, in the second half of the seventeenth century work usually began at 6 a.m. at Hull in the summer months: workmen were paid extra for working before that time.[44] At Chester in 1725 a complaint was made at a meeting of the gild of joiners that journeymen had refused to work the usual hours of 6 a.m. until 8 p.m., 'having an allowance of usual time at dinner'.[45] The working day of some twelve hours, which was the lot of the journeymen joiners, was similar to that laid down for the York carpenters in the early seventeenth century: they were ordered to work a twelve-hour day or forfeit 6s 8d for every hour lost.[46] However, comments from the early 1580s suggest that the twelve hours may have included meal breaks. Some York carpenters and bricklayers were working outside the city at Kirkby Misperton and the rector suggested that they were more expensive than local men, and that part of the problem was that:

By the custom of the City of York bricklayers and carpenters have not usually wrought daytale work any longer than from six of the clock in the morning til six at night, or from five in the morning until seven at night at the furthest. But bricklayers and carpenters of the country usually have wrought and work from sun rising til sun setting their daytale work and sometimes longer.[47]

At Hull in the later seventeenth century the working day was relatively short: workmen who started at six a.m. in the summer received extra pay for staying beyond six in the evening.[48] The only possible hint of a change in the length of the working day comes from the records of St Mary's, Chester. In 1606 the sexton's fee was set at 20s a year for keeping the clock in order and for 'ringing four of the clock in the morning and eight of the clock in the evening', and for keeping the church clean. Half a century later his successor was paid 10s a year for ringing the bell at five in the morning and eight at night, and for mending the bell ropes.[49] The shift in the timing of the morning bell

---

[42] YCR VII, 140; TWAS, 543/19, fos. 153r and v.   [43] *Liverpool Town Books* I, 3.
[44] HCRO, BRF/3/20, p. 684.
[45] CCRO, G14/2.   [46] YCA, B34/186b.   [47] Purvis 1947, 335–6; Palliser 1979, 283.
[48] HCRO, BRF/3/20, pp. 601, 604, 669, 682, 714, 782, 844.   [49] CCORO, P/20/13/1.

may indicate a change in work patterns with the start of the working day moving from 5 to 6 a.m.

The northern accounts say nothing about the length of breaks taken by workmen during the day, although the acts of 1495 to 1563 allowed them to stop for two and a half hours in mid summer, and up to two hours at other times. A lengthy stoppage was needed since the main, heavy meal was usually taken at midday.[50] The longer break in summer was to allow workers to take a siesta 'from the midst of May to the midst of August' amounting to 'half an hour at the most'. At places like Hull, where the working day was only from 6 a.m. to 6 p.m., such long breaks would have driven the hours worked each day below ten.

Extra payments for overtime were made in most northern towns from time to time, although they were not common. At Newcastle in 1594 the masons were paid 'for rising early to receive the carriage' of sand and stones, while at Hull in 1635 some labourers working on one of the defensive banks were paid an extra 1s 'for seven of them staying longer than their time', and in 1668 two of them were given 9d for 'housing sand after they left work'.[51] Some workmen, and especially labourers, were given the opportunity to earn extra money by working at night, although the gilds did not approve of the practice for craftsmen since working out of hours was felt to constitute unfair competition.[52] In some cases it is difficult to decide whether or not a worker was 'on nights' or simply working long hours of overtime. Thus Thomas Ragg, who was mending two of the Lincoln Cathedral bells in 1665, was paid 2s 'for a gratuity for coming from home at two of the clock in the morning and working late at nights'.[53] Some men can be observed working the whole night, often as watchmen: at Newcastle three men were employed 'for watching the common pit three weeks for knowledge of stealing of the ropes' in 1591; in April 1566 the mayor gave 2s 'to six men that watched the Queen's majesty's treasure one night when it went to Berwick'; and at York in 1603 William Best was paid 13s 4d for 'watching 20 days and 20 nights at staithe for vessels from Hull for danger of sickness'.[54] The most frequent use of night-watchmen was at Hull in the 1650s and 1660s when members of the 'town's labourers' often stayed out at night to make sure that nobody interfered with the drinking-water channel. The men, who

---

[50] Weatherill 1988, 152.
[51] TWAS, 543/18, fo. 103v; HCRO, BRF/3/19, fo. 43v; BRF/3/20, pp. 604, 629. See also LAO, Bj/1/13.
[52] TWAS, 802/16 for 1599; 802/2 for 1685.   [53] LAO, Bj/1/8.
[54] TWAS, 543/18, fo. 194r and v;/15, fo. 241v; YCA, CC11, fo. 63r. See also LAO, St Benedict, L1/7/1; *Louth Accts*, 199, 208, 220, 225; YBI, PR/Y/MS/2, fo. 112r; PR/Y/MG/20, fo. 49r; YCA, CC5, fo. 108r; CC8, fo. 55r; TWAS, 659/448; 543/19, fo. 68v.

were paid 10d for a day's work, received 6d a night, although it is clear that they did not need to stay awake all night: often the same men worked a full day and then 'watched' at night, sometimes for weeks on end.[55] In most cases night-watching earned a lower rate of pay than daytime working. Apart from watching, night work was resorted to only when absolutely essential. Sometimes the tide called the tune: thus at Hull in October 1677 fourteen labourers and carpenters were assembled 'for weighing a pile at the bridge they being at work by two in the morning being tide time'.[56] Workmen were also paid for the continuous task of burning plaster through the night, and no doubt many privies and cesspits were relieved of their 'night soil' in the wee small hours: in June 1660 six Hull labourers were paid at the high rate of 2s a night each for three nights 'for dressing the privy adjoining on the town's hall', plus 12d a night between them for ale and tobacco, and a shilling 'for earnest'.[57]

Legislators assumed that the working day would be shorter in the winter than in the summer. Little information is available about the hours worked during the winter months, but it must be assumed, since candles were rarely bought, that a very short day, from dawn to dusk, was worked in the dead days of winter. And it seems likely that the shortness of the working day was a major factor in damping down the demand for labour through the winter.

Labourers and building craftsmen were nearly always employed for complete days. When they were employed for the odd half day, they were usually paid pro rata, or for an hour or two, or 'for a piece of a day': in 1494 a Beverley tiler and his son, who usually got 10d a day, were paid 23d for two days and two hours; at York in 1599 William Woodward, a carpenter who usually got 12d a day, was paid 3s 10d for 'four days lacking a little'.[58] But the infrequency of such payments for broken days is remarkable. The weather must have interfered seriously with outdoor work on many occasions, as it does today, and it must be presumed either that workmen were often given a full day's pay for an incomplete day's work or that they were expected to continue their work even during the most atrocious weather conditions. Or perhaps the paymasters pocketed money not passed on to the workmen. The only recorded instance of reductions in pay due to adverse weather comes from the accounts of the York council: in 1594 a

55 HCRO, BRF/3/20, pp. 28–9, 40, 58–9, 66–8, 103, 346, 359, 382, 604.
56 HCRO, BRF/3/20, p. 930.
57 DFC, CC/190075 fo. 1r; HTH, II, fo. 42v; HCRO, BRF/3/20, p. 272. For candles provided for some privy cleaners at Durham in 1548 see DFC, CC/190075, fo. 4r.
58 HCORO, BC/II/6/15; YCA, CC10, fo. 84B. For other examples of broken time see also CUMROK, WSMB/K; HTH, III, fo. 269r; HCRO, BRF/3/20, pp. 679, 869.

tiler and his boy were paid 15s 2d for working for thirteen days at 14d a day, although the accountant added that 'there was some rainy days which he is to allow or abate for about 6d'.[59] No doubt workmen were laid off for days on end during periods of particularly foul weather, but, according to the accounts, they rarely lost pay on days when work began in the morning. This is surprising. Earlier in the present century, when labourers and building craftsmen were paid by the hour rather than by the day, time lost to the weather was not paid for fully by the employer.[60]

Whatever the length of the basic working day there is no doubt that it was relatively long by modern standards: in most cases it was more than ten hours and somtimes longer than twelve. But long hours do not necessarily lead to higher output. Indeed, 'it seems fairly certain that in most trades any extension beyond nine hours would lower and not increase the total daily or weekly output',[61] and this seems to have been recognised at Newcastle in the 1560s where the monotonous task of pumping water out of a town pit was conducted around the clock by three separate gangs of labourers working eight-hour shifts seven days a week. In October 1562 they were referred to as 'the first shift for eight hours of the night shift', 'the second shift for eight hours of the night shift at the same pit for water drawing', and 'the day shift for eight hours'.[62]

The strength and stamina of manual workers at any time in the past is extremely difficult to assess. It has been suggested that the physical development of the lower orders in the early-modern period was seriously affected by inadequate nutrition and that the rich 'must have been taller, heavier, better developed and earlier to mature than the rest'.[63] Moreover, the short week worked by many 'may have been one aspect of an equilibrium situation determined partly by a high prevalence of debilitating disease and by low and unpredictable supplies of food'.[64] There may be much truth in these suggestions, although some men were capable of working a regular six-day week and some, like the Newcastle pit-drainers, a seven-day week of fifty-six hours.[65] Some men were also capable of handling heavy equipment: at Newcastle in

---

[59] YCA, CC8, fo. 62A.
[60] As late as 1960 Hull labourers received half the usual hourly rate if confined to the lobby, unable to work because of adverse weather, and they could be sent home if they were inactive for a consecutive period of four hours. Thus, their take-home pay for the day could be for two hours only. For a further discussion of the effect of the weather on patterns of work see below, pp. 135–7.
[61] Dobb 1960, 85–6.   [62] TWAS, 543/14, fos. 134r, 141v, 143r and v.
[63] Lis & Soly 1982, 81 quoting Laslett.
[64] Freudenberger & Cummins 1976, 1.   [65] See below p. 131.

the 1560s 'a sinking mell weighing two stones' was wielded by the pit-sinkers, and a 17lb. hammer was bought for Newcastle Trinity House in 1642.[66] Some men were driven extremely hard by those who set them to work. At Levens, near Kendal, the cutting and moving of stones proved onerous in the later seventeenth century: 'I got all the stones ... removed ... upon Saturday last, but I had ten men from Tuesday til Saturday with all our horses, and every day there myself. I have almost killed both men and horses they were so great stones.'[67]

There are a few hints in the northern accounts relating to the amount of work which might be expected from a worker in a day, although often the evidence is insufficient to allow any conclusive analysis. Thus, at Hull in 1663 two labourers were paid for 'housing' sand at 1d a ton, at a time when they were earning 10d a day, but unfortunately we are not told how far the sand was being moved.[68] Similarly, at York, it was laid down in 1656 that labourers were not to carry more than 120 turfs in a poke at a time: this load sounds substantial, but the size of an individual turf is not known.[69] However, some insights into the intensity with which early-modern craftsmen worked can be gained by comparing the daily rates of pay and the piece-rates offered to bricklayers and tilers. This should give some indication of what contemporaries considered a fair day's work and can be contrasted with the amount of work accomplished by twentieth-century bricklayers and tilers. Such a direct comparison is meaningful since the techniques employed by tilers and bricklayers have not changed for centuries and, perhaps, for millennia, although some of the materials have changed. When the late-twentieth-century bricklayer spreads a trowelful of cement on top of the last course and adds another brick, his actions are exactly those of the Tudor and Stuart bricklayer and his medieval forebears.

In the late fifteenth century Richard Bothe worked at Hull Trinity House as a tiler and bricklayer. He was paid 20d a thousand for laying 16,000 'thacktile', but on other occasions received 6d a day for his labour.[70] This suggests that he was expected to take more than three days to lay 1,000 tiles, at the rate of 300 a day. Similarly, in the 1630s Thomas Harpham and Thomas Wright were paid 14s for 'laying four thousand tiles on two outshots of James Fairburn and Widow Allwood houses at 3s 6d per thousand'.[71] This suggests that they were expected to lay some 286 tiles a day each, since 12d was the going daily rate for

[66] TWAS, 543/14, fo. 131v; 659/446.   [67] *Levens Letters*, 91.
[68] HCRO, BRF/3/20, p. 430.
[69] YML, QQ80/5/1; YCA, B37/88, 112b, 124.   [70] *Hull Trinity House Building*, 161.
[71] HCRO, BRF/3/19, p. 122.

tilers. If these men were simply attaching the tiles to the laths nailed across the roof timbers the piece-rates they received suggest either that their pace of work was extremely leisurely, or that the piece-rates were excessively generous. Modern tilers can lay 'a thousand flat tiles a day, no bother'.[72] However, it is possible that the piece-rates were not merely for attaching the tiles: the tilers may have been expected to fix the laths, render the underside of the tiles with mortar, and, perhaps, pay for an assistant. Tilers' men earned 8d a day at Hull during the 1630s, so that a tiler and his man together earned 20d a day, which would imply that they were expected to fasten at least 476 tiles a day between them.

A further comparison of piece and day-rates can be made from the Hull wage assessment for 1570. A master bricklayer was to receive no more than 10d a day in summer and not more than 3s 4d for laying a thousand bricks: in each case he was to provide his own food.[73] Again this seems to suggest a low level of productivity, with the master bricklayer needing to lay no more than 250 bricks when on piece-rates to earn the equivalent of the daily wage. Late-twentieth-century brick-layers, if assisted by a labourer, can lay 500 face-work bricks in eight hours without difficulty and in the early part of this century 750 was regarded as a reasonable day's effort.[74] However, bricklaying was a slower process in the early-modern period. Bricks made by traditional methods were inconsistent in shape, size, and colour, and needed to be selected carefully by the bricklayer. The process of laying the bricks was also slower. Lime mortar was used in larger quantities than would be common today, and it needed more working than modern cement. Moreover, the irregularly shaped bricks took longer to lay than today's products. As a result, 250 bricks a day may not have been bad progress in the sixteenth century.[75] However, it is possible that the piece-rate was intended to cover the cost of a labourer as well as the bricklayer: in which case a combined daily wage of 16d would imply that at least 400 bricks needed to be laid.

The small amount of information relating to the pay of the Hull tilers and bricklayers may suggest that they worked in a rather sedate fashion. However, it is possible that the respective piece and day-rates were customary and had evolved over a considerable period of time, and that contemporaries may not have been fully aware of the

[72] Derived from a discussion with Gordon Rawlinson, a local builder, on 23/8/1990.
[73] *Tudor Proclamations*, II, 338.
[74] These are average figures: a blank gable end can be constructed more quickly than a wall with windows.
[75] I am grateful to Robin Lucas of the University of East Anglia for placing his encyclo-paedic knowledge of bricks and bricklaying at my disposal.

relationship between the two rates. Something of this nature is suggested by the 1570 Hull assessment: when the customer provided food for the master bricklayer the piece-rate was to be no more than 20d for 1,000 bricks, and the day-rate 6d, which suggests that it was expected that 300 bricks would be laid in a day. As we have seen, when the bricklayers fed themselves they were expected to lay only 250 bricks.[76]

Contemporaries rarely discussed the length of the working week since there was a general presumption that labouring men and women would work six days out of seven, taking their rest on the seventh or sabbath day.[77] None of the accounts suggests that a short day was worked on Saturdays, but everyone was expected to attend divine service the following day: it was 'the one day of the average week in which extended recreation could be taken'.[78] Only essential work could be done. At Chester, blacksmiths might only work in the Queen's service or 'set shoe upon a horse'.[79] At times drainage of the Newcastle town pits had to continue throughout Sunday, and lime-kilns had to be serviced every day: during 1596–7 the limeburner and his labourer worked forty-four seven-day weeks, but not at all during the remaining eight weeks.[80] Occasionally Sunday work was necessitated by an accident. At Kendal in January 1661 a thatcher was paid a shilling 'for beer to himself and another he procured to himself to save the thatch on the mill, kiln and stable on the windy sabbath-day'.[81] Although it is likely that more Sundays were worked than we have record of, it is evident that Sunday working was unusual and that most labourers and building craftsmen were able to take their rest or pursue other activities on the Lord's day.

The working year

In theory, 313 weekdays were available for work each year, less a number of days set aside for holidays. It is generally believed that holidays were numerous in pre-Reformation England, amounting to

---

[76] *Tudor Proclamations*, II, 338. Medieval weavers 'seem to have proceeded very slowly': Dyer 1989, 224.

[77] Holidays will be discussed in the next section, below pp. 131–3.

[78] Phythian-Adams 1979, 79.

[79] 79 CCRO, G20/1, ordinances of 1592. See also Phythian-Adams 1979, 79; HCRO, BRF/3/19, fo. 216r; BRF/3/20, pp. 73, 525, 594, 619, 875. Even droving stopped on a Sunday: Woodward 1977, 43.

[80] TWAS, 543/14, fos. 133v–135r; 543/18, fos. 140v, 141v; 543/19, fos. 7v–61r. The weeks they did not work fell in December and January (a consecutive four-week lay-off which included the Christmas and New Year period), February (2), June (1) and July (1). See also 543/18, fos. 113v, 117v, 126r–139r, 250r–252r.

[81] CUMROK, WSMB/K. See also CCRO, TAV/1/7; YCA, CC33, fo. 11v.

between forty and fifty days a year, and that the Reformation, by reducing them, raised the number of days available for work.[82] According to Phelps Brown and Hopkins, the decline in the number of holidays 'raised by a fifth the number of days available for work in the year'.[83] This is impossible. Even if fifty days had been lost each year in medieval England and recovered at the Reformation the gain would have been less that 20 per cent,[84] and, of course, post-Reformation workers continued to take some holidays. Perhaps less days were lost to holidays after the Reformation, but the change was less dramatic than some historians have believed.

Unfortunately, the northern accounts tell us little about the prevalence of holidays, although taking time off at Christmas, Easter, and Whitsun was common practice. During 1661/2 two carpenters – Edward Skelton and George Vickers – worked almost continuously at Lincoln Cathedral, although they each took off six days over Christmas and New Year, two days at Easter, and three at Whitsun. The remaining eleven days they were absent from work were spread throughout the year and may or may not have been related to formal holidays.[85] At Newcastle, labourers were paid 'for drawing down water in the seven holidays in Christmas' in 1596, while at Chester a full week was taken for Easter during the building of the new quay in 1568.[86] In contrast, at Hull in 1622 only three days were lost at Easter, and a further two days at Whitsun.[87] An unspecified number of days was lost for Whitsun at Newcastle in 1596: the pit ropes were removed lest they be stolen, but the work of draining the pit had to continue unabated.[88] In addition to the breaks which can be deduced for the three major festivals, the accounts contain a few references to unspecified holidays: holidays in April, June, and October were mentioned at Hull, and three days were lost at Newcastle in June. At Kendal the chamberlains paid 1s 6d in August 1636 for the 'table' of a wheelwright and his men on 'Bartholomew Day, when they wrought not'.[89] In the

---

[82] Dyer 1989, 222; Knoop & Jones 1949, 118–21. Rogers argued that medieval labourers took very few holidays: Rogers 1908, 181. For continental comparisons see Small 1989, 324, and Goldthwaite 1980, 289. In late-medieval Florence workers took about fifty days a year as holidays.

[83] Brown & Hopkins 1981, 64. This is repeated by Walter in Walter & Schofield 1989, 88.

[84] 365 minus 52 Sundays = 313 minus 50 holidays = 263 days available for work. If all the 50 holidays were regained after the Reformation, and of course they were not, there would have been a gain of 19 per cent.

[85] LAO, Bj/1/8.

[86] TWAS, 543/19, fo. 14v; *Chester Haven*, 108. The week 19–24 April was taken off at Chester: Easter day was 18 April 1568.

[87] HCRO, BRF/3/10.   [88] TWAS, 543/18, fos. 34v, 298r.

[89] HCRO, BRF/3/19, fos. 119r, 130r, 136r; TWAS, 543/18, fo. 139r; CUMROK, WSMB/K.

Table 5.2. *Chief carpenters at Hull, 1618–29*

Name	Smallest number of days worked in a particular year	Largest number of days worked in a particular year (1625)	Mean number of days worked p.a.
Robert Iveson	49 (1621)	192.5	114
James Brasbrick	32 (1626)	185.5	99
William Watherton	20 (1621)	210	107

The figures for Brasbrick are based on an eight-year period; the other two worked throughout the period.
Source: HCRO, BRF/3/19.

late-medieval period some masons, and especially the cathedral masons, were given paid holidays, but there is no evidence to suggest that other workers received holiday pay between 1450 and 1750. The statutes of 1445, 1495, and 1514 specifically forbade such payments.[90] The annual work patterns of early-modern labourers and building craftsmen are difficult to investigate since the extant accounts were not those of the workers themselves.Sometimes individual workmen were occupied for most of the year: in 1673 William Newlove, one of the Hull carpenters, worked for the council for all but eighteen of the workdays available.[91] But workmen rarely stayed so long with a single customer. Occasionally the same workman can be observed in the accounts of different institutions during the course of a single year. At Hull the carpenter William Whelpdale worked for both the town council and Trinity House during the 1560s and 1570s, and others did likewise.[92] Similarly, at York, the same workmen can be found in the records of the city council and of various churches. But such discoveries do little more than confirm the obvious fact that most workers were hired by different customers during the year. In most cases workers do not remain in view for more than a few days or weeks each year, and it is impossible to say what they were doing on other occasions: such 'lost' time was filled by a combination of other work, holidays, periods of unemployment, and sickness.

Salzman remarked on 'the astonishing fluidity of labour',[93] and, even for trusted workers, the employment offered by a particular

[90] Knoop & Jones 1949, 118–19; Rogers 1908, 327–8; YML, E3/27–38; 23 Henry VI c.12; 11 Henry VII c.22; 6 Henry VIII c.3.
[91] HCRO, BRF/3/20. Between 1670 and 1679 he did an average of 217 days a year for the council, topping 250 days in five years.
[92] HTH, II; HCRO, BRF/3/2–4.   [93] Salzman 1952, 59–60.

institution could fluctuate widely from season to season, and from year to year. This is demonstrated clearly by table 5.2 which shows the activities of a Hull carpenter and two of his associates between 1618 and 1629 when they were responsible for about two-thirds of the carpentry work required by the council.

Gaps in the employment records of individual workers are rarely explained in the accounts. When all workmen, or a sizeable group, stopped work simultaneously it is obvious that a particular job had finished or was being run down. But if one or two individuals simply disappeared from a gang we are left in the dark: they may have been sacked, sick or injured, too drunk to work, or absent on some more pressing business. Some insights into the unreliability of workers can be gained from the letters written during the restructuring of Levens Hall, near Kendal, in 1693:

13 March: The Wallers is not comed yet but hath promised to come some time this week.

10 April: The Kendal wallers went off upon Friday last but hath promised to come again within a week.

5 June: ... the wallers promised to be here tomorrow, if fail not (as often they do).

8 June: I wrote in my last about the wallers. They came but this day, they are very ill natured, crossgrained knaves, they will do nothing but what they are forced to do.

18 June: Thomas Knots hath been here plastering ... but was sent for last Saturday night but his man is here about plastering the granary and slaughter-house. I expect himself in five days. His only son 'was adyeing', that was the reason he went away.[94]

Some workers were always prepared to 'swing the lead' but, in an age innocent of most effective medicines, the experience of a north Yorkshire mason in the mid eighteenth century must have been commonplace: he 'came to work having been absent not well about sixteen days'.[95] Even a relatively minor ailment could disrupt work. In April 1673 a Carlisle brickmaker explained to Sir John Lowther why there had been a break in his work: 'I did begin to make bricks about ten days ago and the weather had been so cruel, cold and sharp that I am forced to leave it off again til the Lord send me warmer weather, for two of my workmen have gotten a great cold and are not able to work for the present.'[96]

Because of our ignorance of work patterns it is impossible to esti-

---

[94] *Levens Letters*, 27, 34, 43, 45, 89–90.   [95] *Two Yorkshire Diaris*, 207.
[96] B.C. Jones 1983, 125.

Table 5.3. *The seasonality of employment at Hull, 1653–78*

	Winter December– February %	Spring March–May %	Summer June–August %	Autumn September– November %	Number of man days
Labourers	11.8	22.6	38.2	27.4	26,104
Wrights	13.3	25.9	35.8	25.0	19,866
Bricklayers	11.0[a]	22.3	38.2	28.5	5,710
Overall	12.3	23.9	37.2	26.6	51,680

[a] The winter figure for the bricklayers is slightly exaggerated by the very high level of activity in the first two months of 1661. In other years they did only 10 per cent of their work in the winter.
Source: HCRO, BRF/3/20.

mate the annual income which could be derived from wage-earning and, hence, get a more meaningful insight into shifts in living standards than has been possible in the past. We might assume that if real wages were falling, as indeed they were for much of the sixteenth and seventeenth centuries, workers would have been inclined to work for more days during the year in order to maintain their real incomes. This may have been what the workers would have wanted, but most labourers and building craftsmen were dependent on their customers to set them on work and could do little to influence the level of demand for their services. The number of days available for work may have increased as holiday-taking declined after the Reformation, but was extra work available for the urban wage-earner? Indeed, 'it is necessary to confront contradictory assumptions. While the abolition of holy days after the Reformation would have increased the available days for employment ... this theoretical gain needs to be set against the growing problems of under- and un-employment.'[97]

Seasonality

The changing seasons affected labourers and building craftsmen in two main ways: less work was available in the winter months than at other times of the year, and the reduction in the hours of daylight meant that at least some workers were paid at lower daily rates during the winter.

[97] Walter & Schofield 1989, 88. For a further discussion of the labour supply and employment opportunities see below pp. 191–3.

Most historians of outdoor work have remarked on the relatively low levels of activity during the winter months.[98] The northern accounts confirm their findings. This is shown in table 5.3. At New-castle Trinity House, which was being altered during the 1630s, only a small amount of work was done during the winter: 10.7 per cent of the money laid out on refurbishment was spent during winter, 12.8 per cent in the spring, 46.0 per cent in summer, and 30.4 per cent in the autumn.[99] On an earlier occasion the picture had been even more extreme: when a new quay was being built for the council in 1594 work did not begin until mid March and petered out in September.[100] However, there was at least one period at Hull when the normal pattern did not apply to all workers. During the later 1630s the employment of labourers by the council was spread more evenly through the year: 20.1 per cent of the work was done in winter, compared with 29.5 per cent in spring, 27.3 per cent in summer, and 23.0 per cent in autumn.[101] The explanation for this unusual pattern is that the labourers were employed in the winter mainly to clean the fresh-water dikes, a job which was much easier to do once vegetation on the banks had died back. But it was much more usual for employ-ment to be reduced substantially during the deepest days of winter: in 1659 labourers were not employed at all in January, and almost 85 per cent of labouring work took place between April and September.[102]

One country-house builder intended to sack all his men the day after Michaelmas, although he added that 'you shall not need to let the workmen themselves know it'.[103] And the letters of Hugh James who was in charge of the refurbishment of Levens Hall illustrate graphi-cally the problems involved with trying to press on with building operations during the winter of 1692–3. As early as 14 November he complained that the wallers were not able to work: 'now it's a frost and they cannot work'. On 5 December he was waiting for some Kendal wallers to arrive hoping that 'if God would be pleased to send three or four fine days' he could get the walls up and then 'they shall work no more this season'. The wallers duly arrived, and on 10 December he

---

[98] Knoop & Jones 1949, 131–2; Tomlinson 1973, 13–14; Gilboy 1934, 20; Smith 1989, 25; Airs 1975, 171.

[99] TWAS, 659/447. Total expenditure over the five years was £373. Because of the structure of the accounts the seasons are as follows: winter – mid-November to the end of February; spring, to late May; summer, to the middle of August; autumn – to mid-November.

[100] TWAS, 543/18, fos. 79ff.   [101] HCRO, BRF/3/19.

[102] HCRO, BRF/3/20. The same was true in 1660. In 1661 the main labouring season was June to October; in 1662 it was March to August plus November; in 1663 it was March to October.

[103] Airs 1975, 171.

reported that fine weather was needed so that he could get the job finished and 'the walls levelled and covered' against frost. That was accomplished by 9 January, although he was fretting again within a fortnight and hoping for 'seasonable' weather so that the wallers could 'fall on'. On 13 February he was frustrated again: 'it is now here a frost and likely to be a snow. The weather is so uncertain I dare not fall upon walling as yet.' At the end of the month he confessed that 'the frost is so hard they cannot work'. The severe weather continued into March, and the wallers were not at work until the end of the month, although the preparatory work of collecting stones had continued during the bad weather. By 7 April the wallers were 'going on with all speed'.[104] Working conditions could become very unpleasant, and some workers probably took matters into their own hands like the East Riding thatchers observed by Henry Best: 'They give over their trade usually about Martinmas (11 November), or soon after, so as frosts and cold wet weather begin to come in, for it is an occupation that will not get a man heat in a frosty morning, sitting on top of a house, where the wind commeth to him on every side.'[105] Routine, non-urgent tasks could always wait until the return of more clement weather, although there were some jobs which could not be left. Damage to wharfs, jetties, and other property had to be made good without delay. At Hull in January 1661, 8s 4d was paid to John Silkwood for five days 'at the Charity Hall tiling and at the Grammar School repairing a wall fallen down the windy Saturday', while at Durham in February 1549, money had been laid out 'for repairing a chimney blown down by great wind'.[106]

The demand for workers in the outdoor trades was also affected by the length of the working day. Henry Best explained that at the start of November the thatchers 'come to work ... by that time they can well see about them in the morning, and they leave not work at night so long as they can see to do anything'. In contrast, indoor or workshop based craftsmen could often continue after dark: indeed, cobblers who were paid at the same rate in winter and summer were 'to work with a candle after supper til such time as they go to bed'.[107] Late working was often not possible for labourers and building craftsmen, and many customers determined to wait for spring or early summer rather than begin a job in the middle of winter. The relatively low levels of winter employment for labourers and building craftsmen coincided with

---

[104] *Levens Letters*, 11–33; see also 132–8. See also Tyson 1984, 70–1.
[105] *Henry Best*, 152.
[106] HCRO, BRF/3/20, p. 312; DPK, MC7120. See also DFC, CC/190075, fo. 2v.
[107] *Henry Best*, 149, 152.

slack times in other trades. At Hull seasonal demands for shipping led
to heavy winter unemployment: indeed, 'Hull froze with the Baltic'.[108]
Many belts were tightened in the northern towns during the winter.
By contrast, the high levels of employment available in the towns
during the warmer months coincided with the peak of activity in rural
society. Occasionally this caused a problem. At Levens, a job had to be
postponed since, as the agent put it, 'I am afraid I shall not get any to
undertake it 'til harvest be over'.[109] According to the Statute of
Artificers, 'in the time of hay or corn harvest', the Justices could order
'all such artificers and persons as be meet to labour' into the fields.[110] In
practice, however, the vigour with which urban projects were often
pursued through the summer months, and into the autumn, suggests
that labour shortages were acute only in exceptional circumstances.

Historians approaching early-modern wage accounts for the first time
would expect to find lower daily rates offered to labour in the winter
months. Such a belief would be based on a reading of the standard
texts and a knowledge of the labour legislation of the fifteenth and
early sixteenth centuries. Knoop and Jones explained that the Vale
Royal accounts of the thirteenth century recorded that in November
'the payments are decreased on account of the short days', and that
the lengthening days of early February brought higher levels of pay.[111]
At York in the following century the masons' ordinances indicated a
change in rates at Easter and Michaelmas, although Salzman pointed
out that in practice lower levels of pay were almost invariably given
from All Saints (1 November) to the Purification (2 February).[112] Nevertheless, the labour statutes of 1445, 1495, and 1514 laid down that rates
should change at Michaelmas and Easter, although, given its movable
nature, Easter was an odd date to stipulate. A brief acquaintanceship
with the wage assessments made by JPs after 1563 would also show
that they often expected winter rates to be relatively low.[113] But
seasonal variations in wage rates were not invariable. In the fifteenth
century seasonal differentials were not found on all building sites, and
when they were introduced at London Bridge and at Eton the workers
benefited since the change was effected 'not by reducing the winter
rates, but by increasing the summer rates'.[114] The failure to apply

[108] Jackson 1972, 175, 280, 318–19.
[109] *Levens Letters*, 101. See also Tomlinson 1973, 18.
[110] 5 Elizabeth I c.4.   [111] Knoop & Jones 1949, 116–17; Dyer 1989, 225.
[112] Salzman 1952, 58–9; Knoop & Jones 1949, 117; Swanson 1983, 18.
[113] Continental experience would suggest likewise: Goldthwaite 1980, 322–4; Sonenscher 1989, 182–4.
[114] Knoop & Jones 1949, 118.

seasonal differentials as an invariable rule was also noted by Rogers and Salzman.[115] Moreover, a close examination of post-1563 wage assessments indicates that, while differentials were laid down for many classes of labour, building workers were often assessed at a single rate for the whole year.[116] The northern accounts reveal that the situation was extremely complex: summer–winter differentials were paid in some places at certain times, but not at others; or they were paid to some workers, but not to others. It is difficult to discuss the subject systematically, since relatively little information is available for the winter months. Moreover, the problem is exacerbated by the failure of many accountants to date individual entries. A further difficulty arises from the fact that some jobs were rewarded at a relatively high level during the winter months because of difficult working conditions, which masked any tendency towards seasonal variation. These problems, and the fragmentary nature of many of the accounts, mean that it is not possible to give more than the most tentative indication of changes over time in most northern towns.

Among the larger towns the accounts of York Minster provide the earliest evidence of seasonal differentials: from the late 1460s to the mid 1530s the top mason and the chief carpenter were paid level rates throughout the year, although ordinary craftsmen and labourers moved from the summer rates of 6d and 4d, to 5d and 3d respectively during the winter.[117] Similar differentials were paid at St Michael's, Spurriergate, during the 1520s and 1530s.[118] However, some scrappy evidence for the 1620s and 1630s suggests that differential rates were no longer being offered at the Minster, and at the Restoration most workmen were paid 18d a day, winter and summer alike.[119] The York council accounts for the late 1590s indicate that skilled men moved from 12d in the summer to 10d in winter, and that labourers moved from 7d to 6d. This situation was only partially confirmed in the autumn of 1601. A group of pavers and labourers worked from late September to the end of December: the skilled men got 12d a day during the first month but, inexplicably, moved to 13d from early October and received that rate of pay until the end of the year. But the labourers, who began the period at 7d a day, moved to 6d on 17 October and remained at that rate thereafter. The only unchanged rate

---

[115] Rogers 1908, 327–8; Salzman 1952, 68. For varying practices in Western Europe see Small 1989, 324.
[116] Roberts 1981, 312.
[117] The rates for apprentice masons moved from 5d to 4d in the winter.
[118] YBI, PR/Y/MS/1.   [119] YML, E3/57–65.

was that paid to 'young Harrison' who got 6d throughout. In 1603 labourers and craftsmen seem to have received the same rates throughout the year, although some craftsmen were paid at a reduced rate in the winter of 1610.[120] Thereafter the York material becomes extremely thin and seasonal fluctuations cannot be charted.

For Hull in the second half of the sixteenth century the small amount of information available is also somewhat contradictory: in 1563 carpenters and labourers received the same rates throughout the period January to September, although in the spring of both 1585 and 1586 a small group of carpenters moved from the winter rate of 9d to 10d in early April.[121] Similarly, the accounts for the later 1620s provide mixed information. In 1625 three carpenters – Robert Iveson, William Rawlyn, and James Brasbrick – were paid 10d a day from January to the first week of March. In the week beginning 7 March they moved to 12d and were paid at that rate through the summer. However, on Monday 21 November Rawlyn moved back to 10d, although Iveson and Brasbrick did not move to 10d until the end of the month. Rather oddly, the labourers who were paid 6d during the winter did not progress to 8d until early July, although their return to 6d was delayed until the end of November. The same levels of pay were recorded for the following year, although in the years 1627–9 differentials disappeared for the craftsmen, but remained in place for the labourers. The situation seems to have been the same in 1635, although in the following year level rates were paid for craftsmen and labourers alike. Down to 1640 most workers were then paid at level rates and this continued until the end of the century.[122] Seasonally adjusted rates made something of a comeback in the eighteenth century: in the 1740s some carpenters, but not all, were paid 24d a day in the summer but only 18d in winter. In some years labourers were paid a flat rate of 12d, but some who moved to 14d in the summer of 1742 were reduced to 12d for the winter.[123] Newcastle data for the period from the late 1580s to the 1630s, with only a single exception, paint a consistent picture. The contract paver, William Benson, and his man moved to a lower rate of pay during the winter months, but all other workers remained at the same rate throughout the year.[124] Similarly, at Chester in the later seventeenth and early eighteenth centuries, most skilled men and labourers were paid at level rates. Only in the case of a group of 'stone-getters' is there evidence of a seasonal reduction in rates: during

[120] YCA, CC5–12.   [121] HCRO, BRF/3/2, 5.   [122] HCRO, BRF/3/13–21.
[123] HCRO, BRF/6/538–9, 542–3, 546–51, 553, 577, 594, 660–2.
[124] TWAS, 543/14–26; *Newcastle Accts*, 55–6, 59.

1729–30 they received 16d a day in summer and 12d in winter for working in the quarry.[125]

Unchanging rates were paid at Lincoln Cathedral during the early decades of the seventeenth century, and they were still being paid in the early 1660s when the whole question of pay was investigated in an extensive enquiry conducted in 1663–4 into the accounts of Henry Mansford, who had been Clerk of the Fabric since at least 1643.[126] The investigation led to the adoption of lower rates for the winter for some workers, which suggests that Mansford may have been colluding with the workforce to pay rates higher than the local norms. The plumbers were the most affected by the new ruling, moving from the flat daily rate of 30d, to a new summer-only rate of 30d and 20d in the winter, rates they continued to receive through the 1660s. Glaziers moved from a flat 20d a day to the differential rates of 20d and 18d, although in the winters of 1664–5 and 1665–6 they were paid only 14d a day, and the low flat rate of 12d throughout 1667–8. During the 1660s most labourers were switched to a winter rate of 8d from the flat rate of 10d, but masons and ordinary carpenters, after receiving seasonally differentiated rates during the first two years of the new regime, moved back to level rates. The master carpenter got an undifferentiated 16d throughout the 1660s. This fascinating sequence of events suggests that the Masters of the Fabric of Lincoln Cathedral believed that wage rates were too high, especially for the winter. Only in the case of the glaziers were they able to impose lower rates throughout the year, although they reduced overall labour costs by imposing lower winter rates for most classes of labour. However, at some time in the following decades these seasonal differentials disappeared, and by the 1720s level rates were once more being paid throughout the year.[127]

The evidence for Beverley, Durham, Hull, Louth, and York suggests that lower winter rates were quite common – although by no means invariable – during the later fifteenth and sixteenth centuries:[128] thus, the intentions of the acts of 1445 to 1514, which laid down lower winter rates, were not being fulfilled in all instances. Evidence for the seventeenth and eighteenth centuries suggests that the payment of level rates became more common, although differentials were paid in some places from time to time. However, it must be stressed that these conclusions are based on relatively little evidence.

The frequent failure to reduce nominal rates for outdoor workers

---

[125] CCRO, MUV/1/3, 23, 30, 41, 54; /3/34, 36–8, 56, 66–7, 77, 84, 123; TAB/1; TAR/3/58A; TAV/1/3, 5–7, 9–11, 15, 18–19, 21, 23, 29, 31, 33–4.
[126] LAO, Bj/1/7–8. See below pp. 143–4. [127] LAO, Bj/1/11.
[128] HCORO, BC/II/6/15; *Louth Accts*, 23–6, 137; DPK, MC 2802–3245.

during the short days of winter cannot be easily explained. Where level rates were paid workers received relatively high *hourly* rates in winter, a time of high unemployment. In the absence of any contemporary discussion of the issue various explanations can be suggested. It is possible that although the number of hours worked declined in the winter the total amount of work did not, or at least was not reduced in the same proportion as the number of hours worked: such a hypothesis would rest on the assumption that the pace of work in early-modern England was extremely leisurely, and that by speeding up the job in winter it may have been possible to do as much, or nearly as much, as in the longer days of summer.[129] Secondly, those workers who were hired regularly may have had an implicit contract with their customers which ensured that they would be paid at level rates throughout the year. Thirdly, there may have been an increasing reluctance on the part of labour to accept any reduction in nominal rates during winter, especially in the context of the long-term erosion in real wages down to the middle of the seventeenth century. Finally, it is possible that some customers recognised that the wage rates on offer were by no means generous, even in the summer, and that a further reduction, at a time of the year when the prices of many necessities were relatively high, did not exhibit that degree of Christian solicitude recommended to them from the pulpit.

The provision of non-food perquisites

Perquisite: Any casual emoluments in addition to salary or wages. (1565)

Perquisite: Any article that has served its primary purpose, which subordinates or servants claim a customary right to take for their own use. (1709)

Perquisite: A customary 'tip'. (1721)[130]

There is some confusion, both in dictionary definitions and in common usage, as to whether perquisites, or 'perks', were regular and expected payments, or irregular and unexpected. In the discussion which follows a perquisite will be defined as a payment – often in kind – over and above the basic wage, which may or may not have been regular, and which may or may not have been anticipated by the recipient. The whole question of perquisites has assumed enormous significance for social historians of the eighteenth and nineteenth centuries who have

---

[129] See the discussion of work intensity above, pp. 129–31.
[130] *Oxford English Dictionary.*

conducted an exhaustive search for the origins of true proletarians or wage-slaves. It is widely believed that true wage-earners solely dependent for survival, or very largely so, on their money wages only emerged in the nineteenth century.[131] For earlier periods it is argued that the widespread provision of perquisites makes it difficult, if not impossible, to chart movements in living standards since we do not know the full extent of earnings derived from wage work.[132]

Any attempt to assess the significance of perquisites other than food and drink is made extraordinarily difficult by the wall of silence presented by most records: indeed, 'little is known of workplace appropriation and – given the intractability of the sources – little is likely to be known'.[133] Nevertheless, many historians have assumed that non-food perquisites were an important part of the remuneration of wage-earners, and they turn to a small number of frequently repeated examples to support their claims. These include: the free coal received by miners; the waste cloth taken by tailors; the thrums accumulated by weavers; and the 'chips' or small offcuts of wood appropriated by the carpenters of the royal dockyards.[134] The absence of more extensive evidence may suggest that the practice of taking perquisites was so commonplace that it was normally ignored by the officials compiling institutional accounts: thus, the money paid to workers would be recorded as wages and the perquisites would be hidden in the purchase price of the appropriated raw materials. But the shortage of evidence could also suggest that the receipt of perquisites was less common than has often been supposed.

The northern accounts provide a few examples of the type of perquisites which early-modern workers are believed to have received in such profusion. At the building of the headquarters for Hull Trinity House in the 1460s the chief carpenter, Robert Paget, was paid 20d 'for chips and old timber bought for burning plaster', although some wood was bought in for the same purpose on a later occasion.[135] The only other example of the kind came to light at Lincoln Cathedral in the 1660s during the enquiry into the behaviour of Henry Mansford: he claimed 'that he may receive these casual fees and privileges ensuing, as he conceiveth his predecessors formerly did'. They included:

---

131 Rule 1986, 116–19.   132 Abel 1980, 137; Gilboy 1934, 19.
133 Schwarz 1989, 22.
134 Dobson 1980, 27–8; Rule 1986, 116–17; Schwarz 1985, 33. For a detailed discussion of 'chips' at the Royal dockyards see *VCH Kent* II, 347, 358, 386. In eighteenth-century France the removal of pieces of wood was widespread among wheel-wrights, carpenters, and joiners. The married men in particular valued this source of easy fuel. Sonenscher 1989, 208–9, 256–64.
135 *Hull Trinity House Building*, 159.

All the chips and pieces of wood under one yard in length.

All the pigeon manure.

For every lb. of solder which he maketh himself, 8d.

The keeping of three cattle upon the commons.

He also asked 'that he may be allowed the benefit of all the lead ashes, both past and present and future during his continuance in his said office as he conceiveth his predecessors formerly were'. The enquiry conducted by the Masters of the Fabric denied his right to chips, arguing – with impeccable logic – that, if confirmed, 'he may cut what wood he pleaseth to that shortness, and then take it for his fee'. Their case was bolstered by appeal to ancient precedent. They discovered in the accounts that Humfrey Ireland, Clerk of the Fabric from 1519 to 1537, had accounted for 'chips sold by him'. Thus they concluded that chips were 'none of his fees' and added, 'we think it reasonable that they should be rather employed for melting lead, and refining lead ashes, and other uses for the church'. Mansford replied, vainly, that his predecessors had always had 'chips and old wood and root ends' as part of their fees. The Masters of the Fabric also saw no reason why he should be paid 8d a lb. for solder since '1lb. of pewter (which will cost but 1s) and 3lb. of lead (which will cost but 4d) – in all 1s 4d – will make 4lb. of solder, for which he claimeth 2s 8d'. They also denied his right to the lead ashes.[136]

Mansford's claim to a wide range of perquisites for himself meant that they were not available to the craftsmen beneath him, although he may have been paying some workers, and especially the plumbers, excessive rates in order to gain their acquiescence.[137] Similarly, Robert Paget probably took most of the chips produced at the construction of Hull Trinity House and left little for the rank-and-file craftsmen. The absence of further references to chips in the northern accounts does not mean that they were not taken by some workmen, but it seems unlikely that most workmen in the building trades had regular access to such benefits. Knoop and Jones discussed the provision of food and drink, housing, and clothing for medieval masons, and also cash bonuses, but did not record any examples of their receiving the waste materials generated by their work.[138] Similarly it is difficult to see how bricklayers could have benefited much from the broken bricks and refuse mortar lying around building sites. No doubt they stole bricks and other materials from their customers from time to time, but that is another, even more shadowy story: and building workers of the twentieth century have continued the tradition of embezzlement. We

---

[136] LAO, Bj/1/8. See also above p. 141.   [137] See above pp. 42–3.
[138] Knoop & Jones 1949, 114–16.

are never likely to know much about the prevalence of perquisites on the building sites of early-modern England, but the paucity of hard evidence induces the suspicion that the custom has been exaggerated.

Some workers, especially those hired on annual contracts, were provided with items of clothing. Civic officials and chief workmen were often clad in a special livery to enhance their status: the city mason of fifteenth-century York received a ceremonial gown, and the new master mason at Durham Cathedral in 1488 was to have 'yearly one garment of the said Prior and Chapter and their successors, competent to his degree' together with a rent-free house.[139] At Chester in the early seventeenth century the paver was given a new coat each year 'to show he was the city's servant': in the 1630s it contained a yard and a half of broadcloth, which cost 13s 6d. A century later the paver and the mason were still receiving coats, now made of 'blue shalloone', trimmed with silk thread and five dozen blue buttons between them.[140] At Newcastle there are many examples of such practices. In the later sixteenth century a gown, containing five or six yards of russet, was made for the city limeburner, 'against Easter', and he also received a pair of shoes in 1597. Lancelot Bowmer, the city plumber, did even better. His gown contained three and a half yards of broad cloth, which cost 8s 8d a yard. Other officials to receive clothing in the late sixteenth century included the city paver, the overseer of the town pit, and Jenette Dunne, a street cleaner.[141] Elsewhere, workers were occasionally provided with items of clothing: at York in 1615 two masons were each given a pair of boots; in 1619 the Carlisle mason was given 5s 4d 'to bestow for a frieze jerkin over covenant'; and in the early 1650s stockings, shoes, and shirts were provided 'for the boy which makes the tile'.[142]

Ordinary workers were sometimes given protective gloves. They were often given to medieval masons as they were 'needed to protect the layers' hands from splinters and should, therefore, be regarded as adjuncts to masons' tools, rather than as a badge of office'.[143] Similarly, some stone setters were given gloves at Durham in the 1540s, although most references to gloves in the northern accounts were for carpenters and others when timber-framed buildings or roof timbers were hauled

[139] Swanson 1983, 8; Salzman 1952, 47, 592–4.
[140] *Chester Minutes*, 15. Two weeks later a new paver was refused a coat: *ibid.*, 26; CCRO, TAR/3/47; TAV/1/7, 11, 17, 26. For the sixteenth century see TAR/1/13, 15.
[141] TWAS, 543/18, fo. 292v; 543/19, fos. 31v, 61r; TWAS, 543/19, fo. 190v. See also 543/16, fo. 140v; 543/33, 36; MF557; NCRO, EP13/68, pp. 21, 66.
[142] YCA, CC15, fo. 41v; CUMROC, Ca/4/1, /3. See also CUMROK, WSMB/K. In 1704 the Chester treasurer laid out 2s 6d 'for the hangman's frock': CCRO, TAB/2, fo. 10v.
[143] Knoop & Jones 1949, 69.

into place.[144] Occasionally more unusual perquisites are mentioned in the accounts. At Kendal in the 1650s 'all the men that wrought then at the dam' were given tobacco in addition to bread and drink, while at Hull in 1667 four labourers digging out the privy at the charity hall received 'one penny a day allowance in tobacco and strong water'.[145] At the end of the century some Chester carpenters were given 1s 8d in 'ale and tobacco' when engaged on an unspecified task.[146] Newcastle colliers received 'Christmas coal', and in October 1597 the accountants referred to 'the colliers, their Michaelmas geese this year', which suggests a regular perquisite.[147]

Workers were sometimes given extra cash payments or bonuses. Craftsmen often received a small sum as a 'Godspenny' to seal the bargain when they agreed to do a particular job: the churchwardens of St Mary's, Beverley, gave 4d to Robert Sceale in 1592 'for a Godspenny when we covenanted with him the amending of old Hird's house'.[148] Extra payments were also made to reward workers who had done particularly well. Such bonuses were paid to the chief carpenter at York Minster in the late fifteenth century, and a century later two York labourers were paid an extra 6d for their 'extraordinary pains'.[149] The nature of the extra effort was rarely specified, but at Newcastle in 1576 a workman was given an extra 2s 6d 'in reward for guttering and standing in water to his knees', while Christopher Walmesley, the chief mason at York, was given a bonus of £2 in 1567, because he had worked standing in water 'a good space'.[150] By far the most unusual bonuses were recorded by the accountants at Lincoln Cathedral. In 1634 the bill submitted by the plumber for the previous year amounted to £10 8s 9d for work and materials, but an extra £2 was paid 'by the direction of my Lord Bishop and Mr Chaunter to redeem him from prison'. Amazingly, a similar payment was made over fifty years later to Marmaduke Ryall, the chief carpenter at the cathedral from 1664 to 1696.[151]

The abiding impression derived from the northern accounts is that, apart from the provision of food and drink, perquisites were neither habitual nor commonplace. On the great majority of occasions that

---

[144] DFC, CC/190071, fo. 14r; *Newcastle Accts*, 69; Tyson 1979, 85, 87; Tyson 1980, 117; Tyson 1982, 154, 158; CUMROK, WSMB/K for 1669; CUMROC, Ca/4/3.
[145] CUMROK, WSMB/K; HCRO, BRF/3/20, pp. 272, 566.   [146] CCRO, TAB/1, fo. 98v.
[147] TWAS, 543/19, fo. 52v.
[148] HCORO, PE/1/51 for 1592. See also YBI, PR/Y/MS/1, fo. 181v, PR/Y/MS/2; HTH, III, fo. 396r; YCA, CC14, fo. 69v.
[149] YML, E3/25, 31–2; YCA, CC9, fo. 56v. See also TWAS, 543/19, fo. 5r; CCRO, TAB/1, fo. 98v.
[150] TWAS, 543/16, fo. 114v; *YCR*, VI, 128.   [151] LAO, Bj/1/6/2; Bj/1/9.

labour was hired the only payment recorded was that of the basic money wage, plus, on some occasions, a drink allowance. There is no doubt that some workers expected to take home waste materials, but such activity has left little more trace than the pilfering which may also have been widespread. In the absence of more firm evidence the case for the ubiquity of perquisites in the early-modern economy must be returned as non-proven. Of course, any historian is permitted to make an intelligent guess and my guess is that the level of perquisites given to early-modern workmen has been exaggerated. But it must be recognised that all parties are guessing: no more and no less. However, if perquisites were not everyday occurrences, the building workers and labourers of early-modern England may not have been as far removed from their ninteenth-century descendants as is often imagined.

The provision of food and drink

Whether or not independent workers were provided with food and drink by their customers is a question of central significance for our understanding of living standards in early-modern England. Many historians have argued that through such provision many workers were cushioned against the full impact of the rising prices which were such a characteristic feature of the sixteenth and early seventeenth centuries.[152] The 'tabling' of workers was always more likely to be a feature of country living, although W.G. Hoskins suggested that: 'Even in towns, wage rates were quoted "with meat and drink" and "without meat and drink". A considerable proportion of the labouring class *must have opted* for the meat and drink, though wives and children may consequently have gone short' (my italics).[153] Indeed, many local and national regulations, both before and after 1563, did lay down wage rates in both categories, but the mere provision of such rates on paper proves neither that they were paid nor that workers were presented with a choice by their customers.[154] It was not in the interests of many workers, even in the countryside, to eat at their customers' tables.

Reluctance to accept 'meat and drink' terms undoubtedly stemmed from the fact that these virtually halved the take-home pay of everyone, be he master or man. Such terms might have been acceptable to a self-indulgent single man but they offered a one-sided bargain to a workman with a family to support. While he feasted, his wife and children starved.[155]

[152] See the discussion in Woodward 1981, 29–30.   [153] Hoskins 1976, 224.
[154] Woodward 1981, 30.
[155] Smith 1989, 23.

The kind of problems which a married man could run into were neatly illustrated by Henry Best in the 1640s. He pointed out that:

Thatchers have (in most places) 6d a day and their meat in summer time ... yet we never give them above 4d a day and their meat in summer, because their diet is not as in other places, for they are to have three meals a day ... and at each meal four services, viz. butter, milk, cheese and either eggs, pies, or bacon and sometimes porridge instead of milk. If they meat themselves they have usually 10d a day.[156]

But workers were rarely fed by their customers in the northern towns. Many labourers and building craftsmen were given allowances of drink, and sometimes bread, but the provision of meals was reserved, almost without exception, for those who had to travel away from home for their work.

Knoop and Jones found little evidence of the regular 'tabling' of workmen:

Although most municipal wage regulations and statutes fixing wages in the Middle Ages laid down one rate of wages with meat and drink and another, and higher rate, without meat and drink, we have actually found very few cases of employers paying masons their wages partly in kind ... As a rule, on big building operations the masons appear to have been paid their whole wages in money, though occasionally ale and, very rarely, bread, may have been supplied as a kind of bonus or special allowance.

Thorold Rogers was in broad agreement.[157] Nevertheless, some workers were habitually fed by those who set them on work. Apprentices and an unknown proportion of journeymen lived with their masters and were fed by them, although it is impossible to say anything further on the subject. However, unless there was a significant change in the quality and quantity of the fare offered to apprentices and journeymen, the cost of feeding them must have consumed a higher proportion of the income derived from their labour during the period of rising prices.[158] That is, the residual value to the master of living-in apprentices and journeymen declined during much of the sixteenth and seventeenth centuries.

The northern accounts provide a very large number of examples of the provision of drink to workmen, and, more occasionally, food. Early-modern society was awash with alcoholic drink, partly because it made very good sense to avoid drinking water, especially in the towns. At one extreme, a few workers were paid entirely in kind, usually for

---

[156] *Henry Best*, 144.
[157] Knoop & Jones 1949, 114; Rogers 1882–7, V, 637–8. For similar comments about the situation on the continent see Goldthwaite 1980, 291–6.
[158] For a similar comment see Sonenscher 1989, 194.

small one-off tasks. At Kendal 8d 'in beer' was given 'to eight men for drawing a plank to the bridge' in 1653, and at Newcastle in 1574 half a barrel of beer was given by the mayor 'to those that were helping the ship that was sunk'.[159] Few workers were paid entirely in kind, but many did receive some drink at work and the subject will be discussed in three categories. First, treats were provided to mark important staging-posts in a particular job. Secondly, some workers, but by no means all, were given an allowance of drink and sometimes bread: such payments took the form of a wage supplement. Thirdly, small numbers of men were fed by their customers, chiefly when they were obliged to work away from home and could not rely on the support of their wives and families.

Treating

Treats were scattered throughout the life of a building project and were expected by the workmen. Sometimes they began before the job had even started. The churchwardens of Holy Trinity, Goodramgate, York, devised a fine explanation for their expenditure of 12d in 1633: 'Laid out at several meetings to know what work we should do in the church before we could set any on work.'[160] Further expense could be incurred when workmen arrived to 'view' or weigh-up a particular job and deliver their expert opinion: at Kendal in 1664 6d was paid 'for drink for the workmen when they first met to consider how the mills might be mended'.[161] A few workmen were given drink as a 'Godspenny' to seal the bargain when they were hired.[162] Further treats could follow at various crucial phases of the work. The raising of a timber-framed structure was one much-favoured occasion for drinking, and sometimes the fare was substantial. Large amounts of ale and beer, and bread, were given on various occasions to the labourers who helped to carry timber and raise the new Trinity House at Hull in the late fifteenth century: these basics cost 9s 7d, and they were supplemented by some 'fresh fish', 'fresh flesh', 'fresh herring', and cheese which cost 1s 10d in total.[163] The most exotic account of such festivities relates to the construction of a new barn at Rydal in 1670:

---

[159] CUMROK, WSMB/K; TWAS, 543/16, fo. 106r. See also HCRO, BRF/3/5; CCORO, P/20/13/1; Laughton 1987–8, 123; CCRO, TAR/3/58A; CUMROC, Ca/4/3.
[160] YBI, PR/Y/HTG/12.
[161] CUMROK, WSMB/K. See also CCORO, P/20/13/1; YML, E2/22; HCRO, BRF/3/20, p. 129; TWAS, 543/15, fo. 242r; YBI, PR/Y/HTM/17 for 1690.
[162] YBI, PR/Y/HTG/12, /13; PR/Y/HTM/17; HCORO, PE/121/37.
[163] *Hull Trinity House Building*, 157; Airs 1975, 111. See also YML, E3/54; Wigfull 1929, 67, 70; TWAS, 543/18, fo. 109v.

This day was raised the corn barn at Rydal, they began about nine in the morning, at twelve all the bearers had a dinner, about five in the afternoon they had a great cheese cake, 4s in ale (besides that which was sent and two pails full of our own) and five pounds of tobacco (viz. I gave one pound to the wrights, one pound to the wallers and two pounds to the other bearers and my wife gave one pound amongst the women) which comes to 4s 2d, in all 8s 2d.[164]

Any extraordinary effort could induce a liquid response. At Carlisle in 1684, 4s 6d was spent 'for drink and bread and cheese at bringing on the upper millstone, there being a great many men', and a similar treat was provided two years later when pipes and tobacco were added for a total outlay of 12s 6d.[165] Elsewhere, drink was occasionally provided to compensate workers for toiling in unpleasant conditions. Men labouring at the Kendal mill-dam got extra drink in the late sixteenth and seventeenth centuries, and some Chester masons received 2s 'for ale, being working in the water' in 1709.[166] Hull labourers were sometimes given extra drink when cleaning out the sewers or cesspits, 'because of the noisesomeness of the smells', and the twenty men who formed a pit-rescue team at Newcastle in October 1592 were paid 10s for their efforts, and a further 5s 2d was spent 'for bread, drink and candle to the men which sought the three men that was wanting in the common pit'.[167] Treats were also provided on occasion either to encourage workmen or to reward them for some sterling effort. At Newcastle 4s 4d was paid in 1592 'for bread and drink to the wrights and armourer for making better haste of their work', and some Hull men were rewarded in 1675 with 3s 'to drink working all the day, not ceasing til they had done'.[168] Treats were sometimes provided when a project came to an end. On 16 September 1515, when the weathercock was set upon the new spire at Louth, the priests sang a *te deum*, the churchwardens ordered the bells to be rung, and 'caused all the people there being to have bread and ale. And all to the loving of God, Our Lady and All Saints.'[169] But usually the final treat was a more restrained affair, restricted to the workmen and, perhaps, a few officials.[170]

In May 1634 the accountant of Newcastle Trinity House added the

---

[164] Tyson 1980, 116. For similar feasts see Tyson 1982a, 154, 158.
[165] CUMROC, Ca/4/3. See also CUMROK, WSMB/K for 1595; TWAS, 543/18, fo. 117v; LAO, Bj/1/7.
[166] CUMROK, WSMB/K; CCRO, TAV/1/6. See also at York in 1599: YCA, CC10, fo. 77r.
[167] HCRO, BRF/3/20, p. 365; TWAS, 543/18, fo. 115v.
[168] TWAS, 543/18, fo. 233r; HCRO, BRF/3/20, p. 846. See also CUMROK, WSMB/K for 1632; CCORO, P/20/13/1 for the early 1660s; TWAS, 543/19, fo. 39v.
[169] *Louth Accts*, 181.
[170] CUMROK, WSMB/K; LAO, L1/5/12, fo. 59r; Bj/1/13; TWAS, 543/18.

note, 'spent with the workmen when we paid them their wages at several times'.[171] This unique reference suggests that other small, unexplained payments for drink, which are scattered through the accounts, were made when workmen received their wages. This was probably the case at Chester during 1711 and 1712. A small gang of between three and five men, working on the city walls, was paid 1s a week 'for ale'. In the early eighteenth century a shilling would buy a gallon of ale, or slightly less, which suggests that the workmen were being given a weekly treat, perhaps on payday.[172]

Treats were intermittent and erratic in their incidence. They were provided on some jobs, but not at all on others, and they cannot be regarded as a regular part of any workman's remuneration. At times they seem to have been given simply because the mayor or some other official turned up to monitor the work and ordered some liquid refreshment: at Hull in 1653, 1s 6d was 'given by the mayor's order to the labourers to drink when he and some of the aldermen went to view the work and gave order for making the cross bank at Hessle Gate'.[173] At other times treats seemed to drop from heaven, like manna, unexplained, but welcome nevertheless: in 1494 a penny was laid out at Beverley 'in bread and ale to said workmen as a gift'.[174] Treats could never be relied on and many workers probably went weeks or months without receiving such a windfall, but they probably helped to maintain a degree of optimism among hard-pressed workmen.

Food and drink as a wage supplement
An immense amount of information is available relating to the provision of modest amounts of food and drink at the workplace, or the substitution of a monetary allowance, but reality was extremely complex.[175] However, in most cases where a daily allowance or 'lowance' was made for beer or ale, and sometimes for bread also, the amount of sustenance provided was insufficient to provide workers with their total dietary needs for the day.[176] Indeed, such allowances fell short of the comprehensive provision intended by those who framed the national wage regulations, or by the JPs who drew up the post-1563

171 TWAS, 659/447.
172 CCRO, MUV/1/23, 30, 41, 54. For the price of ale and beer see appendix 3.
173 HCRO, BRF/3/20, p. 25, see also pp. 26, 109 and CUMROC, Ca/4/3.
174 HCORO, BC/II/6/15.
175 What follows is somewhat different from the analysis in Woodward 1981, 30, where the impression is given that food and drink was very rarely given to workers. Certainly the provision of a full diet was unusual, so the criticism of Hoskins stands in that respect, but the provision of some drink and, more occasionally bread, was fairly common.
176 For a discussion of the cost of living see below pp. 215–22.

wage assessments. In the seventeenth century, when allowances were specified, they usually amounted to a penny or two on top of the basic wage. But in many cases, building-site workers were simply given a single cash payment for each day's work. However, it could be argued that in such instances a drink allowance had been built silently into the wage. This can be seen clearly at Kendal in 1657. John Ward, a carpenter, was sometimes given a specific allowance, but sometimes not, although the total daily payment was always the same: he was paid either 16d a day, or 14d plus a 2d-a-day allowance for beer. This suggests that drink was not actually being given to the workman.[177] Thus it is possible that in those accounts which rarely specified allowances the wage offered was a composite one which incorporated a small payment in lieu of drink. However, the Hull case indicates that this was not always so. In the middle of the seventeenth century the council began to give the bricklayers and their labourers an allowance of a penny a day on top of their basic cash wages. This gave the bricklayers a penny more than the carpenters, and the labourers a penny more than they got when not working alongside the bricklayers.[178] Only towards the end of the seventeenth century did the carpenters receive the allowance: on occasion they got tuppence, although in most cases it was simply built into the basic payment of 24d a day.[179] What seems to have happened at Hull is that the council began to give an allowance to the bricklayers, for some unspecified reason, from around the middle of the seventeenth century: at a later date it was offered to other craftsmen, including the carpenters. However, on many occasions the allowance was simply built into the wage.

There are also some signs that allowances became more common at York during the seventeenth century, although the accounts are more fragmentary than those for Hull.[180] The churchwardens' accounts for St Michael's, Spurriergate, which survive from 1518, only occasionally recorded payments for food and drink. Other churches provided occasional treats in the sixteenth century, and the city council gave both treats and occasional allowances, but policy was not consistent. The Minster accounts from the late fifteenth century record some treats, but little in the way of regular allowances.[181] It is possible that workmen expected to be given drink at work, or receive a cash equivalent, and that such provision was commonly given in the

---

[177] CUMROK, WSMB/K.   [178] HCRO, BRF/3/20.   [179] HCRO, BRF/3/21.
[180] YBI, PR/Y/ASN/10; /HTG/12–13; /MCS/16–18; /MG/19–20; /MS/1–2, 5.
[181] YBI,PR/Y/MS/1,fos.165r,173r;PR/Y/HTG/12;/MCS/16;/MG/19;YCA,CC5–10;YML, E3/24–65.

private sector. In 1597 William Woodward, a carpenter, submitted a bill to the council for materials and his own labour and for some work he had subcontracted: he claimed 12d a day for the craftsmen and 10d for their men, adding 'they demand this for that they had nothing to drink'.[182] This suggests that the workmen were accustomed to receiving a lower basic cash wage topped up by a drink allowance, and that the wages claimed on that occasion were recognised as composite rates with an inbuilt drink allowance. Perhaps private customers plied workmen with drink on a regular basis, although large institutional employers probably avoided the logistical difficulties of supplying drink to workmen by building the drink allowance into the basic wage.

What the accounts of York and other places make clear is that allowances were not always consistent: often they varied from one worker to another, and from year to year. It is unusual to get any indication of the forces which helped to determine the level of allowances, although a remarkable series of entries in the churchwardens' accounts for St Martin's, Coneygate, York, provide some telling insights. On a number of occasions in the late sixteenth and early seventeenth centuries the auditors were highly critical of the accounts. In 1601 they struck a despairing note: 'Also we find in divers places in the account that they [the churchwardens] ask allowance for ale and other charges unreasonably, and yet we passed them, hoping they will the next year be better husbands for profit of the parish.' They were not, and in 1602 the auditors reported that they had found, 'very unreasonable allowance of bread and ale, whereof warning was given, and yet no amendment, but rather worse'.[183] In 1675 the churchwardens of St Martin cum Gregory recovered 3s 6d which 'by an oversight in the workmen's note paid them more in their drinking than they ought'.[184] It is possible that in all these instances the churchwardens had been lining their own pockets by recording excessive allowances for the workmen.

The situation in other northern towns was no less varied. At Carlisle the chamberlains varied their practice from year to year in the seventeenth century, although the fine set of workmen's vouchers for the first half of the eighteenth century indicate that any allowances were normally built into the wage by that date: of the eighty-four bills submitted only three mentioned drink, including one case where the

---

[182] YCA, CC9, fo. 63a.
[183] YBI, PR/Y/MCS/17, fo. 47r. In 1589 they had been critical of the treat given to workers at the rehanging of the bells. A marginal note reads 'no beef is to be allowed': *ibid.*, fo. 14r. Similar complaints were made on other occasions: *ibid.*, fos. 49r, 115v.
[184] YBI, PR/Y/MG/20.

mayor had treated the men to ale which cost a shilling.[185] Similarly, the paymasters in late-sixteenth-century Kendal rarely specified allowances, although such payments began to creep in from the early seventeenth century.[186] In late-sixteenth-century Beverley the council gave few allowances, although the churchwardens of St Mary's did so from time to time, and continued the practice in the seventeenth century.[187] On the estates of the Bishop of Durham in the late fifteenth and sixteenth centuries most workmen were paid in cash: the Dean and Chapter of the cathedral did the same.[188] The Dean and Chapter at Lincoln did likewise, although the town's churchwardens adopted various strategies: in the seventeenth century allowances were often specified at St Michael's in the Mount, as they were at St Martin's, but very rarely at St Benedict's. This meant that at times the total pay received by the same class of labour could vary by a penny or two, although on occasion wage packets were the same, presumably because a notional drink allowance had been built into the cash wage.[189] At Newcastle the council accounts for the sixteenth century rarely noted extra allowances for drink, although it is possible that they began to be paid in the following century: by the 1620s Newcastle Trinity House was giving regular drink allowances, usually of 2d a day, and it is possible that the town council followed suit.[190] At Chester in the seventeenth century the city officials sometimes recorded drink allowances, but sometimes not.[191] The impression given by the 'selected vouchers' of the eighteenth century is that drink allowances were commonly specified, although they were by no means invariable. Thus, a bill for 1740 refers to 'drink as the carpenters had when repairing the bridge gate £6 19s'.[192] Unfortunately, because the vouchers were 'selected' by an earlier generation of archivists it is not possible to estimate the number of man-days for which the allowance was paid, nor is it known whether the impression given by the surviving vouchers fairly represents the whole body of material which originally existed.

The picture presented by the northern accounts is both highly complex and somewhat confusing. Individual institutions did not always follow consistent policies and it must be suspected that the

185 CUMROC, Ca/4/3; Ca/4/vouchers.   186 CUMROK, WSMB/K.
187 HCORO, BC/II/31–42; PE/1/51–95.
188 See the large number of accounts in the Miscellaneous Charter collection at DFC.
189 LAO, Bj/1/6–8; St Michael on the Mount, L1/7/1–2; St Martin, L1/5/12; St Benedict, L1/7/1–4.
190 This is not certain since the accounts went into summary form in the early seventeenth century.
191 CCRO, TAB/1; TAR/2/23–41; TAR/3/42–56.   192 CCRO, TAV/1/30.

particular path followed had much to do with the individuals chosen to supervise the accounts in a particular year. The larger institutions were reluctant to provide drink for their workmen throughout the period, a policy which made a great deal of sense, especially when large numbers of workers were involved. Cash allowances probably became more common in the seventeenth century than earlier. It is possible that they were being demanded more insistently by labour and were being used as a lever to raise the overall level of pay. Evidence from churchwardens' accounts suggests that the smaller institutions were more prepared to provide drink for workmen, and the limited amount of information relating to the private sector would suggest likewise.[193] It seems likely that early-modern workmen expected to be offered some refreshment by their customers, but that they often had to be satisfied with a cash equivalent or, in some cases, with nothing at all. 'Drink', whether in the form of liquid refreshment, a specific cash allowance, or a swollen basic wage was common in the north. However, whichever form it took it was usually a relatively small part of the daily reward, generally amounting to about 10 per cent of the money wage, sometimes more but often less.

Occasionally the accounts provide some insights into the way drink was provided for workmen. The thirst of some Kendal haymakers in 1632 is almost tangible: 3d was paid to William Wilkinson's wife 'for drink which they sent for that day'.[194] There are other references to women, and occasionally men, supplying drink to workmen, although in most cases the supplier was not named. A number of women supplied drink at All Saints', North Street, York, in the later seventeenth and early eighteenth centuries: they included Mary Conn, the widow of George Conn, a bricklayer and former churchwarden and house-tenant of the church.[195] In 1637 Newcastle Trinity House cut out the middle-woman by spending 4s 6d on 'half a barrel of beer for the workmen's drinks', and the Chester treasurers paid £1 8s in 1730 'for drink delivered to the workmen at the charity school'.[196] Alternatively, at Carlisle in 1742 payment was made for 'ale drunk at Robert Knaggs for the workmen'.[197] Such references are unusual and we rarely know whether the drink was delivered to the workmen or vice versa. Similarly, we rarely know the time of day when drinks were taken. However, at Kendal in 1635, 1s 4d was 'paid in drink to the workmen

[193] *Hull Trinity House Building*; Laughton, 1987–8, 113; Wigfull 1929, 69–73.
[194] CUMROK, WSMB/K.
[195] YBI, PR/Y/ASN/10. For other accounts of women supplying drink see YBI, PR/Y/MS/2; LAO, L1/5/12, fo. 59v; HCORO, PE/1/55.
[196] TWAS, 659/447; CCRO, TAV/1/22.   [197] CUMROC, Ca/4/1742.

forenoon and afternoon'.[198] At Chester in 1695 the city paver and his gang were paid 2s 'to morning draughts', and in the 1740s 'morning drinks' or 'morning draughts' at around a penny a head were mentioned on five occasions.[199] These references suggest that, as in London, the allowances paid to workmen were to provide them with a modest breakfast.[200] However, depending on the nature of the drink, an allowance of one or two pence could have provided the lubricants for more than one session. At Hull in 1731 the inbuilt allowance of 2d given to many craftsmen could have bought a gallon of small beer, but less than two pints of ale.[201]

Some York evidence suggests that a drink allowance was sometimes paid to induce workmen to stay at work for the whole day. In 1526 the churchwardens of St Michael's, Spurriergate, gave 4d 'for ale to the workmen because they should not go home at noon'. Similar payments were made on various occasions during the next few decades, and in 1547 two tilers and their men were given 5½d in drink 'at divers times because went not at noon to their dinners'.[202] Clearly, there were occasions when customers would not want workmen to be absent for an hour or two in the middle of the day: this was the case at Hull in 1673 when the carpenters and labourers were given a shilling 'to drink when they took up the great timber, not coming home to dinner'.[203] Similarly, it is possible that the small allowance given to the Hull bricklayers and labourers from the mid seventeenth century was to induce them to remain at work and not go home. It was probably important to restrain bricklayers from wandering home, since mortar deteriorates if not worked regularly and a heavy shower could wreak havoc with newly laid bricks. However, it is also possible that the extra allowance was to compensate the bricklayers for working in dusty conditions. This is suggested by the penny-a-day allowance given to two labourers in 1679 when they were slaking lime.[204]

This discussion of the provision of drink at work does scant justice to the complexity of the issue. Alcoholic beverages played an important part in the lives of most early-modern people, and it seems likely that all but a handful of workers drank beer or ale at work. It was procured in many different ways. Some customers provided it from their own resources or bought it in for the occasion; others sent the workmen out

[198] CUMROK, WSMB/K.
[199] CCRO, MUV/3/89, 91, 96, 104; TAB/1, fo. 92r; TAV/1/32.
[200] Boulton 1987b, 10–11. [201] See appendix 3.
[202] YBI, PR/Y/MS/1, fos. 55r, 144r, 147r, 164r, 173v, 215r.
[203] HCRO,BRF/3/20, p. 769; see also p. 207. For the length of the working day see above pp. 123–7.
[204] HCRO, BRF/3/20, p. 961.

to a nearby alehouse; but many merely provided a wage supplement. Some made no provision at all.

The 'tabling' of workmen

Some urban labourers and craftsmen were fed by their customers. But it was not in the interest of most workers to receive about half of their pay in kind, nor was it necessarily to the benefit of the customer. When Rose Castle Chapel, near Carlisle, was being rebuilt in 1675 the accountant recorded that: 'if any ... could have had tabling elsewhere, the Bishop would not have had any of them in his house at table, but corn being so very dear ... did force [him] ... either to table them in his own house or let the building cease'.[205] The need to table workers was greater in the countryside,[206] especially where skilled men had to be brought some distance, and also in the smaller towns where there were fewer specialists than in larger places. At the building of Louth steeple in the early sixteenth century, glaziers were hired at 4d and 5d a day, plus an extra 2d for their board, and the master mason 'made a bargain' for the board of himself and his apprentice.[207] Board wages were paid for some workers at Sheffield when a new house was being erected in 1575/6, and a skilled Nantwich joiner and his men were given three meals a day at 2d a meal when they set up some prefabricated wainscot at Chester in 1613. This was exceptional: 'diet was not considered a normal element in the wage packet of Cestrian craftsmen'.[208] The cost of providing a full diet for workmen varied. A boatbuilder and his man were tabled by the Dean and Chapter of Durham for 4s a week in 1571, or 3d a day assuming a six-day week, but two mill-wrights were tabled at 8d a day each at Kendal in 1594.[209] However, when a mill-wright and his man worked at Whitehaven in 1649 he was paid £2 4s 8d 'for his diet and his man's 23 days at 2s a day except Sundays at 16d'.[210] This exceptional entry recognised the fact that manual workers need a higher calorific intake on working days. A century later, Hugh Tyson, a Lakeland joiner, charged 10d a day when fed by his customers, but the extraordinary sum of 3s a day 'without meat':[211] few customers could have afforded to let him fend for himself, although perhaps he was a legendary trencherman.

[205] Tyson 1983b, 69.
[206] Airs 1975, 166–7; *Hornby Castle Accts*, 104, 110; *Tattershall Castle Accts*, 43; *Henry Best*, xlviii–ix.
[207] *Louth Accts*, 67, 128, 198.
[208] Wigfull 1929, 67–8; Laughton 1987–8, 112–13. Meals were not regularly offered at Hull in the late fifteenth century: *Hull Trinity House Building*, passim.
[209] DPK, MC/3049; CUMROK, WSMB/K.   [210] Tyson 1988, 184.
[211] Moorman 1950, 159.

Relatively few of the accounts mention the cost of lodging, although when Hugh Tyson stayed away from home he charged extra: 'lay down at Thomas Hodgson's 3d'. In those cases where lodging was not stipulated perhaps the cost of board also covered the cost of a bed for the night, although workmen may often have been accommodated at the work place. When Kendal mill was repaired in the years around 1600 the absence of any reference to lodging suggests that the workmen may have slept in the mill, or in one of the out-buildings.[212] Certainly that was the case on an East Yorkshire farm. When harvest workers were hired from a distance, 'they usually make three beds ready for them in the folks' chamber', but 'if there be any more, they make the rest in the barn, kiln, or some other convenient house for that purpose'.[213]

Some of the most interesting entries relating to the feeding of workmen come from the Kendal mill accounts. During October 1582, 'George the milnwright' received 39s 'in full for all their wages', plus 20s 'more coming and going to Kendal and fro', 5s 'drinking money for him', and the same for his man. William Judson's wife received 11s 'for the rest of the milnwright table in full', and 5s was paid 'for carriage of wright tools to Wakefield'.[214] Major repairs were not needed every year, but there was a great deal of activity during the 1590s when the wife of James Airey, himself a town official, provided many of the meals for the mill-wrights and their men. Other women provided a similar service on occasion. The cost of meals varied – from about $4\frac{1}{2}$d to 8d a day during the 1590s – although the most common charges were 5d or 6d. The practice of tabling the mill-wrights continued in the first two decades of the seventeenth century. In 1619 George Fell took over as chief mill-wright. He and his gang were fed by William Baxter's wife: in the spring of 1620, when he and his three men worked for three days, 8s was laid out 'for their table and drinks'. Fell next appeared in the accounts in January 1622 when 4d was spent 'for going to Windermere for milnwright'. The gang duly arrived and worked for ten days dressing and setting the mill stones, and a Mrs Alderis was paid 18s 8d for their table. George Fell probably moved to Kendal some time after 1622 and continued to work for the council until 1640. He was usually paid 12d a day, although he sometimes got 10d in winter, and from time to time he received a small drink allowance. But he was not tabled after 1622. Clearly the burgesses of

212 CUMROK, WSMB/K.
213 *Henry Best*, 50. See also p. 121 for a discussion of their bedding. See also Airs 1975, 164–6.
214 CUMROK, WSMB/K.

Kendal had to pay less for the upkeep of their mill once they had a skilled man in their midst. Only when he went out of town to buy new mill stones was he given a subsistence allowance. In the late autumn of 1635 he went 'three several times to Kellet [in Lancashire] ... to see the mill stones', and was reimbursed for the cost of his horse feed and for his own diet 'at Dragon' where a supper cost 4d.

Subsistence allowances were sometimes given when townsmen were sent to work away from home. At Newcastle in 1510 20d was paid 'for half a barrel of beer and bread and fish' for the carpenters working in a wood outside the town, and four men sent from Durham to repair Hett Mill, some four miles south of the town, received 'board wages' of 4d a day in 1552 on top of their basic wages of 4d or 5d.[215] Provision for those working away from home was made most frequently by Hull Trinity House. In the second half of the sixteenth century the institution became responsible for placing and repairing buoys and beacons to aid navigation along the Humber. Workmen were recruited, boats hired, and sufficient food and drink put on board for the journey downstream. When the first beacon was installed in 1568 food was not mentioned, although a kilderkin of beer was provided. But in 1572 a female caterer provided 'victuals to the men that set the beacon' for 8s. In 1599 details of the provisions were given for the first time: the boat was stocked with two quarters of pork, three cakes of butter, two cheeses, some veal which cost 2s 2d, a barrel of beef, and some bread. In 1606, probably during Lent, a floating feast of beer, oysters, two couple of fish, 'mustard seed to the fish', three dozen of bread, and four cakes, and a pot of butter were sent down the Humber. Even better was to come. In 1615 the aquatic picnic comprised fish, 9lb. of 'Holland cheese', oysters, four quarts of sack, together with some bread and butter, vinegar, and half a kilderkin of beer. The men who braved the river in the winter of 1646/7 were treated to two and a half stones of beef and a quarter of mutton. Some tobacco and sack were also provided.[216] The provision of such fine fare was, no doubt, partly a reflection of the growing wealth and importance of the institution, but it was also due to the fact that brethren of the gild usually supervised the work: the ordinary workmen benefited from the desire to provide an appropriate diet for their betters.

215 *Newcastle Accts*, 139; DPK, MC3006; 3008/1, 6–7: YML, E3/52. See also DPK, MC3009/1; 3010/2; 3056/7; 3092/1; LB25–6: DFC, CC/190094–7; 190100, fos. 2v, 5r: HCRO, BRF/3/20, pp. 708, 742, 750–1.
216 HTH, II, fos. 81r, 93r, 99v, 185r and v, 210r, 230r, 235r; III, fos. 6v, 15r and v, 16r, 64r, 151v; IV; V.

Welfare provision

The earnings of early-modern workmen were affected not only by the erratic demand for their labour, but also by the high incidence of ill-health, injury, and early death. In the fifteenth century, when earnings were relatively high, 'they ceased immediately if the worker was injured, ill, or old',[217] and the same was true throughout the early-modern period. No doubt many workers could expect support from their wider families in times of trouble, together with some assistance from casual charity and, as the period progressed, increasing support from the poor law.[218] Craftsmen might also expect to receive some help from their gilds or from those who had set them on work. The Kendal and Newcastle accounts reveal a number of instances in which the councils relieved needy workmen. At Kendal in 1591/2 a woman was paid a shilling, 'for healing Hew's head', while in 1596/7 two suppers were given to 'old Lyndaye ... when he came to put one of the workmen's arms into joint'. On neither occasion was there any mention of compensation to the worker. After this brief flurry of philanthropy the Kendal accounts fall silent on the issue.[219] During the early decades of Elizabeth's reign the Newcastle chamberlains occasionally made payments to needy workmen: in 1562 a collier 'that was hurt in the pit' received 3s 4d; in 1567 a street cleaner got a shilling 'for Godsake being sick', and a surgeon was given 5s 'for healing of certain labourers hurt in the town's work'; in 1576 a labourer was given 2s 'in recompense of his hurt that he took the last week at the quarry in the town's work', and a slater got 10d 'in relief' at the end of the year.[220] Pastoral support reached its peak in the last decade of the century. Four carpenters, who were felling timber at various times, and a labourer were recompensed for their injuries with average sums of just over 2s apiece, including the carpenter and a 'poor labourer' who each got a shilling for their broken arms, amounts equivalent to a day and a half and two days' pay respectively. But when 4s was paid in 1591 'for healing of a wright's leg that was hurt in Gateshead Park felling of the town's timber' he seems to have received nothing. Between 1591 and 1593 seven colliers were 'hurt in the common pit' or had 'hurt a leg', and five of them were each given a shilling: the other two got 8d and 2s. Finally, seven men associated with the building trades were given financial aid during bouts of sickness: payments varied from 6d to 2s 6d, and included two payments of 12d given to

---

[217] C. Dyer 1989, 233.   [218] On the effectiveness of the Poor Law see Slack 1988.
[219] CUMROK, WSMB/K.
[220] TWAS, 543/14, fos. 131v, 133r; 543/15, fos. 274r, 277r; 543/16, fos. 114v, 115r and v.

Robert Ruderforth, a paver, who was 'lying sick' in December 1593. The affliction proved terminal and the council paid 3s 4d towards his burial the following February.[221] The council also awarded an unusual pension to William Benson, the town's paver. In August 1594 he was referred to as 'William Benson paver [as] was [who] is fallen blind', but he continued to receive his quarterly retainer of 20s until February 1600, when, presumably, he died.[222] After 1600 the chamberlains stopped recording such pastoral payments, except in the summer of 1608 when 3s 4d was paid in three instalments 'to Elizabeth Hall in reward, widow, her husband being slain in the town's work'.[223]

In failing to make more frequent provision for sick and injured workmen the Newcastle chamberlains were not alone. However, it is possible that these accounts are not the correct place to look for such payments. This is indicated by the printed minutes of the York council which occasionally mention pastoral payments to workers. In 1578 it was agreed that a porter 'who was lately hurt by chance in the fore part of his head shall have 10s towards his surgery', and ten years later Peter Wilkinson, a carpenter, 'who at this present is lunatic' was to have 8d a week during his illness.[224] But even the York minutes say little about such support. Injuries, fatal or otherwise, have always come easily in the building trades, and they were commonplace in early-modern England. At Durham in January 1542, 22d was spent 'watching of one man that was slain in the quarry with 8d given for fetching the coroner'.[225] The career of one of the Chester joiners was terminated abruptly in 1672 when he fell to his death from a high 'periel' in St Oswald's.[226] However, the shortage of references to death and injury suggests that most workers and their dependants could expect little financial assistance from their customers. After all, their relationship existed so that one party could perform a specified task for the other party: serious injury or death made that impossible and effectively cancelled the agreement.

It has been suggested that the gilds played a useful role by distributing charity and minimising the potential burden on other sources of relief.[227] This was true in the case of the richer gilds like the Hull Trinity House which ran its own *maison dieu* for needy and

---

221 TWAS, 543/18, fos. 67r–297v. The council paid 3s for the burial of a glazier/painter in 1596: *ibid.*, fo. 289r.
222 TWAS, 543/18, fos. 98v–175r. For references to Benson's contract see above p. 37.
223 TWAS, 543/21.
224 *YCR*, VII, 171; IX, 23–4. See above p. 98 for the wench who hurt her finger.
225 DFC, CC/190071, fo. 22r. See also *Louth Accts*, 203; *Two Yorkshire Diaries*, 126.
226 CCORO, P/20/13/1; Laughton 1987–8, 113.
227 Walker 1981, 6–7.

ancient mariners and their wives or widows, and supported large numbers of out-pensioners. As customers they also compensated a few workmen when they were injured, including 'a labourer the which happened to be hurt at the raising of the Trinity House' who was given 5d.[228] But many gilds, and especially the relatively impecunious building-trade gilds, had slender resources, and what money they managed to accumulate was spent mainly on giving the active members a good time and protecting their trade interests. The records of the northern building-craft gilds provide very few examples of financial aid being given to members or their dependants. Such direct financial support was extremely marginal for most members and there were hardly any such institutions to relieve common labourers.

Labour mobility

The extent to which labourers and building craftsmen moved from place to place in search of work is uncertain since only on rare occasions do the accounts indicate their place of domicile. Nevertheless, there are enough scattered references to men working away from home to make it plain that the practice was fairly common. Medieval masons were necessarily mobile, moving from job to job across the country, and the builders of early-modern country houses were similarly peripatetic.[229] In the smaller towns there were often insufficient specialists to deal with all situations. Many of the masons employed at the building of Louth steeple in the early sixteenth century were outsiders. The bells were made in Nottingham and the clappers were made and repaired by smiths in Boston and Hull.[230] Even in the larger towns, with their more sophisticated occupational structures, outsiders were frequently brought in, especially when more specialist skills were needed. Masons in particular continued to be highly mobile.[231] Other types of craftsmen were recruited from outside as required: a Grimsby man 'came to this city [York] to view the spring for making of a conduit in this city' in 1599; 20d was spent at Newcastle in 1593 'for seeking a man in Yorkshire for the mending of the common bell in St Nicholas's church'; a year later the chamberlains there laid out 20s to a man 'in part of his charges at London for the providing of a

228 *Hull Trinity House Building*, 158. See also HTH, II, fo. 58r; V.
229 Knoop & Jones 1949, 142–4; Airs 1975, 42, 62, 64, 134–41; *Naworth Accts*, 33; *Levens Letters*, 173–6. For a discussion of the situation on the continent see Small 1989, 339–40.
230 *Louth Accts*, 20, 79, 92, 102, 128, 179. See also Lloyd 1961, 11; A. Dyer 1973, 148.
231 Salzman 1952, 46; YBI, PR/Y/MB/34; Colvin 1982, 474; DFC, CC/190069, fo. 6r; LAO, Dviii/3/8/41; TWAS, 543/15, fos. 257v, 264r; Howell 1967, 296–7.

carpenter for mending the bridge'; a Lancaster clockmaker was hired at Kendal in 1608; and a London paver was at work in Hull in the summer of 1659.[232]

In East Yorkshire there was an exchange of workmen between Hull and Beverley. On at least three occasions in the late fifteenth century Beverley plumbers were employed on the leads of the new Trinity House at Hull. Two Beverley bricklayers worked on the Hull defences in 1571, and in 1655 a Beverley smith supplied nails to the council on a number of occasions. Moving in the opposite direction, the church-wardens of St Mary's, Beverley, paid 3s 2d to a Hull man in 1646/7 'for his direction for mending the chimes'.[233] These few references suggest that the interchange of labour between the two towns was a common feature of life in the area. Certainly many goods destined for Beverley and beyond arrived in the port of Hull. The 'great fair' held at Beverley in May was supplied by London merchants, and the York grocers arrived 'to furnish themselves with such commodities as they want'.[234] In July 1637, when the plague began to rage in Hull, the Beverley council ordered that contact between the two towns should cease: contagion was feared 'by reason of the commerce between the inhabitants of Beverley and the inhabitants of the said town of Hull'.[235] Workmen were also drawn to Hull from elsewhere in the region. They included: Robert Paget, the chief carpenter at the new Trinity House; the appropriately named William Playsterer of Gainsborough, who both supplied plaster and applied it to the walls of the same building; a glazier who was given 2d 'for his ferry over Humber'; and a number of Cottingham wheelwrights.[236] Conversely, the influence of some of the town's workmen spread further afield: some bricklayers had building contracts in the surrounding countryside.[237]

There was a similar two-way traffic of skilled men at York. During 1577 the council agreed to establish two mills at St Anthony's Hospital for setting 'roguish and idle persons on work', and a Beverley carpenter called Edward Porter, 'who seemeth to be skilful in making of the said mills', was engaged to do the job. Thirty years later, a Hull man was given 5s 'for his pains in searching the foundation of the staithe'.

---

232 YCA, CC10, fo. 64a; TWAS, 543/18, fo. 60v, 543/18 fo. 78v; CUMROK, WSMB/K; HCRO, BRF/3/20, p. 241. For more examples of workers from outside see Tyson 1984, 77–8, 80–4.

233 HTH, I, fos. 47r, 107v; *Hull Trinity House Building*, 166; HCRO, BRF/3/3; BRF/3/20, pp. 104–5; HCORO, PE/1/55.

234 *Henry Best*, 118.   235 *VCH Hull*, 155–6; HCORO, BC/II/7/4, fo. 65r.

236 *Hull Trinity House Building*, 156, 164; HTH, II, fo. 21v; HCRO, BRF/3/3, 5, 14. In 1622 two 'Western workmen' did a substantial amount of piling on the river bank: HCRO, BRF/3/10.

237 *VCH Hull*, 150.

But incomers were not always so welcome. William Jackson, his wife, and children were included in a list of labourers thrown out of the city in 1577: they were 'to go to Hull immediately from which they came'.[238] York craftsmen were also employed in the surrounding countryside. The services of the highly regarded glaziers were in great demand in the north from an early date, and the city's carpenters and bricklayers also found country work.[239] At Durham the position is even clearer since, in the early part of the period, the bishopric estate included large numbers of country properties which needed frequent attention, and a steady stream of craftsmen flowed out of the town to Bishop Auckland, Chester le Street, Darlington, Gateshead, Stockton, and elsewhere.[240]

The frequent use of the same workmen year after year by the councils and other institutions of northern England indicates that the majority of urban labourers and building craftsmen did most of their work in their home towns, although there was also a substantial movement of workers between towns, and between town and country; this was especially true of the journeymen joiners at Chester.[241] And those master craftsmen with less common skills were more mobile than others. Movement from town to town helped to keep workers aware of conditions and wage rates elsewhere. This may go a long way to explaining the relatively close relationship between wage rates in neighbouring towns. In particular, the almost parallel movement of rates at Hull and Beverley suggests that the two towns did not possess totally independent labour markets, but that they were closely interrelated, with wage rates moving more or less in step with each other.[242]

The supervision of workers

Much of the day-to-day supervision of the work on building sites fell to the leading craftsman. When Louth steeple was built in the early sixteenth century, 2s was spent 'for to get a master mason for to take charge'.[243] On occasion a single man might agree to organise the whole project from start to finish. In 1632 the Hull council decided to build a two-storied, brick gildhall and John Catlyn, a local builder and architect, was commissioned to supervise the project, which was

---

[238] *YCR*, VII, 145, 148, 159–61; YCA, CC13, fo. 55v.
[239] Bartlett 1959–60, 19; Palliser 1973b, 48; Purvis 1947, 334–6; Palliser 1979, 283; YML, E3/51.
[240] DFC, CC/190045–8, 190054, 190066–7, 190069, 190071–2.   [241] See above pp. 68–71.
[242] See above p. 163 and also below pp. 202–3.
[243] *Louth Accts*, 20–1, 79–80, 90, 113, 119, 127–8, 137, 161, 179.

eventually completed in 1636.[244] In some cases responsibility for a building project was split: at the rebuilding of Rose Castle Chapel near Carlisle in the 1670s, John Lowther worked 'overseeing and paying workmen', while the more skilled work fell to William Thackeray the contractor, referred to as 'architect'.[245] But most jobs were much less imposing and remained under the control of more humble practitioners. In all cases, however, the ultimate controller of a job was not the chief craftsman, but the customer, whether a private individual or institution: it was the customer who held the purse strings, paid the piper, and called the tune. The supervision they provided was often casual and amateurish, but it did require workmen to glance over their shoulders, if only occasionally. Supervision often fell to annually elected town chamberlains and churchwardens, many of whom probably had no more experience of controlling labourers and building craftsmen than the oversight of their own house repairs. Their presence is rarely acknowledged in the accounts, but in 1552 the York city fathers explicitly placed the chamberlains in charge of paving a stretch of road, and at Carlisle in the seventeenth century a chamberlain was paid 12d a day for 'my own attendance' when keeping an eye on the work.[246] They did not always do a good job. In 1610 the auditors of the accounts of a York church felt that the churchwardens had not been 'good stewards'. They had paid the glazier 6d a foot for setting new glass, although there were others 'who will do the like work as well, but better cheap'.[247] At some churches the job of watching over workmen was given to the parish clerk, which provided an element of continuity.[248]

The difficulty of ensuring adequate supervision is well illustrated by the various strategies adopted by the Chester council during the building of a new quay in the mid sixteenth century. In 1557 it was 'agreed and ordered for the better setting forward the work of the haven that there should be a master of the work, a treasurer and two overseers of the work to be done, and for that time was nominated and appointed John Smith alderman for the master of the work, Thomas Aldersey alderman treasurer, and William Leche alderman and Thomas Stuerde overseers of the said work'. When the job was reorganised in 1565 Anthony Hurleston, a gentleman, was appointed overseer and he received 3s 4d a week 'in consideration of his dili-

---

[244] *VCH Hull*, 433; Neave 1983, 8–10.   [245] Tyson 1983b, 72–4.
[246] *YCR*, V, 71; CUMROC, Ca/4/3.
[247] YBI, PR/Y/MCS/17.
[248] CCORO, P/65/8/1. See also the accounts of St Michael, Spurriergate, York, where the same man supervised work throughout the 1520s and 1530s: YBI, PR/Y/MS/1.

gence'. The arrangement did not last, and in January 1568 the council
ordered that each week one of the aldermen or common councillors, at
the nomination of the mayor and 'upon his own proper costs', should
go down to the quay to supervise the work. He was assisted by a site
foreman referred to as 'master of the work'.[249] Such attempts to
establish a formal structure of supervision had long been customary on
the larger building sites. In the medieval period clerks of works were
engaged for the erection of large stone buildings, and the organisation
on some royal sites could be quite complex. At the repair of Carlisle
Castle in 1557 ordinary carpenters were paid 7d a day, compared with
the 12d paid to the master carpenter in charge of them. There was also
a 'treasurer of work' and a clerk of works, earning 4s and 1s a day
respectively, and two clerks – one to the treasurer who got 12d a day,
and one in the quarry who received 6d.[250] The Dean and Chapter at
many cathedrals employed a Clerk of the Fabric to oversee the constant programme of maintenance.

Town councils also employed regular overseers, and the practice
seems to have become more common in the seventeenth century. The
Hull council acquired an overseer on the cheap when a former sheriff
was given a pension of 40s a year in 1595 on the grounds of his
poverty; he had to earn it by supervising the town's works.[251] During
the 1660s and 1670s Matthew Hardy was the overseer and general
organiser of work. His jobs included: 'setting workmen awork about
the causey'; 'measuring ground paved in this town and collecting
money'; going out 'to measure timber'; and riding 'to Swine Wood to
make choice of 240 trees'. He received a quarterly fee of 10s plus
expenses and a daily allowance.[252] At York, Mr William Pacoke,
engaged when the 'causey without Monk Bar' was repaired in 1610,
was called the 'overseer of same work', and from 1611 to 1623 James
Gibson was employed as 'overseer of the city's works'. He was paid an
annual fee of £5 and extra sums from time to time.[253]

The authority of overseers was given a substantial boost by the
labour statutes of the late fifteenth and sixteenth centuries. The act of
1495 established that, 'if any artificers or labourers retained in service
with any person for building or reparation, make or cause to be made
any assembly to assault, harm or hurt any person assigned to control
and oversee them in their working, that he or they so offending have

[249] *Chester Haven*, 87–8, 90–1, 95–7.
[250] Knoop & Jones 1949, 21, 24–5, 37, 91, 146, 149, 190, 192, 203; PRO, E101/483/17.
[251] Gillett & MacMahon 1989, 117.   [252] HCRO, BRF/3/20, pp.404, 425, 626–7, 704–6.
[253] YCA, CC13–18. His rate of pay cannot be determined since he submitted composite
       bills. See also YCA, CC29–30; CCRO, TAV/1/15; TWAS, 543/18, fos. 309v–310v and
       passim; 543/19, fos. 10r, 12v, 13v.

imprisonment for a year . . . and further to make fine at the king's will'. This clause was repeated in the acts of 1514 and in 1563, when it was also made an offence for a workman to make 'any assault or affray upon his master, mistress or dame'.[254] The effectiveness of such regulations is, of course, unknown, but building craftsmen were occasionally imprisoned.[255] As on modern building sites, the mere existence of overseers did not guarantee that the work would proceed smoothly, nor that the job would be well done. Like Henry Mansford, some overseers may have been more interested in feathering their own nests than in protecting the interests of the customer.[256] However, the long service of some men, such as Matthew Hardy at Hull and James Gibson at York, suggests that at least some of them gave reasonable value for money, and the quality of Henry Mansford's work was not questioned.

Reflections

Both labourers and building craftsmen endured irregular patterns of employment: all outdoor workers suffered from a low level of demand for their labour during the winter months. Additionally, some, although by no means all, received relatively low rates of pay during the dead days of winter. Unfortunately, the nature of the sources means that it is impossible to determine with any degree of accuracy the number of days a year worked by individuals. Only occasionally can a workman who disappears from the accounts of one institution be traced in other accounts during the same year. Their disappearance was often due to the ending of a particular job, although there can be little doubt that ill-health and injury frequently played a part. However, few workmen could expect to receive much support from their former customers and were thrown back on more general sources of charity. Although some building craftsmen were able to spend part of their time in their own workshops preparing materials, many worked away from home for much of the time. Once at the building site they became clock-watchers, knocking off at specified times and receiving overtime payments for working early or late. When a job was in full swing early-modern workers were expected to remain at their posts every day except Sunday. During the year workmen moved from site to site and from one customer to another, and there were also

---

[254] 11 Henry VII c.22; 6 Henry VIII c.3; 5 Elizabeth I c.4.
[255] See pp. 29, 146, 183. See also TWAS, 543/15, fo. 258v. The kind of records which could reveal more cases relating to labour difficulties have not been researched in depth for this project.
[256] For Mansford's career, see pp. 43, 141, 143–4.

flows of labour from town to town and from the towns to the country-side: such flows kept workers abreast of conditions of work and wage rates elsewhere in the region. There are some signs that the pace of work was often relatively leisurely in the early-modern period and that when it was not – as in the case of the Newcastle pit-drainers – a much shorter day was worked.

The northern evidence suggests that most workers received the bulk of their remuneration in cash. Drink was a frequent accompaniment of the work process – many workers, especially in the seventeenth century, received a daily drink allowance, and workers were given treats of food and drink when crucial phases of the work were completed – but workers were provided with their full dietary needs only when they worked away from home. It was neither in the interest of the workers to have a substantial proportion of their wages deducted to cover the cost of full diet, nor in the interest of customers – and especially institutional customers – to get involved in the complex logistics of providing the food. Nor did the average worker receive much in the way of non-food perquisites. Regular workers who were paid a retainer to ensure their future cooperation were sometimes given items of clothing, and some of the senior workmen were allowed to remove surplus materials from the workplace: such practices left little over for the rank-and-file workmen. Cash bonuses for extra effort were also paid from time to time. However, there can be little doubt that such perks formed a very small part of the pay received by the average northern worker.

Shifts in the level of wage rates in the north of England are discussed in the next chapter, the second part of which wrestles with the difficult question of why rates moved in the manner they did at the times they did.

6

Wage rates in the northern towns

This chapter is based on the wage data presented in appendix 1. For each town the information is introduced by a discussion of the quality of the source material and any particular problems relating to the individual series. Unlike in the work of some earlier historians, the town series have been kept apart and not spliced together to form a regional picture.[1] Moreover, each series has been compiled according to the same set of rules so that the rates paid in different towns can be compared.[2] The rates presented were the daily rates paid to workers in the summer months without the provision of full diet, but with the addition of a daily drink allowance, or cash equivalent, when it was paid. Winter rates are not represented in the appendix, partly because the bulk of the work of building craftsmen and labourers was done in the warmer months, and also because seasonal differentials in wage rates were not paid in all places. The wage series relate to the main body of building craftsmen and labourers. The craftsmen included carpenters and joiners, bricklayers and pavers, wallers and masons, tilers and slaters, and they were usually paid at similar levels within the same town. In some cases the skilled men were paid at the same rate, although in other instances they were paid at varying levels determined by their skill, experience, and responsibility. To some extent the appearance of different rates of pay is due to the fact that it is sometimes difficult to distinguish between the skilled journeyman and his master, who may or may not have received a few pence more each day. However it is plain that most men – both masters and journeymen – were paid within a relatively narrow range in the northern towns. Nevertheless, there were those who, because they

---

[1] Brown & Hopkins 1981, 1–12. See Gilboy 1934, 250–1, for the problems which come from trying to manufacture a composite index.
[2] On the problems of comparing series for different towns see Abel 1980, 135.

were in a position of authority or possessed a rare skill, earned significantly more than the common herd. The rates paid to such aristocrats of labour have not been included in appendix 1.[3] Similarly, rates have not been included for the occasional member of a skilled team who was paid at an unusually low level: it must be assumed that such men were either young, unusually weak, incompetent, or aged. Despite excluding such outlying rates there can still be problems in comparing wages from year to year, even within the same town. Recorded wages could vary and explanations were rarely proffered. At Hull in the 1570s most craftsmen were paid between 8d and 10d a day, although in 1571 the range was 9d to 11d. The high rate of 11d was paid to Thomas Cook, one of the carpenters, although he only received 10d a day in both 1572 and 1573, and both 9d and 10d in 1574 when there may have been a seasonal adjustment in his pay.[4] It would be a mistake to regard 1571 as a high-wage year in Hull, although the accounts do not provide any clue as to the reason for Cook's generous recompense that year: perhaps he was paid at a relatively high level for accomplishing some particularly taxing job.

Within particular towns different customers usually paid similar rates to the same class of labour. They paid at a customary or going rate which was acceptable both to themselves and to the workmen involved, and widely known in the town. The point can be illustrated most clearly from the Hull records.[5] The accounts of Trinity House cover almost the whole of the period under review, while those of the council run in a broken sequence from the middle of the sixteenth century, and it is possible to trace many individual craftsmen, and some labourers, who worked for both institutions in the same year. During the period 1563–87 they nearly always paid craftsmen between 8d and 10d a day, although there was an occasional difference in the way labourers were treated. Throughout the early part of Elizabeth's reign the council gave them 6d a day, except in 1572 when they were given 5d, 6d, and 7d. Trinity House hired labourers on relatively few occasions and usually paid them 6d, but in the summer of 1573 the gild paid for 13 man-days at 4d. This suggests that wage rates were not set in concrete, although it is possible that the labourers were either young or old, or perhaps did not work full days. But such divergencies were most unusual, and at Hull and elsewhere different institutions within the same town usually paid the same rates. This means that it is possible to establish a wage series for an individual town by splicing

---

[3] See above pp. 41–3.   [4] HCRO, BRF/3/3.
[5] The same was true of Lincoln, Newcastle, and York. Detailed references to the accounts will not be given when discussing wage rates: see the series in appendix 1.

together data taken from a range of sources. This is essential, since no institution has a completely unbroken run of detailed accounts.

This chapter is divided into two main parts. It begins with a description of changes in nominal rates. The three centuries under discussion break down in a surprisingly symmetrical fashion: the period 1450–1540 was a time of wage-rate stability, with the majority of workers receiving similar rates of pay; a period of turbulence followed from 1540 to 1560, or thereabouts, when rates rose everywhere; between 1560 and 1640 wage rates remained stationary over long periods, but drifted upwards from time to time; another period of turbulence followed down to the Restoration, when rates again rose sharply in most places; the final period of ninety years was, once again, a period of relative stability with some wage drift. The second part of the chapter contains an analysis of those factors which may have influenced changes in levels of pay: the regulation of wage rates by national and local authorities; changes in the supply of labour; possible shifts in the demand for labour; and the role of custom. It is a difficult discussion, conducted in the absence of many of the facts which would be present in an ideal world, and it is hedged about with much uncertainty.

Changes in wage rates

Although the northern data are relatively thin for the years from 1450 to 1540, the overall picture is not in any doubt. It was a period of remarkable stability in wage rates. Nominal rates had increased during the previous century following the Black Death and they seem to have edged upwards, in York at least, in the mid fifteenth century.[6] Thereafter they mostly stayed at the same level until the 1540s. At Durham, craftsmen received 5d or 6d a day from the 1460s to the 1530s, while labourers got 3d or 4d until the 1510s, but a flat 4d in the 1530s. Similar rates were paid at Newcastle between 1508 and 1511, and at Hull from the 1460s to the 1520s, although in the third quarter of the fifteenth century some labourers received only $3\frac{1}{3}$d a day.[7] Other scattered evidence supports this picture of consistency: at Tattershall Castle in the 1470s labourers received 4d and craftsmen 6d, while at Louth in the early sixteenth century the most common rate for craftsmen was 6d, and most labourers received 4d a day.[8] As always the chief craftsmen got rather more. The remarkable stability in northern wage rates

---

[6] Swanson 1989, 85.   [7] See also the rates for Beverley in 1494 and Berwick 1538.
[8] *Tattershall Castle Accts*, 78; *Louth Accts, passim*.

before about 1540 was paralleled elsewhere in the country. As Thorold Rogers observed of the fifteenth century:

The wages of the artisan during the period to which I refer were generally, and through the year, about 6d a day. Those of the agricultural labourer were about 4d. I am referring to ordinary artisans and labourers. Persons who plied a craft in which greater skill was needed, perhaps one which was rarely procurable except from a distance, received more ... Nor is there any material difference, with one notable exception, in the payments made for labour all over England. It is equally well paid throughout the country. The exception is London, where the wages were from twenty-five to thirty per cent over the rates paid in other places.[9]

This was all equally true of the early decades of the sixteenth century.

Wage rates moved ahead almost everywhere during the 1540s and 1550s. Once more there are tantalising gaps in the northern data. At Chester craftsmen earned 6d both in 1548 and 1553. Some labourers moved to 5d in the later year, and by 1558 they had moved to 6d. When craftsmen reappear in the early 1560s they were earning 8d or 10d a day compared with the 6d paid still to labourers. Similarly at Hull, the old rates of 6d and 4d were still being paid in the 1540s, but by the early to mid 1550s they had moved to 8d or 9d for craftsmen, and 5d for labourers. By 1557 craftsmen were receiving between 8d and 10d a day, and labourers had moved to 6d by 1563. Rates can also be seen rising in Lincoln and York. The richest information comes from the Durham accounts. During the mid 1530s most craftsmen were paid 5d or 6d, although in 1539 some of them broke through the traditional barrier to earn 7d a day. The rates for skilled men remained in the range 5d to 7d during the early 1540s, but had advanced to 7d or 8d by the mid 1550s. The rates for labourers hardly moved during the 1540s, although one labourer received 5d a day in July 1545.[10] They then moved on to 5d in 1550 and to 6d a year later. By 1551 most craftsmen – including carpenters, daubers, tilers, glaziers, and wallers – were getting 8d a day, and they gradually consolidated their position during the 1550s: most received 8d or 9d in the early 1560s. Labourers, on the other hand, failed to protect their gains and 5d a day became standard during the 1550s, although some got 4d and others 6d. Throughout the north of England by the spring of 1563 wage rates for labourers and building craftsmen were significantly higher than they had been throughout the early decades of the sixteenth century and, hence, above the maxima – 6d for craftsmen, 4d for labourers – specified by the Act of 1514. The general increase in nominal rates formed the context for the review of wage control undertaken by the second

[9] Rogers 1908, 327; Airs 1975, 186.　　[10] DPK, MC2875.

Elizabethan parliament which culminated in the Statute of Artificers of 1563.

Between 1560 and 1640 wage rates moved ahead in most places, although there were long periods when they failed to rise, often for decades at a stretch. The most impressive gains were at Newcastle. Craftsmen, who had mostly received 8d a day in the 1560s, had moved to between 16d and 18d by the later 1630s: labourers went from 5d or 6d in the 1560s to 10d on the eve of the Civil War. Only in York did the labourers do as well, although the craftsmen did comparatively less well receiving between 12d and 14d from the 1610s to 1640. Hull craftsmen, who had been receiving between 8d and 10d a day in the 1560s, had advanced to between 12d and 16d by the 1630s. Labourers remained on 6d a day from the 1560s to 1587, but had moved on to 8d by 1617, a rate they remained at until 1640. Away from the three large towns of north-eastern England craftsmen tended to do rather less well: at Carlisle craftsmen got between 10d and 12d from the late sixteenth century to the 1620s, before moving on to between 12d and 14d on the eve of the Civil War; the Chester men received from 10d to 12d in the 1600s and mostly 12d in the 1620s; Kendal craftsmen remained on between 10d and 12d from the late 1610s to 1640, as did the Lincoln men. With only one exception – some Carlisle labourers received 10d a day in 1639 – the less specialised men did not get more than 8d a day for their efforts before the Civil War. They reached 8d as early as the 1580s at Carlisle, but fell back to between 6d and 7d during the 1610s. At Chester, labourers reached 8d in 1608, as did the Lincoln and Kendal men during the next decade. On the eve of the Civil War most labourers received 8d a day for their efforts, that is double the rate their forebears had received in the early decades of the sixteenth century, although at York and Newcastle they were doing rather better. The experience of craftsmen in the different towns was rather more varied. Most received at least 12d a day by 1640, or twice the rate normally paid a century earlier, although in some of the smaller towns such as Lincoln and Kendal some only got 10d a day. But at Hull, York, and Newcastle, and probably at Beverley also, craftsmen were getting 12d or more a day by 1640, and significantly more in some cases.

Like the situation a hundred years earlier, the middle decades of the seventeenth century witnessed substantial turbulence in northern wage rates. By the outbreak of the Civil War the northern towns had begun to separate out into two groups with Hull, Beverley, Newcastle, and York emerging as relatively high-wage economies – as far as building craftsmen were concerned – and Lincoln, Durham,

Chester, Kendal, and Carlisle as relatively low-wage economies.[11] Wage-rate movements during the middle decades of the century exacerbated those differences and by the 1660s most craftsmen in the high-wage towns were being paid between 18d and 22d a day: maximum rates were 20d at York, 21d at Beverley, and 22d at Hull and Newcastle. By contrast, in the low-wage towns most craftsmen were paid in the range 16d to 18d: the highest rate was paid at all places except Kendal – where the highest paid men got only 16d a day – while a few of the Carlisle men got 19d. However, at Lincoln and Kendal the bottom rate was only 12d. Labourers generally did less well. This, combined with the greater increases which went to the craftsmen, led to a widening of the differentials between the pay of labourers and craftsmen in some of the northern towns, which will be discussed later.[12] By the Restoration, after about a century and a half of sustained commodity-price inflation, many craftsmen were earning three times as much as their predecessors of the early sixteenth century, although some were earning only double the earlier rates. Similarly, in some places labourers were earning 12d a day, that is, three times the going rate in the earlier sixteenth century, but in most towns the labourers earned no more than 10d, often less.

The experiences of building craftsmen in the northern towns after 1660 were mixed. At Hull the gains achieved in the middle of the century were built on: craftsmen were paid a uniform 24d a day from the late 1690s down to 1750. Beverley men were also paid well, receiving between 20d and 23d in the same period: and high rates were probably paid at Newcastle, although little information is available. At York, however, the small amount of data available suggests that some of the gains of the seventeenth century may not have been retained in the following century: but it must be stressed that the limited amount of evidence available makes this uncertain. Away from the larger towns of the north-east, craftsmen were doing less well. In the north-western towns, together with Durham and Lincoln, craftsmen rarely received more than 18d a day, and often less. Thus, while the Hull men were getting four times as much a day as their early Tudor forebears, others were getting no more than three times that amount. And some, like the slaters and plasterers of Cockermouth,[13] were getting only double the earlier rate.

Labourers were also paid at different levels in the northern towns in the final period, although variations in their pay were not as marked as among the craftsmen. Hull men, who began the period on 10d a day,

[11] See below pp. 202–3.   [12] See below pp. 176–7.   [13] CUMROC, PR136/152.

moved on to 12d from the mid 1680s, and received between 12d and 14d from the mid 1730s. Beverley labourers got between 10d and 12d from the 1680s to 1740, and then moved on to a steady 12d. The Newcastle men were getting 14d in the 1710s, but, unfortunately, nothing is known of their rates later in the period. At York the labourers reached 12d a day in the early eighteenth century, while the Lincoln men, after sticking at 10d from the 1660s to the 1730s, moved on to 12d in the 1740s. After falling behind in the mid seventeenth century and getting only 8d a day at the Restoration, Durham labourers advanced to 10d by the early 1680s, and to 12d from the 1710s or 1720s. The progression took longer at Chester: labourers mostly received 10d a day from the 1660s to the 1720s, moved on to between 10d and 12d in the 1730s, and to 12d in the 1740s. Only at Carlisle were labourers paid less than 12d in the middle of the eighteenth century. And the detailed story is unusual. Most labourers received the high rate of 12d a day from the 1650s to the late 1680s. There is then a gap in the records until the 1720s, but from then until the middle of the century labourers were recorded as receiving between 8d and 11d a day, with 9d being the most common rate. By the middle of the eighteenth century most labourers in the towns of northern England received 12d for a day's work, that is they were getting three times the rate which went to their early-Tudor ancestors. This means that their rates of pay had advanced less than the pay of building craftsmen in the relatively high-wage economies of Hull, York, Newcastle, and Beverley, although their progress was in line with the increase in the rates paid to the craftsmen in the lower-wage towns of Lincoln, Durham, Chester, Kendal, and Carlisle.

Wage-rate movements followed broadly similar paths across the country throughout the early-modern period. Southern wage rates were extremely 'sticky', often remaining at the same level for decades, and there was an 'extraordinary absence of falls'.[14] Similarly, northern rates were often unchanged for long periods and gains were rarely reversed. There may have been short periods when wage rates fell back – perhaps in response to a sudden fall in prices – although such movements are difficult to detect. The only apparently clear-cut, long-term reduction in rates comes from the Carlisle accounts. For thirty years beginning in 1659 labourers received 12d a day, but only 9d or 10d in the second quarter of the eighteenth century. There may have been a general reduction in the rates paid to labourers, but the expla-

---

[14] Brown & Hopkins 1981, 7–8.

nation may have had more to do with the nature of the work being done in the different periods. Most of the evidence for the seventeenth century comes from the accounts of the chamberlains who, for the most part, paid for work at the town mills, which often involved repairing the weirs and dams: perhaps the labourers were paid at a high level to compensate them for working in difficult conditions. Occasionally, as in the mid 1670s, some labourers were paid at a lower level which suggests that a two-tier system of payment may have been in operation. Evidence for the eighteenth century comes from the bills submitted to the council by the master craftsmen, which included claims for the payment of labourers doing various jobs around the town.[15] There may have been a reduction in the general level of labourers' pay, but we cannot be certain.

There were two major changes in the structure of wage rates in the northern towns during the seventeenth century: significant differences emerged in the rates paid to workers in different towns, especially for the more skilled men; there was also an associated shift in differentials between craftsmen and labourers in some places. It is commonly believed that there was a 'remarkable stability of the differentials between the rates of the craftsman and his labourer', which persisted from the Black Death to the First World War. This view, articulated by Phelps Brown and Hopkins, was echoed by Hobsbawm, who argued that the differential was one of 'great antiquity and persistence'. However, whereas Phelps Brown and Hopkins put the ratio between the rates for craftsmen and labourers at 3:2, Hobsbawm put it at 2:1.[16] Evidence to support both views can be found in the accounts of northern England, although only at Chester and Kendal did the ratio remain unchanged at 3:2 throughout the period. Across the region, and in the south of England also, the ratio – endorsed by the national maxima laid down in the acts of 1495 and 1514, of 6d for craftsmen and 4d for labourers – stood at 3:2 before 1540, and in most places it changed little during the following century. But some changes began to occur: at Hull in the 1630s skilled men received between 12d and 14d, with some of them getting 16d, compared with the 8d which went to the labourers. However, it was during the middle decades of the century that the major changes took place, especially in Hull, Beverley, York, and Newcastle where the rates for craftsmen advanced rapidly. By 1660 the ratio was approaching, or even exceeding 2:1, and the situation was most clear-cut at Hull where craftsmen had advanced to 24d by the end of the seventeenth century,

15 CUMROC, Ca/4, vouchers.
16 Brown & Hopkins 1981, 8; Hobsbawm 1964, 346; Rule 1986, 111; Clarkson 1971, 223.

Table 6.1   *Northern wage rates compared with those for southern England (in pence)*

	c. 1560	c. 1640	c. 1660	c. 1700	c. 1750
(a) Craftsmen					
Beverley	—	14–18	19–21	20–3	20–3
Carlisle	—	12–14	18–19	—	18–20
Chester	8–10	12–14	14–18	15–18	16–18
Durham	7–9	—	16–18	16–18	18
Hull	8–10	12–16	18–22	24	24
Kendal	—	10–14	12–16	14	—
Lincoln	—	10–14	12–16	18	18–20
Newcastle	7–8	16–18	20–2	—	—
York	7–8	14	18–20	18–22	—
Southern England	8–10	12–16	18	18–20	24
(b) Labourers					
Beverley	6	—	—	10–12	12–14
Carlisle	—	—	12	—	10
Chester	6	8	10–11	10–12	12
Durham	5–6	—	8	10	12
Hull	6	8	10	12	12–14
Kendal	—	8	9–10	10	—
Lincoln	—	8	8–10	10	12
Newcastle	5–6	10	12	10–14	—
York	6	10	10–14	12	—
Southern England	6–8	10–12	12	12–14	16

Source: Brown and Hopkins 1981, 11, and see appendix 1 for the northern rates.

but labourers only to 12d. From the late 1730s some of the labourers began to make up lost ground by moving up to 14d a day when the craftsmen were still on 24d: but other labourers in the town remained on 12d. Only at Durham did the ratio move in both directions. By 1660 labourers were getting a mere 8d a day compared with the 16d to 18d going to the craftsmen. However, by 1700 labourers were getting 10d a day, and 12d by the 1720s, although the craftsmen's rates had hardly changed. That is, the original sixteenth-century ratio of 3:2 had moved to 2:1 by the Restoration, but edged back towards 3:2 in the early decades of the eighteenth century.

Northern labourers and building craftsmen were always paid at significantly lower levels than their counterparts in London. By the early seventeenth century London craftsmen were earning 18d a day compared with the 8d to 12d earned in the northern towns, and London labourers got 12d compared with the northern rate of between

6d and 8d.[17] In the middle of the eighteenth century most craftsmen in the metropolis received 36d a day and labourers 24d, whereas the most highly paid northerners were the Hull craftsmen who got 24d a day, with the labourers receiving a maximum of 14d.[18] However, most northerners fared better throughout the period than their southern cousins outside the metropolis. The data are summarised in Table 6.1.

Only in 1750 did the typical southern craftsman earn as much as the most highly paid northerners. However, it is possible that the New-castle men were earning more than 24d by 1750, although adequate records are not available to support this suggestion. Similarly, the most highly paid northern labourers did quite well compared with their southern counterparts, at least down to 1700, although the absence of worthwhile data for York and Newcastle obscures the picture in the later period.

For the eighteenth century it is possible to make more comparisons, especially with the work of Elizabeth Gilboy, and the more recent findings of Hunt and Botham for Staffordshire. In each case the authors used median wage rates rather than the spread of rates adopted here. Moreover, Gilboy produced rates only for labourers and journeymen craftsmen, which means that her rates often need to be compared with the lower rates for craftsmen in the northern towns. For north Staffordshire, Hunt and Botham found that labourers were paid 10d or 11d in the early 1750s, that is at a level a little lower than was commonly paid in the northern towns, while both the carpenters and bricklayers got no more than 16d, a poor return compared with that achieved by most northerners.[19] Gilboy's findings for the north are broadly consistent with the data provided here, although much of the evidence she collected from quarter-sessions papers related to rural projects, and especially to road and bridge building. She believed that although there was some tendency for wage rates to rise in the first half of the eighteenth century, especially in Lancashire, most of the increase took place after 1750. Similarly, wage rates seem to have risen little in the northern towns in the first half of the century. In the industrial areas of West Yorkshire labourers were paid at a flat 12d a day throughout the first half of the eighteenth century, although in the more rural areas they got between 8d and 10d in the early years of the century rising to 12d in the 1740s. Rates were a little lower in the North Riding where most labourers were paid 10d a day in the last two

[17] Rappaport 1989, 145–53, 407; Gilboy 1934, 39–70.
[18] Schwarz 1985, 37; Gilboy 1934, 8–9.
[19] Gilboy 1934, xxviii, 9–15, 251–3; Hunt & Botham 1987, 387, 389–91.

decades of the period, although the range of median payments was from 8d to 11d. In Lancashire labourers moved from between 8d and 10d in the first two decades of the century to 12d thereafter. Most of the journeymen craftsmen were paid 18d throughout the first half of the century in the North and West Ridings of Yorkshire, although rates were somewhat lower in Lancashire: between 1700 and 1730 they received between 12d and 18d, and mostly from 16d to 18d during the next two decades. The discovery of rather lower rates for craftsmen west of the Pennines ties in with the discovery that rates were relatively low for such workers in the towns of the north-west during the same period. Gilboy accepted that rates were relatively low in Lancashire in the early eighteenth century, and she pointed out that: 'The wage set by the justices at Manchester in 1725 was 1s (without meat and drink) for the journeymen, and 1s 2d for the masters, in all the building trades. This was probably not far from the current wage, as far as we can tell, at that time, except possibly in the industrial centres.' Such rates would have been considered very low by building craftsmen in most of the northern towns, even in Kendal where urban craftsmen were paid at the poorest level, although the Manchester justices made it plain that they expected craftsmen in the more northerly parts of Lancashire to take even lower wages than those prescribed.[20]

Comparison with the wages given to workmen elsewhere suggests that the labourers and building craftsmen of the northern towns were being paid at a relatively high level. In 1750 craftsmen at Hull received the same daily rates as their southern counterparts, and the Beverley men – and almost certainly those of Newcastle – were not far behind. In the towns of the north-west, and also in Durham and Lincoln, craftsmen were paid at a lower rate, many of them receiving no more than three-quarters of the Hull rate. The contrast between the situation at Hull and the north-western towns was even more extreme around 1700 when the Hull men received twice the rate going to some of the Kendal men. But even the men of Chester, Carlisle, Durham, and Lincoln seem to have been relatively well paid compared with their colleagues in North Staffordshire. Some northern labourers were earning rates not far short of those earned in the south, and higher than those being paid in North Staffordshire. And as Gilboy showed, labourers repairing the country roads and bridges of northern England were paid at broadly similar rates. It has always been assumed that wages were higher in the south of England than in the north during

[20] Gilboy 1934, 160, 166, 168–9, 177–80, 183–4, 220.

the early-modern period. This is certainly true if a comparison is made with London rates: in terms of wage levels the metropolis was always an outlier, with wage rates markedly higher than elsewhere. But southern rates outside London, as revealed by the work of Phelps Brown and Hopkins, and Gilboy, were not markedly higher than the rates paid in the high-wage northern towns.

The determination of wage rates

What factors played the largest role in determining the level and pattern of wages in an early-modern economy?[21]

This is a very difficult question to answer, and one which has not been seriously debated for the early-modern period. It is relatively simple to establish the level of wages paid to different varieties of labourers and building craftsmen, and this has now been accomplished for the northern towns to add to our knowledge of conditions in the south. Nominal rates rose everywhere from the middle decades of the sixteenth century, although the timing and degree of change varied from place to place, and from one class of labour to another. Local conditions, often hidden from the gaze of the inquisitive historian, played their part in shaping the particular wage profiles of different places, but the broad similarity of movements, and their correspondence to trends elsewhere in the country, indicates that larger forces were at work.

As Leslie Clarkson has observed, 'There were, broadly, three sets of influences at work' in the fixing of wages: 'the interaction of supply and demand, the force of custom, and statutory regulations'.[22] But further discussion of the subject is hampered by our ignorance of the essential variables: especially our limited knowledge of the demand for labour and, to a lesser degree, its supply. Some decades ago Donald Coleman argued that the economy of early-modern England was characterised by a substantial degree of unemployment and under-employment.[23] His views have stood the test of time and the mismatch between the supply of labour and demand for it helps to explain why nominal rates failed to keep pace with the inflation in commodity prices, especially for foodstuffs, which was such a marked feature of the sixteenth and early seventeenth centuries. Those who were pre-dominantly dependent on wage-earning for their livelihoods in the

[21] Vries 1978, 87. A version of the following argument appears in Woodward 1994.
[22] Clarkson 1982, 17.
[23] Coleman 1955–6.

England of Charles I had to endure a substantially lower standard of living than that enjoyed by their forebears of the early sixteenth century. But if a general overstocking of the labour market can help to explain why the price of labour failed to advance in line with the rise in the price of foodstuffs, it cannot explain why, in most instances, nominal rates failed to fall back to help to clear the market of surplus labour, nor why they moved upwards at particular times.

The discussion which follows is divided into five parts. The first section deals with the regulation of wages by central and local governments. However, it will be argued that the chief factor determining the level of wages was not such regulation, but rather the interaction between the supply of labour and the demand for it, in the general context of an over-stocked labour market. These questions will be confronted in the second and third parts of this section respectively. Custom, that great stand-by of the social historian and frequently invoked explanation for all that is difficult to understand, will be investigated in the fourth section, and a series of conclusions will be offered in the final part of the chapter. However, what follows is necessarily somewhat tentative since much of the information needed for a complete analysis of the problem is not available.

The regulation of wages

The earliest recorded attempt to regulate wage rates was in London in the early thirteenth century, but it was the effects of the Black Death which brought involvement by the state.[24] The ordinance of labour of 1349, and the Statute of Labourers of 1351, instituted a programme of wage control which remained in place until the early nineteenth century. From the middle of the fourteenth century to the middle of the sixteenth century the wages of a broad spectrum of the labour force were subject to nationally established maxima: the one exception was the Act of 1389/90 which gave JPs the right to establish local rates 'according to the dearth of victuals'.[25] In the first part of the period under review wages were expected to conform to the maxima laid down in the Acts of 1445, 1495, and 1514, as follows:

1445 Free mason and master carpenter	$5\frac{1}{2}$d
Master tiler, slater, rough mason, carpenter, and 'other artificers concerning building'	$4\frac{1}{2}$d
Every other labourer	$3\frac{1}{2}$d

---

[24] Knoop & Jones 1949, 123–4; Hutchins 1900, 404. [25] 13 Richard II, stat. 1 c.VIII.

1495   Free mason, master carpenter, rough mason,
       bricklayer, master tiler, plumber, glazier, carver,
       and joiner   6d
       The master mason and master carpenter which
       shall take the charge of the work having under
       them six men   7d
       Every other labourer and artificer not afore named   4d[26]

The 1495 rates were reiterated in 1514.

By the middle decades of the sixteenth century the rates laid down
for provincial workers in 1495 and 1514 had become unrealistic, and
the Statute of Artificers of 1563 re-established the sliding scale first
adopted at the end of the fourteenth century.[27] At Easter the JPs were
ordered to:

assemble themselves together ... calling unto them such discrete and grave
persons of the said county or of the said city or town corporate as they shall
think meet, and conferring together respecting the plenty or scarcity of the
time, and other circumstances necessary to be considered, shall have authority
... to limit, rate and appoint the wages ... of the said artificers, handicraftsmen,
husbandmen or any other labourer, servant or workman whose wages in time
past hath been by any law or statute rated and appointed.

The effects of the national maxima established before 1563 are
imperfectly understood. It is usually thought that the legislation of the
mid fourteenth century was ineffective, although the relatively
modest wage increases of the period suggest that some restraint was
being effected.[28] However, it has been argued that 'it may be assumed
that wage restrictions on builders were for the most part a dead letter
in late-medieval York'.[29] Indeed, this was the case not only at York, but
also at Durham, Hull, and Beverley: in all four places in the later
fifteenth century labourers and building craftsmen were paid above
the rates laid down in 1445. The same was true in other parts of the
country.[30] The accounts of Selby Abbey provide some interesting
insights into the working of the 1445 Act. During the mid 1430s a
thatcher and a plumber received 6d a day, and carpenters and roofers
5d, and similar rates were paid in the early 1440s: that is, workers were
being paid above the rates authorised in the subsequent act. But the act

[26] 23 Henry VI c.12; 11 Henry VII c.22; 6 Henry VIII c.3.   [27] 5 Elizabeth I c.4.
[28] Dyer 1989, 218–19.
[29] Swanson 1983, 27.
[30] Rogers 1908, 327. Only a few scattered references to the enforcement of labour
    regulations have been found for the second half of the fifteenth century, although
    this may be more a reflection of the fragmentary nature of the records than of reality:
    Swanson 1983, 27. See also PRO, KB9/325, membranes 39, 41, for York in 1469 and
    1470: I am grateful to R.W. Hoyle for providing me with this reference.

made no difference. During 1446/7 carpenters got 6d a day, roofers 5d and 6d, and daubers – who did low-grade work akin to that of labourers – got 4d or 4½d.[31] The Act of 1495 raised maximum wage rates to more realistic levels, close to those prevailing in the market place. The situation was well summarised by Thorold Rogers who argued that, despite the attempt to curb wages in 1445, 'the rate keeps steadily high, and finally becomes customary, and was recognised by Parliament [in 1495]'.[32] Across the country the new rates – a maximum 6d for craftsmen and 4d for labourers – remained the norm for most outdoor workers until about 1540, despite the onset of inflation in the early decades of the century. Although the 1445 Act failed to control wages, those of 1495 and 1514 probably helped to stabilise rates at the same level until the 1540s. Certainly, in the mid sixteenth century commentators assumed that the legal maxima were the going rates for labour.[33]

By the middle of the sixteenth century commodity-price inflation had made the maxima of 1514 increasingly unrealistic, and contemporary observers wondered how wage-earners were able to subsist.[34] Part of the answer was that many were being paid at higher rates, and remedial action was necessary if the authorities were to regain control of the situation. At York matters came to a head in 1552 when the building workers went on strike, refusing to accept the old rates newly insisted on by the city council: the craftsmen claimed that they had been getting 8d a day without food rather than 6d as laid down in 1514. The leaders of the strike were thrown in gaol. Unfortunately, the council records reveal nothing further about the dispute, although in 1556 building craftsmen were getting 8d a day, the rate claimed as the going wage in 1552.[35] Elsewhere in the country a more flexible approach was adopted. In 1551 London building workers were allowed to take higher rates than those authorised in the special act of 1515, although they were told to 'work better cheap than they now do', while the Coventry wage assessment of 1553 laid down maximum rates above the old level.[36]

The problem of rising wage rates was not likely to go away, and it may have been exacerbated by the demographic crisis of the mid to late 1550s, which is said to have created a tightness in the labour market.[37] The government needed to act if it was to regain control. The

---

[31] *Selby Accts*, 104–6, 225–8, 245–7. Daubers and plasterers were paid 4d a day and the 'mates' of craftsmen between 2d and 4d.
[32] Rogers 1908, 326.   [33] Roberts 1981, 228.   [34] *Discourse of the Commonweal*, 33.
[35] Woodward 1980b, 7–9. For a more detailed discussion of the events of 1552 see below, pp. 198–9.
[36] Woodward 1980a, 33.   [37] Fisher 1965: see below, pp. 193–5.

first Elizabethan parliament met in the early months of 1559 and considered various matters relating to the regulation of the labour market. A well-known document belonging to this session has survived among the papers of William Cecil, and this series of 'Considerations delivered to the Parliament, 1559' contains a suggestion that the statute of 1389, which allowed local flexibility, should be re-instated.[38] In April 1559 'The Bill for wages of servants and labourers' was given a second reading, but it got no further: the first Elizabethan parliament had enough to do voting taxes, settling the religious issue, and securing the realm.[39]

When parliament met again in 1563 it passed the massive Statute of Artificers, which laid down the framework of wage regulation and control of the labour market for two and a half centuries.[40] But the hiatus between the parliaments of 1559 and 1563 had been a period of experimentation. Discussion of government policy is complicated by the gap in the Acts of the Privy Council from May 1559 to May 1562 so that it is necessary to piece together government intentions from the reaction in the provinces to central directives. But it is clear that the government adopted a two-pronged strategy, attempting to enforce a rigid policy in the north (insisting on the implementation of the maxima of 1514), but experimenting with a more conciliatory and flexible approach in the south and midlands. Wage assessments, allowing rates above the 1514 level, were issued for Northamptonshire and Worcester in 1560, Buckinghamshire in 1561, King's Lynn in 1562, and the Cinque Ports in the early 1560s.[41] In August 1560 the mayor and aldermen of Hull received a letter from the Council in the North which said that 'we be informed that there is much disorder within our town of Kingston upon Hull by labourers, artificers, and workmen much against our laws and statutes therefore provided'. Appended to the letter was a list of articles to be observed 'concerning the order of servants of husbandry, labourers and artificers', which echoed earlier acts and pointed ahead to many of the provisions of the Statute of Artificers. It was followed by the statement, 'None to take more wages than hereafter is declared', and the rates of 1514 were reiterated. At the Hull council meeting of 24 August the proposals were fully accepted.[42] The York city fathers ignored the orders. In June 1561 they received a letter from the council asking why they had been 'very negligent in the accomplishment of your duties in the execution of the former articles

[38] *TED*, I, 325–30.
[39] *House of Commons Journals*, I (1549–1647), bills 54, 56, 58–61; Woodward 1980a, 34–5.
[40] 5 Elizabeth I c.4.   [41] Woodward 1980a, 32–44; Roberts 1981, 21–2.
[42] Woodward 1980a, 36–7; Woodward 1979, 101–4.

and instructions heretofore sent you touching servants, labourers, regrators and others'. Again they failed to act, but in August they were spurred into action by another letter which mentioned that the laws for 'servants and labourers' were to be enforced. At the sessions of January 1562 the details of the 1514 Act were written into the record, and 113 workers were indicted for receiving excessive wages. Building craftsmen were accused of taking 7d or 8d a day in summer without food – the rate claimed by the strikers of 1552 – and labourers 6d.[43] Scattered data for other provincial towns between 1559 and 1563 indicate a general interest in the regulation of labour markets: at Liverpool reference was made to 'common labourers [who] have of late taken great and excessive wages for their labours'.[44]

But more radical action was needed if a coherent national policy was to emerge. It came with the Statute of Artificers, the preamble of which recognised that the wage rates laid down in 1495 and 1514 were no longer appropriate:

chiefly for that the wages and allowances limited and rated in many of the said statutes, are in divers places too small and not answerable to this time, respecting the advancement of prices of all things belonging to the said servants and labourers, the laws cannot conveniently without the great grief and burden of the poor labourer and hired man be put in good and due execution.

Henceforth wages were to be assessed annually by local JPs.

The immediate response of the justices in the northern towns was to raise rates above the levels laid down in 1514. At York the mayor and aldermen, 'having consideration of excessive prices of all manner of victual and other necessaries in these north parts', established a maximum rate of 10d a day in summer 'without meat' for the free mason or master carpenter 'taking the charge of the work and having under them three servants at the least'. Other building craftsmen were to take no more than 8d, and labourers were to have no more than 5d a day throughout the year without their diet. Similarly, Lincoln building craftsmen were not to get more than 10d a day and their servants or labourers 7d.[45] The few wage rates available for Lincoln workers in 1563 suggest that the rates assessed as maxima were close to the market level, and the same was broadly true at York, although labourers generally got 6d a day compared with the assessed maximum of 5d. Assessments for other northern towns have not survived for 1563, although the Newcastle justices assessed rates on at least three occasions during the 1560s. Wage assessments have survived for Hull and

---

[43] Woodward 1980a, 37.   [44] *Ibid.*, 39.   [45] *Tudor Proclamations*, II, 223–7.

Table 6.2. *Maximum wage rates assessed at Chester, 1570 and 1575 (in pence, without food and drink)*

	1570	1575
Master carpenter	12	8
Carpenter's servant	6	4
Sawyer	8	8
Joiner	8	5
Rough mason, plasterer	6	$4\frac{1}{2}$
Bricklayer	4	6
Slater	4	4
Tiler	4	5
Thatcher	4	3
Mowers of corn: Best sort	3	10
Second sort	2	—
Third sort	2	—

Source: Tudor Proclamations, II, 339, 392–3.

Chester in 1570.[46] At Hull master craftsmen were to receive no more than 10d a day in summer without food, and junior craftsmen 8d. The authorities had taken the advice of 'divers discreet and sage men of the said town' about the appropriate level of wages, 'having respect as well to the plenty as to the scarcity of things that is very likely to be in these parts this year following'.[47] The Hull authorities, along with those at Lincoln and York in 1563, confirmed the existing market rates as the allowable maxima. That is, they took the view that the market rate – which was well above the old 1514 level – was fair and, hence, that they needed to do no more than rubber-stamp current practice. However, there are signs that, in some of the towns, the new powers were soon being used to try to hold down wages. At York the rates assessed in 1563 were re-issued for more than twenty years, and by the 1580s the authorities were battling to hold the line against wage increases: in May 1581 the leaders of four of the gilds were ordered to observe the assessed rates.[48] From at least 1570 the Chester justices took a severe line and attempted to peg wage rates. During the late

---

[46] Minchinton 1972, 208–9; TWAS, 543/15, fos. 224v, 296r. For the 1580 assessment see *ibid.*, 543/16, fo. 133r.
[47] *Tudor Proclamations*, II, 337–9.
[48] YCR, VI, 83, 101, 126, 137; VII, 30, 140; VIII, 11, 46, 101.

Table 6.3. *Maximum wage rates assessed at Chester, 1597 (in pence)*

	With meat and drink	Without meat and drink
Master carpenter	$3\frac{1}{2}$	9
Carpenter's servant	1	7
Rough mason	2	8
Plasterer	$1\frac{1}{2}$	8
Slater	1	8
Bricklayer	2	7
Sawyer and tiler	$1\frac{1}{2}$	7
Thatcher	1	7
Joiner	$1\frac{1}{2}$	$6\frac{1}{2}$

Source: Tudor Proclamations, III, 173–4.

1560s craftsmen got between 8d and 10d in the town, but the authorities laid down maxima of between 4d and 8d a day for ordinary building craftsmen in 1570. This measure may have had some effect in pulling down nominal rates, although most craftsmen were paid at higher levels. In 1575, having considered 'the plenteousness and cheap of things at this present', and despite their earlier failure to lower wages, the Chester justices reduced the allowable maxima still further.[49] The rates for 1570 and 1575 are set out in table 6.2.

Despite the wording of the assessment, it is difficult to believe that the rates for some workers – and especially for the mowers of corn in 1570, or the thatcher in 1575 – were exclusive of diet. Moreover, there seems to be no logic in the shifting rates from one type of worker to another: consider the positions of the carpenter's servant and the bricklayer.

The Chester justices returned to their task in the 1590s, although in 1593 and 1596 they only stipulated daily rates when food was provided for the worker. The rates for both years seem very low: most were to receive not more than between 1d and $2\frac{1}{2}$d a day when fed at work. The only exceptions were the mill wright who was given a maximum of 3d, and the master carpenter who could take 4d. In 1597, apparently spurred by the escalating food prices of the mid 1590s the mayor and other justices 'with respect and consideration had of the great dearth and scarcity of things at this present' raised the rates for workers hired

[49] *Tudor Proclamations*, II, 339, 392–3. According to data, mostly for the south of England, 1573 was a poor harvest year but that of 1574 average. According to the prices presented by Peter Bowden the average price for all grains stood at 313 for 1563–72, but hit 478 in 1573 before falling back to 334 in 1574: Hoskins 1964, 37, 39; Thirsk 1967, 819.

by the year who fed themselves, and also laid down rates in both categories for workers hired by the day (see table 6.3).[50]

These rates were out of line with market-place reality in Chester: during 1598 slaters earned 8d a day when feeding themselves, the rate laid down in the assessment, but sawyers and carpenters got 12d. This suggests that the Chester authorities were attempting, unsuccessfully, to control what they regarded as excessive rates of pay, as they had in the early 1590s when the carpenters and slaters were condemned for their 'great exactions of the citizens'. The aldermen and stewards of the gilds had been called before the mayor 'for remedy of all such wrong, oppression and injuries by them and their companies formerly committed'. They were told to 'receive and give from time to time such wages as shall be appointed by the mayor for the time being'.[51]

From the limited amount of evidence available it seems likely that most wage assessments in northern England tended to mirror the rates prevailing in the local labour market. It is possible in the case of York that the reiteration of the same rates for twenty years had the effect of curbing further increases, although the market rate for skilled men advanced from a predominant 8d in the 1560s, to between 8d and 10d in the 1580s. Only for Chester is there clear evidence of an attempt to peg rates below the market level. However, after the turn of the century the York city fathers tried to do likewise. During the first decade of the new century the most common daily rate for craftsmen in the northern capital was 13d, although the range was from 10d to 14d between 1605 and 1610, while labourers were paid at a level 8d. But in four assessments between 1605 and 1610 the justices attempted, unsuccessfully, to pull down rates to a lower level. Craftsmen were not to take more than 8d or 10d in the summer according to the assessments of 1605 and 1607, and not more than 10d or 12d following the assessments of 1609 and 1610. All four assessments laid down a maximum of 6d for labourers, a rate they had not been getting since the 1580s.[52]

After this brief flurry of activity in York the civic authorities of northern England seem to have intervened rarely in the process of wage determination. This was true also in other parts of the country, and urban assessments became particularly rare after 1660.[53] There was, however, some quickening of interest in the regulation of wages during the middle two decades of the century which was probably

[50] *Tudor Proclamations*, III, 117–18, 158–9, 173–4.   [51] Morris 1893, 436.

[52] YCA, B32, fos 362r and v; B33, fos. 66r–67r, 163r–164r, 200v–201v.

[53] Roberts 1981, 9, 66. Assessments in London ceased after the 1590s: Rappaport 1984, 109.

Table 6.4   *Rates assessed at Hull for the summer (in pence, without food and drink)*

	1669	1683	1721
Master joiner	20	20	20
His servant	14	—	—
Master carpenter	18	20	20
His servant	12	14	14
Master bricklayer, tiler or paver	18	20	20
Their servants	8	12	—

Source: HCRO, CAR/1–3.

connected with the substantial increase in the level of prices in the mid to late 1640s, and their subsequent decline in the 1650s, together with significant increases in most wage rates. At York a committee was established in 1646 to consider the wages of carpenters and bricklayers, and the wages of the main building workers were set at no more than 16d in 1651.[54] Since the going rate for skilled labour was between 18d and 20d in the late 1640s and early 1650s it would appear that the council was batting on a losing wicket. Two years later, a minute in the Chester Assembly Book recorded that building craftsmen should not take more than 14d in the summer and their men 12d.[55] Again the attempt to peg wage rates failed and skilled men received between 13d and 18d at Chester in the 1650s. At national level there was a flurry of assessment activity in the mid 1650s, and a committee of the House of Commons was asked to investigate the 'more effectual execution of existing wage statutes'. Nothing came of the initiative.[56]

After 1660 only the justices of Kendal and Hull attempted to regulate the pay of building workers, although the chief concern of the Hull magistrates was to control the cost of carriage around the town: highly detailed schedules were laid down for the porters according to the distances that goods were carried. The rates for building craftsmen were added to the main body of the assessment almost as an after-thought (see table 6.4)[57]

These maxima were somewhat lower than the prevailing market rates being paid by the council itself and other customers: this seems to have been a classic case of the right hand not knowing, and perhaps not caring, what the left hand was doing. If the intention was to reduce

[54] YCA, B36/200; Roberts 1981, 196.   [55] CCRO, AB/2, fo. 102v.
[56] Roberts 1981, 40–1.
[57] HCRO, CAR/1–3.

wage rates the policy was a resounding flop. Assessments were drawn up at Kendal in 1667 and 1719, although they were headed 'Westmorland' and may well have been intended chiefly for implementation in the countryside: nevertheless, the 1719 assessment did stipulate that the rates laid down were 'not to be exceeded in the Barony of Kendal', which suggests that the town was included. However, the rates laid down in both assessments were unrealistic. In 1667 master builders were not to take more than 8d a day in the summer 'without meat and drink', and they were to have 7d for their assistants over the age of 18. But most building craftsmen received between 14d and 16d a day at Kendal during the 1660s. The allowable maxima were raised in 1719: skilled men were to take as much as 10d or 12d a day, and their older journeymen 10d. General labourers were not specified, although agricultural labourers were not to get more than 8d a day.[58] Market rates are very scarce for Kendal in the early eighteenth century, although once again the allowable maxima seem to have been lower than the wages actually received in the town.

At the end of the last century Thorold Rogers believed that from 1563 to the early nineteenth century 'a conspiracy, concocted by the law and carried out by parties interested in its success, was entered into, to cheat the English workman of his wages, to tie him to the soil, to deprive him of hope, and to degrade him into irremediable poverty'. Indeed, the Statute of Artificers had the effect of making his wages small 'by allowing those who are interested in keeping him poor to fix the wages on which he shall subsist'.[59] And many historians have agreed that 'the State everywhere exerted its influence on the side of low wages'.[60] But the effect of such control, especially after 1563, was probably minimal. The Act of 1445 had failed to control wage rates in the later decades of the fifteenth century, although the more realistic maxima established in 1495 and 1514 were generally adhered to during the first three or four decades of the sixteenth century. But these could not be maintained during the mid-Tudor inflation. The Statute of Artificers, with its inbuilt flexibility of locally determined maxima, allowed the gradual emergence of wage differentials from place to place and may – at least in the sixteenth century – have done something to curb excessive wage inflation. But after 1600, and especially after 1660, wage assessment was rarely used in the towns and where it was used – as in the case of Hull – the assessed maxima were below the market level. However, it has been argued that wage control was not simply a matter of economic control, and that the authorities were

---

[58] CUMROK, WD/Ry, Box 31; WQ/I/4.   [59] Rogers 1908, 398–9.
[60] Coleman 1955–6, 281 quoting Heckscher.

more concerned with the maintenance of social order and hierarchy than with the achievement of economic ends.[61] That may have been the case, although, if so, the Chester justices changed their minds dramatically between 1570 and 1575 about the pecking order between the various building trades.

The supply of labour

Knowledge of the labour supply in any society is always bound to be partial. By 'labour supply' we mean the total number of hours of work that the population is willing and able to provide. Other things being equal, the labour force will expand if the population grows, as it did in England for much of the sixteenth and early seventeenth centuries. Moreover the supply of labour for any sector can rise if resources are switched from one area to another. The population of England more than doubled after 1500 to reach an estimated 5.2 million in 1650: it then fell back to just over 5 million in 1700, before rising to some 6 million in 1750.[62] Growing numbers meant that more hands were available to guide ploughs and shuttles, and to accomplish the numberless back-breaking tasks of a relatively unmechanised society. The ranks of wage-earners grew both relatively and absolutely during the period, although many, especially in the countryside, were not totally dependent on their wages for their support, and many by-employments sprang up to provide work for idle hands.[63] The proportion of the population available for wage work will vary depending on a number of factors, including the age structure, attitudes to child and female employment, and the availability of effective relief for the young and old, lame and sick. The productiveness of labour will depend not only on the volume of capital employed and the quality of organisation in the work place, but on the physical attributes of individual workers which will be related to the abundance and variety of the diet, the length of the working day, general levels of health, and attitudes to work. The size of the labour force cannot be determined simply by adding up the total number of those apparently available for work. In every society there are those who would rather beg, borrow, or steal for their livelihoods and early-modern England was no exception. Moreover, labour can voluntarily withdraw from the productive process, or threaten to do so, and the attitudes of workers to their conditions of work, and especially to their levels of remuneration,

---

[61] Roberts 1981, abstract.   [62] Wrigley & Schofield 1981, 531–3.
[63] Thirsk 1967, 399; Thirsk 1978.

probably played a crucial role in the determination of wage rates in early-modern England.

For Thorold Rogers 'the fifteenth century and the first quarter of the sixteenth were the golden age of the English labourer ... At no time were wages, relatively speaking, so high, and at no time was food so cheap.' Modern historians still see the late Middle Ages as a period of relative prosperity.[64] At York 'wages for all labour, and particularly for unskilled and semi-skilled labour, rose very considerably in the later Middle Ages, sustained at this higher level by a shortage of manpower until the early sixteenth century'.[65] This situation was caused by the great fall in the national population following the Black Death and its failure to recover in the fifteenth century. But numbers began to increase from the late fifteenth or early decades of the sixteenth century, and commodity prices began to rise. Historians believe that for much of the following two centuries the English labour market was well-stocked and that – apart from exceptional periods such as that following the demographic crisis of the late 1550s – the economy was characterised by a substantial degree of unemployment and under-employment: this can be illustrated by the great seasonal fluctuations in employment levels for both labourers and skilled men, and also by the high levels of poverty which are said to have characterised the flourishing ports of Hull and Newcastle towards the end of the period.[66] The over-stocking of the labour market was reflected in the long-term deterioration in real wages, and in the long periods during which nominal rates failed to rise.

At least by the 1540s, and perhaps earlier, the English economy was exhibiting many of the features of the labour-surplus economy analysed by W.A. Lewis. He argued that in many economies 'an unlimited supply of labour is available at a subsistence wage'.[67] However, the concept of a subsistence wage is extremely illusive. Whose subsistence would such a wage provide for? Would it cover the man and his wife, and a number of children? Would the man have to work for six days a week throughout the year to guarantee the survival of the household unit? It would be difficult in early-modern England to point to a time when wages were at the subsistence level, since nominal rates often remained the same for decades at a time while their real value was being eroded by inflation. If a labourer's wages were set at the level of a 'bare physical subsistence standard', as Maurice Dobb suggested,[68]

---

[64] Rogers 1908, 326; C. Dyer 1989, 276.   [65] Swanson 1989, 152.
[66] Howell 1967, 314–19; Jackson 1972, 319–26.
[67] Lewis 1959, 448. See also Clarkson 1982, 17–18; Dobb 1960, 147–51; Wootton 1962, 22.
[68] Dobb 1960, 134.

they must have fallen well below the subsistence level after some years or decades of inflation. What we can say is that a plentiful supply of labour was available in early-modern England at the going rate: whether or not that was at subsistence level must remain an open question, which will be reconsidered in the next chapter.

Both the gilds and the town authorities tried to regulate the supply of labour by restricting entry into the towns, albeit with different motives. Gild regulations were aimed chiefly at controlling entry to the ranks of the master craftsmen rather than curbing the total number of men working in a particular craft. Any success which the gilds had in restricting the number of skilled men improved their bargaining position, and it is possible that the widening wage differentials between craftsmen and labourers in some of the northern towns was due, to some extent, to the deliberate restrictions placed on recruitment to the skilled ranks. However, differentials became most marked at Hull where the gild structure was relatively weak.[69] The desire of the town authorities to inhibit immigration was related to fears about the numbers who might call on civic support in times of distress. At Hull newcomers were to be tolerated only if they were 'not likely to become chargeable to the body politic', and similar considerations were expressed at Chester and Grimsby.[70] But town authorities found it extremely difficult to restrain undesirable settlement – as in York during Elizabeth's reign, or Hull in the 1640s, when the population expanded rapidly[71] – and it seems unlikely that such policies affected wage levels to any marked extent.

The most substantial discussion of the effect of changes in the supply of labour on wage rates in early-modern England came from the pen of F.J. Fisher in 1965. He argued that 'the catastrophic harvests of 1555 and 1556 were followed by one of the major influenza epidemics in English history', which may have reduced the national population by almost a fifth and which had the effect of raising wage levels and slowing down the increase in grain prices. Acknowledging that his statistics were none-too-reliable, he added that, 'since a considerably smaller fall than a fifth would be enough to affect wage rates, it demonstrates that no wildly improbable demographic implications lie hid in the proposition that one effect of the famines and epidemics of the 'fifties was to give a temporary buoyancy to wage rates'.[72]

[69] See above pp. 30–1.
[70] Gillett & MacMahon 1989, 128–9; Davies 1956; *Chester Minutes*, 55; Gillett 1970, 112.
[71] Palliser 1979, 125; see below p. 201 for a discussion of the population of Hull.
[72] Fisher 1965, 125, 127.

Table 6.5 *Median daily wage rates of building workers in southern England*

	Cambridge, Canterbury, Dover and Devon (Fisher)		Oxford (Brown)	
	Carpenter	Labourer	Carpenter	Labourer
1500–4	6	4	6	4
1540–4	7–8	5	6–7	4
1560–4	12	8	10	6–8
1630–4	12–20	10–14	12–16	8–10

Source: Fisher 1965, 122; Brown and Hopkins 1981, 11.

Moreover, the upwards pressure on wage rates increased the impetus to reorganise the labour market and contributed to the genesis of the Statute of Artificers. These views have taken on the authority of orthodoxy.[73] The reality of the crisis is not in any doubt. The work of Wrigley and Schofield indicated that by 1561 the national population was some 5.5 per cent lower than it had been in 1556, although a recent article has suggested that their analysis masks the severity of the crisis, which was nearer the order of magnitude suggested by Fisher.[74] But the effect of the crisis on the pattern of wage-rate movements remains in doubt. Fisher used data from the Beveridge archive to support his views and suggested that material presented by Phelps Brown and Hopkins showed broadly similar trends, albeit at a slightly lower level (see table 6.5).

Both series show a substantial increase in wage rates between the early 1540s and the early 1560s, although it is impossible from such data to determine the timing of the changes. In fact, up and down the country much of the increase took place before the outbreak of influenza in 1557. In Oxford craftsmen's wage rates began to edge upwards from a standard 6d a day to between 6d and 7d, and occasionally 8d, in the later 1530s and early 1540s, while in 1549 and 1550 they stood at 8d or 9d. The year 1551 was an extraordinary one for the Oxford men: they were paid between 12d and 14d in that year of financial uncertainty. Thereafter from 1552 to 1559 rates mostly fell in the range 8d to 10d a day, and then hardened to 10d from 1560.[75] Similarly in London the wages paid to skilled men and labourers rose

[73] Woodward 1980a, 33; Corfield in Fisher 1990, 12; Roberts 1981, 198–9; Foot 1980, 2; Palliser 1983, 53.
[74] Wrigley and Schofield 1981; Moore 1993.   [75] Rogers 1882, III, 606–36.

by 50 per cent between 1543 and 1551, but by smaller proportions from 1555 to 1563: skilled rates rose by 16.6 per cent and those for labourers by 25 per cent.[76] Unfortunately, data for the north of England are less plentiful for the middle decades of the century, although there is enough evidence to suggest that much of the upward movement occurred before the demographic crisis of 1557–9. At Durham much of the increase came before 1555, and relatively high rates were paid at Gateshead in 1551: most carpenters and sawyers got 9d a day, although one man received only 8d. Across the river at Newcastle two men were paid 8d a day for mending walls.[77] Workmen at the royal works at Berwick still received the statutory rates of 6d for craftsmen and 4d for labourers in 1538, although in the early months of 1557, before the onset of the infection, wages were considerably higher. Labourers got 5d in the winter and 6d in the summer, although craftsmen received level rates regardless of the season. Their pay ranged from 7d to 8d for the carpenters; 8d for the joiners, slaters, some masons and hard-hewers; up to 10d a day for the masons; while the 'hard-hewers occupied at the hard stone quarry' got 10d or 11d.[78] In September 1557 quarriers at Carlisle got 6d a day, carpenters 7d, and masons 8d, although the labourers had not moved on from the statutory 4d.[79] Elsewhere in Cumbria some masons engaged in bridge repair in 1554 got 8d a day, and the labourers 6d: some other skilled men received 10d a day in 1559, although the labourers were still on 6d.[80] The fragmentary data available for Hull and York suggest that wage rates rose in the early 1550s, although some further movement occurred in the later 1550s and early 1560s. Thus, the demographic crisis of 1557–9 may have helped to fuel demands for higher wage rates, but the main tide of mid-century increases had come before 1557. Fisher's influenza may have culled the population to a remarkable extent, but its effect on wage rates was modest, at best.

If a major national demographic crisis failed to have a significant impact on the level of wage rates it may be imagined that more localised crises, which struck individual communities with awesome effect, would have had major repercussions on local labour markets, forcing up wage rates here and there in piecemeal fashion. This was the case in London where wage rates shot up temporarily in response to the moderate plague of 1636, and again in the mid 1660s under the dual stimulus of a swingeing reduction in the labour supply following the plague of 1665 and a massive increase in the demand for labour

[76] Rappaport 1989, 405.   [77] DFC, CC/190076.   [78] PRO, E101/483/14; 16.
[79] PRO, E101/483/17.
[80] G.P. Jones 1953, 89–90.

after the fire of the following year. In each case, however, rates returned to their previous levels once the crisis had passed. The great London plague of 1625 may have helped to raise metropolitan rates to a new and enduring level in the mid 1620s.[81] But it seems that, as in so many areas of economic and social life, the metropolitan experience was unique. In the north, major urban demographic crises did not disturb market wage rates.

Perhaps the most severe northern crisis occurred at York in 1604. During Elizabeth's reign the city had been free of plague, but the outbreak of 1604 wiped out an estimated 30 per cent of the population.[82] Rates of pay were not affected. Perhaps a similar proportion of the Newcastle population died in the plague of 1588/9, but for most of the 1590s wage rates remained at the level of the previous decade. Likewise, the devastating visitations of 1597 and the mid 1630s seem to have had no effect on wage levels.[83] At Hull in 1637 perhaps an eighth of the town's population died, but again wage rates remained undisturbed. Nor were they affected at Chester following the heavy death toll of 1603–6.[84]

At first sight the stability in wage rates during and after a massive fall in a town's population is puzzling. Perhaps the iron grip of custom precluded any movement. But a more likely explanation relates to shifts in the demand for labour, and in its supply. In the short term urban economies were devastated by such demographic crises, and especially by the fierce assaults of bubonic plague. At Newcastle during 1588/9 the business of the town was said to be at a standstill, as it was at Hull in 1637. Markets were suspended, townsfolk quarantined, and most jobs involving labourers and building craftsmen ground to a halt. Very little work was done for the Hull council during July, August, and October 1637, and none at all in September. Traditionally these were busy months. Those not allowed to leave their houses included the mother and father of Andrew Marvell, the Hull MP and poet.[85] Strict quarantine measures must have made it very difficult, if not impossible, for traders and artisans to maintain their businesses and support their families.[86] Everywhere plague 'stopped work and destroyed wealth', not least because many citizens, and especially the richer tradesmen who were so crucial to the

[81] Boulton 1987b, 13–14.   [82] Palliser 1979, 124–5; Palliser 1973a, 54–6.
[83] Shrewsbury 1971, 241–2; Palliser 1973a, 52; Clark & Slack 1976, 89; Howell 1967, 6–7; Clark & Slack 1972, 7.
[84] Data on Hull from the CAMPOP files; Alldridge 1986, 8.
[85] Barnes 1891, 171; Gillett & MacMahon 1989, 162; HCRO, BRF/3/19; *VCH Hull*, 155–6.
[86] Archer 1991, 198.

vitality of early-modern towns, took flight for the duration of the outbreak.[87]

Major mortality crises did create some extra employment. At Newcastle in 1597 the gravemaker was kept busy, and George Hindmers and his assistant rounded up and executed roaming dogs, together with small numbers of swine and geese. Hindmers – a 'butcher and beadle for the poor' – claimed to have exterminated 150 dogs between February and April 1597, at 2d a head. Extra hands were also needed to carry food and coal to the infected, and some carpenters were busy making 'lodges' for the sick. In March two men were paid 6s 'to put new-comed beggars out of town'.[88] But there can be no doubt that the disruption to normal businesses far outweighed the effects of plague as a job-creator, and that 'plague totally disrupted the life of a town, causing unemployment and bringing its markets to a standstill'.[89] As far as the building trades were concerned, few customers were likely to contemplate beginning a new project, and all but the most urgent of existing jobs were likely to be shelved. Given that contemporaries believed that the plague could be passed from person to person, few would be prepared to welcome a potential plague-carrier into their homes unless it was absolutely vital.

Thus, although plague, or any other major epidemic, could deliver a devastating blow to a town's labour supply – and the short-term loss could be much greater than the eventual death toll since many suffered weeks of debilitating illness before recovering – it also dramatically reduced the demand for labour in the short run. Whether or not the supply of labour or the demand for it fell more steeply cannot be determined, but the reduction was not sufficiently asymmetrical to affect wage levels. In the medium term – that is, the year or so after the outbreak – things got back to normal. Markets reopened, abandoned trade routes were re-established, and the economic tempo of the town quickened. At that point we might expect an upward pressure to be exerted on wage rates as demand re-asserted itself. But, except in the case of London, this did not occur since urban populations, and hence the supply of labour, recovered quickly even after the most severe crises.[90] Demographic recovery can be best illustrated from the experience at York in 1604 where perhaps a third of the population died. But recovery set in quickly,[91] and the revival of economic hope was

---

[87] Slack 1985, 188–9; Willan 1983, 33–4; Supple 1964, 25–6, 99–102.
[88] TWAS, 543/19, fos. 17r–25v, 59r. For pest houses elsewhere see *VCH Hull*, 155; Slack 1985, 45–7, 276–7, 282–3.
[89] Clark & Slack 1976, 89.   [90] Slack 1985, 190.
[91] See various York parish registers including those of St Michael le Belfry PR; St Martin, Coney St., PR.

reflected in the scramble of townsmen and outsiders to join the ranks of the city's freemen. Immigrant admissions which had averaged 45 a year during the 1590s fell to 15 in 1604, but rose to 82 in 1605 and remained at that level for three years: citizen admissions, which had averaged 27 in the 1590s, rose to 90 in 1605 before gradually declining to their former level.[92] Thus, it was 'business as usual' at York within a remarkably short interval after the crisis of 1604, and the same was true at Chester after the outbreak of 1603–6: within a year or two 'numbers were back to normal'.[93] Rapid recovery also took place at Hull after the plague of 1637. Such demographic resilience relied on high levels of immigration. The ability of urban economies to bounce back rapidly after the most appalling loss of life meant that any shortfall in the labour supply was made good before any increase in the demand for labour could make itself felt sufficiently to impose an upward pressure on wage rates.

Wage rates tended to move upwards in the sixteenth and seventeenth centuries during or after periods of rapid inflation, especially in the prices of basic foodstuffs, which suggests that the increase in nominal rates may have been connected with the refusal of labour to accept further reductions in their living standards. The clearest examples come from the middle decades of both the sixteenth and seventeenth centuries. The relatively modest inflation curve of the early decades of the sixteenth century steepened dramatically during the debasement of the 1540s,[94] and by the end of the decade wage rates were moving upwards throughout the country. Statutory wage controls, last imposed in 1514, became irrelevant and an attempt to re-impose the old rates at York in 1552 was met with agonised disbelief. In their petition of 12 July 1552 the leaders of the York building crafts argued that they could not subsist on the old rates:

It is so that all things are so dear and out of the way that we are not able to work for that wage unless we should be forced and constrained to run out of the city or else our wives and children and our servants to go on begging for ever. Wherefore, we ... beseech you ... to suffer ... us to take our wages as they that do set us on work and we can agree or else to license us to complain us further, for the truth is, do with us what so ever shall please you for we will not work for that wage that will not find us unless you do rate all manner of tools and tool-makers and all victuallers as you do your poor orators.[95]

---

[92] Palliser 1973a, 57.
[93] CAMPOP holds transcriptions of the registers of the two Hull churches and I am grateful to them for providing me with copies.
[94] Rappaport 1989, 132; Outhwaite 1982, 12–16; Thirsk 1967, 816–19; Rogers 1908, 343–5, 428.
[95] Woodward 1980b, 9.

This passage is worth quoting in some detail because at no other point can the demands of labour be heard so clearly. And it was just this situation which the Act of 1548 'touching victuallers and handicraftmen' had been designed to avoid.[96] It laid down that:

if any artificers, workmen or labourers do conspire, covenant or promise together or make any oaths that they shall not make or do their works but at a certain price and rate, or shall not enterprise or take upon them to finish that another hath begun, or shall do but a certain work in a day, or shall not work but at certain hours and times, that then every person so conspiring, covenanting, swearing or offending being lawfully convicted thereof by witness, confession or otherwise, shall forfeit for the first offence ten pounds to the King's majesty ... or else shall suffer for the first offence twenty days' imprisonment and shall have only bread and water for his sustenance.

That such a measure could control all such activity was a forlorn hope. Workmen everywhere were feeling the pinch and customers were forced to pay wages higher than the legal maxima if workers were to remain healthy or, perhaps, if they were to remain at work at all. Whether workmen outside York withdrew their labour in the early 1550s is not known, but in many cases the mere threat of action or, perhaps, the sight of a half-starved workman may have been sufficient to induce the payment of higher rates.

Strikes were rare in early-modern England,[97] and much of the negotiation for higher wages was conducted in private, away from the prying eyes of official record keepers and modern historians. One such incident can be detected from the detailed accounts of Hull Trinity House. During the 1610s the cost of transferring a chaldron of coal from on board ship to the quayside suddenly jumped from between 14d and 17d to about 30d, and the increase was due almost entirely to a substantial rise in the labour charge, rather than to the cost of boat hire.[98] Unfortunately, the town council minutes are entirely silent about the issue, and we can only guess at the haggling which had taken place.

After the rapid inflation of the middle decades of the sixteenth century food prices rose more gently for some time, although they climbed steeply following the poor harvests of the mid 1580s, and the string of near-disastrous harvests of the mid to late 1590s. Wage rates for workers who fed themselves rose modestly during the 1590s and early 1600s, although not in line with the increase in food prices. In London, labourers' rates which had been frozen since 1560 began to

---

[96] 2 & 3 Edward VI c.15.
[97] Rappaport 1989, 10; Howell 1967, 292–3. See also E. Hughes 1952, 16; Dobson 1980, 22.
[98] HTH, III.

rise in 1593, although the rates for craftsmen, which had not moved since 1576, did not begin to rise until two years later.[99] Thorold Rogers also detected some upward movements in southern England during the same decade,[100] Unfortunately, the northern accounts are mostly too fragmentary to be able to chart shifts in nominal rates with any degree of accuracy. However, there are signs of movement in the accounts of both Beverley and Kendal, and an even clearer picture emerges from the records of York and Newcastle. At York skilled men received between 8d and 11d during the late 1580s and early 1590s, but by the early seventeenth century they were getting between 11d and 13d: the rate of 12d was first recorded in 1596. Labourers moved from 6d or 7d in the mid 1590s, to between 6d and 8d in 1599, and to 7d or 8d in the early seventeenth century. At Newcastle between 8d and 10d was paid to skilled men from 1590 to 1598, and between 10d and 12d from 1599: labourers remained on 6d until 1600, and then moved to 8d in 1601.

By the outbreak of the Civil War nominal rates had risen substantially, although real wages were significantly lower than they had been a century and a half earlier. It seems plausible to suggest that, despite the pools of surplus labour in many towns and in the countryside, workers could not afford to let living standards decline too disastrously, and that periodic refusals to accept out-moded levels of pay had helped to nudge nominal rates upwards. But there were limits. Labour was never in a sufficiently strong postion to be able to insist on rates which kept pace with the inflation.

By the early 1640s the price of grain was some six times the level it had been in the late fifteenth century, but prices raced upwards again in the second half of the decade: in 1646 prices were about a third higher than in the early 1640s, and for the three years 1647–9 they were fully two-thirds higher.[101] Alarm bells rang in the homes of many wage-earners, and, once again, in a period of escalating prices, wage rates moved upwards. Many years ago Lipson suggested that 'the Civil War, among its other economic effects, caused a rise in prices which necessitated an advance in wages':[102] he may not have been completely right about the cause of the renewed inflation, but he was correct in believing that there was a substantial rise in nominal rates. London rates rose during the years 1640–3, and during 1649–59, and, overall, 'the steepest rise in wages took place in 1640–56 … followed by a plateau which remained until the early 1690s'.[103] Northern rates also

---

[99] Rappaport 1989, 405–7.   [100] Rogers 1887, VI, 614–22.
[101] Thirsk 1967, 815–21; Thirsk 1985, 828.
[102] Lipson 1934, III, 260.   [103] Boulton 1987b, 13.

rose substantially during the middle years of the seventeenth century. For some of the northern towns – including Carlisle, Chester, and Hull – the data are too thin to be able to pin-point the years when rates moved upwards, although at both Kendal and Newcastle higher rates were paid from 1647, and at York the pay of labourers rose in 1646.

The evidence of rising nominal rates during the 1640s and 1650s provides further support for the suggestion that the reluctance of labour to accept the old rates at a time of rapidly rising prices was a major factor in determining the upward movement in wage rates. It is possible that changes affecting the number of workers available also played a part. Some of the northern towns endured debilitating out-breaks of disease during the 1640s,[104] although it seems unlikely that they suffered from serious shortages of labour. The full impact of the conflict on urban society has yet to be fully assessed, although it has been suggested that 'immigration into the larger walled towns acceler-ated as activists fled from the enemy and ordinary villagers sought refuge from armed conflict'.[105] That was certainly the case at Hull. Recovery after the plague of 1637 was swift but, instead of settling back to a demographic equilibrium which was close to the old situation, the town's population continued to grow. Baptisms, which had averaged less than 200 a year in the earlier 1630s, were some 50 per cent higher through the 1640s. To judge from the level of baptisms, the population grew marginally during the 1650s, but then fell away after the Restor-ation. It could hardly be argued that Hull was suffering from an overall shortage of labour during the middle years of the seventeenth century, although the influx probably did more to swell the ranks of potential labourers rather than those of the craftsmen, thus helping to improve the rates of pay of craftsmen relative to those of the labourers.

After 1660 conditions were very different from those of the previous 150 years. The inflation ended in the middle decades of the century, and the national population fell marginally down to 1700, but rose thereafter. Those circumstances may have had a two-fold effect on wage levels: a tightening of the labour supply may have helped labour to resist any attempts to reduce wage rates, and the levelling off of prices probably made customers increasingly reluctant to accede to demands for higher wages. It is possible in the new demographic regime of the later seventeenth century that any sudden reduction in the supply of labour may have affected wage rates, and a demographic crisis between 1679 and 1681 may have affected large parts of eastern and northern Yorkshire: it has been argued that the wages of servants

[104] Howell 1967, 319–20; *VCH Hull*, 156; Alldridge 1986, 8; *VCH York*, 173.
[105] Clark 1981, 15.

hired by the year were pushed up, and that the authorities were stimulated into issuing a new wage assessment and prosecuting offenders against the labour code.[106] But the crisis, which can be monitored in the increased mortality figures for Hull during 1679 and 1680, had no effect on the level of wages in Hull, Beverley, or York.

The demand for labour

Discussion of shifts in the demand for labour is fraught with difficulties. There is no doubt that the growth of population down to the middle of the seventeenth century – in the context of an economy which was expanding and diversifying, albeit slowly – brought an increase in the demand for goods and services, and hence, given the minimal advances in labour productivity, an increase in the demand for labour. Moreover, the building trades benefited from the shifts of economic advantage which tended to favour middle-income groups who spent freely on building new houses and refurbishing the old: there was a nationwide surge in house building in the half century centred on 1600 and, perhaps, an even greater increase around 1700.[107] But it is extremely difficult to move from such broad generalisations to a discussion of changing levels of demand in local labour markets.

One possible clue about differing levels of demand in different markets comes from the broad patterns of wage rate movements in the northern towns. As we have seen, by the outbreak of the Civil War the northern towns had begun to separate out into two groups, as far as the wages of building craftsmen were concerned, with Hull, Beverley, York, and Newcastle emerging as relatively high-wage economies and the others – Lincoln and Durham, and the north-western towns of Chester, Kendal, and Carlisle – as relatively low-wage economies.[108] Differences became more marked in the later seventeenth century. Such variations in levels of pay suggest differences in the relationships between the supply of building craftsmen and the demand for their services in the different towns, and it is noticeable that at least three of the towns in the high-wage group seem to have enjoyed a higher level of economic vitality than the towns in the low-wage group. In the case of the fourth member of the high-wage group – Beverley – building craftsmen seem to have benefited from the town's proximity to Hull: workmen moved freely between the two towns and it seems probable that wages in Beverley – the less vital of the two communities – simply

---

[106] Kelsall 1939, 310–16.   [107] Hoskins 1963; Machin 1977.
[108] See above pp. 173–4.

shadowed the rates paid in Hull.[109] But, of course, any really meaningful analysis of demand would necessitate a detailed investigation of
shifts in the levels and distribution of income, and changes in the
pattens of expenditure in the different towns. This is not possible.
Moreover, the task is made more difficult because we know so little
about changing levels of building activity in the different towns. The
available records, rich in detail though they sometimes are, relate to
only a part, and sometimes a relatively small part, of the total building
activity in a particular town. Thus, it is possible to demonstrate that the
amount of labour required by one of the larger institutions varied
considerably from year to year, but the relationship of that expenditure to the total outlay on building activity in the town is unknown.
Nevertheless, the brief review of economic conditions in the northern
towns and the discussion of shifts in wage rates suggest that those
towns in the high-wage group (with the exception of Beverley) were
larger than those in the low-wage group (with the exception of
Chester), and that their economies were more buoyant. The combination of greater population size and economic buoyancy was perhaps
instrumental in allowing building craftsmen to press for wage rates
which were higher than those achieved in the north-western towns,
together with Lincoln and Durham.

   The rates paid to labourers did not follow the same pattern. Wages
were lowest at Durham and Beverley around 1660, being 8d and 9d
respectively, and highest at Carlisle and Newcastle where they got 12d
a day. They received between 8d and 10d at Lincoln, 8d and 11d at
Chester, 9d or 10d at Kendal, 10d at Hull, and between 10d and 12d at
York. However, the traditional ratio between the rates paid to craftsmen and labourers was breaking down in some places by the middle of
the seventeenth century, and especially in the high-wage towns. This
suggests that the demand for skilled labour, relative to its supply, was
greater than that for labourers in some towns. This would hardly be
surprising, and it is only remarkable that the traditional ratio between
their levels of pay survived in so many places for so long.

   It might be expected that an abrupt increase in the demand for
labour would exert an upward pressure on wage rates. Such occurrences are difficult to detect, although it has been suggested that a
major fire could have raised rates in a particular town.[110] Early-modern
towns with their predominantly timber-framed buildings were particularly susceptible to devastation by fire, and, as Londoners discovered in 1666, both the price of labour and the cost of materials could

[109] See above pp. 163–4.   [110] This was suggested to me by Brian Outhwaite.

escalate after a major conflagration: it was reported in November 1666 that materials were so dear 'that where I had formerly agreed for a small building at £80, they now demand £300'.[111] However, there is no doubt that the Fire of London had a greater impact than usual since the devastation was so widespread, and since it followed the plague of the previous year which, at least temporarily, had cut such swathes through the city's labour force. Evidence of major fires in the north is not plentiful, but Chester was hit hard in 1564,[112] although the full extent of the damage is not known. Unfortunately, the extant accounts are not sufficiently detailed to show clearly whether there was a sudden jump in wage rates: there may have been some upward movement in craftsmen's rates, but it is impossible to be certain. Similarly, Stratford-upon-Avon was ablaze in both 1594 and 1595, but the limited amount of information available in the town accounts suggests that wage rates were unaffected.[113] Although the evidence is extremely thin, and further local research may reveal some interesting and perhaps contrary results, it would not be surprising to learn that wage rates did not rise in response to sudden, short-term surges in the demand for labour. Town economies were not closed and extra labour could be drafted in from other towns, or from the surrounding countryside, as required.[114] Moreover, most – if not all – towns contained pools of underemployed labourers and craftsmen who could be called on to work for longer periods in a crisis. A sudden increase in the demand for labour was more likely to raise workers' average incomes by providing them with more work over the course of a year than to lift their nominal rates of pay.

It is possible that the increase in wage rates during the later 1640s and 1650s was connected with the higher levels of building activity associated with post-war reconstruction. Chester, Hull and Newcastle were all besieged and damaged during the Civil War, and Lincoln and York suffered substantial disruption.[115] Such activity may have stretched existing supplies of labour, although in at least one of the beleaguered towns – Hull – the population rose rapidly during the war years, almost certainly due in large part to an influx from the surrounding countryside. But on balance it seems likely that the increase in nominal rates in the middle decades of the seventeenth century had more to do with the refusal of workers to accept a further deterioration

---

[111] Slack 1988, 38; Kitching 1981; *HMC Hastings*, 1930, 372.   [112] Clark & Slack 1972, 7.
[113] *Stratford Minutes*, IV and V.   [114] See above pp. 162–4.
[115] *Chester Minutes*, I; *VCH Hull*, 105; *VCH York*, 189–90; Howell 1967, 122, 132–4, 153–4, 159–60, 274; J.W.F. Hill 1956, 162–4.

in living standards during a period of escalating prices than with an increased demand for labour.

The role of custom

'Custom' is a very useful concept for economic and social historians since it can be invoked whenever other explanations seem inadequate. Any unusual social configuration or seemingly bizarre economic behaviour can be laid at its door. But customary practices, no matter how strange they may seem to the beholder, did not simply emerge from the ether. Customs as they evolved were related to man's perception of his world, including the social and economic arrangements which surrounded him. Differentials in remuneration between one class of labour and another in early-modern society were often reflections of finely graduated concepts of social hierarchy,[116] and modern differentials owe much to such legacies. One post-war economist could see 'the contemporary wage and salary structure of this country as the accumulated deposit laid down by a rich mixture of economic and social forces, operating through considerable periods of history'.[117] The low rates of pay given to most women in the early-modern period were rooted in convictions – underscored by biblical authority – about their physical, economic and social, intellectual and political inferiority (especially in the eyes of men) which has characterised English society into the present century. Female rates of pay were not simply reflections of the supply of their labour and the demand for it.

Most customs relating to pay had the advantage of being time-saving. Customs such as the accepted differentials in levels of pay between one grade of labour and another obviated the need for constant haggling over rates. There was no need to discuss the relationship between one rate and another: it was taken for granted. But customs were not immutable. In medieval society there was a tendency for wage levels to respond to shifts in commodity prices: they moved up when prices rose and were reduced when they fell.[118] But it can be argued that a new custom emerged from the labour shortages of the later fourteenth and fifteenth centuries. Workers were in a relatively strong position, and they became increasingly reluctant to accept any reduction in their wage rates. No doubt this attitude was stiffened by the inflation of the sixteenth and seventeenth centuries, which meant that any fall in nominal rates would exacerbate the

[116] Roberts 1981, 226.   [117] Wootton 1962, 160.
[118] Bolton 1980, 78, 214.

deterioration taking place in real wages. But, if workers balked at any reduction in their rates of pay, the overstocked labour market meant that wage rates responded to rising prices only after a substantial lag. As at York in 1552, workers were likely to resist attempts to force down their rates of pay, and those magistrates who tried to do so after 1563 by assessing rates below the market level failed. The refusal to accept any reduction in nominal rates helps to explain the characteristic ratchet effect of wage-rate movements: rates moved up at relatively rare intervals, and then remained at the same level for years or even decades on end.[119] Only in London did short-term shocks to the supply of labour disturb this pattern.

Eventually, in the middle decades of the seventeenth century the inflation came to an end, but, as Roger Coke explained in 1671, workers were reluctant to work for lower wages in years when provisions were cheap.[120] This did not prevent modest reductions for craftsmen in the north-western towns during the 1680s, although elsewhere rates for craftsmen did not fall, nor did the rates for labourers in any of the northern towns. The failure of nominal rates to move downwards in the new price environment may be explained, in part at least, by the force of the custom forged during previous centuries. Thereafter, the defence of existing wage rates became a central feature of British labour attitudes. As Keynes explained: 'workers will usually resist a reduction in money-wages', although 'it is not their practice to withdraw their labour whenever there is a rise in the price of wage-goods'.[121]

It may be wondered why those hiring labour were prepared to accept the custom of non-reducing wage rates when they must have been fully aware that alternative supplies of labour were available for hire, sometimes at lower rates of pay. There is no totally satisfactory explanation for this: just a range of theoretical possibilities. Customers tended to hire the same trusted workmen year after year. The men were unlikely to have been prepared to accept varying rates of pay, and customers were probably reluctant to take a chance with a new set of lower-paid workmen who might turn out to be totally inadequate. Also, it could have occurred to those hiring labour that they did not need to reduce rates in order to benefit from cheaper labour, since the onward march of commodity prices for much of the period rendered labour relatively cheaper as the decades passed. Finally, it is possible that some customers, as practising Christians, were sensitive to the

---

[119] Levels of poor relief moved upwards in a similar fashion: Slack 1988, 179.
[120] Quoted in Lipson 1934, III, 276.
[121] Keynes 1960, 9.

plight of struggling wage-earners and were reluctant to contribute to a further deterioration in their economic circumstances. Whatever the reasons – and they would vary from place to place, and from one period to another – the custom of non-reducing wage rates was accepted by customers and workmen alike and, in all but a few isolated instances, it held firm. Other customs affecting income levels and the conditions of employment for labour remain largely hidden from view. Craftsmen in some of the northern towns worked relatively short hours compared with their rural counterparts, although the process by which workers negotiated such an advantage is unknown

Although they remain cloaked in mystery, it is clear that many labour-market customs were produced by market forces, by the subtle interplay between those who wished to employ labour and the workmen who were prepared to sell themselves. Unlike the other factors of production, labour had a voice – both collective and individual – and could respond either positively or negatively to any offer of work. Of course, for some workers custom was so strong that no amount of complaining could produce the desired result. Thus, only in truly exceptional circumstances could female labourers earn as much as the men toiling alongside them. Male labourers were hardly ever able to earn as much as craftsmen: in many places their pay remained in a fixed ratio to that of the more specialised men, sometimes for centuries on end. But relativities could change and the traditional ratio of 3:2 between the pay of craftsmen and labourers broke down in some places until it stood at 2:1. And any custom could be transformed by the compelling force of the market place. The shifting relativities between craftsmen and labourers were probably due to the extreme overstocking of the market for labourers – as at Hull in the mid seventeenth century – and the relative shortage of craftsmen.

Reflections

There can be little doubt that the chief influence on the level of wage rates in early-modern England was the interaction between the supply of labour and the demand for it. For much of the period, and especially in the era of rising population from the early years of the sixteenth century to the mid seventeenth century, labour markets were overstocked, real wages drifted downwards, and workers found it increasingly difficult to support themselves and their families by wage-earning alone. Custom – in part the product of the interplay of economic forces, but also the product of perceptions of social hierarchy

– also played a role in determining the level and movement of nominal wages, and so too did government policy. But regulation was probably the least important factor. And belief in the ineffectiveness of government policy has been expressed not only for England but for the whole of western Europe:

> In spite of severe wage taxation and labour regulations prevailing in many countries, wages during the late fourteenth century and fifteenth century increased not only nominally but also in relation to silver and grain. Consequently it must have been economic forces that caused the relative decline in wages in the sixteenth century. No law or agreement can adequately account for it.[122]

There were probably times when local or national wage regulation helped to stiffen the resolve of customers against demands for higher wage rates, but – as the events of the 1550s demonstrate – no amount of coercion could hold rates back in the face of extreme opposition on the part of labour. Similar attempts after 1563 to use wage assessments to peg wage rates also failed.

Although the mechanisms cannot be clearly discerned, changes in the demand for labour probably help to explain the development of two phenomena in the north during the seventeenth century: the increasing divergence of nominal rates between towns; and the widening of the differential between labourers and craftsmen within some towns. But it is impossible to explain the long-term failure of nominal rates to match the rise in the price of basic foodstuffs without reference to the supply of labour. Every increase in nominal rates improved real wages, at least for a short time, but, until the later part of the seventeenth century, rising prices quickly ate away any benefits. Labour markets were simply too well stocked to allow workers to insist on nominal rates which kept abreast of rising prices, except in the most exceptional circumstances. Even a major national demographic crisis – like that of the later 1550s – had at most only a modest impact on wage levels, and the most devastating local crises caused barely a ripple. Nevertheless, inflation made workers increasingly reluctant to accept any reduction in nominal rates, thus underpinning a custom of some solidity. But despite such determination on the part of workers it was the lot of those predominantly dependent on wage-earning to endure increasingly uncomfortable living conditions for at least half of the period.

[122] Abel 1980, 140.

7

Towards an understanding of living standards

If we want to discover not the nominal wage, i.e. the money paid for a certain time or for a certain piece of work, but the actual wage, together with its purchasing power, we are tackling a difficult and complicated problem the solution of which can only be obtained by comparing a number of different data. We ought first to know a man's total wage for a month, a season or a year, and how far it was reduced by either voluntary or compulsory unemployment. For a man may be well paid and yet earn very little, if he does not work every day. Then we should know whether he had any other source of income, as was the case with village workers, who when comparatively well off cultivated their plots of land or grazed their cows on the common, and who when very poor received help from the parish. We should also want to know what each member of the family contributed to the annual family budget. Then, even assuming that we have been able to solve that part of the problem, a no less difficult problem remains to be solved, for we should want to find out how this income was actually spent. And it would not be enough to know what were the price of foodstuffs and the rents. For unless we knew what kinds of food were actually consumed, and the relative quantities of each which the needs and habits of the consumers demanded, such a list of prices would not be of much use. In order, therefore, to be able to draw any conclusions we should need to have at our disposal a great collection of facts which nearly always are missing, except for our own times. We are really able only to grasp some rough relationships between the phenomena.[1]

Mantoux's incisive summary of the difficulty we face when trying to establish shifts in living standards could hardly be bettered, and this book can illuminate only a few of the dark corners which remain. Some valuable insights have been gained already. The use of a wide range of northern sources fully confirms the view that master craftsmen were not true wage-earners in the modern sense of the word.[2] They were petty entrepreneurs who supplied not only their own labour, but also that of their apprentices and journeymen. The

---

[1] Mantoux 1961, 420; quoted in Gilboy 1934, xxvi.   [2] Woodward 1981.

typical firm in the provincial building trades remained small throughout the period, but the extent of the extra profits available to the master depended on the proportion of the wage which he passed on to his subordinates, the cost of their subsistence when they lived in, and on his success in acquiring work for them. Master craftsmen could also profit by supplying the raw materials with which they worked, especially for smaller projects funded by non-institutional customers. Labourers were a different breed. In most cases they supplied only their own labour and rarely, if ever, any of the raw materials with which they worked. Some were employed for a large part of the year, but others flitted in and out of employment.[3]

It is commonly believed that wage-earners benefited substantially from the provision of food and drink at work, but only those obliged to work some considerable distance from their homes could expect to be 'tabled' by their customers. Nevertheless, drink was frequently provided, both in the guise of treats at crucial stages of a job and in the form of wage supplements, which probably became more common during the seventeenth century. But drink allowances provided only a small proportion of the dietary needs of a workman and his family. Historians have often regarded the acquisition of non-food perquisites as one of the characteristic features of early-modern labour markets, differentiating them from the more modern forms of remuneration which emerged in the nineteenth century. This may have been the case in some areas of work, but perquisites were rarely on offer to the labourers and the rank-and-file building craftsmen of northern England.[4] Knowledge of the number of days worked is essential if we are to convert wage rates into annual incomes: but this is one of the most intractable of problems.[5] Apart from a few instances where we know that labourers or artisans worked for most of the year, it is plain that employment was 'irregular and discontinuous in the extreme and consistently inadequate': indeed, they did 'a good deal of floating about'.[6]

It is often suggested that, in periods of falling real wages, workers would be keen to work for more days in the year in order to maintain levels of consumption. This is highly plausible and ties in with the notion that contemporaries had high leisure preferences and would cease work once their earnings were sufficient to satisfy a narrow range of needs.[7] It is perfectly logical to imagine that the relatively

[3] See above pp. 1–2.   [4] See above pp. 142–57.
[5] Brown & Hopkins 1981, 13; Fisher 1990, 138; Lindert & Williamson 1983, 3; Scholliers 1989, 42–3; Penn & Dyer 1990, 368; Levine & Wrightson 1991, 254–7.
[6] Blockmans & Prevenier 1978, 24; Goldthwaite 1980, 297.   [7] Clarkson 1971, 43–4.

high real wages of the later fifteenth century induced many labourers and artisans to work a relatively short year.[8] But as inflation took hold in the early decades of the following century the situation changed: real wages were driven down, workers were forced to work harder to protect their living standards and, fortuitously, the number of days available for work was increased by the adoption of Protestantism which reduced the number of holy days. Indeed, it has been suggested that 'real earnings almost certainly fell by less than did [real] wage rates, as people worked longer hours and took less time off in order to try to maintain the purchasing power of what they received'.[9] But the desire to work harder does not necessarily mean that increased employment opportunities will present themselves. Urban labourers and building craftsmen played an essentially passive role, responding to the demands of their customers. Certain types of craftsmen – including joiners – could make some of their products ahead of demand and hope that a display of their wares would attract custom. But such advertising was rarely possible for the carpenters and bricklayers.[10] Whether or not the majority of labourers and building craftsmen were able to find more work as the grip of the Tudor and early Stuart inflation tightened must remain an open question.

Movement through the life-cycle had a very substantial effect on the living standards of early-modern workmen and their families. Unfortunately much is hidden from us, but it is not difficult to imagine new masters struggling to establish their businesses in the face of a range of costs: of gild membership; of becoming a freeman; of setting up a new business and home; and of marriage. The arrival of children brought further economic problems. Most men did not live long enough to enjoy a well-earned retirement. About half of the Chester joiners did not get beyond their mid forties and only a few lived to a ripe old age. But the family business did not necessarily disappear on the death of its leader. Widows played an important part in preventing families from descending into destitution.[11] The remainder of this chapter will be devoted to an attempt to say rather more about shifts in living standards for labourers and building craftsmen in the towns of northern England between 1450 and 1750. The first section, on the cost of living, opens with a review of the existing literature, and moves on to discuss the cost and provision of food and drink, fuel, and housing. The second section attemps to outline the myriad sources of

---

[8] C. Dyer 1989, 224–5.   [9] Clay 1984, I, 217; see above, pp. 131–3.
[10] Some shoemakers carried enormous stocks of ready-made goods: Woodward 1968b, 75–6.
[11] See above, chapter 3.

family income, which added to the wages earned by the man of the house.

The cost of living

Introduction

For nearly forty years early-modern historians have relied heavily on the real wage index produced by Phelps Brown and Hopkins. The picture they painted was a gloomy one with real wages tumbling in the sixteenth century and failing to recover in the early decades of the following century. Only in the later seventeenth century, as the price revolution stuttered to an end, did wage-earners recoup some of the lost ground, although in the early eighteenth century real wages were still significantly lower than they had been in the late fifteenth century.[12] Other historians have often used their work with uncritical enthusiasm. Thus, we are told that:

there was a savage depression of the living standards of the lower half of the population, since food and fuel prices rose more sharply than those of other commodities. In the building industry real wages in the later sixteenth century were less than two-thirds of what they had been in 1510, and in the fifty years before the civil war they were less than half. The mass of the population was forced down to a diet of black bread.[13]

Not all historians have used the Phelps Brown and Hopkins index in such a cavalier fashion. Peter Ramsey in particular found it difficult to swallow the story presented by the statistics:

It seems hardly possible that such a drop can have taken place without far greater outcry than we have record of. To accept the figures at their face value would mean that urban workers were dying of starvation in thousands at the end of the sixteenth century and in the early Stuart period. Some factors have surely been left out of account.[14]

Indeed, various buffers which protected workers from the full force of the inflation needed to be considered: the subsistence production of foodstuffs in field or garden; the provision of food and drink at work; and family earnings over and above the wage of the head of the household.[15] An additional problem was that the index was based predominantly on wholesale prices and, as J.U. Nef explained many years ago, 'men did not eat hay or straw, or even oats or wheat'.[16]

[12] Brown & Hopkins 1981, 29–30.   [13] C. Hill 1967, 64.   [14] Ramsey 1963, 137–8.
[15] Woodward 1981, 29–31.   [16] Nef 1966, 120.

Phelps Brown and Hopkins were fully aware of the distortions which this could cause:

Processed products like bread and beer will not have risen in price so much as grain and malt: the price of the loaf, for example, will have had to cover not the cost of grain only but wages for milling, transporting, and baking, and as these did not go up as much as grain, the loaf will have gone up rather less too. This consideration is important. If the prices wage-earners paid at retail were made up, say, as to two-thirds of such wholesale costs of foods and materials as we have used, and as to the other third of wages, an English index of retail prices starting at the base of 100 in 1451–75 would have gone up to only 380 by the end of the sixteenth century, against the 475 of our index, and the basketful would be well over 50 per cent of its initial size instead of around 40.[17]

For London at least this suggestion has been confirmed recently by the work of Steve Rappaport. He collected more than 4,000 food, drink, and fuel prices from the records of the London livery companies and his composite price index stands at 334 in 1600 compared with the Phelps Brown and Hopkins figure of 459.[18] By combining his new price series with a new wage-rate series he concluded that the real wage index for 1600 stood at 69 rather than the 44 suggested for southern building workers. His figures show that London living standards were undoubtedly being squeezed, but not to the extent suggested by the old series which hit a low point of 29 in the crisis year of 1597 compared with a figure of 59 for London workers according to the new index.[19]

Some northern price data – for food and drink, fuel, and housing – will be deployed later in this chapter, but it has not proved possible to compile a composite price index of the kind available for London and southern England. Thus, it will not be without interest to look at the general movement of northern wages in the light of the two southern price series. Table 7.1 lays out the decadal averages presented in the two series from the late fifteenth to the early seventeenth century. Both show the steep rise in prices of the mid sixteenth century and the surge of the 1590s. These were periods of considerable difficulty for wage-earners throughout the country when nominal rates tended to edge upwards, slowly following the rising prices.

The data from table 7.1 are combined in Table 7.2 with some of the northern wage data to provide a very rough indication of shifts in real

---

[17] Brown & Hopkins 1981, 64.
[18] *Ibid.*, 29; Rappaport 1989, 123–8, 401–7. Brown & Hopkins 1981 used the years 1451–75 for their base whereas Rappaport used 1457–71: thus the series start very much from the same point. For a similar analysis suggesting a less steep rise in prices than that offered by Brown & Hopkins see Loschky 1980.
[19] Rappaport 1989, 407; Brown & Hopkins 1981, 29.

Table 7.1. *Average price movements in southern England and London,*
1450–1609

Decade	Southern England (Brown & Hopkins)	London (Rappaport)
1450–9	99.2	—
1460–9	104.1	—
1470–9	94.3	—
1480–9	116.0	—
1490–9	101.3	98.4
1500–9	104.3	101.0
1510–19	111.2	107.6
1520–9	148.0	115.1
1530–9	155.1	121.5
1540–9	192.1	145.2
1550–9	289.2	212.3
1560–9	278.8	223.9
1570–9	314.7	240.9
1580–9	357.0	256.8
1590–9	472.0	315.7
1600–9	474.9	332.0

Sources: Brown and Hopkins 1981, 29; Rappaport 1989, 403–7.

Table 7.2. *Northern wage rates compared with southern prices*

Date	Northern wage rate (pence per day)[a]	Real wage at: Southern prices	Real wage at: London prices
(a) Craftsmen			
Early sixteenth century	6	95.8	99.0
1530–9	6	66.2	82.3
c. 1600	8	28.2	42.2
	10	35.3	52.8
	12	42.4	63.4
(b) Labourers			
Early sixteenth century	4	95.8	99.0
1530–9	4	62.2	82.3
c. 1600	6	31.8	47.5
	7	37.1	55.4
	8	42.4	63.4

Note: [a] For northern wages, see appendix 1.

wages in the north of England. Of course, it is not being suggested that northern prices behaved in the same fashion as southern prices, but the exercise will provide a useful comparison when northern prices are discussed in the next section of this chapter.

Highly questionable though this process may be, it suggests that, unless prices were very markedly different in the north of England than in the south – and it is unlikely that they were – real wages deteriorated in northern parts during the course of the sixteenth century. The same was true of the early seventeenth century. Although much more work needs to be conducted into the history of northern prices, it has been possible to assemble sufficient material to confirm these broad generalisations. It may not have been black bread for all, but there can be little doubt that life became more difficult for wage-earners in Tudor and early Stuart times, and that 'an optimistic view of the English economy at the end of the sixteenth century runs counter to all the available evidence'.[20]

The cost of food and drink

Although it is not currently possible to establish a composite price index for the north of England, a series of food prices for Lincoln and Hull makes it possible to estimate shifts in the cost of diet for wage-earners in the two towns from the middle of the sixteenth century. The data are laid out in appendix 2, which opens with a discussion of the methods used and the assumptions made. The calculations are based on the assize prices for grain at Lincoln from 1513 to 1712, and for Hull after 1708, together with the prices paid for beef and cheese bought for the feasts held regularly at Hull Trinity House. The cost of feeding a single worker is based on a seventeenth-century diet presented by Drummond and Wilbraham, which would provide nearly 3,000 calories a day: 2 lb. of bread, 9 oz. of peas, and $3\frac{1}{2}$oz. of cheese.[21] This would be enough to ensure survival, although such a diet would not allow a man to work flat out at a strenuous task for six days a week. However, most men and women, and many children, would add extra calories to their diet by consuming beer or ale. Since the cost of small quantities of peas cannot be calculated with any degree of accuracy, oats have been substituted. Additionally, beef has been substituted for cheese, either when cheese prices are not available or when beef was cheaper per pound, as it often was. Once the diet of a single man has been

---

[20] Slack 1988, 6.
[21] Drummond & Wilbraham 1964, 465–7. See appendix 2 for a discussion of the methods used.

established the cost of feeding a family of varying size can be calculated and set against the wage rates of labourers and craftsmen.

The cost of feeding an adult male rose from about a penny a day or less in the middle of the sixteenth century, to more than 2d a day in the early seventeenth century, and to almost 3d in the 1630s. That is, the cost of providing this relatively nutritious diet was significantly less than allowed for in most post-1563 wage assessments. This underpins the belief that it was rarely in the interest of workers to be fed at work.[22] These tentative estimates of basic dietary costs are consistent with contemporary assessments of minimum levels of support for the poor. They include the York survey of the poor of 1588 which insisted on everyone having 'at the least 1½d the day, under which sum a poor creature cannot live'.[23] At Easter 1588 2 lb. of bread could have been bought at Lincoln for just under a penny, and the price had dropped by nearly 20 per cent by Michaelmas: that is, Lincoln folk could have purchased their daily bread out of the dole provided by the York authorities, although little would have been left for other needs. Such levels of support seem to have been common: at Ipswich during the 1590s, and at Salisbury in the 1630s the authorities 'appear to have assumed that 8d to 1s a week was the cost of subsistence for an adult, and 4d to 6d a week for a child; and they used the dole to bring family income up to at least that level'.[24] Similarly at Kendal in 1654 the cost of feeding a prisoner was set at 2d a day.[25]

Other evidence, such as the prices paid for feeding workers away from home, or the food allowances made in wage assessments, suggest higher costs. However, such allowances bear little relationship to the cost of basic home catering. Eating out was always more expensive than home cooking. In 1561 the York authorities – who a quarter of a century later put the basic cost of survival at 1½d a day – ordered innkeepers not to take more than 4d a meal from a poor man, and the fare was to include bread, drink, herring, and salt fish with some kind of pottage. Gentlemen, and the better-off who wished to eat more heartily, were to pay 6d, or more if they called for extra dishes.[26] On the eve of the Civil War York prices were enhanced by the presence of the king and his retinue, although one visitor argued that excellent dinners were available at various inns for as little as 6d.[27] At Carlisle in 1650 the council paid the hefty sum of 12d for the supper and breakfast of a Scotsman 'which was robbed on the seas', and four years later 4d

[22] See above, pp. 147–8.
[23] *YCR*, VIII, 157–8. For a discussion of the situation in London see Archer 1991, 190–2.
[24] Slack 1988, 80–1.   [25] CUMROK, WSMB.   [26] *YCR*, VI, 6.
[27] *York Descriptions*, 20.

was spent on 'a cripple's supper'.[28] Many similar examples could be provided from the northern records, but they have little relevance to the struggle that labourers and building craftsmen had in trying to feed their families. Very occasionally, when out of town on official business, they were entertained to a meal in an eating house, but the cost of such meals bears no closer relationship to the cost of daily survival than it does in the late twentieth century.

Like all indices of the cost of living in early-modern England, the data presented in appendix 2 suggest that many workers became progressively worse off during the century or so before the Civil War. Single men could cope without too much difficulty throughout the period. At Hull unmarried craftsmen could always earn their basic diet in less than 100 days, and the best-paid men never needed to work for more than 75 days to reach the target: the situation facing Lincoln craftsmen was broadly similar. Single labourers did less well. By the 1590s they needed to work for more than 100 days to cover their basic food needs, and their position continued to deteriorate down to the Civil War. Indeed, although the situation eased somewhat for the best-paid craftsmen at Hull in the 1620s and 1630s, it worsened for most classes of labour down to the middle of the seventeenth century. The position was critical for men with families. Labourers with a wife and four children in the 1630s would have needed to work for 520 days to earn enough to pay for the basic family diet, and at Hull even the best-paid craftsmen would have needed to work for more than 300 days in the 1610s. From the middle of the seventeenth century conditions began to ease. Most workers enjoyed improved nominal rates of pay, and all workers – and particularly the more specialised men – needed to work for less days in order to provide an adequate diet than they had in the dark days before the Civil War. Moreover, the behaviour of grain prices at Hull suggests that conditions remained favourable in the first half of the eighteenth century: average wheat prices were 16 per cent lower than they had been at Lincoln in the last four decades of the seventeenth century, although the price of oats was some 13 per cent higher.[29]

For more than a century before the Civil War those dependent on wage-earning, to some extent or another, for their livelihoods, were placed in extremely difficult circumstances by the upward movement of food prices combined with the sluggish response of nominal wage rates. As the years passed a higher and higher proportion of the wage packet had to be devoted to the basic cost of staying alive. No doubt

---

[28] CUMROC, Ca/4/3. On the cost of 'tabling' workmen see above, pp. 157–9.
[29] J.W.F. Hill 1956, 225–6; Kelsall 1938.

Table 7.3. *The number of days worked by a Lincoln labourer*
to pay for a basic oatmeal diet (to the nearest whole day)

Date	Wage (pence per day)	Single man	+ Wife	Children + 1	+ 2	+ 3	+ 4
1540–9	4	37	65	93	122	148	158
1550–9	4	71	124	177	230	265	301
1560–9	6	44	77	110	143	165	187
1590–9	6	62	108	154	200	231	262
1600–9	8	42	74	105	137	158	179
1610–19	8	65	115	164	213	245	278
1620–9	8	53	94	134	174	200	227
1630–9	8	72	126	180	234	270	306
1650–9	10	60	105	150	195	225	255
1660–9	10	48	83	119	154	178	202
1670–9	10	42	74	106	137	158	179
1680–9	10	45	79	113	147	169	193
1690–9	10	46	81	115	150	173	196

Source: See appendix 2.6.

many belts were tightened: indeed, 'it is hard to believe that food was not constantly on the minds of a large percentage of the working population'.[30] Any shortfall in dietary needs would have contributed to the low levels of productivity which were probably a feature of the period. Even if they retreated to the extremely monotonous diet of Scottish labourers, who could function on an intake of 30 oz. of oatmeal a day plus a little kale,[31] they still needed to work long and hard simply to place enough oatcakes or porridge on the table. This is demonstrated by Table 7.3, which gives the number of days a Lincoln labourer needed to work to buy enough oatmeal to feed his family.

The data presented in the table and in appendix 2.6 demonstrate dramatically the effect of the life-cycle on wage-earners. After marriage, conditions began to deteriorate once children arrived and did not improve until they were able to earn at least a part of their keep: and this is assuming that neither the wife nor husband was placed in an early grave. Indeed: 'Bachelors were least threatened with hunger, but families generally existed in a state of chronic need. Marriage for most workers brought misery, and the unskilled in particular had to tighten their belts at marriage. Working-men's children

[30] Shammas 1990, 148.   [31] From information provided by Christopher Smout.

suffered permanent malnutrition.'[32] Although specific information is not yet available, it may be imagined that many labourers and less successful craftsmen delayed marrying and perhaps contributed to the growing number of never-marrieds of early Stuart society.[33] Moreover, it would only make sense if, once married, they took steps to limit the size of their families so that, as with medieval peasants, 'family sizes varied with wealth'.[34]

Family men would not only be obliged to reduce their consumption of the less essential items of diet, they would also need to keep an eye on the market and switch from one bread grain to another as relative prices changed. This remained a requirement well beyond the end of our period, especially in years of high prices:

The choice of cereal was price and income elastic, and that pre-industrial patterns endured until at least the early nineteenth century is verified by the government enquiries of 1796 and 1800, which show not only a marked decline in *per capita* cereal consumption, but also a widespread substitution of barley, and to a lesser extent, of oats, pulse, and rye, for wheat, and of browner for whiter flours.[35]

A century and a half earlier Henry Best had explained that: 'Poor folks put usually a peck of peas to a bushel of rye, and some again two pecks of peas to a frundell of masseldine, and they say that these make hearty bread. In many places they grind their after-loggings of wheat for their servants' pies.'[36] Such expedients were more likely to be followed in years or seasons of great scarcity. At Lincoln in the mid 1580s few of the poor could have afforded to eat wheaten bread. The price of wheat, which stood at 17s 6d a quarter at Michaelmas 1585, rose to 25s 6d the following Easter, to 36s by the next Michaelmas, and to 54s 6d by Easter 1587: a rise of over 200 per cent. In contrast the price of oats rose only by 122 per cent, from 6s to 13s 4d, so that by the end of the period a quarter of wheat cost four times as much as a quarter of oats. Prices rocketed again during the mid to late 1590s until the price ratio between the two grains stood at a record 5.3:1 at Easter 1598.[37] Similar conditions prevailed at Hull in the 1590s, and in 1597 the council acquired a stock of rye which was sold to the poor at below the

---

[32] Lis & Soly 1982, 19–20.   [33] Wrigley & Schofield 1981, 260.
[34] C. Dyer 1989, 134.
[35] Collins 1975, 104.
[36] *Henry Best*, 109. A 'frundell' was a dry measure probably of two pecks; 'masseldine' was maslin – a mixture of grains, especially wheat and rye; 'after-loggings' were the coarse flour that remained after the fine flour had been sifted.
[37] J.W.F. Hill 1956, 224. During the second half of the sixteenth century the price of wheat generally rose more between Michaelmas and Easter than that of oats: see appendix 2.8.

market price.[38] Indeed, everywhere these were 'lean and difficult years'.[39] Although price series are not available for other northern towns, it is evident that the high prices were common throughout the north in the difficult years of the 1580s and 1590s. These, along with the early 1620s and 1630s, were the years of crisis identified by Andrew Appleby.[40] One of the Chester merchants recorded that in 1586 'corn grew marvellous dear', and two of the city's merchants were despatched to Hull to buy a cargo of rye. A year later the merchants sought permission 'to traffic to Dansk and other places in those countries' which had a surplus of grain. Again, in the mid to late 1590s, 'corn grew very dear ... and also other victuals, likewise at a great price, not only here but generally through this land'.[41] There can be no doubt that poor consumers would switch from one basic foodstuff to another as relative prices changed, and there can have been few of the poor who ever tasted wheaten bread.

Any discussion of diet is hampered by the fact that we know very little about what ordinary people ate. As a result, some of the assumptions made in this book may not be justified. Thus, the prices presented in appendix 2.2 suggest that single men and those with small families in Hull would have been able to eat beef and cheese from time to time. No doubt they also consumed other items, either because prices were sufficiently low at a particular season to allow consumption of more than just grain, or because prices were so high that people were forced to consume unpalatable foodstuffs normally eaten by livestock. Wage-earners may have consumed a wider range of foodstuffs than we imagine, although the prices laid down at York in 1558 for a range of delicacies and some more basic foodstuffs suggest that few wage-earners could afford to be very adventurous in their eating habits, except on special occasions (see table 7.4).

All workers, and many of their dependants, acquired part of their sustenance and calorific intake by drinking ale or beer, which was provided either by their employers and customers, or out of their own pockets. The northern evidence suggests that the price of such beverages rose less than that of other foodstuffs: prices are laid out in appendix 3. Before 1550 traditional unhopped ale could be bought at Boston, Hull, and York for 2d a gallon or less, while at Chester in 1552 the price of a gallon of 'best beer' was set at $1\frac{1}{3}$d. Few labourers would have been able to afford more than a pint or two of the new-fangled beer called 'ale' which sold at a shilling or more a gallon

[38] Gillett & MacMahon 1989, 130; Davies 1956.   [39] Rappaport 1983, II, 128.
[40] Appleby 1973, *passim*.
[41] Woodward 1970b, 49–53.

Table 7.4. *Prices laid down at York, 1558 (in pence)*

Item	Price
Best capon	10
Best pig	10
Best goose	10
Best hen	5
Six eggs	1
Couple of coneys	8
Woodcock	4
Plover	3
Teal	2
Mallard	4
Partridge	3

Source: YCR, V, 170.

Table 7.5. *The volume of ale or beer which could be purchased with a day's wage*

Date	Place	Drink	Price per gallon (in pence)	Labourer		Craftsman	
				Wage (in pence)	Number of gallons	Wage (in pence)	Number of gallons
Strong drink							
1464/5	Hull	Ale	2	4	2.0	6	3.0
1540	York	Ale	2	4	2.0	6	3.0
1547	Boston	Best beer	1½	4	2.7	6	4.0
1552	Chester	Best beer	1⅓	4	3.0	6	4.5
1664	Hull	Strong beer	6	10	1.7	20	3.4
1675	Hull	Ale	10	10	1.0	20	2.0
1696	Hull	Ale	12	12	1.0	22	1.8
1730	Hull	Ale	16	12	0.75	24	1.5
1731	Hull	Ale	10	12	1.2	24	2.4
Weak drink							
1572	Lincoln	Ordinary beer	1	6	6.0	10	10.0
1667	Hull	Small beer	1.8	10	5.6	18–22	10–12.2
1686–1731	Hull	Small beer	2	12	6.0	24	12.0

Source: See appendix 3.

at Hull in the late seventeenth and early eighteenth centuries.
However, much cheaper drink was always available. At Lincoln 'single
beer' and 'ordinary beer' were priced at 1d a gallon in 1562 and 1572
respectively. And at Hull in the later seventeenth and early eighteenth
centuries small beer cost only 2d a gallon, the price their forefathers
had paid for strong ale at the end of the fifteenth century. Such weak
beer 'was the daily liquor of the lower classes and servants, and it was
this which was usually sold off the premises for domestic consumption'.[42] Anyone prepared to slake his thirst with small beer could do so
for little cost. The price of ale or beer in relation to wage levels is
summarised in table 7.5.

Although the prices rose less than those of other foodstuffs, even the
cheapest drinks would strain the pockets of the very poor. But those in
regular work would have been able to buy enough to ensure health.
However, no doubt there were always those who put their own thirst
above the needs of their families and consumed more than was strictly
necessary from a dietary point of view. When the York authorities laid
down the cost of basic subsistence at $1\frac{1}{2}$d a day in 1588 they hoped to
be able to prevent the wives and children of labourers from begging,
and restrain their husbands 'from the alehouse, where they drink all
that should maintain their poor wives and children at home'.[43]

The cost of fuel

The main types of fuel used for domestic purposes in early-modern
England were wood, peat, and coal. However, as the price of wood
soared in many parts of the country during the sixteenth and seventeenth centuries, coal came into more general use for domestic heating
and cooking.[44] At York wood had been used in the medieval period,
although in the second half of the sixteenth century it was increasingly
replaced by peat and coal. The council even considered running its
own colliery, but the idea was dropped and by the end of the century
'sea-coal' from Newcastle was the most important item in the city's
coasting trade. However, references to peat, or 'turves' as they were
known in contemporary accounts, became even more numerous. They
were used for domestic purposes at all levels of society and by 1597
were described as 'now the greatest part of our fuel'.[45] Chester had
easy access to coal produced by the pits of North Wales,[46] and most of
the northern towns considered in this study could tap supplies of

[42] Clark 1983, 97–8.   [43] YCR, VIII, 158.   [44] Hatcher 1993, 31–55.
[45] Palliser 1979, 194, 273.
[46] Woodward 1970b, 17–18.

Table 7.6. *A decadal index of coal prices at Hull, 1471–1740*
(to the nearest whole number)

Years	Number of years	Index	Years	Number of years	Index
1471–99	13	100	1620–9	10	444
1520–9	8	139	1630–9	9	485
1530–9	5	140	1640–9	10	739
1540–9	8	183	1650–9	10	626
1550–9	10	263	1660–9	8	552
1560–9	7	288	1670–9	10	581
1570–9	10	354	1680–9	10	487
1580–9	8	359	1690–2	3	688
1590–9	8	400			
1600–9	10	428	1714	1	621
1610–19	10	444	1730–9	5	577
			1740	1	560

Note: The base of 1471–99 was used, which gives an average price of 42. 86d per chaldron. For year-by-year details see Hatcher 1993, 176–9.

water-borne fuels. Hull hearths were warmed either by 'coals from Newcastle', or by turves, and the accounts of Trinity House give prices for both fuels in most years: they were used to heat the public chambers and the small cells which housed pensioners. Although the great bulk of the coal came from Newcastle some also came from Sunderland, and occasional cargoes of 'Scottish coal' and 'Western coal' from the West Riding arrived in the port.[47] The coal was transferred from the ships by ketch, shovelled onto the quayside, and then carted to the House. The prices paid for coal arriving in the port are summarised in table 7.6.

Prices began to rise in the early sixteenth century, accelerated in the middle decades, and rose more gently thereafter down to the Civil War: indeed average prices rose by just over 70 per cent between the 1560s and the 1630s. Prices then rose substantially in the 1640s due to the war-time dislocation of the Newcastle trade and they were affected in each of the next three decades by the impact of the wars against the Dutch which helped to raise freight costs. By the 1680s – the last decade for which there are adequate data – prices had fallen back to their pre-Civil-War level. Clearly there were periods when people in straitened circumstances would not have been able to afford coal.

The turf-price series for Hull has a peculiarity which cannot be fully

[47] Based on HTH, I–V. The town council occasionally bought such west country coals: HCRO, BRF/3/19.

Table 7.7. *The decadal average price of turves at Hull, 1544–1692*
(in pence per thousand turves: to the nearest penny)

	Number of observations	Price		
		Minimum	Mean	Maximum
1544–9	8	8	13	20
1550–9	8	11	21	32
1560–9	8	27	34	46
1570–9	22	25	30	48
1580–9	12	25	36	52
1590–9	17	20	32	43
1600–9	8	22	33	44
1610–19	24	20	33	46
1620–9	34	22	32	46
1630–9	44	25	34	48
1640–9	38	31	44	78
1650–9	37	28	36	48
1660–9	35	22	30	48
1670–9	31	18	27	43
1680–9	51	18	23	36
1690–2	10	18	22	28

Source: HTH, II–V.

explained: prices varied substantially over short periods of time, often within the same year. This is illustrated in table 7.7 which lays out both the mean price of turves in each decade, and also the minimum and maximum prices recorded.

The most likely explanation for the variations in prices – which were not seasonal in nature – is that the town was supplied from different sources with a product which varied substantially in quality. Perhaps the cheaper turves were inferior local products, and the more expensive from further afield. However, the accounts reveal the origin of the turves on only one occasion: in the autumn of 1551 turves were acquired at source:[48]

	s	d
Paid to Edmund Johnson for the boat to Keadby for 4,000 turves	1	6
Paid for the said 4,000 turves there	2	8
Paid to two women for carrying the same turves in a 'mawnde' from the waterside unto the Trinity House		5
Paid to two men that went with the boat for the said turves	1	0
[Total]	5	7

[48] HTH, II, fo. 26r.

On that occasion the turves had come from Keadby in Lincolnshire, four miles south-east of Crowle on the river Trent, and they cost nearly 17d a thousand, compared with an average price of 11½d a year earlier. The experiment proved too costly, and in future turves were bought at the quayside.

After a significant increase in price in the middle decades of the sixteenth century, the price of turves rose hardly at all during the next 150 years. There can be little doubt that the Hull poor would have been more likely to buy turves than coal to heat their homes, especially since the effective use of coal as a domestic fuel involved expenditure on grates, chimneys, and other equipment. Coal could be burnt without a purpose-built grate or chimney,[49] although the occupants of the dwelling would have suffered a great deal, and it seems unlikely – given the movement of prices – that coal would have been used in some of the very small dwellings described in the next section. It is impossible from the available evidence to estimate the cost of domestic heating and cooking at Hull, although the trend in the price of turves, after the middle of the sixteenth century, indicates that costs fell relative to wage rates. Nothing is known about the price of turves in other northern towns, although the literary evidence for York suggests that the product was also relatively cheap there, and in both Carlisle and Kendal 'turf remained a popular domestic and industrial fuel down to the eighteenth century';[50] and coal remained inexpensive in places within easy reach of a colliery. At Newcastle the price of coal rose significantly less than it did at Hull during the course of the sixteenth and seventeenth centuries,[51] and the increase was probably little greater than the advance in the wage rates of building craftsmen. Too little is known about the cost of fuel in the various northern towns being studied to come to any definite conclusion, although it seems likely that in many places the cost of fuel increased less than that of basic foodstuffs, and that in some places – and especially in Hull – the price of some fuel fell in real terms.

The cost of housing.

On the side of outlay we know little or nothing about some important costs, notably rent.[52]

Historians working on early-modern living standards have always left house rents out of account, and the same has been true until very recently in the long-running debate relating to the period of industria-

---

[49] Hatcher 1993, 409–18.   [50] *Ibid.*, 50.   [51] *Ibid.*, 573–4.
[52] Brown & Hopkins 1981, 13.

lisation.[53] Nevertheless, a great deal can be said about rent in the early-modern north, although it has not proved possible to put together a satisfactory rent series. In part this is because rents did not behave like other prices. Properties were leased out for periods of several years on level rents so that changes in market conditions were not reflected immediately. Thus, the churchwardens' accounts of St Martin's, Coney Street, York, record that James Stubbs rented a property – known variously as a 'tenement', 'his dwelling house', or the 'tenement in the churchyard' – for 3s 4d a year from 1569 to 1604. The property then passed to a Mr Young, and he and Mrs Young paid 13s 4d a year for it until 1621.[54] That is, the rent quadrupled when the house changed hands in 1604. It is also difficult to compile a meaningful series because house rents – unlike agricultural rents which relate to a relatively homogeneous commodity – cover an enormous range of types of property from hovels to mansions, and there is no standard unit of account like the acre. Some individuals and institutions often owned a number of properties across the quality range, so that it is difficult if not impossible to calculate an average price which has any real meaning: the property owned by All Saints, North Street, York, in the third quarter of the seventeenth century ranged from bedsitters, let for 2s a year, to houses fetching rents of up to £10 a year.[55]

Entry fines are also a problem. They are rarely mentioned in the accounts, but it is clear that they were levied from time to time in early-modern England, at least for the more substantial properties. A rare example was recorded in the accounts of St Martin's, Coney Street. Peter Williamson paid £2 a year for a property from 1585 to 1635: it was called 'the tenement in his occupation', or 'his now dwelling house'. However in 1599 he paid £3 6s 8d 'for the fine of his house to increase the lease to 21 years which the parish hath granted': if this was for the full term it amounted to just over 3s a year or 8 per cent on top of the yearly rent. As we shall see later, some fines were paid in late-sixteenth-century Hull, although they featured hardly at all in the late-medieval period.[56] It must be suspected that fines played little part in the leasing of low-grade housing which often attracted very low rents.

The various problems associated with the leasing of housing, and the attempt to compile a meaningful price index, can be illustrated further from the history of a single property in York which belonged to

[53] On London rents see Power 1972, 254–5; Rappaport 1989, 150. See also Lindert & Williamson 1983, 8–9; Hunt & Botham 1987, 386, 388.
[54] YBI, PR/Y/MCS/16.   [55] YBI, PR/Y/ASN/10.
[56] See below, p. 231; *Hull Rentals*. On the problem of entry fines see Willan 1980, 34–5.

the church of St Martin's, Coney Street. In 1552 a tenement was leased out to Richard Baysborne at 8s a year, which he continued to pay until 1569 when he was succeeded by his widow, who paid for the next year. They were followed by Robert French, a cook, who held the property from 1571–7, and by Thomas Metcalf from 1578–89: in 1581 the property was described as 'a tenement in the occupation of him and others'. During the years 1590–2 the 8s rent was paid by a Mr Bestson, although in 1591 the property was said to be in the occupation of Ellis Carr, a dyer, and he paid 20s for the second instalment of rent in 1592: the property was then referred to as 'that house wherein he dwelleth being the same which Mr Bestson had from French by lease'. Clearly the churchwardens were in the process of raising the rent, and in 1593, 26s 8d was paid for the year by Sir James Foxgill who continued to pay it until 1602. He was followed by a Mr Claphamson who paid 26s 8d in 1603 'for the rent of his house in Coney Street late tenure of James Foxgill clerk'. Claphamson, who became a churchwarden in 1606, remained the tenant at the same rent until 1635 when he was succeeded by a Mr Paley. Clearly it would be no easy matter to create a price series from a group of such properties. This house in Coney Street, which seems to have been a property of some size, passed from one tenant to another, was subject to multiple occupation on at least one occasion, was sublet for part of the period, and had its rent raised substantially in 1593.

But the inability to create a meaningful rent series at this stage is not a serious problem. Evidence from a range of northern rentals from the late fifteenth century to the late seventeenth century makes it plain that property was available at low rents for those who were prepared to tolerate cramped and inadequate living conditions.

Rents probably became cheaper in most places in absolute terms down to the middle decades of the sixteenth century. At Hull in 1465 out of fifty-nine properties owned by the council eighteen were let for an annual rent of 10s or less, although it has been pointed out that 'by comparison with other rentals the average town rent was high', and that the council did not own much of the lower-class housing in the town – 'it was left to private landowners to provide housing for the lower classes'.[57] By the 1520s the situation had changed somewhat. A larger stock of council housing provided many cheap dwellings and over half of the properties were leased for 5s or less in 1527/8. The details from the town rentals, together with those for the private estate of William Sydney in 1538, are summarised in table 7.8.

[57] *Hull Rentals*, 21–2.

Table 7.8. *Rents at Hull, 1465–1538*

	Rents				
Date	Over £1	Over 10s	Over 5s	5s or less	Total
1465	22	19	17	1	59
1527/8	3	10	36	73	122
1538 (Sydney)	14	21	36	72	143

Source: Hull Rentals, 111–33. I am grateful to Rosemary Horrox for giving me a copy of her transcription of the Sydney rental.

During the 1520s and 1530s the combined council and Sydney estates had 53 properties earning a rent of 3s or less, and a further 92 with rents of less than 5s, while the Gild of Corpus Christi was renting out 'little houses' for 2s, and others for between 4s and 8s in 1524. It would have taken a craftsman earning 6d a day only ten days to cover a rent of 5s, and a labourer just 15 days: cheaper property would have involved even less effort. There is no doubt that property was relatively cheap in the early sixteenth century. By the 1520s many of the council rents were said to be 'in decay', that is reduced – often considerably – and there were empty houses available in both Beverley and York.[58] One response of private landlords in York was to demolish properties, and in 1547 it was reported that 'there is so many tenements within this city of 20d and 2s farm [rent] by year that vagabonds and beggars cannot be avoided', and those who could not pay even those small rents could squat in vacant property. Property values also declined in Newcastle in the later fifteenth and early sixteenth centuries.[59]

Although the growth of population probably reduced the number of vacant houses, low-grade housing continued to be available at low rents in the towns of northern England after the middle of the sixteenth century. At St Martin's, Coney Street, in the 1550s six dwellings out of a total of ten were leased for 5s or less a year, and in 1600 two out of the seven leases fell into the same category. Similarly at Beverley in 1592, fourteen out of fifty-four dwellings were leased for annual rents of 5s or less, and a further nineteen for 10s or less. Fourteen of the dwellings were in the churchyard and comprised two tenements, five cottages, and seven 'chambers' – the equivalents of modern bed-sitters

[58] *VCH Hull,* 41, 72; *VCH Beverley,* 87–8; Palliser 1979, 205–6, 214.
[59] Palliser 1979, 215; Swanson 1989, 161–2; Butcher 1978, 69.

– and the fourteen lettings carried a mean rent of less than 4s a year.[60] Nearly fifty years later, 79 out of 198 dwellings were rented out in the manor of Bridlington for 5s a year or less, and a further 88 for 10s or less.[61] Between 1647 and 1685 the authorities at All Saints', North Street, York, leased a house for 5s a year, and four rooms in two cottages each carried a rent of 2s a year throughout the period. In contrast the rents of all but one of the more expensive properties rose during the period: nine of them carried rents of more than £1 a year and the increase in rents amounted to 65 per cent on average. Some scattered evidence suggests that house rents in the countryside could also be very low in the later sixteenth and early seventeenth centuries: cottages, often with access to small amounts of land, were available in some places at low rents, often well below the 5s mark.[62]

Some of the low urban rents may have been the result of parish paternalism, a desire to accommodate the deserving poor of the community as cheaply as possible.[63] Thus at All Saints', York, in the middle of the seventeenth century the two small tenements or cottages were usually leased out to widows. In 1647 Widow Bayley paid 2s a year for a 'tenement', and the same was paid for 'one chamber over the said cottage in the occupation of Widow Dresser'. Another cottage housed Anthony Raper on the ground floor and Anne Dawson in the room above: again they each paid 2s a year. In 1650 Anne Dawson was replaced by two women who each paid 1s a year, and they remained together in the single room for eight years. Some element of parish paternalism may also have been in play with the churchyard dwellings at St Mary's, Beverley, although the frequency with which small properties were available at very low rents suggests that there was a market in low-grade housing which went far beyond the charitable impulses of the parish authorities.

Relatively little is known about the nature of such primitive dwellings, partly because their fabric has not survived. The cottages erected in many churchyards were no doubt flimsy structures, although they were probably better than the refuge put together for 'Manx Tom' at Chester in 1603. In the late sixteenth century he did odd jobs at St Mary's, and was given a salary of 2s 6d 'for keeping the churchyard clean all year'. The churchwardens laid out 21d 'for making a cabin for Tom'.[64] This may have been similar to the 'lodges' or 'hovels' used as temporary housing for pitmen at Whickham, the 'sheds' erected in

60 HCORO, PE/1/51.   61 *Bridlington Charters*, 97–104.
62 *Bankes Family*, 40; *Hornby Castle Accts*, 39–40, 46, 49–50, 73.
63 Archer 1991, 85, 192.   64 CCORO, P/20/13/1.

many London parishes, or the one-roomed hovels which still existed in York in the late nineteenth century.[65]

As the evidence relating to some of the York parocbial cottages indicates, many of the poor did not live in dwellings dedicated to the use of a single family unit. Indeed, as the national population grew in the sixteenth century, and the surplus housing stock of an earlier generation was absorbed, multiple occupancy became common. Few new houses were built in Elizabethan York and the growing numbers were accommodated through the subdivision of existing properties, and by cramming more people into them, as well as by erecting cottages in yards and gardens.[66] At Chester in 1628 a complaint was made about the 'multitude of poor vagrant and idle people' flocking to the city, and a search for lodgers was ordered. Two years later a feltmaker called Richard Vause was reported for converting a kiln into houses, and he had modified another building to make it suitable for multiple occupancy 'to the prejudice of the city and contrary to ancient orders'.[67] A similar worry was expressed at Lincoln in 1636. It was argued that the construction of cottages, the conversion of barns, stables, and outhouses, and the division of houses had facilitated 'a great confluence and resort of poor people from foreign places'. In future, strangers were not to be taken as tenants without the express permission of the mayor and common council.[68] But it is the nature of subdivision and subtenancy – in both town and country – to avoid public scrutiny, and only rarely do we meet co-habitees in rentals: one example comes from Hull in 1527/8 where a rent of 4s was paid 'for a tenement that two shipwrights dwelled in'.[69]

Low-grade housing was readily available in the towns of northern England for those who needed it. Such housing was, no doubt, often mean, damp, and constricted, but it made survival considerably easier in a relatively hostile climate. How many labourers and building craftsmen lived miserably cannot be estimated, but some, like Thomas Cole a York carpenter, clearly did: he died in 1520 and his house consisted of a hall, and a 'bowting house' in which he slept and stored 'his stuff that pertaineth to his occupation, as axes and other things'.[70] But not all lived in such cramped conditions. Robert Bridghouse, a Manchester joiner, occupied a well-furnished house of ten rooms in Elizabeth's reign, and John Newlove, a Hull carpenter, paid Trinity

[65] Levine & Wrightson 1991, 189–90; Power 1978, 171; Palliser 1979, 27–8, 33–5; Shammas 1990, 160–1. Michael Power has confirmed that in London even sheds carried relatively high rents.
[66] Palliser 1979, 285.   [67] *Chester Minutes*, 152–3, 160.
[68] J.W.F. Hill 1956, 138. See also Slack 1988, 68; Power 1972, 256–8.
[69] *Hull Rentals*, 132.   [70] Palliser 1979, 33.

Table 7.9. *Leases to Hull labourers and building craftsmen*

Date	Name	Occup-ation	Nature of property	Entry fine	Length of lease (years)	Rent p.a.	Wage (pence per day)	Days
1592	Robt. Banks	J	Messuage or cottage	£1	21	5s	10	6
1593	Wm. Whelpdale*	C	Messuage	£4	21	8s	10	10
1596	Ricd. Haslam	J	Building plot		61	1s	—	—
1600	Ricd. Kitching	B	Messuage		21	£4	10	96
1608	Hy. Thompson*	C	Shop		21	£1	12	20
1609	Xt. Maxwell*	B	Building plot		80	1s	—	—
1611	Garrat Simson	L	Messuage		21	£1	8	30
1644	Mtt. Rowton*	C	Messuage		21	£1 2s	18	15
1645	Robt. Thompson	B	Messuage		21	£1 6s 8d	18	18
1646	Jo. Bracebridge	C	Messuage		10	£1 6s 8d	18	18
1654	Robt.Somerscales	L	Messuage and garth		21	£2 10s	10	60
1659	Wm. Sanderson	B	2 mess- uages and close		21	£9	—	—
1664	Thos. Jackson*	B	Messuage		21	£1	22	11
1671	Jo. Elliott*	S	2 messuages		21	£3	—	—
1731	Thos.Rosendale	B	Messuage		21	£2 10s	24	30
1736	Wm. Hudson	P	Messuage		21	£12	—	—

Note: An asterisk is attached to the name of a man who appears in the Hull accounts. Occupations are given as follows: B, bricklayer; C, carpenter; J, joiner; L, labourer; P, plumber; S, smith.
Source: HCRO, BRN 55, 78, 82, 116, 118, 132, 226, 235, 238a, 273, 318, 339, 377, 501, 513; WG 38.

House a rent of £2 12s in the 1680s for his house: at his usual wage of 22d or 24d it would have taken him twenty-six days or slightly longer to earn his rent.[71] Henry Hunter, who laid down graves at St Michael's, Spurriergate, York, rented a house for £4 a year, plus a 'warehouse' or 'storehouse' for a further 10s, in the mid seventeenth century, although he received a retainer of £4 a year from the church.[72] These scattered references suggest that some building workers were able to afford more comfortable houses than the miserable hovels which could be rented for a few shillings a year, and the point is underlined by the fine set of leases preserved in the council archives at Hull. The

[71] Willan 1980, 108–12, 121; HTH, V.   [72] YBI, PR/Y/MS/5.

leases which relate to labourers and building craftsmen are presented in table 7.9.

The table suggests that some men, like the bricklayer Richard Kitching or the labourer Robert Somerscales, contracted to pay relatively high rents in relation to their wages, although it is possible that they sublet part of the property. Of the remainder, the highest rents were paid by men who seem to have had greater access to profit-making than the others: William Sanderson made bricks, John Elliott was one of the blacksmiths employed most regularly by the council, and William Hudson was a plumber. For the rest, the rents they agreed to pay could be accumulated by wage-earning for between one and five weeks. The ability to pay such rents indicates that these men were above the very bottom rung of the social ladder.

Not all labourers and building craftsmen rented their dwellings. Some owned property although they cannot have acquired it simply by saving out of their wages. It has been suggested that in the middle of the fifteenth century it would have cost 'no more than £12' (my italics) to build a smallish house in Hull, and another house was built in 1499 for £15 16s.[73] However, it would have cost a craftsman getting 6d a day the earnings of 480 days to pay for the cheaper house, and a labourer considerably longer. No doubt savings could be amassed through a combination of hard work, profit-taking, family earnings, inheritance, and marriage – and borrowing probably played its part – but clues are rarely given. However, we are told that in the later seventeenth century, Thomas Hartness, a Carlisle bricklayer was able to buy a small property for £31 because, allegedly, 'he had thrived sufficiently'.[74] The meaning of this statement is not clear. All we really know is that Hartness bought a house: the means by which he was able to do so is totally unknown.

Wills often contain interesting information relating to the ownership of property. In some cases the inventory reveals a man of apparently little means, although the will can suggest otherwise. Leon Wigsley, a Lincoln labourer who died in 1631, was such a man. His inventory listed goods valued at only £3 14s 5d, but he left 8s a year to his wife Mary 'out of the house that my mother Wigsley now dwells in so long as she shall keep her my wife'.[75] The will gives a different impression from the inventory. Most other property owners were rather better off than the Wigsleys, although they were not necessarily rich men. Richard Richardson, a Boston carpenter who died in the

[73] Gillett & MacMahon 1989, 36.
[74] B.C. Jones 1983, 126. John Railton, another Carlisle bricklayer, bought a house in 1690.
[75] LAO, Inv. 138/4; LCC, 1631/60.

winter of 1609–10, possessed goods valued at £10 16s 8d, although he
owed £5 13s 10d including 10s to the butcher and 1s 4d for three pecks
of barley. But his will reveals a totally different aspect of the family
economy: he left 'all those my three tenements in Bargate, Boston' to
his wife. He and his wife lived in one of the properties and the other
two were rented out.[76] The estate of John Wyley, a Boston bricklayer
who died a few months later, was similar: his goods were valued at
£13 11s 4d, although they included three head of cattle valued at £6 10s
and an old mare worth 10s; and his household possessions were
valued at £4 13s. His debts almost balanced – he was owed £8 12s, just
17s 10d more than he owed others. But the will reveals that he owned
'my mansion house wherein I now dwell', which he gave to his wife
and after her to his son Richard, who was a minor. Richard also
received 'one cottage or tenement in the tenure of Widow Westgate',
and two other cottages or tenements. The two servants – perhaps
journeymen – got a shilling each.[77] John Haggas, a Whitby mason, was
much richer. He made bequests totalling over £180 and 'left all my
house with the appurtenances thereunto belonging where I now
dwell in Baxtergate in Whitby' to his son Lawrence.[78]

In north-west England five out of a group of seven carpenters for
whom probate records are available owned properties in the late
seventeenth and early eighteenth centuries. The first was John Nicholson of Penrith who died in 1669 leaving goods worth just under £10,
according to his inventory. He left his wife Frances: 'all that my
messuage and tenement with the appurtenances thereunto belonging
situate in Burrowgate in Penrith aforesaid where I now dwell, with the
house on the backside of the same, and one garth and shop thereunto
adjoining during her natural life and so long as she liveth'.[79] Thomas
Watson who died in 1712 was less generous to his wife. He gave 'all
that messuage or dwelling house and garth with the appurtenances in
which I now dwell ... unto my loving wife Jane for the term of three
years from and after my decease, if she shall live so long'. Clearly he
felt that she was living on borrowed time.[80] Robert Wilson of Penrith
and John Blamire of Carlisle who died in 1744 and 1748 respectively
also owned houses, but by far the most interesting of the north-
western wills was that made by Thomas Hartness, the Carlisle bricklayer who had bought a house in the late seventeenth century.
According to the inventory his possessions were worth just over £13,

[76] LAO, Inv. 109/112; LCC, 1610/479.   [77] LAO, Inv. 109/102; LCC, 1610/124.
[78] St Ninian's Papers, Whitby, NW/U/4. I am grateful to Rosalin Barker for providing me
    with this information.
[79] CUMROC, P1669.   [80] CUMROC, P1712: an inventory has not survived.

and in his will he made explicit provision for his widow's accommodation:

I do leave and bequeath to my wife Jennet Hartness the room that Nicholas
Lowther lately lived in, and also one little buttery joining to the same room
and one loft or chamber above the buttery ... and also one little shop joining to
Widow Smallwood's now dwelling house. And my will is that my son Thomas
shall allow my wife free liberty to the aforesaid bequeathed loft and if he find
that inconvenient I do oblige my said son Thomas to make and build for my
said wife sufficient stairs out of the buttery into the aforesaid loft at his own
proper cost and charges, my said wife enjoying all the aforesaid premises
during her natural life without the disturbance of my son or any other person
whatsoever. As for the goods in my Mansion House I do bequeath them to be
equally divided between my wife and my son Thomas.

If the will was followed to the letter the loft and buttery would have
been rather congested with Jennet's half share of the four bedsteads,
two feather beds, three tables, two cupboards, three chairs, three
stools, and a long settle, together with kitchen and table-ware, curtains,
napkins, and bed linen.[81] Although the amount of space allocated to
her was not over-generous Jennet Hartness was set to enjoy a relatively well-furnished widowhood, although it is not made clear where
her income was to come from.

The probate records of some men reveal that even those with
considerable assets sometimes preferred to rent property. Thus James
Lawes, a rich Lincoln plumber who died in 1630, whose inventory
listed possessions and outstanding debts amounting to nearly £800,
owned 'the lease of the dwelling house with the lease of other houses'
valued at £20. The outstanding lease of John Jobson's house was worth
twice as much. He was a Lincoln mason who died in 1612 leaving
possessions valued at just over £28, in addition to the lease.[82] Clearly
this was a lease with a long time to run, like that of Randle Hall, a
Chester mason who died in 1633: the inventory of his goods listed 'the
interest of the lease of the decedent's dwelling house yet in being for
nineteen years or thereabouts' valued at £50. He also possessed 'the
interest of a lease of two houses in the Fleshmonger Lane for seven
years or thereabouts yet in being' said to be worth £21, and the
reversion of a lease for 21 years in two houses in St Nicholas Street
valued at £20. Most of this additional property was sublet, and was at
least partly furnished: the 'dwelling house of Jane Pue in St Nicholas
Street' contained a cupboard and a little table valued at £1; 'the
dwelling house of Thomas Lloyd in Fleshmonger Lane' contained

[81] CUMROC, P1705.   [82] LAO, Inv. 136/354; 112a/286.

furniture and other goods valued at £5 2s; and the furniture in 'the house of John Sellars in Fleshmonger Lane' was worth £2 2s 8d.[83]

These few examples – and a thorough trawl through the northern probate repositories would reveal many more similar stories – demonstrate that some labourers and building craftsmen owned property, and in some cases were able to benefit by leasing part of it out to others. Some also acquired property in connection with their trades. This was the case with the two Hull men who leased building plots from the council in the late sixteenth and early seventeenth centuries, although more detailed insights are available only in the case of John Farthing, a Hull bricklayer. In March 1670 he bought a messuage and little garden in Lowgate for £46 5s, but mortgaged the property for £20 with the vendors a day later. Then, in January 1671, he recouped much of his original outlay by selling land in Lowgate, together with some building materials, to the council for £37 5s.[84]

It seems unlikely that the majority of building workers, and especially labourers, owned the houses they lived in. However, it is evident that low-grade dwellings were available in the northern towns at low rents for those who needed them. Of course, for those close to the margin of subsistence having to pay rent at any level would create difficulties: if poor widows in York were expected to live on 1½d a day, an annual rent of 2s would involve tight budgeting. Elsewhere, multiple occupancy could be both a benefit to the poor and a source of profit to the owner. For those in work the very low rents on offer in most towns could be earned in just a few days, and even the rents of the more substantial properties occupied by some of the Hull craftsmen could be earned in a few weeks. The preparedness of some men to pay rents which would take up to five weeks to earn is in itself an indicator of how far they were from the margin of subsistence, and anyone capable of paying the higher rents could always fall back on a cheaper, nastier letting if the household economy faltered. Those for whom even the lowest rents were too high were able to squat in unoccupied buildings or sleep in some unoccupied corner. Perhaps many junior tradesmen slept in their workplaces, like William Stout the Lancaster shopkeeper. As an apprentice he slept in his master's shop, and he recalled that 'we apprentices laying in the shop were early called up'. Later, when he set himself up in business in 1688, 'I took off the shop a small room, for a bed, table and a small light, where I lodged'. As he went on to explain: 'I went to board with Alderman Thomas Baynes at

83 CCORO, WS1633, Randle Hall. See also LAO, Inv. 144/156; 154/57; LCC, 1647–8/601; 1636/153.
84 HCRO, BRA/78.

the price of five pounds a year, victuals and washing. But lodged in the shop ... for in my apprenticeship, and some time after, we were frequently called up at all times of the night to serve customers, which obliged us to have a bed in the shop.' When he took an apprentice of his own two years later, he 'lodged with me in the shop'.[85]

Accommodation was rarely cost free in early-modern England,[86] but dwellings of one sort or another were available for rents which could be extremely low. It seems likely that for many of those in work only a small proportion of the annual income was spent on rent, and this is a conclusion which Eden and Davies subscribed to in the later eighteenth century.[87] Those who owned property, whether it was acquired by inheritance or by dint of hard work, enjoyed a substantial buffer against the ravages of the price revolution down to the middle of the seventeenth century: they did not pay rent, they could earn money by leasing out their property, and, in an emergency, they could realise their capital by selling.

Family income

Artisans seldom restricted themselves to one branch of manufacture ... Nor did they limit themselves to manufacturing; indeed if they were to make any money at all it was imperative that they did not. Artisans worked in the service industries, kept livestock, ventured into the victualling trades, in short took any opportunity they could to earn a little extra money.[88]

Many years ago Maurice Dobb suggested that 'when we talk about the standard of living of the worker and his family, we are concerned with the total *earnings* of the family-unit over a whole week or a whole year',[89] and the emphasis on family earnings has become one of the commonplaces of early-modern historiography. Indeed, 'questions about work and earnings by women and children have always been lurking in the wings throughout the standard of living debate'.[90] But it is one thing to recognise the problem and quite another to take it fully into account. Employment beyond the basic occupation of the male head of household is often difficult to trace, although it is evident that many urban craftsmen and traders pursued a wide range of business activities in addition to their basic occupations. Labourers and building craftsmen were no exception to the rule. Wives and children also

85 *Stout Autobiography*, 75, 80, 90, 97, 99.
86 Miners sometimes received free housing: Hatcher 1993, 396–7.
87 This point was made to me by Richard Wall of CAMPOP.   88 Swanson 1989, 6.
89 Dobb 1960, 27.   90 Lindert & Williamsn 1983, 17.

contributed to the household income, although their activities have left relatively few traces in official records. Occasionally the wives and offspring of building workers were able to contribute to the family business, but opportunities were probably less than in the predominantly shop-based trades: most of their work was probably done elsewhere. Although the evidence is patchy, and it is impossible to estimate the extent to which the families of labourers and building craftsmen were dependent on 'outside' earnings, enough examples can be given to demonstrate that such activities were common and spread over a wide area of economic activity.

Throughout the country agriculture was the most important by-employment for those not primarily engaged in farming. Before 1640 about a quarter of rural labourers were 'cottage farmers', and at Stiffkey in Norfolk in the later sixteenth century most labourers retained a 'toe-hold' in the land over and above the small plots which went with their cottages, and they had enough pasture to keep livestock.[91] Similarly, village craftsmen in the building trades in the later sixteenth and early seventeenth centuries had a considerable interest in agriculture: the sixty carpenters living in rural Lincolshire in the later sixteenth century who left probate inventories were all involved in agriculture to some extent, as were all but one of a group of north-western carpenters.[92] Town labourers and building craftsmen were less likely to maintain their ties with the soil, although the divorce between town and country was much less pronounced than it became as a result of industrialisation: fourteen out of twenty-four urban building craftsmen had at least some farming interests.[93] At times the involvement was minimal, as can be seen from the inventories of three Lincoln men: Francis Halliday, a carpenter who died in 1610, had a cock and two hens; Edward Houlton, a labourer who died in 1636, had 'two little pigs'; while George Shewsmith, a glazier and plumber at the Minster who died in 1672, possessed a single cow.[94] Others were in an intermediate position owning a few head of cattle or sheep, and maintaining some interest in arable agriculture. For some the involvement was much more substantial. The contrasts can be seen clearly at Chester: three joiners who died in the first half of the seventeenth century had no interest in agriculture, whereas Thomas Stanier, a carpenter who died in 1611, owned a mixed farm valued at £27 13s. The wills and inventories of a group of twenty-two building craftsmen

---

91 Everitt in Thirsk 1967, 401–6, 420; Smith 1989, 367–8.   92 Woodward 1981, 40.
93 *Ibid.* For information on the extensive farming interests of other types of urban artisans see Woodward 1968b, 89–91.
94 LAO, Inv. 109/296; 144/150; 175/201.

from the north-western towns of Appleby, Carlisle, and Penrith reveal that at least fifteen of them had some interest in agriculture.[95] The proportion of urban labourers and building craftsmen who possessed farming stock is unknown, although the probate records for labourers and building craftsmen must lead us to assume that only a minority did so.

Labourers, building craftsmen, and their families frequently pursued other business activities in addition to their basic trades and their interests in agriculture. Some jobs, such as brewing and spinning, were essential parts of many household economies, especially in the earlier part of the period, and only occasionally were they of sufficient importance to be classified as by-employments. In the sample of Lincolnshire probate inventories for the later sixteenth century, more than a third of the carpenters possessed spinning wheels, and more than two-thirds of the families in Lancashire and Cheshire also owned a wheel or two. Additionally, out of the 132 inventories of building craftsmen from the three counties 15 reveal the existence of genuine, non-agricultural interests.[96]

Among townsfolk the provision of drink was one of the commonest extra activities. In mid-fifteenth-century York those fined as brewers included glaziers and masons, and in 1596 nearly 8 per cent of the city's licensed victuallers were building craftsmen: surprisingly, labourers were not involved in 1596 although they featured prominently in the drink trades in other parts of the country.[97] Such systematic information is not available for other northern towns, although there are scattered references to building craftsmen running ale-houses or fully fledged inns. At Hull, a tiler who kept an alehouse was imprisoned for forty-eight hours in 1576 'because he had allowed a young unmarried couple to lodge for the night and commit fornication'. John Blamire, a Carlisle carpenter who died in 1748, was also in the trade: his inventory listed a lead and brewing vessels in the brewhouse worth £3, twelve bushels of malt valued at £3 10s, and ales in the cellar worth £6.[98] Even more deeply involved was William Rea, a Carlisle bricklayer who died in the winter of 1720–1. He left £120 to his two daughters, adding that: 'if my personal estate after my debts and funeral expenses are defrayed shall happen to fall short and insufficient to pay the aforesaid legacies she my said wife will be so kind as to make up such deficiency out of the freehold messuage and tenement

95 CCORO, WS1611; CUMROC, P1625–1750.
96 Woodward 1981, 39.   97 Swanson 1988, 34; P. Clark 1983, 76–7.
98 Gillett & MacMahon 1989, 126; CUMROC, P1748.

in the city of Carlisle aforesaid called the *George'*. His inventory suggests that it was a large, well-equipped establishment: it had eight rooms including a brewhouse. Additionally the unspecified contents of the cellar were valued at £50, and his stock of malt was worth £40. The swine, which may well have been fed on the waste left over from the brewing process, were valued at £2 17s 6d.[99] James Lawes, the Lincoln plumber who died in 1630, probably ran a sizeable inn, although this was not stated explicitly. The brewing gear in the brewhouse was valued at £6 5s, and 'in divers malt rooms' he had 120 quarters of barley and malt valued at £200. His silver-ware was valued at £45, and the thirty-seven pairs of sheets seem more in keeping with a hostelry than with a private house.[100]

No doubt these few references to the involvement of building workers in the victualling trades are the tip of a substantial iceberg.[101] In addition, many women were involved in the provision of the food and drink supplied to labourers and building craftsmen either as treats or on a more regular basis.[102] But much of that activity was hidden away in the accounts under headings such as 'drink supplied to the workmen'.

Labourers and building craftsmen turned their hands to other tasks as opportunities presented themselves. Sometimes this amounted to the maintenance of businesses of some importance. Thus Robert Bridghouse, a Manchester joiner, dealt in yarn,[103] while John Billing, a Manchester glazier who died in 1588, had irons in several fires in addition to a passing interest in agriculture. He seems to have had a thriving career as a glazier – he had five cases of glass valued at £6, 'made glass' valued at £1, plus a vice and various other tools. He also ran a general store in Manchester, which contained a range of items including pots, trenchers, and points, and he may have traded in yarn and have operated as a small clothier: there were seven 'weaving looms' in the house which may have been used to make the considerable quantities of inkle and points he possessed, including £16 worth of inkle which was in London. Additionally, the goods 'in his shop in Rochdale' were valued at £1 14s 7½d: they comprised small quantities of pewter, brass, and iron ware.[104] At Chester a few men combined the occupations of bricklayer and linen-draper, and some building craftsmen hired out a horse, or a horse and cart: Charles Boswell, the Chester city paver in the late seventeenth century, hired out two teams on one occasion.[105]

---

[99] CUMROC, P1720.   [100] LAO, Inv. 136/354.   [101] See Laughton 1987–8, 113.
[102] See above, pp. 155, 158.   [103] Willan 1980, 85, 128.   [104] LCRO, WS1588.
[105] *Chester Freemen I*, 128, 150; CCRO, TAB/1, fos. 66r, 84r, 99r. See also YCA, CC12.

No doubt others had similar interests outside their basic occupations, but for many the opportunities were more casual and intermittent. At Hull the trusty labourers supplemented their earnings by emptying the 'tubs of office' (toilets), and by doing other odd jobs.[106] There are many references in the northern accounts to payments for such casual employment, and it seems almost certain that the men involved were drawn from the lower segments of society, including labourers, although the occupations and names of those participating are rarely given. Some men possessed unusual skills which could be used to boost family earnings. Thus in the late 1590s John Hardcastle, a Newcastle glazier, was paid 40s a year 'for helping divers and sundry poor people of hurts and diseases in this town'.[107] In 1605 Jane Gill, the wife of a York carpenter, cured the head of a young child orphaned in the plague of the previous year: subsequently the couple agreed 'to bring up the child with meat, apparel and other things, so as she shall not be chargeable to this corporation or any parish of this city' and they received a reward of 20s for doing so.[108]

Although the process cannot be charted in great detail there is no doubt that, as in the medieval period: 'for the urban masses there was a multiplicity of small jobs and chances for retail trade, none of which would have been especially rewarding in themselves, but which in combination gave families the ability to make a living. The attractions of town life for migrants lay in the range of opportunities unavailable in the countryside.'[109] Future work on individual towns, like that on York in the late Middle Ages,[110] will reveal a much more dense earnings' network for labourers and building craftsmen, although inevitably much will remain hidden. No doubt many labourers and some of the building craftsmen received assistance from the poor-law authorities, and other sources of charity, and there were those who turned to crime. Few early Quarter Sessions records have survived for the north, but those for Chester in the mid sixteenth century provide a small insight into the activities of two building craftsmen. Stephen Watton, a carpenter, was the greater villain: he stole clothing, bedding, and table linen valued at nearly £9. This seems to have been a premeditated offence in which his wife was involved. William Robinson's crime appears to have been more opportunistic: he was a slater and stole a pewter dish said to be worth 10d.[111]

A few men added to their family incomes by making investments

---

[106] See above, p. 105. [107] TWAS, 543/19, fos. 4v, 107v.
[108] YAO, CC12, fo. 113A.
[109] C. Dyer 1989, 208. [110] Swanson 1983, 1988, 1989.
[111] CCRO, QSF/17, fo. 16r; /24, fo. 7r.

which probably did not involve them directly in any work. This seems to have been the case with John Haggas, the wealthy Whitby mason who died in 1637, whose will referred to 'one quarter and a sixteenth part of one ship or hoy called the *Welcome* of Whitby wherein Robert Missell is master'. Similarly, William Williamson the Chester joiner who died just after he had been elected alderman of his gild for the first time, left goods valued at just over £96, plus £63 16s 3d 'owing unto him that he laid out concerning a barque'.[112] In two other cases the involvement with the sea was at a much lower level: William Belvish, a Grimsby carpenter who died in 1569, left 'one boat with all that belongeth thereunto' valued at £1, while a Newcastle smith who died in 1583 referred to his fishing boats, nets, and gear valued at £2.[113]

Early-modern economic relationships were sustained by a highly intricate network of indebtedness. In many cases when goods were exchanged, or services rendered, cash did not follow immediately, either because the customer could not afford to pay until money owed to him was forthcoming, or because credit was so ubiquitous that hardly anyone paid on the nail. Robert Sevell's situation was probably typical of many young workers: when he died in 1605 he was owed £10 2s 10d in thirteen separate debts, plus an unspecified amount owed by Sir Thomas Stanley for work done. He had only joined the Joiners' Gild in 1599, and was still struggling to establish himself in business: this was reflected in the £36 19s 2d which he owed, including a £25 loan 'to the city'.[114] Those with few possessions could have a substantial proportion of their total estate bound up in debts: Roger Woodcock, a Chester plasterer who died in 1648, was owed £20, although his household possessions and tools were valued at only £3 12s 4d.[115] These debts may well have accrued through normal business dealings, but some men seem to have been owed money by others to a much greater extent than could be explained by the need to offer credit to customers. Indeed, money-lending seems to have been a common outlet for the surplus funds of some of the more successful building craftsmen, and outline details of the estates of nine such men are set out in table 7.10. What is remarkable about many of them is the high level of the debts owed to them compared with the value of their moveable possessions.

Unfortunately, except in the case of John Billing details of the debts are not available: he had ninety-six outstanding debts, ninety-one of which were recorded in his 'debt book' – the remaining five were 'by

112 St Ninian's Papers, Whitby, NW/U/4; CCORO, WS1641.
113 LAO, Inv. 48/31; *Durham Wills*, 66–7.
114 CCORO, WS1605.   115 CCORO, WS1647.

Table 7.10. *Money owed to northern building craftsmen (to the nearest pound)*

Date	Name	Town	Trade	Goods £	Money owed to him £
1588	John Billing	Manchester	G	222	103
1630	James Lawes	Lincoln	P	517	268
1633	Randle Hall	Chester	M	213	90
1637	Ralph Davenport	Crewe	C	36	177
1677	John Wighall	Lincoln	B	97	220
1730	Thomas Milburn	Appleby	M	42	105
1744	Robert Wilson	Penrith	C	55	223
1746	Thomas Watson	Penrith	C	109	186
1750	Isaac Monkhouse	Carlisle	M	67	322

Note: B = bricklayer; C = carpenter; G = glazier; M = mason; P = plumber.
Sources: CUMROC, P1730, 1744, 1746, 1750; LAO, Znv. 136/354, 219A/183; LCRO, WS1588; CCORO, WS1633, 1637.

bonds and bills'. The unsecured book debts were mostly small – only sixteen were for more than £1 – whereas the five secured debts were all for larger amounts, and they totalled £22 2s 9d. A few of the debts were specified as being for work done or for glass supplied, but the great majority were simply owed by named individuals. What proportion of the debts, if indeed any, were loans rather than debts incurred for work done cannot be determined. But Randle Hall was probably involved in general money-lending. His inventory of 1633 listed 'debts owing to the decedent' amounting to £80 15s, and among the artefacts listed were various items which had been pawned, valued at £8 19s 7d. The appraisers made fourteen such entries which included kitchen gear, bedding, two little chests, a brass mortar and pestle, a pewter flagon, 'one old red petticoat', and 'two silver spoons in pawn'. It is possible that he had received these goods in temporary payment for work done, although it seems more likely that he was operating as a local money-lender and proto-pawnbroker. Others may have done the same.

Some building craftsmen also had considerable sums of money in their houses. Of the men who appear in the table of creditors, Ralph Davenport of Crewe had £30 16s 'in ready moneys', while Thomas Watson had £60 'cash'. Robert Widowes, a Manchester carpenter who died in 1623, had possessions valued at just over £65 which included £22 'in coin', but the man with the largest stock of cash was William

Sharman, a Salford plumber who died in 1633. He was owed £40 2s 5d in thirteen debts, the most substantial of which was for £17 18s from 'the Right Honourable the Lord Strange', and his material possessions were valued at £188 11s 4d, which included £96 'in ready money'.[116]

In 1644 the Hull bricklayers sent a petition to the council complaining about a man from Amsterdam who claimed to be making improved chimneys in the town: his activities were said to be to 'the hindrance and impoverishment of them, their wives, children and servants, *who have no other means to live and maintain themselves, but by their occupation*' (my italics).[117] This was patently not true for many building craftsmen in northern England, although no doubt there were some who found it difficult to come by 'outside' earnings. Unfortunately it is impossible to know the proportion of families which benefited from multiple sources of income, largely because the official record-keepers were so little interested in the process. However, it is clear that 'individuals and family units did not restrict themselves to one occupation'.[118]

Historians have been hampered in their attempts to understand how those towards the bottom of the social hierarchy survived partly because they have found it difficult to reject assumptions relating to the work-practices and lifestyles of their own times. Since industrialisation most workers, and especially those in the towns, have earned the greater part of their income from a single, regular source, or, if the wife was working, from two sources. In the early-modern period it was unusual to try to survive by pursuing a single occupation, and the same remained true in the countryside for even longer. When George Bourne (Sturt) came to observe the villagers living around him in the early years of the twentieth century he was at a loss to know how they managed to survive. He soon began to realise that the labourer's life was 'one continuous act of unconscious self-reliance'.[119] The men laboured long and hard in the fields, but took on extra jobs after 'work', tended their gardens, and looked after their pigs. The women took in washing, did needlework, went charring, and occasionally worked in the fields: their work-patterns were irregular, and pregnancy interrupted their earnings potential. The children helped out from an early age by doing odd jobs, and they left school at fourteen or earlier. Obviously the parallels cannot be pushed too far, but until modern times most families could not hope to survive on the pay-packet of a single 'bread-winner', and the earnings of the women-folk

[116] LCRO, WS1588.   [117] HCRO, BRL, 1458.
[118] Swanson 1988, 37; Swanson 1989.
[119] Bourne 1966, 19.

could bring much needed support to the family, as they have increasingly in the later twentieth century.

Reflections

Two different approaches have been used in this discussion of the living standards of labourers and building craftsmen. Both approaches are deeply flawed. Any attempt to establish a meaningful series of real income founders on our ignorance of the number of days worked in the year. Moreover, far too little is known about consumption patterns. Nevertheless, the direct comparison of wage rates and commodity prices for the north of England broadly confirms the traditional view that English labour suffered a significant deterioration in real wages during the period of the price revolution, and only recovered some of the losses during the next century. The picture presented is a dynamic one. In contrast, the attempt to build up a profile of the lifestyles and sources of income available to labourers and building craftsmen is essentially static. The type of evidence available means that it is possible to establish that some individuals were markedly better off than others, and thus were able to ride out the vicissitudes of erratic price movements more easily, but how they fared in relation to other occupational groups cannot be measured with any degree of accuracy. Labourers are particularly difficult to discuss in any detail. Anyone could drift in and out of labouring work and, except in a few exceptional cases – as at York, where certain types of labourers were licensed for particular tasks, or at Hull, where a group of dominant labourers emerged in the seventeenth century – they remain a shadowy group. On the other hand, more can be said about the building craftsmen, who were named in the accounts more frequently.

Much of the evidence in the second section of this chapter was drawn from wills and probate inventories. The various problems associated with their use are too well known to need more than summary treatment here.[120] Inventories provide a snapshot of a person's stock of possessions within a few days of death, but they tell us relatively little about the process by which those belongings had been acquired, nor about how old the dead person was, and whether or not married with a family. Some of these problems are alleviated if a will is also available: bequests were usually made to relatives, which gives some idea about an individual's age, and any real estate holdings

[120] Riden 1985; Spufford 1990.

were usually mentioned. Information about debts is provided in many inventories, although this was by no means obligatory, and it was more common to list debts owed to the estate than those owed by the dead person. In some cases a list of debts was appended to the will, but problems remain. A recent study has shown that the rank ordering of a group of inventories according to the value of the possessions listed could change substantially when debts, funeral charges, and other costs had been taken into account by the executors in order to reveal the final net worth of the moveable estate.[121]

Unfortunately, many people in early-modern society – and especially the poor – did not leave wills, and their few possessions were allocated informally among relatives. This makes it impossible to study the full range of experience of those occupational groups whose members occupied the lower rungs of the social ladder. In sixteenth-century Worcester the probate records of building workers amounted to only 2.1 per cent of the total body of records, and only 1.0 per cent of inventories sampled for the period 1675 to 1725 in a recent national survey were for labourers. In late-medieval York relatively few building workers left wills: they 'only survive for 7 per cent of all builders made free in the fifteenth century; this in itself is an indication of their limited resources when compared to crafts like tanners or pewterers where 20 per cent and 23 per cent respectively of free craftsmen made wills which survive'.[122]

The probate material which has survived for northern building workers covers a wide spectrum of wealth. At the base were men like Robert Shaw, a Stockport carpenter who died in 1599. After specifying a few bequests he gave 'all the rest of that little portion of goods that God hath blessed me withall' to his two daughters, one of whom was made the executrix alongside a neighbour. Shaw's estimation of his estate was not a case of false modesty: his household possessions comprised some pewter and brass, 'a little ark', a coffer, a pair of bedstocks, a little board, treen ware, kitchen gear, and bedding; his clothes were valued at 10s: in total, £2 4s 8d. His will also refers to 'one cutting axe' which does not feature in the inventory. We may wonder why Robert Shaw bothered to make a formal will. The answer is simple: his wife was dead and he wished to ensure that his possessions went where he desired. In particular he wanted some of his clothing and other small items to go to 'Robert Shaw my base begotten son'.[123] Robert Shaw senior can stand proxy for a large number of other building craftsmen and labourers who did not leave wills, although no

---

121 *Ibid.*   122 A. Dyer 1973, 82; Weatherill 1988, 168; Swanson 1983, 28.
123 *Stockport Inventories*, 24–5.

doubt there were some who had even fewer possessions, perhaps owning only the clothes they stood up in, and a few rudimentary tools. This may have been the case with Moses Dalbie, a Chester glazier who died in 1649. His widow administered his estate, paying a debt of 30s, although the accounts recorded that 'the said accountant doth charge herself with the sum of 12s 6d of good and lawful money of England being the total sum of the inventory taken of the goods of the said deceased'.[124] To judge by modern standards Robert Shaw, and no doubt Moses Dalbie and his wife, lived in sparsely furnished dwellings, but this does not tell us the whole story of their lifestyles. We cannot tell how often they went hungry, how often there was insufficient fuel on the fire, and whether or not their clothing was adequate to keep out the winter weather.

Above Robert Shaw in the pecking order of wealth were men with possessions worth £10 or so. They included Francis Halliday, a Lincoln carpenter who died in 1610, and left 'my cloak, my best breeches and my best hat' to his brother and some tools to two nephews. The residue, 'after indifferent appraisement thereof made by honest neighbours chosen to that purpose', was to be divided equally between his wife and his daughter, when she reached the age of twenty-one. The house was modestly, but comfortably, furnished with goods valued at £8 9s 4d: his 'apparel and money in his purse' came to £1 6s 8d; he had a cock and three hens worth 1s 4d; and his tools and the stock connected with his trade were valued at £3 8s.[125] Higher still were the men with deep pockets who were often owed large sums of money. Included among their number was James Lawes of Lincoln, prince of the northern building workers. He seems to have retired from the plumbing business, since the inventory of 1630 does not list any lead, tools, or other gear connected with the trade: but he was owed a great deal of money and seems to have been running a brewery, and probably an inn.[126] Other men of impressive financial standing include John Haggas, the Whitby mason/shipowner, who made bequests amounting to £185, and William Sharman, the Salford plumber, who had £96 in ready money. He had a small farm, and possessed £46 8s 7d invested in almost four tons of lead which was partly at Bolton and Rochdale, but mostly in his Salford shop. His possessions were valued at £188 11s 4d, excluding debts.[127]

By diligent trawling through the diocesan record repositories of northern England it would be possible to add substantially to the

---

[124] CCORO, WS1649. [125] LAO, Inv. 109/296; LCC 1610, 439.
[126] LAO, Inv. 136/354.
[127] LCRO, WS1633.

number of wills and inventories relating to labourers and building craftsmen. But to what effect? There would be more detail and, no doubt, new by-employments would be discovered to add to the list, but little of substance would be added to our knowledge of shifts in living standards. More would be known in detail about the lives of some building craftsmen and labourers, but nothing of the large number whose affairs were kept out of the probate courts. Perhaps greater insights can be gained by returning briefly to the direct evidence relating to wages and prices.

Whether or not they could afford to buy enough of their daily bread was the chief problem facing many labourers and building craftsmen in early-modern England. All of the series of grain and bread prices – for both northern and southern England – indicate a substantial degree of inflation between the early decades of the sixteenth century and some point in the mid seventeenth century. During that period, when nominal wage rates rose only sluggishly, conditions deteriorated for those predominantly dependent on wage-earning for their livelihoods. There is no doubt that using the Phelps Brown and Hopkins cost-of-living index exaggerates the degree to which living standards declined – and this has been confirmed by the recent work on London – but there is also no doubt that the quality of life for many was deteriorating. The price data for Lincoln and Hull indicate that for many workers improvements did not occur before the later seventeenth century. Calculations based on a notional diet which would have given an adult male around 3,000 calories a day – exclusive of their drink intake – suggest that, even in the 1630s when conditions were at a low ebb for many, single men could earn their diet relatively easily, although the acquisition of a wife and the arrival of children quickly made matters difficult unless the extra family members – and especially the wife – were able to make a considerable contribution to their keep. In addition to the cost of food, many urban workers had to buy their drink, fuel, housing, and clothing on the market. But the acquisition of all those extra necessities cost less than is often imagined. Some varieties of drink became cheaper compared with the price of other commodities, and also in relation to wages. Similarly, if the Hull peat-price series is any guide to conditions elsewhere, those towards the bottom of the social ladder were able to buy relatively cheap fuel. Nor does housing seem to have been a problem. For those who needed to rent the roof over their heads, and doubtless they were the great majority, low-grade dwellings were available at low rents which could be earned by a labourer making just a few days' effort. Finally, anyone close to the poverty line was unlikely to buy new clothing: they were much more likely to benefit from the constant process of recycling of old, cast-off garments and shreds of material.[128] This is not to suggest that all labourers and building craftsmen spent their days in rags, but that there were cheap sources of clothing available – as indeed there are today – for those who wished to take advantage of them. Such processes formed an important part of the survival strategies of the poor.

One of the main problems in trying to estimate the difficulty faced by labourers and artisans striving to meet the daily costs of survival is that the degree of dependence on wage-earning is unknown. Master craftsmen, supplying raw materials and the labour of others from time to time, were not totally dependent on their wage-earning potential, and the evidence presented in the second part of this chapter makes it plain that many families had more than one source of income. But there are many questions which cannot be answered by a study of this nature. In particular, in the absence of the account books kept by the building craftsmen themselves, the number of days worked each year and the degree of dependency on wage-earning will never be known with any degree of accuracy. And it is unlikely that such records will be found. If historians wish to explore these matters further, worthwhile advances are more likely to come through intensive studies of individual towns based, in the first instance, on a thorough family reconstitution of the parish registers, and continued through an exhaustive investigation of freemen's rolls, council minutes, gild records, town accounts, probate records, and other material.[129] Such a town, with an impressively full array of records would not be easy to find, and there is not a perfect example in the north. To take one case: Hull has an excellent, if broken, series of accounts, good parish registers for each of the two churches, and adequate council minutes; but the freemen's rolls are weak, gild records almost non-existent, and, as throughout much of Yorkshire, few inventories are available before the 1690s. There are similar weaknesses in the spread of records available for other northern towns: at Chester, Lincoln, and York there were too many churches to make family reconstitution feasible; the accounts for Beverley and Lincoln are weak for long periods, and there is little information relating to gild activity; the accounts for Newcastle and York, which are good for the sixteenth century, fade in the seventeenth century; and the records of the towns of the far north-west are too fragmentary to offer much encouragement.

The final conclusions on shifts in the living standards of northern

[128] Woodward 1985, 177–9.
[129] For an attempt to reconstruct life in a circumscribed rural area see Smith 1989.

labourers and building craftsmen between 1450 and 1750 hold few surprises. After a comfortable start in the later fifteenth century, conditions deteriorated down to the Civil War, but eased somewhat thereafter. Supplements to family income, from a range of sources, and the relatively low prices of at least some of the basic necessities of life made survival easier than an excessive concentration on the movement of food prices would suggest. Conditions were never easy and many felt the gnawings of hunger, sometimes on a daily basis, although others managed to live at a substantially higher level. Labourers had the most difficult time: they were unspecialised, rarely benefited from the provision of raw materials and employment of others, got little support from the gilds, and invariably received lower wages than the craftsmen working nearby. But they did survive and in some cases they can be traced in the records over long periods of time. Although they were on average less well off than building craftsmen,[130] those who remained fit enough to work were above the very bottom stratum of urban society which included the poor widows subsisting with difficulty in cheerless parish rooms. Building craftsmen were a rung or two higher on the urban social ladder, and a few clawed their way to much greater heights, although as a group they remained among the more lowly of the urban crafts.[131]

[130] Based on information supplied by Mark Overton relating to probate inventories in different parts of the country.
[131] Swanson 1983, 28–31.

Appendices

Appendix 1 Wage rates paid in the towns of northern England, 1450–1750

Wage-rate data for labourers and building craftsmen are given for each of the northern towns in a consistent form. Either a single rate is given or, where more than one rate is quoted, the lowest and the highest rate. Outlying rates which are either exceptionally high or low have not been included but they have been discussed at the appropriate point in the text above. Only rarely is the quoted rate the only one available for the year: in most instances a number of rates is available and frequently they are very numerous. For most towns the series for the craftsmen is dominated by the rates paid to carpenters and brick-layers although the rates paid to joiners, glaziers, sawyers, tilers, and masons have also been included. The series for each town is prefaced by a short introduction.

Some of the documents do not give the dates of transactions and present the data in a split year: e.g. most of the churchwardens' accounts run for a year from Easter – viz. Easter 1602 to Easter 1603. In a case like this the data in the series will be logged under 1602 unless the source gives a specific date for the entry.

As discussed in chapter 5 the accounts vary enormously in terms of the treatment of the drink allowance: in some cases it was explicitly stated; elsewhere it was built into the basic wage; and on some occasions it seems to have been missing altogether. Since the allowance was sometimes built into the wage the policy adopted here is to add the explicit drink allowance to the basic wage whenever it is mentioned. However, the allowance was usually no more than one or two pence and, in the seventeenth century (when it was most common), did not comprise a sizeable proportion of the total wage.

In all of the series data will be given for each year unless the data are identical for two or more years when a sequence of dates will be given in the left hand column: viz. 1660–2 means that the same data are given for the three years 1660, 1661 and 1662. When there is a gap in the data from one year to another a horizontal line appears in the left hand column:

1660

1662.

There is a brief discussion of the source material for each town, but in order to get a full appreciation of the records used it is necessary to consult the bibliography.

Appendix 1.1   Beverley

Sources

1   The Corporation account rolls: the series begins with a fine roll for 1494 which produces useful wage data, but the next roll – for 1502–3 – sets the format for the rolls which follow: they are in a more summary form which rarely produces evidence of individual wage rates (just one rate is given in 1573 and two in the following year). The series is broken: there are just six annual rolls for the first half of the sixteenth century and nineteen for the second half.

2   The Corporation minute books: these cover part of the period from 1558 to 1660. For the sixteenth century this is a more useful source: the first two books which cover the years 1558–73 produce some interesting data about the operation of the Beverley labour market, including wage rates for some years. But again the data are relatively thin.

3   The accounts of the churchwardens of St Mary's: they take two forms: a broken series of annual rolls for the period 1592 to 1734, which comprises the best single source for Beverley, although the quality of the information deteriorates from the 1690s; and an account book for 1732–81 which produces only a small amount of information.

Relatively few wage rates are available for Beverley and the series is weaker than that for most other towns. It has been necessary to make an adjustment to many of the rates quoted in the accounts of St Mary's in the later seventeenth century. From 1650 to the early 1670s craftsmen and their assistants were paid a standard allowance of 3d a day on top of their basic wages, as on occasion were labourers. After a break the records begin again in 1678, but there is no mention of the allowance until it reappears for the two years 1689/90 and 1690/1 after which it again disappears. There are three possible explanations for this:

(i) that the allowances continued to be paid although they were not recorded in the accounts;
(ii) that the allowances were not paid;
(iii) that the allowances were paid but that they were built silently into the basic wage.

The problem with the second and third explanations is that they would have involved a reduction in the level of pay which, on the evidence for other places in the north, does not seem to have been very likely. It would also mean that there had been a shift from year to year. The solution to the problem which has been adopted here, for those years when the allowance was not recorded, is to give the rate paid as the lowest rate and to add a standard allowance of 3d to give a higher rate. There is a similar problem with the pay of labourers although the level of the allowance is less clear cut. When the sexton worked as a labourer he received an allowance of 3d a day although it is not clear that this was standard for other labourers.

There is another problem in trying to establish the rates of pay of Beverley labourers in the seventeenth century. At St Mary's most of the casual labouring was done by the sexton, who received a yearly retainer and was then paid for labouring at a daily rate. There are some indications that the sexton was paid a daily rate below the usual market rate. Thus in 1645/6 the churchwardens paid the sexton 6d a day for five days' work; the corporation account roll for 1644/5 recorded that labourers were paid at 9d and 10d a day for ditching. Through the 1650s and 1660s the sexton was paid mostly at 9d a day, although occasionally he only got 8d, whereas in 1652 six labourers were paid 51s 3d for 47 days, that is, just over 13d a day if they were all paid at the same rate. Since most of the rates for labouring work relate to the sexton it is possible that the going rate for labourers in Beverley was higher than the series suggests: in order to indicate the problem clearly the rates given to the sexton are given in brackets.

The Beverley wage series (in pence)

Date	Craftsmen	Labourers	
1494	6	3–4	
1548	6	4	
1563	—	6	
1565	—	6	
1573	—	6	
1574	8	6	
1584	—	6	
1592	8	—	
1595	8	6	
1602	8	—	
1604	—	6	
1623	16	6	(6)
1642	14–18		(6)
1644	—	9–10	
1645	—		(6)
1646	16–20		(6–8)
1647	20		(6)
1650–1	19		(8–9)
1652	19	13	(9)
1653–5	19		(9)
1656	19–21		(9)
1657	19	11	
1658	21	11	(8)
1659	—		(9)
1660–2	21		(9)
1663–8	19–21		(9)
1669	19–21	—	
1670	19	—	
1672	16–21	—	
1678–81	16–21	—	
1684	18–21	—	
1686–7	18–21	—	
1688	—	12	
1689–90	21	—	
1691	20–3	10	
1692	18–23	10–12	
1693	20–3	10–12	
1695	20–3	—	
1697	20–3	10–12	
1705	20–3	10–12	
1706	—	10–12	
1707–8	20–3	10–12	
1710–12	20–3	10	(8)
1713	20–3	—	
1715	20–3	10	
1717–8	20–3	10–12	
1721–3	—	10–12	
1740	—	10–12	
1741	20–3	12	
1742–5	—	12	
1749	—	14	

Appendix 1.2   Carlisle

Sources

1   The chamberlains' accounts, which run in a broken sequence from 1602 to 1739. They are relatively uninformative, often providing composite entries and the final volume covering the years 1695–1739 contains little of value for this project.

2   The chamberlains' vouchers, which were the bills submitted by the workmen for work done. There are eighty-four vouchers which contain some very useful data and have been drawn on a number of times in the text above. The vouchers cover the period from 1688 to 1750 although all but two of them are for the period after 1712.

3   Some data are available for the years 1577–95 from the accounts of royal building activity. The rates paid were relatively high, probably above those paid by the council and other employers in the town in the later sixteenth century.

The Carlisle wage series is a relatively poor one. The accounts often specify the nature of the work in hand and the term 'workman' seems to have been used for both skilled men and labourers. The seventeenth-century accounts often provide information relating to the provision of food and drink at work although sometimes such data are missing. The recording of the allowance seems to have varied from one chamberlain to another: when not recorded it was usually built into the basic wage. The vouchers on the other hand mention food and drink only as an extra treat and the workmen seem to have built the drink allowance into the basic wage on all occasions.

The Carlisle wage series (in pence)

Date	Craftsmen	Labourers
1577	10–12	6
1584	12	8
1586–7	12	8
1595	12	8
1603	—	6
1616	—	6–7
1617	—	6
1618	—	6–7
1621	10	6
1622	10–12	6
1628	12	8
1639	14	—
1640	12	10
1642–3	14	6
1650	—	11–12
1651	18	8–12
1659	—	12
1660	18	12
1661	19	12
1662–5	—	12
1666	18–19	12
1671	18	—
1672	18–20	12
1673	—	12
1674	20	12
1675	—	8–12
1676	—	9–12
1677	18	10–12
1684	16–19	12
1686	16	12
1688	—	12
1689	16–18	12
1694	16	—
1721	18	—
1722	16–18	9
1723	18–20	—
1724	18	9
1725	18	8–10
1726	20	—
1727	18–20	—
1728	20	—
1729	18–20	10
1730	18–20	8–10
1731	18–20	—
1732	18–20	9
1733	16–20	9–11
1734–5	18–20	9
1736	18	9
1737	18	—
1739	18	9
1741	18–20	—
1742	16–18	—
1747	20	9
1748	18	10
1749	18	—

Appendix 1.3   Chester

Sources

The Chester series is based on two main sets of records:

1   The financial records of the city authorities, chiefly the treasurers' accounts and the muragers' accounts. These survive with gaps from 1553, and until the late seventeenth century take the form of annual accounts which often provide details of payments made to individual workers. From the late seventeenth century they are supplemented by the 'selected vouchers' submitted by the workmen.

2   Churchwardens' accounts for various churches.

Throughout, the series is relatively fragmentary both in terms of the number of years covered and the richness of the data available. However, the various accounts tell a relatively consistent story and there are no significant differences in the level of pay given to the different types of craftsmen and the series for them is drawn from the rates for masons, carpenters, and bricklayers.

The Chester wage series (in pence)

Date	Craftsmen	Labourers (male)	Women
1548	6	4	—
1553	6	4–5	2
1558	—	6	—
1562	8	—	—
1564	10	6	—
1565	9	—	—
1568	9–10	5–5.5	3
1569	8–10	—	—
1572	8	6	—
1573–4	—	6	—
1579	9	—	4
1583	8	6	—
1587	8–10	6	—
1588	—	6	—
1598	8–12	—	—
1604	10–12	6	—
1605	10	—	—
1607	12	—	—
1608	—	8	—
1610	10–12	8	—
1611	12	—	—
1613	12–14	—	—
1614	—	8	—

The Chester wage series *(in pence)* (cont.)

Date	Craftsmen	Labourers (male)	Women
1615	10	8	—
1617	12–14	—	—
1618	12	8	—
1619	12	7–9	—
1620	—	9	—
1622	12	—	—
1623	—	8	—
1624	12	—	—
1626	12–15	8–9	—
1627	12	8	—
1633	12–14	8	—
1634	—	8	—
1637	12–14	—	—
1638	—	8	—
1639	13	—	—
1641	12	—	—
1645	12	8	—
1652	13–15	—	—
1653	14	—	—
1654	14	8	—
1655	—	8	—
1656	13–16	—	—
1658	14–18	—	—
1660	16	—	—
1661	17–18	11	—
1664	18	10	—
1669	14–18	8–10	—
1670	—	9–12	—
1672	14–18	9–10	—
1675	18	10	—
1683	16	—	—
1684	14	10	—
1687	—	12	—
1690	16	—	—
1692	—	12	—
1695	18	10	—
1697	—	9–11	—
1698	16–18	9	—
1699	16	9	—
1700	16–18	—	—
1701	15–18	10–12	—
1702	15–18	10	—
1703	—	10	—
1704	16–18	9–10	—
1705	—	9–10	—
1707	—	10	—

The Chester wage series (in pence) (cont.)

Date	Craftsmen	Labourers (male)	Women
1708	18	10	—
1709–10	16–18	10	—
1711	16–18	8–9	—
1712	16–18	9–10	—
1713	16–18	10	—
1714	16	10	—
1715	16–18	10	—
1716	16–18	—	—
1717	16	—	—
1718	16	10	—
1720	16	10	—
1721–3	16–18	10	—
1725–6	16–18	—	—
1727	16–18	10	—
1728	16–18	—	—
1729	14–18	10	—
1730	14–18	12	—
1731	16–18	10–12	—
1732	15–18	—	—
1733	16–19	12	—
1734	16–18	10	—
1735	16–18	10–12	—
1736	17–19	10–12	—
1737	16–18	—	—
1739	16–18	10–12	—
1740	17–19	—	—
1741	16–19	12	—
1742	16–18	11–12	—
1743	16–18	—	—
1745	18–19	12	—
1746	17–19	12	—
1747	16–18	—	—
1748	16–18	11	—
1751	16–18	12	

Appendix 1.4   Durham

Sources

Some information has been gathered from the churchwardens' accounts kept at the County Record Office and from the Abbey account rolls printed in three volumes by the Surtees Society. But the series is based predominantly on two main sets of records:

1   The financial records of the Dean and Chapter of Durham Cathedral kept in the Prior's Kitchen, which fall into three categories:

(a) the Dean and Chapter treasurers' books, which run in a broken sequence from 1554 to beyond the end of the period studied. Many of the accounts are in summary form and provide relatively little information;

(b) a collection of records known as miscellaneous charters which include many documents relating to repair work in the Cathedral and further afield. They run from the 1540s to the 1570s and are particularly strong for the 1540s and 1550s;

(c) the audit bills which are relatively few in number and relate to the late seventeenth and early eighteenth centuries.

2   The financial records of the Bishop of Durham's estates kept at Five the College which fall into two groups:

(a) the Clerk of Works' accounts which run from the 1470s to the 1580s; again they are particularly strong for the middle years of the sixteenth century. Work was often undertaken outside the town by Durham men and they were paid the same basic rates regardless of venue: this means that wage rates relating to other places can be used as a proxy for Durham rates when they are missing;

(b) two boxes of miscellaneous material known as Loose Box 25, which contains material for the 1540s to 1590s and for the late seventeenth century, and Loose Box 26, which has material for the late seventeenth and eighteenth centuries.

Data are plentiful for the sixteenth century and particularly for the 1540s and first half of the 1550s: this is especially valuable since it provides insights into the movement of wage rates during those decades of monetary instability. After the mid 1560s the series becomes more fragmentary although the information for the 1590s is good. Thereafter little is known about wage rates until the 1680s and 1690s, after which the evidence becomes rather thin but generally consistent.

The Durham wage series (in pence)

Date	Craftsmen	Labourers (male)	Women
1450	6	—	—
1456	5	—	—
1465	5–6	—	—
1468	4–5	—	—
1470	6	—	—
1472–3	—	3–4	—
1475	5–6	4	—
1477	5–6	3–4	—
1480	5–6	3–4	—
1489	5–6	3–4	—
1493	5–6	—	—
1494	5	—	—
1501	4–5	—	—
1503	5	—	—
1513	5–6	3–4	—
1515	5–6	3–4	2
1519	5–6	4	—
1534–5	5–6	4	2
1538	5–7	4	2
1541	5–7	4	2
1542	5–7	3–4	—
1543	5–7	4	2
1544	6	4	—
1545–6	6–7	4–5	2
1547	6	—	2
1548	6–7	4	2
1549	7–8	—	—
1550	6–8	5	—
1551	7–9	6	—
1552	6–9	5	2
1553	7–8	5	2
1554	7–8	5	—
1555	7–8	5	2
1557	7–9	4–6	2
1561	9	5–6	—
1562	8–9	6	—
1564	8–10	—	—
1571	7–8	—	—
1573	7–8	—	2
1574	8	—	2
1577	7–9	6	3
1584	8–10	5–6	2
1589	8	6	2–3
1590	8	5	2–3
1591	8	5	2–3
1592	8	5–6	3

The Durham wage series (in pence) (cont.)

Date	Craftsmen	Labourers (male)	Women
1593	8–9	5–6	3–4
1594	8–9	5–6	3
1596	8–9	6	3
1597	9	6	3
1663	18	8	—
1666	16	8	—
1681	16–18	—	—
1682	—	10	—
1683	16–18	—	—
1684	16–18	10	6
1685	16–18	10	—
1686	18	—	—
1687–92	16–18	10	—
1694	16–18	—	—
1695	6–18	10	—
1696	18	—	—
1700	16–18	10	—
1701	18	10	—
1704	16–18	—	—
1705	16–18	10	6
1709	16–18	10	—
1710	18	12	—
1724	16–18	12	—
1727	—	12	—
1728	18	10–12	—
1729	—	12	—
1730–1	18	12	—
1739	18	—	—
1740	18	12	—

Note: Until 1538 all of the accounts relate to a split year, 1538–9; the information in the series has been logged under the leading year.

Appendix 1.5   Hull

Sources

The Hull series is based on two major and three minor sources:

1   The accounts of the Hull Trinity House which date from the 1460s. Five detailed account books cover the period down to 1692: thereafter the accounts were entered in annual volumes but only in summary form. However some of the vouchers submitted by the workmen have survived for the early decades of the eighteenth century. The accounts of the late fifteenth and early sixteenth centuries have some gaps and some of the years which are covered do not provide usable material: this explains why the series is fragmentary for that period. The accounts rarely provide a detailed dating of events although the accounts were kept on a quarterly basis so that it is usually possible to determine the season of the year being covered.

2   The accounts of the town council, usually referred to as the Town Husbands' Accounts. They begin in 1563, but are not continuous. However, when they are on stream they provide an enormous amount of information of unparalleled value for the north of England. This is especially true of the accounts for the third quarter of the seventeenth century. From the later seventeenth century a great deal of information can be derived from the surviving workmens' vouchers.

3   The Hull chamberlains' account roll for 1464–5 printed in *Hull Rentals*, 91–109.

4   The accounts of the Corpus Christi Gild for the 1520s.

5   The churchwardens' accounts for St Mary's, Lowgate, for the period from 1657. As with all such accounts the data are spotty and sometimes difficult to interpret.

The quality of the information varies from time to time: for some years only a few entries are available whereas in other years entries relate to many hundreds of man-days – the wage rates for the third quarter of the seventeenth century relate to more than 60,000 days' work. However, the high degree of consistency in the data provided from year to year – including moving from years of very full documentation to those with much more skimpy evidence – encourages the belief that the evidence is generally reliable. The Hull series is the most solid of those collected in this appendix.

The Hull wage series (in pence)

Date	Craftsmen	Labourers
1467	6	3.3–4
1470–2	6	4
1476	—	3.33
1486	6	4
1496	6	—
1522	6	—
1523	6	4
1525	6	4
1529	6	4
1541	6	4
1548	6	—
1550	6	5
1551	9	5
1554	8	5
1557	8–10	5
1563–5	8–10	6
1566	8–11	6
1568	9–10	6
1569	8–10	6
1571	9–11	6
1572	8–10	5–7
1573	8–10	4–6
1574	9–10	6
1575	10	—
1578	10	6
1579	9–10	6
1580	8–10	6
1581	—	6
1583	10	—
1584	8–10	6
1585	9–10	6
1586	10	6
1587	9–10	6
1596	10	—
1605	10	—
1606	10–12	—
1609	12	—
1611	12	—
1614–15	12	—
1616	10	—
1617	12	8
1618	12	6–8
1619–21	12	8
1622	10–12	8
1623–4	12	8
1625–6	12	6–8
1627	12	8
1628	10–12	6–8
1629	10–12	7–8
1630	12	7–8

The Hull wage series (in pence) (cont.)

Date	Craftsmen	Labourers
1632	—	8
1635	12–14	8
1636–7	12–16	8
1638	12–14	8
1639	12–16	8
1640	12–14	8
1652–3	18–21	10
1654–5	18–19	10
1656–60	18–21	10
1661–75	18–22	10
1676	18–22	10–12
1677	20–4	10–12
1678	18–24	10
1679	18–21	10
1680	24	—
1681	20–4	10–14
1682–5	24	—
1686	24	12
1687	22	12
1689	—	12
1691	22–4	12
1692	21	12
1693–4	22	12
1695	22–4	12
1696	21–4	12
1697	20–4	12
1698–1700	24	12
1708	24	12
1709	24–6	12
1710	24	—
1711	24	12
1713–14	24	12
1715	24	—
1720	24	—
1725	—	15
1729–31	24	12
1732	24	12–18
1734	24	—
1735	24	14
1736	24	12
1737	24	—
1739–40	24	—
1741–2	24	14
1743	24	12
1744	24	14
1745	24	—
1746	24	12–14
1747	24	—
1748	24	12
1749–50	24	—

Appendix 1.6 Kendal

Sources

The borough of Kendal was incorporated in 1575 and the chamberlains' accounts began seven years later and run through to 1734, although the last useful information on wages appears in the account for 1712. Many of the data relate to the repair of the town mill and associated dam together with some repairs to the bridge and other council property. As will become apparent from the wage series presented below the accounts are broken in various places.

The whole series is of a relatively poor quality, certainly compared with the series for Hull, and it is more scrappy for the period after 1660. Thatchers appear regularly in the Kendal accounts and they were usually paid about 2d less than other building craftsmen; because they appear so rarely in the accounts of the other towns they have been omitted from the series. The thatchers were aided by a server who was usually paid at the same rate as common labourers and their rates have been incorporated in the series when labourers' rates are missing.

The chief problem with the series relates to the drink allowance. Workers at Kendal were frequently given drink or a money allowance at work, especially in the seventeenth century. The most common allowance was 2d a day although the amount was not always stated. Sometimes the allowance was added silently to the basic wage although on some occasions there was neither reference to the allowance nor an enhancement of the basic wage. It is possible, of course, that the drink was given to the workmen but accounted for elsewhere; if so, this will have the effect of depressing some of the rates recorded in the series.

Appendix 1

The Kendal wage series (in pence)

Date	Craftsmen	Labourers
1582	8	6
1583	9	6
1586	8	—
1590	8	6
1592	8	—
1593	8–10	—
1594–6	8	6
1597	—	6
1598	8	—
1599–1600	8–10	—
1602	—	6
1603	8–10	6
1604	8–10	—
1605	8	—
1608	8	—
1609	8–10	8
1613	8–10	—
1614–15	—	6
1616	—	7
1617	10–11	—
1618	12	8
1620	12	8
1622	13	9
1624	10–12	—
1625–6	10	—
1627	10	6
1628	10–12	6
1629	10–12	6–7
1630	10–14	—
1631	12–14	—
1632	12	—
1633	12	8
1634	10–12	6–8
1635–7	10–12	6
1638	12	8
1639	10–12	8
1640	10–14	8
1641	12	—
1644	10–12	9–10.5
1645	12	—
1646	11–12	8
1647—8	14	9
1649	14	—
1650	12	—
1651	12–16	—
1652	14–15.5	—

The Kendal wage series (in pence) (cont.)

Date	Craftsmen	Labourers
1653	16–18	—
1654	13	10
1656	14–16	—
1657	14–16	9–10
1658	14–16	8
1659	14–16	—
1660	12–15	—
1661	14–16	10
1662	—	10
1663	14–16	9
1664	14–16	10
1665	14–18	—
1666	16	—
1667	14–15	—
1669	13.5–14	12
1679	13–18	—
1681	14	—
1683	14	—
1684	14–16	—
1686	12–14	—
1688	14	—
1690–1	14	10
1692	14	—
1712	15	—

Appendix 1.7   Lincoln

Sources

The Lincoln series is relatively fragmentary since no single source dominates. There are three main sources:

1   The accounts of the Dean and Chapter relating to the cathedral. The early sixteenth century accounts have been heavily repaired and contain little of value for this project. For the seventeenth and eighteenth centuries they are much more valuable, especially for the 1660s.

2   Churchwardens' accounts: as usual they are very varied in quality but contain much of value.

3   The chamberlains' accounts which run from the late seventeenth century and contain little of any real worth.

As with the Beverley series some of the payments for labouring were made to a sexton and these rates – which were probably below the market rate – are given in brackets.

The Lincoln wage series (in pence)

Date	Craftsmen	Labourers	
1554	6–8	4	
1600	—	6	
1602	10	6–7	
1606	10–14	7–8	
1612	—		(6)
1613	10–12		(6)
1614	—		(6)
1616	12	—	
1617–18	10–12	8	
1619	10–12	7–8	
1620	10–12	8	
1622	10–12	8	
1623	12	7–8	
1624–7	12	8	
1628	10–12	7–8	
1629	10–14	8	
1630–1	12	8	
1632	12	7–8	
1633	10–12	8	
1634	12–14	8–11	
1636	14	8	
1639	12	—	
1654	—	8	
1655–6	16	10	
1657	15	—	
1659	16	10	
1660	12–14	8–10	
1661	12–16	8–10	
1662–3	12–18	8–10	
1664–9	12–18	10	
1672	16	10	
1673–5	—	10	
1676	16–18	10	
1677–82	—	10	
1688	—	12	
1694	18	10	
1696	—	10	
1703	18	10	
1705–6	18	10	
1711	18	10	
1716–17	18	10	
1722	20	10	
1723	—	10	
1726–9	—	10	
1730	18	10	
1738	18	10	
1739	—	10	
1740	18–20	10–12	
1741–50	—	12	

Appendix 1.8   Newcastle upon Tyne

Sources

The Newcastle series are relatively disappointing. There are some chamberlains' accounts for the early sixteenth century which have been printed but the main series does not begin until 1561. For some five decades the accounts provide some very valuable material but from the early seventeenth century they move into summary form and thereafter rarely provide any detailed wage data. The wage series are continued in the seventeenth century by the accounts of Newcastle Trinity House and then from the later seventeenth century by the churchwardens' accounts of St Nicholas's. The series is especially thin from the middle of the seventeenth century, which is a great shame considering the significance of the Newcastle area in the development of early-modern England.

The Newcastle wage series (in pence)

Date	Craftsmen	Labourers
1508–11	5–6	3–4
1560	7–8	6
1561–3	8	5
1565	8	5
1566	8–9	5–6
1567	8–10	5–6
1568	8	5–6
1574	8	5
1576	8–10	5–6
1580–1	8–10	5–6
1590–8	8–10	6
1599–1600	10–12	6
1601	10–12	8
1606	12	8
1607–8	10–12	8
1633	16	8–10
1634	16–18	8–10
1635–8	16–18	10
1639	14–18	10
1640	16–18	10
1642	16–18	12
1643	18	10
1645	16	10
1646	18	12
1647	20	—
1648–50	—	12
1651	21	12
1652	—	12
1654	22	12
1655	20–2	12
1656	22	12
1657	20–2	12
1659–60	20–2	12
1670	20	—
1687	18	—
1702	—	10
1703	18	—
1707–8	—	14
1713	24	—
1715–16	—	14
1719	22	—
1720	—	14
1724	22	—

Appendix 1.9 Penrith

Sources

The Penrith series comes from the churchwardens' accounts and hence, as usual, is fragmentary although it tells a consistent story: wage rates were considerably lower than in other northern towns. It is possible that rates were similarly low in other small towns away from the mainstream of economic life although there is little supporting evidence. In places the records are difficult to interpret since it is not always clear what individual workmen were doing. In addition, a composite drink allowance was sometimes paid but it is impossible to tell how much was going to individual workers: where an unknown amount of drink went to a worker a plus sign has been added to the basic wage.

The Penrith wage series (in pence)

Date	Craftsmen	Labourers
1655	12–13	—
1662	12	—
1666	12	—
1683	13	—
1685	10–12 +	—
1693	—	8
1695	12	—
1697	12	8
1700–2	14	6
1703–4	12	6–8
1705	12	8
1706	12	—
1711	12	8
1713	—	6
1715	—	8

Appendix 1.10   York

Sources

The York series are based on three major sources:

1   The Minster fabric rolls: these annual accounts which begin in the late fourteenth century have been used for the period from November 1469–70 (for such split years, data are logged under the second named year). They are the only source for wage rates until the St Michael, Spurriergate, accounts begin in 1518. The survival of the Minster accounts is patchy: from the 1520s to the 1580s only between two and five years are covered in each decade and from 1590 to the Civil War accounts have survived for only six years. From the middle of the seventeenth century the accounts become increasingly summary and rarely provide any detailed wage data. The rates quoted in the craftsmen's series are for carpenters, masons, tilers, and glaziers: once again plumbers have been omitted.

2   The chamberlains' accounts: which begin in 1559 and run through to the middle of the eighteenth century. Again the accounts are fragmentary: after providing good data for the years 1559 and 1565 there is a gap until 1584 – data are then available for twenty-six of the years from 1584 to 1621. Until 1621 the accounts provide a considerable amount of useful information, although there are years when little can be learned: after 1621 they take an increasingly summary form and provide wage data for only a few years.

3   Churchwardens' accounts: due to the inadequacy of the Minster Accounts after 1590 and the chamberlains' accounts after 1621 the York series relies heavily on the fragmentary data gleaned from the numerous churchwardens' accounts which have survived for York. The most useful are the accounts for St Michael, Spurriergate, which begin in 1518: the early accounts are a particularly rich quarry since the church owned a considerable number of houses. Unfortunately the churchwardens' accounts took an increasingly summary form in the later seventeenth and early eighteenth centuries and the York series is extremely thin for that period.

The York wage series (in pence)

Date	Craftsmen	Labourers
1470–1	6	4
1473	6	4
1475	6	4
1479	6	4
1482	6	4
1485	6	4
1498–9	6	4
1505	6	4
1508	6	4
1510	6	4
1516	6	4
1518–20	6	4
1522–48	6	4
1550	6	4
1554	7	4
1556–7	8	—
1559	7–8	6
1560	8	—
1565	7–9	6
1566–7	8	6
1568	8	—
1569	8	6
1571	8–9	6
1573	8	—
1574	8	6
1576	8	6
1578–9	8–10	6
1580	8–10	—
1581–2	8–10	6
1583	8	—
1584	8–10	6
1586	8–10	6
1587	10	6
1588	8–11	6
1589	11	—
1590	8–11	7
1592	11	—
1593	—	7
1594	9–11	6–7
1595	9–10	6
1596	8–12	6–7
1597–8	10–12	6–7
1599	12	6–8
1600	12	7
1601	11–13	7
1602	12–14	8
1603	12–13	7–8
1604	13	8
1605	13	7
1606	13–14	7–8
1607	10–14	—
1608	13	8
1610	12–13	8
1611	10–14	8
1612	14	8–9

The York wage series (in pence) (cont.)

Date	Craftsmen	Labourers
1613	13	8
1615	12	—
1616	12–14	8–9
1617–18	14	9
1619	12–14	7–9
1620	12–14	9
1621	12–14	8–9
1623	12–14	—
1624	12–15	7–10
1625	—	8
1628	12–14	8
1630	12	8
1631–2	14	10
1633	14	9–10
1634–6	14	—
1637	14	10
1639–41	14	10
1643	21	—
1644	16	—
1645	16	10
1646	20	12
1647	18	12–14
1648	21	12
1649	18–20	—
1650	18	10
1651	20	—
1654	18–20	10
1655–6	18	—
1659	18	10
1660	18	10–14
1662	18	10–12
1663	20	12
1666	—	12
1669–72	18	—
1673	18–20	—
1674	18	—
1675	20	12
1677	—	13
1678	18	12
1681	20	12
1682	22	—
1684	18–22	12
1692	20	—
1694	20–2	12
1695	22	12
1696	18	—
1697	20	12
1699	—	12
1700	20	12
1703	20	12
1707	20	12
1710	20	12
1727	18	—
1742	18	—

Appendix 2

The cost of diet at Hull and Lincoln

The tables which follow are based on the assize prices for grain laid down at Lincoln down to 1714, and at Hull from 1710 to 1749, and the prices paid for cheese and beef for the feasts held at Hull Trinity House. Unfortunately it is not possible to provide a price series for each town separately since grain prices were not collected at Hull until the early eighteenth century[1] and few meat prices are available for Lincoln. The price of wheat, oats, and peas for Lincoln are laid out in appendix 2.1 and the Hull prices in appendix 2.2. At Lincoln three prices of wheat were given each year and the middle price has been used here in the calculations since that was the price used to set the price of bread.[2]

The calculations of diet are based on the daily diet laid down by Drummond and Wilbraham: they suggested that a typical 'seventeenth-century diet when "White Meats" became scarce' comprised $3\frac{1}{2}$ oz. of cheese, 2 lb. of bread and 9 oz. of peas a day which would provide 2,850 calories. The same diet without the cheese would provide 2,450 calories a day.[3] In the tables which follow most of the calculations are made in relation to this basic diet although appendix 2.3 also gives the daily price of the grain diet only.

The price of 2 lb. of bread has been calculated in the following fashion: a bushel of wheat weighs approximately 60 lb. and will yield 48 lb. of flour which will produce about 67 lb. of bread (3 lb. 2 oz. of wholemeal flour will make five 14 oz. loaves: i.e. 50 oz. of flour will make 70 oz. of bread).[4] Thus a quarter of wheat (eight bushels) would yield enough bread for 269 days so that the cost of a man's daily bread has been calculated by dividing the price of a quarter of wheat by 269.

[1] *Hull Prices*; Kelsall 1938.   [2] A.H. Taylor 1917, 291.
[3] Drummond & Wilbraham 1964, 465–7.
[4] Collins 1975, 108. From information provided by Mrs Stephenson, a Cottingham baker.

This is in line with the suggestion by Gilboy that a family of six would eat half a peck of wheat a day if dependent on wheaten bread (half a peck of wheaten flour would produce about $8\frac{1}{2}$ lb. of bread).[5]

Since it has proved impossible to estimate the cost of 9 oz. of peas (the weight of a bushel is not known nor the yield of eatable produce from such a bushel) oats have been substituted for peas in the diet calculated here. A bushel of oats weighs about 40 lb. and would produce some $22\frac{1}{2}$ lb. of edible oatmeal so that the price of 9 oz. of oatmeal can be calculated easily from the price of a quarter of oats. Of course in some northern areas the basic staple of life would be oats rather than wheat, although this may not have been the case at Lincoln and it has been suggested that the Hull diet was more dependent on wheat than on oats.[6] However, it would not always make a great deal of difference to the calculations if oats were substituted for wheat, since the prices of the two grains moved together in a more or less synchronised fashion as shown in appendix 2.8. The wheat calculations above suggest that a man needed about $1\frac{1}{3}$ quarters of wheat a year or about 4 quarters of oats: Scottish labourers 'could survive on 30 oz. of oatmeal, plus water and a little kale, but began to get weak on this diet at, say, 25 oz.' ($22\frac{1}{2}$ lb. of oatmeal, the produce from a bushel of oats, divided by 30 oz. = 12 days: 365 days divided by 12 = 30.4 bushels or 3 quarters and 6.4 bushels or nearly 4 quarters).[7] However at Lincoln the price of wheat was generally about three times the price of oats in the middle decades of the sixteenth century so that the cost of each item in nutritional terms was roughly the same. With the ratio between the prices of the two grains at 1:3 consumers would be more or less indifferent as to which grain they consumed although when the ratio fell below that level, as in the 1550s when prices stood at 1:2.5 many consumers would switch to wheaten bread: similarly, when the ratio rose above 1:3 in the later sixteenth century many would be tempted to eat more oatmeal. The consumption of larger quantities of oatmeal when wheat was relatively expensive would alter the calculations in the tables which follow. Moreover, consumers were likely to switch from one grain to another not only from one year to another but also within the year.[8]

In arriving at the cost of feeding it has been assumed that consumers would be likely to switch from cheese to beef if the latter was significantly cheaper, as it often was in seventeenth century Hull: where only one price is available that has been used but where both are

---

[5] Gilboy 1934, 193.   [6] Collins 1975, 102.
[7] From information provided by Christopher Smout in a letter of 7 March 1990.
[8] Collins 1975, 103–5.

available the lower (invariably the beef price) has been used. This is based on the assumption that cheese and fat meat contain approximately the same number of calories.

In calculating the cost of feeding a family it has been assumed that a woman will consume 75 per cent as much as a man, that each of the first two children will consume at the same level, and that the third and fourth children will together eat as much as the father. Obviously these are heroic assumptions and can give no more than a very general guide to the cost of feeding a family. It has been argued that women routinely received less to eat than men in the early-modern period and only those teenagers who were in regular work are likely to have been given as much to eat as men when times were hard.[9] Moreover it is likely that all received more calories a day than implied by the diet assumed here since no allowance has been made for drink: this is discussed in chapter 7 and the price of drink is laid out in appendix 3. The calculations of family diet are laid out in appendix 2.4. The annual cost of feeding a family of varying size is presented in appendix 2.5 where the data from appendix 2.4 are multiplied by 365. Appendix 2.6 gives the number of days which had to be worked by men on different levels of pay in order to achieve the notional diet of 2 lb. of wheaten bread, 9 oz. of oatmeal and $3\frac{1}{2}$ oz. of cheese or beef a day.

[9] Shammas 1990, 154.

Appendix 2.1. *Grain prices at Lincoln, 1513–1714, and Hull, 1708–50*
The prices given are for Michaelmas and are given in shillings per quarter to
the nearest decimal place.

Dates	No. of observations	Wheat	Oats	Peas/beans
(a) Lincoln				
1513–18	4	6.9	—	—
1520–9	6	7.1	—	—
1530–9	3	6.5	3.0	4.0
1540–9	6	9.9	3.1	4.5
1550–9	9	14.9	5.9	9.7
1560–9	9	15.7	5.5	9.7
1570–9	10	17.4	5.8	8.6
1580–9	9	18.3	6.3	9.9
1590–9	7	26.3	7.7	15.4
1600–9	2	24.0	7.0	17.0
1610–19	6	35.5	10.9	18.4
1620–9	9	31.4	8.9	16.9
1630–9	5	37.4	12.0	24.0
1650–9	4	40.0	12.5	21.7
1660–9	7	32.7	9.9	19.4
1670–9	8	28.4	8.8	19.1
1680–9	10	25.7	9.4	18.5
1690–9	10	31.9	9.6	19.7
1700–9	6	27.3	9.7	17.7
1710–14	3	35.0	13.2	
(b) Hull				
1710–14		28.8	10.8	
1708–9		31.5	10.6	
1710–19		25.8	10.7	
1720–9		23.3	11.2	
1730–9		24.1	10.3	
1740–9		26.2	10.5	

Source: J.W.F. Hill 1956, 221–6; Kelsall 1938, 56.

Appendix 2.2. *Prices at Hull – cheese and beef plus sugar and tobacco
(prices in pence to the nearest farthing)*

Dates	Cheese per stone	Beef per stone	Sugar per lb.	Tobacco per oz.
1540–9	9	—	—	—
1550–9	12	—	—	—
1560–9	16	12	—	—
1590–9	—	16	—	—
1600–9	—	19.25	23	—
1610–19	56	27.25	21	—
1620–9	—	25.25	16.5	12
1630–9	70	31.5	19.5	10
1640–9	70	—	16	10
1650–9	56	32	17	8.5
1660–9	—	30	10	6.25
1670–9	42	26.5	8	3.25
1680–9	—	25.5	7	1.25
1690–9	—	23.5	—	—

Note: The price of beef at Newcastle was 14d a stone in 1563 and 20d a stone in
1591: TWAS, 543/14, fos. 157v–158r; 543/18, fo. 198r.
Source: HTH, I–V.

Appendix 2.3. *The cost of diet of a single adult male at Hull and Lincoln*
(prices in pence to the nearest second decimal place)

Date	Bread	Cheese	Beef	Oats	Grain only	Cheese diet	Beef diet
	2 lb.	$3\frac{1}{2}$ oz.	$3\frac{1}{2}$ oz.	9 oz.			
1513–18	0.31	—	—	—	—	—	—
1520–9	0.32	—	—	—	—	—	—
1530–9	0.29	—	—	0.11	0.40	—	—
1540–9	0.44	0.16	—	0.12	0.56	0.72	—
1550–9	0.66	0.21	—	0.22	0.88	1.09	—
1560–9	0.70	0.29	0.21	0.21	0.91	1.20	1.12
1570–9	0.78	—	—	0.22	1.00	—	—
1580–9	0.82	—	—	0.24	1.06	—	—
1590–9	1.17	—	0.29	0.29	1.46	—	1.75
1600–9	1.01	—	0.35	0.26	1.27	—	1.62
1610–19	1.58	1.00	0.49	0.41	1.99	2.99	2.48
1620–9	1.40	—	0.46	0.33	1.73	—	2.19
1630–9	1.67	1.25	0.56	0.45	2.12	3.37	2.68
1640–9	—	1.25	—	—	—	—	—
1650–9	1.78	1.00	0.57	0.47	2.25	3.25	2.82
1660–9	1.46	—	0.54	0.37	1.83	—	2.37
1670–9	1.27	0.75	0.47	0.33	1.60	2.35	2.07
1680–9	1.15	—	0.46	0.35	1.50	—	1.96
1690–9	1.42	—	0.42	0.36	1.78	—	2.20
1700–9	1.22	—	—	0.36	1.58	—	—
1710–14	1.56	—	—	0.50	2.06	—	—

Appendix 2.4. *The daily cost of feeding a family at Hull and Lincoln (prices in pence)*

Dates	Single man		+ Wife	+ Children			
	Cheese diet	Beef diet		+1	+2	+3	+4
1540–9	0.72	—	1.26	1.80	2.34	2.70	3.06
1550–9	1.09	—	1.91	2.73	3.54	4.09	4.63
1560–9	—	1.12	1.96	2.80	3.64	4.20	4.76
1590–9	—	1.75	3.06	4.38	5.69	6.56	7.44
1600–9	—	1.62	2.84	4.05	5.27	6.08	6.89
1610–19	—	2.48	4.34	6.20	8.06	9.30	10.54
1620–9	—	2.19	3.83	5.48	7.12	8.21	9.31
1630–9	—	2.68	4.69	6.70	8.71	10.05	11.39
1650–9	—	2.82	4.94	7.05	9.17	10.58	12.00
1660–9	—	2.37	4.15	5.93	7.70	8.89	10.07
1670–9	—	2.07	3.62	5.18	6.73	7.76	8.80
1680–9	—	1.96	3.43	4.90	6.37	7.35	8.33
1690–9	—	2.20	3.85	5.50	7.15	8.25	9.35

Appendix 2.5. *The annual cost of feeding a family at Hull and Lincoln (in pence)*

Dates	Single man	+ Wife	Children			
			+1	+2	+3	+4
1540–9	262.8	459.9	657.0	854.1	985.5	1116.9
1550–9	397.9	697.2	996.5	1292.1	1492.9	1690.0
1560–9	408.8	715.4	1022.0	1328.6	1533.0	1737.4
1590–9	638.8	1116.9	1598.7	2076.9	2394.4	2715.6
1600–9	591.3	1034.8	1478.3	1923.6	2219.2	2514.9
1610–19	905.2	1584.1	2263.0	2941.9	3394.5	3847.1
1620–9	799.4	1398.0	2000.2	2598.8	2996.7	3398.2
1630–9	978.2	1711.9	2445.5	3179.2	3668.3	4157.4
1650–9	1029.3	1803.1	2573.3	3347.1	3861.7	4380.0
1660–9	865.1	1514.8	2164.5	2810.5	3244.9	3675.6
1670–9	755.6	1321.3	1890.7	2456.5	2832.4	3212.0
1680–9	715.4	1252.0	1788.5	2325.1	2682.8	3040.5
1690–9	803.0	1405.3	2007.5	2609.8	3011.3	3412.8

Appendix 2.6. *The number of days worked to feed a family at Hull and Lincoln (to the nearest whole day)*

Date	Wage (pence per day)	Man	+Wife	Children			
				+1	+2	+3	+4
(i) Labourers							
(a) Hull							
1540–9	4	66	115	164	214	246	279
1560–9	6	68	119	170	221	256	290
1590–9	6	106	186	266	346	399	453
1610–19	8	113	198	283	368	424	481
1620–9	8	100	175	250	325	375	425
1630–9	8	122	214	306	397	459	520
1650–9	10	103	180	257	335	386	438
1660–9	10	87	151	216	281	324	368
1670–9	10	76	132	189	246	283	321
1680–9	12	60	104	149	194	224	253
1690–9	12	67	117	167	217	251	284
(b) Lincoln							
1540–9	4	66	115	164	214	246	279
1550–9	4	99	174	249	323	373	423
1560–9	6	68	119	170	221	256	290
1590–9	6	106	186	266	346	399	453
1600–9	8	74	129	185	240	277	314
1610–19	8	113	198	283	368	424	481
1620–9	8	100	175	250	325	375	425
1630–9	8	122	214	306	397	459	520
1650–9	10	103	180	257	335	386	438
1660–9	10	87	151	216	281	324	368
1670–9	10	76	132	189	246	283	321
1680–9	10	72	125	179	233	268	304
1690–9	10	80	141	201	261	301	341
(ii) Hull Craftsmen							
(a) The best-paid men							
1540–9	6	44	77	110	142	164	186
1550–9	10	40	70	100	129	149	169
1560–9	10	41	72	102	133	153	174
1590–9	10	64	112	160	208	239	272
1600–9	12	49	86	123	160	185	210
1610–19	12	75	132	189	245	283	321
1620–9	12	67	117	167	217	250	283
1630–9	16	61	107	153	199	229	260
1650–9	21	49	86	123	159	184	209
1660–9	22	39	69	98	128	147	167
1670–9	24	31	55	79	102	118	134
1680–9	24	30	52	75	97	112	127
1690–9	24	33	59	84	109	125	142

Appendix 2.6. (*cont.*)

Date	Wage (pence per day)	Man	+ Wife	Children			
				+1	+2	+3	+4
(b) The worst-paid men							
1540–9	6	44	77	110	142	164	186
1550–9	8	50	87	125	162	187	211
1560–9	8	51	89	128	166	192	217
1600–9	10	59	103	148	192	222	251
1610–19	10	91	158	226	294	339	385
1620–9	10	80	140	200	260	300	340
1630–9	12	82	143	204	265	306	346
1650–9	18	57	100	143	186	215	243
1660–9	18	48	84	120	156	180	204
1670–9	18	42	73	105	136	157	178
1680–9	20	36	63	89	116	134	152
1690–9	21	38	67	96	124	143	163
(iii) Lincoln Craftsmen							
(a) The Best Paid Men							
1550–9	8	50	87	125	162	187	211
1560–9	10	41	72	102	133	153	174
1610–19	12	75	132	189	245	283	321
1620–9	12	67	117	167	217	250	283
1630–9	12	82	143	204	265	306	346
1650–9	16	64	113	161	209	241	274
1660–9	18	48	84	120	156	180	204
1670–9	18	42	73	105	136	157	178
1680–9	18	40	70	99	129	149	169
1690–9	18	45	78	112	145	167	190
(b) The worst-paid men							
1550–9	6	66	116	166	215	249	281
1600–9	10	59	104	148	192	222	251
1610–19	10	92	158	226	294	339	385
1620–9	10	80	140	200	260	300	340
1660–9	12	72	126	180	234	270	306
1670–9	16	47	83	118	154	177	201

Appendix 2.7. *The quantity of oats which could be bought at Lincoln and Hull for a unit of wheat*

Date	Number of observations	Amount of oats
(a) Lincoln		
1539–49	7	3.1
1550–9	9	2.5
1560–9	9	2.9
1570–9	10	3.0
1580–9	9	2.9
1590–9	7	3.4
1600–9	2	3.4
1610–19	6	3.5
1620–9	9	3.5
1630–9	5	3.1
1650–9	4	3.2
1660–9	7	3.3
1670–9	8	3.2
1680–9	10	2.7
1690–9	10	3.3
1700–9	6	2.8
1710–14	3	2.7
(b) Hull		
1710–14	5	2.7
1708–9	2	3.0
1710–19	10	2.4
1720–9	10	2.1
1730–9	10	2.4
1740–9	10	2.5

Appendix 2.8. *The percentage change in wheat and oats prices at Lincoln from Michaelmas to Easter*

Date	Number of observations	Wheat % change	Oats % change
1550–9	7	+24.1	+14.8
1560–9	9	+17.5	+9.6
1570–9	10	+17.3	+11.6
1580–9	9	+19.8	+16.5
1590–9	7	+13.7	+41.9

Appendix 3

The price of ale and beer in the northern towns

Date	Place	Type of drink	Quantity (in gallons)	Price per gallon (in pence)
1464/5	Hull	Ale	12	2
1540	York	Ale	—	2
1547	Boston	Best ale	—	1.75
	Boston	Best beer	—	1.5
1550	Lincoln	Ale	—	2.5[a]
1552	Chester	Best beer	—	1.33[a]
1553	Lincoln	Ale	—	2[a]
1561	Manchester	Ale	—	4 or 6[a]
1562	Liverpool	Ale	—	6[a]
1562	Lincoln	Beer	—	2[a]
		Single beer	—	1[a]
1572	Lincoln	Ordinary beer	—	1[a]
		Ale	—	2.5[a]
1587	Lincoln	Ale	—	3[a]
1591	Newcastle	London beer	—	6
1593	Newcastle	London beer	—	6
1638/9	Hull	Strong beer	c.70	5 & 6
1639–40	Hull	Ale	266	8
1642	Hull	Beer	c.36	3.75
1647	Hull	Strong beer	20	4.6
1648	Hull	Beer	42	5
1653–91	Hull	Ale	2000+	8
1654	Hull	Strong beer	78	4
1656	Hull	Beer	80	4.8
1661	Hull	Beer	23	6
1664	Hull	Strong beer	26	6
1667	Hull	Small beer	20	1.8
1669	Hull	Beer	40	5.25
1672	Hull	Beer	30	6
1675	Hull	Ale	124	10

Appendix 3 (*cont.*)

Date	Place	Type of drink	Quantity (in gallons)	Price per gallon (in pence)
1679	Hull	Beer	5	3.6
1686	Hull	Small beer	10	2
1691	Hull	Small beer	6	2
		Good ale	10	9
1691/2	Hull	Small beer	26	2
1696	Hull	Ale	60	12
1703	Newcastle	Ale	0.75	12
1705	Newcastle	Ale	0.5	14
1708	Newcastle	Ale	0.5	14
1728–30	Hull	Ale	a large volume	16
1731	Hull	Small beer	12	2
		Ale	12	10

[a] = assize prices

Note: The price for ale at Manchester in 1561 was 4d for out-sales and 6d for ale drunk in the house.

Sources
Boston: P. Clark 1983, 97.
Chester: CCRO, A/B/1, fo. 85r.
Hull: *Hull Rentals*, 97; Davies 1956; HTH, IV, V; HCRO, BRF/3/19–21; HUA, DTR/1/7.
Lincoln: Hill 1956, 82.
Liverpool: *Liverpool Town Books*, I, 195.
Manchester: *Manchester Court Leet*, 68.
Newcastle: TWAS, 547/18, fos. 148r, 197v, 252v; MF/557.
York: YBI, PR/Y/MS/1.

Bibliography

Primary material

Manuscripts

Information is provided in the following format: name of the place to which the information relates; the record repository concerned; a brief description of the manuscripts and their outline dates (where the series is substantially broken more detailed dates are given); the record office reference.

APPLEBY
CUMROC: CW 1585–1630: WSMB/A

BARNARD CASTLE
PRO: Accts of repairs, 1532–3: E101/458/8

BERWICK
PRO: Accts of repairs, 1532–57: E101/483/13–16

BEVERLEY
PRO: Acct of works, 1548–9: E101/458/24
HCORO
    Council minute books, 1558–1660: BC/II/ 7 /2–4
    Town acct rolls, 1494–1728: BC/II/6/15–125
    St Mary, CW, 1592–1750: PE 1/51–114
HUA: Acct Book of the executors of Michael Warton, 1688–9: DP/81

BRIDLINGTON
PRO: Accts of works, 1539–45: E101/622/29; 459/5–6

CARLISLE
CUMROC
    Chamberlains' accts, 1602–1750: Ca/4/1–6
    Probate inventories and wills, 1630–1750: P1630–1750
    Vouchers to accts, 1600–1750: Ca/4/11–126

PRO: Accts of works, 1557–8, 1569, 1576–1602: E101/483/17; 545/16

CHESTER
CCRO
(a) City Finances
Muragers' accts, 1709–50: MUV/1–3
Treasurers' accts, 1554–1672: TAR/1/8–3/59
Treasurers' accts and rentals, 1683–1714: TAB/1–2
Treasurers' vouchers, 1580–1750: TAV/1/1–35
(b) Gild (Company) records
Bricklayers, Company book, 1683–1750: G4/1
Joiners, carvers and turners, acct book, 1728–50: G14/3; Company
book, 1576–1750: G14/1; minute book, 1615–1726: G14/2
Mayors' company papers, 1578–1627: MCP/2
Smiths, cutlers and plumbers, acct book, 1637–1750: G20/2
CCORO
(a) CW accts
Holy Trinity, 1633–84: P1/11
St Mary on the Hill, 1536–1690: P20/13/1, 4–16
St Michael, 1558–1678: P/65/8/1
St Peter, 1626–87: P63/7/1
(b) Probate inventories and wills, various
PRO: Accts of works, 1557–1602: E101/483/17; 545/16

COCKERMOUTH
CUMROC: CW, 1668–1748: PR 136/152–3

DURHAM
DCRO
(a) City records
Acct book of John Dunn, carpenter, 1730: D/X/487/12/3
Mayors' accts, 1720–50: DU 1/42/1–2, 8–9
(b) CW accts
St Margaret's Chapel, 1665–1720: EP/Du.SM/50
St Mary le Bow, 1678–1750: EP/Du.MB/9
St Mary the Less, 1662–1750: EP/Du.ML/6
DFC: Bishopric Estate, Clerk of Works accts, 1475–1586: Box 75/3/190045–78/76/
190102
DPK: (DEAN AND CHAPTER MUNIMENTS) Audit bills (uncalendared), 1709–40:
bundles 15–16, 18
Audit book 5, 1723–46
Loose papers, 1542–1740: Boxes 25–6
Miscellaneous charters, 1541–97: MC 2662–3359, 6792–7121
Treasurers' books, 1557–1710: 1–50

FLAMBOROUGH
PRO: Acct of works, 1541–6: E101/463/17–20

HOWDEN
HCORO: CW accts, 1593–1666: PE 121/37

HULL (KINGSTON UPON HULL)
HCRO
Chamberlains' bills: BRF/6
Chamberlains' accts, 1562–1701: BRF/3/2–21, 52–60
Civic letters, 1576–1690: BRL/1397–1416, 1458, 1512
Corpus Christi Gild acct, 1522–5: BRA/88
Miscellaneous deeds, 1508–1750: BRA/28–50, 78; BRI/17–46; BRK/3;
BRM/79–362; BRN/14b-545; WG38
Wage assessments, 1669, 1683, 1721
HCORO
Holy Trinity order book, 1654–90: PE 158/60
Holy Trinity parish registers: PE 158/1
St Mary, CW, 1684–1750: PE 185/34, 35
St Mary, parish register, 1657–1750: PE 185/2
HTH
Acct books I–V, 1461–1692; HTH, I–V
Order books 1 & 3, 1582–1630, 1665–1703: HTH/OB/1, 5
HUA
Maister acct book, 1714–25: DP/82
Trinity House vouchers, 1714–50: DTR/1/7

KENDAL
CUMROK
Apprentice enrolment book, 1640–1750: WSMB/K/7
Book of indentures, 1680–1736: WSMB/K/8
Chamberlains' accts, 1582–1734: WSMB/K
Probate inventories and wills, various
PRO
Accts of works at Kendal and Penrith, 1577–9: E101/545/19

KIRKBY LONSDALE
CUMROK
CW accts, 1669–1750: WPR/19
Settlement certificates etc., 1698–1750: WPR/19

LANCASHIRE
LCRO: Probate inventories and wills, various

LINCOLN
LAO
(a) City records: Chamberlains' rolls, 1685–1742: Boxes 1–5
(b) Cathedral records: Dean and Chapter fabric accts, 1512–47, 1616–
    1750: Bj/1/6–13; 5/19
(c) CW accts
    St Benedict, 1652–1750: L1/7/1–2
    St Martin, 1554–1634: L1/5/12
    St Michael on the Mount, 1625–80, 1739–50: L1/7/1–4
(d) Probate inventories and wills, various

NEWCASTLE UPON TYNE
PRO: Accts of work, 1558–60: E101/476/21–2
TWAS
(a) City Finances: Chamberlains accts, 1561–1683 : 543/15–60
(b) Gild (Company) records
    Carpenters: Meeting book, 1590–1661: 903/1
    Bricklayers: Agreement with masons, 1654: 817/6
             Account books, 1725–42: 802/7–8; 817/9
             Minute books, 1637–1750: 802/1–5
             Ordinances, 1599–1727: 802/16
    Joiners: Account books, 1652–80: 648/8–9
         Admissions book, 1648–1750: 648/13
         Minute and order books, 1666–1750: 648/3–4, 6, 12
(c) Trinity House records
(d) CW accts, All Saints, 1694–1740: MF557
NCRO: CW ACCTS
    St Andrews, 1663–1750: EP/13/68–9
    St Nicholas, 1684–1720: M/18/31

PENRITH
PRO: Accts of work, 1577–9: E101/545/19
CUMROC: CW accts, 1655–1750:PR/110/1/75

WHITBY
St Ninian's Papers: will of John Haggas: MW/U/4

YORK
YBI
(a) CW Accts: All Saints, North St.,1645–1730: PR/Y/ASN/10
    Holy Trinity, Goodramgate, 1559–1750: PR/Y/HTG/12–13
    Holy Trinity, Micklegate, 1683–1718: PR/Y/HTM/17
    St John, Ouse Bridge, 1705–38: PR/Y/J/18
    St Lawrence, 1674–1750: PR/Y/L/23
    St Martin's, Coney St., 1553–1633, 1725–50: PR/Y/MCS/16–18
    St Martin cum Gregory, 1560–1750: PR/Y/MG/19–20
    St Michael's, Spurriergate, 1518–47, 1594–1710: PR/Y/MS/1–2,5
    St Michael le Belfry, 1636–1729: PR/Y/MB/34
(b) Probate inventories and wills: various
YCA
    Card index of gild records
    Chamberlains' accts, 1559–1750: CC5–38
YML
(a) Minster fabric rolls and accts, 1469–1750: E3/24–65, E4a
(b) Gild records
    Bricklayers: Accts, 1589–1629, 1660–83, 1727–50: QQ80/2/1–3
    Apprentice book, 1654–1750: QQ80/2/13
    Attendance rolls, seventeenth century: QQ80/2/4–6
    Ordinances, 1590–1712: QQ80/2/11
    Carpenters: Orders and ordinances: QQ80/3/2
    Free labourers: Ordinances, 1578–1750: QQ80/5/1–2

Printed primary material

The short title given for each volume is used in the footnotes.

Bankes Family: The Early Records of the Bankes Family at Winstanley, ed. J. Bankes and E. Kerridge, Chetham Society Publications, 3rd series, 21 (1973)

Belfry PR I & II: *The Parish Registers of St Michael le Belfry, York* part I, 1565–1653, ed. F. Collins, Yorkshire Parish Register Society, 1 (Leeds, 1899); part II, 1653–1778, ed. F. Collins, Yorkshire Parish Register Society, 11 (Leeds, 1901)

Bridlington Charters: Bridlington Charters, Court Rolls and Papers, ed. J.S. Purvis (London, 1826)

Builder's Companion: The Builder's Companion and Workman's General Assistant by W. Pain, 3rd edn (London, 1769)

Carlisle Records: Some Municipal Records of the City of Carlisle, ed., R.S. Ferguson and W. Nanson (Carlisle and London, 1887)

Chester Assembly Book: Typescript Calendar of the First Chester Council Assembly Book, CCRO, Cal.A/B/1

Chester Courts: Typescript Calendar of the Chester Crownmote and Quarter Sessions Files, 1488–1566, CCRO, Cal.QSF

Chester Freemen I & II: *The Rolls of the Freemen of the City of Chester*, 1392–1700 & 1700–1805, 2 vols. ed. J.H.E. Bennett, The Record Society of Lancashire and Cheshire, 51 and 55 (1906 and 1908)

Chester Haven: 'The Account Book of the New Haven, Chester, 1567–8', ed. E. Rideout, *Transactions of the Historic Society of Lancashire and Chester*, 80 (1929), 86–128

Chester Minutes: Calendar of Chester City Council Minutes 1603–1642, ed. M.J. Groombridge, The Record Society of Lancashire and Cheshire, 106 (1956)

Clifton Accts: 'The Church and Churchwardens' Accounts of Clifton, Westmorland', ed. C.M.L. Bouch, *Transactions of the Cumberland and Westmorland Antiquarian and Archaeological Society*, 49 (1949)

Coventry Leet Book: The Coventry Leet Book, ed. M.D. Harris, The Early English Text Society, 134–5, 138, 146 (1907–13), continuous pagination

Derbyshire Annals: Three Centuries of Derbyshire Annals, ed. J.C. Cox, 2 vols. (London 1890)

Discourse of the Commonweal: A Discourse of the Common Weal of this Realm of England, ed. E. Lamond (Cambridge, 1954)

Doncaster Records: A Calendar of the Records of the Borough of Doncaster, ed. W.J. Hardy, 4 vols. (Doncaster, 1899–1903)

Dublin Accts: 'A Fifteenth-Century Building Account from Dublin', ed. J. Lydon, *Irish Economic and Social History*, 9 (1982), 73–5

Durham Abbey Accts: Extracts from the Account Rolls of the Abbey of Durham, ed. J.T. Fowler, Surtees Society Publications, 3 vols., 99, 100, 101 (1898–1901)

Durham Wills: Wills and Inventories from the Registry at Durham, part II, Surtees Society Publications, 38 (1860)

East Yorkshire Descriptions: Descriptions of East Yorkshire, Leland to Defoe, ed. D. Woodward, East Yorkshire Local History Society, 39 (1985)

Elizabethan England: Elizabethan England by William Harrison, ed. L. Withington (London, 1976)

Evelyn Diary: The Diary of John Evelyn, ed. W. Bray, 2 vols. (London, 1966)

Family History: 'A Family History begun by James Fretwell', in *Yorkshire Diaries*

and Autobiographies in the Seventeenth and Eighteenth Centuries, Surtees Society Publications, 65 (1877), pp. 163–243

Gild Life: Two Thousand Years of Gild Life, ed. J.M. Lambert (Hull, 1891)

Goodramgate PR: The Parish Registers of Holy Trinity, Goodramgate, York, 1573–1812 ed. R.B. Cook, The Yorkshire Parish Register Society, 41 (York, 1911)

Henry Best: The Farming and Memorandum Books of Henry Best of Elmswell 1642, ed. D. Woodward, British Academy, Records of Social and Economic History, NS, 8 (1984)

HMC Hastings: Historical Manuscripts Commission: Report on the Manuscripts of the Late Reginald Rawdon Hastings, II, ed. F. Bickley (London, 1930)

Hornby Castle Accts: A Sixteenth-Century Survey and Year's Account of the Estates of Hornby Castle Lancashire, ed. W.H. Chippindall, Chetham Society, NS, 102 (1939)

Hull Bricklayers: The Order Book of the Brotherhood of Bricklayers, Tilers, Wallers, Plasterers and Pavers of Kingston upon Hull, ed. W.F.W. Transactions of the East Riding Antiquarian Society, 29 (1949), pp. 49–61

Hull Customs: The Customs Accounts of Hull 1453–1490, ed. W.R. Childs, Yorkshire Archaeological Society, Record Series, 144 (1986)

Hull Deeds: Calendar of the Ancient Deeds, etc. of Hull, ed. L.M. Stanewell (Hull, 1951)

Hull Labour: 'Labour Regulation at Hull, 1560', ed. D. Woodward, *Yorkshire Archaeological Journal*, 51 (1979), 101–4

Hull Plan: The Changing Plan of Hull 1290–1650 ed. R. Horrox (Hull, 1978)

Hull Prices: 'Wheat Prices in Elizabethan Hull', ed. D. Woodward, *Yorkshire Archaeological Journal*, 52 (1980), 173

Hull Registers: Aggregate Analyses from the Parish Registers of Holy Trinity and St Mary, Hull, Cambridge Group for the Study of Population and Social Structure

Hull Rentals: Selected Rentals and Accounts of Medieval Hull, 1293–1528, ed. R. Horrox, Yorkshire Archaeological Society, Record Series, 141 (1983)

Hull Trinity House Building: 'The Accounts of the Building of Trinity House, Hull, 1465–1476', ed. D. Woodward, *Yorkshire Archaeological Journal*, 62 (1990)

Hull Trinity House Order Book: The First Order Book of the Hull Trinity House, 1632–65, ed. F.W. Brooks, Yorkshire Archaeological Society, 105 (1942)

Kirkby Stephen Accts: 'Kirkby Stephen Churchwardens' Accounts', ed. J. Breay, *Transactions of the Cumberland and Westmorland Antiquarian and Archaeological Society*, 49 (1949), 56–65

Levens Letters: 'All Things is Well Here': Letters from Hugh James of Levens to James Grahme, 1692–95, ed. A. Bagot and J. Munby, Cumberland and Westmorland Antiquarian and Archaeological Society, Record Series, 10 (1988)

Liverpool Burgesses: 'The Burgess Rolls of Liverpool during the Seventeenth Century', ed. E.M. Hance and T.N. Morton *Transactions of the Historic Society of Lancashire and Cheshire*, 36 (1887), 129–58

Liverpool Town Books: J.A. Twemlow, *Liverpool Town Books*, 2 vols. (Liverpool, 1918)

Louth Accts: The First Churchwardens' Book of Louth 1500–1524, ed. R.C. Dudding (Oxford, 1941)

Manchester Court Leet: The Court Leet Records of the Manor of Manchester, I, 1552–86, ed. J.P. Earwaker (Manchester, 1884)

Naworth Accts: *Naworth Estate and Household Accounts, 1648–60*, ed. C.R. Hudleston, Surtees Society Publications, 168 (1958)

Newcastle Accts: *The Accounts of the Chamberlains of Newcastle upon Tyne 1508–1511*, ed. C.M. Fraser, The Society of Antiquaries of Newcastle upon Tyne (1987)

Northumberland Accts: *The Estate Accounts of the Earls of Northumberland, 1562–1637*, ed. M.E. James, Surtees Society Publications, 163 (1955)

Norwich Records: *The Records of the City of Norwich*, 2 vols., ed. W. Hudson and J.C. Tingey (Norwich and London, 1910)

Oxford Apprentices: *Oxford City Apprentices, 1697–1800*, ed. M. Graham, Oxford History Society, NS, 31 (1987)

Percy Papers: *The Household Papers of Henry Percy Ninth Earl of Northumberland (1564–1632)*, ed. G.R. Batho, Camden Society, 3rd series, 93 (1962)

Plymouth Accts: *Plymouth Building Accounts of the Sixteenth and Seventeenth Centuries*, Devon and Cornwall Record Society, NS, 12 (Torquay, 1967)

Sandgate Castle Accts: 'Sandgate Castle, 1539–40', *Archaeologia Cantiana*, 20 (1893) 228–57

Selby Accts: *Monastery and Society in the Middle Ages: Selected Account Rolls from Selby Abbey, Yorkshire, 1398–1537*, ed. J.H. Tillotson (Woodbridge, Suffolk, 1988)

Selby Wills: *Selby Wills*, ed. F. Collins, Yorkshire Archaeological Society Record Series, 47 (1912)

Stockport Inventories: *Stockport Probate Records 1578–1619*, ed. C.B. Phillips and J.H. Smith, Record Society of Lancashire and Cheshire, 124 (1985)

Stout Autobiography: *The Autobiography of William Stout of Lancaster*, ed. J.D. Marshall (Manchester, 1967)

Stratford Minutes I–V: *Minutes and Accounts of the Corporation of Stratford-upon-Avon*, I, *1553–66*, ed. E.I. Fripp, Dugdale Society Publications, 1 (1921); II, *1566–77, ibid.*, 3 (1924); III, *1577–86, ibid.*, 5 (1926); IV, *1586–92, ibid.*, 10 (1929); V, *1593–98*, ed. L. Fox, *ibid.*, 35 (1990)

Tattershall Castle Accts: *The Building Accounts of Tattershall Castle 1434–1472*, ed. W.D. Simpson, The Lincoln Record Society, 55 (1960)

TED: *Tudor Economic Documents*, 3 vols. ed. R.H. Tawney and E. Power (London, 1924)

Tudor Proclamations: *Tudor Royal Proclamations*, 3 vols., ed. P.L. Hughes and J.F. Larkin (New Haven and London, 1969)

Two Yorkshire Diaries: *Two Yorkshire Diaries*, ed. C.E. Whiting, Yorkshire Archaeological Society, Record Series, 117 (1952)

YCR: *York Civic Records*, I–IX: ed. A. Raine and D. Sutton, Yorkshire Archaeological Society, Record Series, 98, 103, 106, 108, 110, 112, 115, 119, 138 (1939–53, 1978)

York Descriptions: *York as they saw it – from Alcuin to Lord Fisher*, ed. D. and M.Palliser (York, 1979)

York Freemen: *Register of the Freemen of the City of York vol. I, 1272–1558*, Surtees Society Publications, 96 (1897)

York Memorandum Book: *York Memorandum Book, part II, 1388–1493*, ed. M. Sellers, Surtees Society Publications, 125 (1915)

York Quarter Sessions: 'The Minute Book of the York Court of Quarter Sessions 1638–1662', ed. J.W. Fowkes, *Yorkshire Archaeological Journal*, 41 (1966), 449–54

Secondary sources

Abel, W. 1980. *Agricultural Fluctuations in Europe from the thirteenth to the twentieth centuries*, London

Airs, M. 1975. *The Making of the English Country House, 1500–1640*, London

Alldridge, N. 1986. 'The Mechanics of Decline: Population, Migration and Economy in Early Modern Chester', in M. Reed (ed.), *English Towns in Decline, 1350 to 1800*, Working Paper no. 1, Centre for Urban History, University of Leicester, Leicester

1988. 'Loyalty and identity in Chester parishes 1540–1640', in S.J. Wright (ed.), *Parish, Church and People: Local studies in lay religion 1350–1750*, London

Appleby, A.B. 1973. 'Disease or Famine? Mortality in Cumberland and Westmorland, 1580–1640', *Economic History Review*, 2nd series, 26, 403–32

Archer, I.W. 1991. *The Pursuit of Stability: Social Relations in Elizabethan London*, Cambridge

Arkell, T. 1987. 'The Incidence of Poverty in England in the Later Seventeenth Century', *Social History*, 12, 23–47

Armstrong, P. 1987. *The Archaeology of the Beverley Gate, Hull: Interim Report*, Hull

Armstrong P. & Ayers, B. 1987. *Excavations in High Street and Blackfriargate*, East Riding Archaeologist, 8

Ayers, B. 1979. *Excavations at Chapel Lane Staith 1978*, East Riding Archaeologist, 5

Barnes, H. 1891. 'Visitations of Plague in Cumberland and Westmorland', *Transactions of the Cumberland and Westmorland Antiquarian and Archaeological Society*, 41, 158–86

Bartlett, J.N. 1959–60. 'The Expansion and Decline of York in the Later Middle Ages', *Economic History Review*, 2nd series, 12, 17–33

Barty-King, H. 1991. *A Country Builder: The Story of Richard Durtnell & Sons of Brasted, 1591–1991*, London

Beckinsale, B.W. 1969. 'The Characteristics of the Tudor North', *Northern History*, 4, 67–83

Beier, A.L. & Finlay, R. 1986. *The Making of the Metropolis: London 1500–1700*, London

Ben-Amos, I.K. 1988. 'Service and the Coming of Age of Young Men in Seventeenth-century England', *Continuity and Change*, 3, 41–64

Berg, M. 1987. 'Women's Work, Mechanisation and the Early Phases of Industrialisation in England', in P. Joyce (ed.), *The Historical Meanings of Work*, Cambridge, 64–98

Beveridge, W. 1939. *Prices and Wages in England: I, Price Tables: Mercantile Era*, London

Bindoff, S.T. 1961. 'The Making of the Statute of Artificers', in S.T. Bindoff, J. Hurstfield, and C.H. Williams (eds.), *Elizabethan Government and Society*, London

Blockmans, W.P. & Prevenier, W. 1978. 'Poverty in Flanders and Brabant from the Fourteenth to the Mid-Sixteenth Century: Sources and Problems', *Acta Historiae Neerlandicae*, 10, Hague, Boston, London, 20–57

Bolton, J.L. 1980. *The Medieval English Economy, 1150–1500*, London

Bonney, M. 1990. *Lordship and the Urban Community: Durham and its Overlords 1250–1540*, Cambridge

Boulton, J. 1987a. *Neighbourhood and Society: A London Suburb in the Seventeenth Century*, Cambridge

1987b. 'Constructing a Wage Series for Building Labourers', unpublished paper

Bourne, G. 1966. *Change in the Village*, London

Brooks, F.W. 1939. 'A Medieval Brick-Yard at Hull', *Journal of the British Archaeological Association*, 3rd series, 4, 151–74

1945. 'A Wage-Scale for Seamen, 1546', *English Historical Review*, 60, 234–46

Brown, H.P. & Hopkins, S.V. 1981. *A Perspective of Wages*, London and New York

Brunskill, E. 1951. 'Two Hundred Years of Parish Life in York', *The Yorkshire Architectural and York Archaeological Society, Annual Report 1950–1*, 17–58

Brunskill, R.W. 1970. *Illustrated Handbook of Vernacular Architecture*, London

Burnett, J. 1966. *Plenty and Want: A Social History of Diet in England from 1815 to the Present Day*, London

Butcher, A.F. 1978. 'Rent, Population and Economic Change in Late-Medieval Newcastle', *Northern History*, 14, 67–77

Chalklin, C.W. 1974. *The Provincial Towns of Georgian England: A Study of the Building Process 1740–1820*, London

Challis, C.E. 1989. *Currency and the Economy in Tudor and early Stuart England*, Historical Association, New Appreciations in History, 4

Charles, L. & Duffin, L. 1985. *Women and Work in Pre-Industrial England*, London

Clark, A. 1919. *Working Life of Women in the Seventeenth Century*, London

Clark, P. 1981. *Country Towns in Pre-industrial England*, Leicester

1983. *The English Alehouse: A Social History 1200–1830*, London

Clark, P., Gaskin, K., & Wilson, A. 1989. *Population Estimates of English Small Towns 1550–1851*, Centre for Urban History, University of Leicester, Working Paper no. 3, Leicester

Clark, P. & Slack, P. 1972. *Crisis and Order in English Towns 1500–1700*, London

1976. *English Towns in Transition 1500–1700*, London

Clarkson, L.A. 1971. *The Pre-Industrial Economy in England 1500–1750*, London

1975. *Death, Disease and Famine in Pre-Industrial England*, London

1982. 'Wage-Labour, 1500–1800', in K.D. Brown, *The English Labour Movement 1700–1951*, Dublin, 1–27

Clay, C.G.A. 1984. *Economic Expansion and Social Change: England 1500–1700*, 2 vols., London

Clemens, P.G.E. 1976. 'The Rise of Liverpool, 1665–1750', *Economic History Review*, 2nd series, 29, 211–25

Coleman, D. 1955–6. 'Labour in the English Economy of the Seventeenth Century', *Economic History Review*, 2nd series, 8, 280–95

Collins, E.J.T. 1975. 'Dietary Change and Cereal Consumption in Britain in the Nineteenth Century', *Agricultural History Review*, 23, 97–115

Colvin, H.M. 1975. *The History of the King's Works*: III, *1485–1660*, London

1982. *The History of the King's Works*: IV, *1485–1660*, London

Cooney, E.W. 1955–6. 'The Origins of the Victorian Master Builders', *Economic History Review*, 2nd series, 8, 167–76

Corfield, P.J. 1982. *The Impact of English Towns, 1700–1800*, Oxford

Cross, C. 1987. 'Northern Women in the Early Modern Period: The Female Testators of Hull and Leeds, 1520–1650', *Yorkshire Archaeological Journal*, 59, 83–94

Crossley, D.W. 1972. 'The Performance of the Glass Industry in Sixteenth-Century England', *Economic History Review*, 2nd series, 25, 421–33

Cunningham, H. 1990. 'The Employment and Unemployment of Children in England, *c.* 1680–1851', *Past and Present*, 126, 115–50

Cunningham, W. 1894. 'Dr Cunningham and His Critics', *Economic Journal*, 4, 508–18

Davies, W.J. 1956. 'A Description of the Trade and Shipping of Hull during the Seventeenth Century', unpublished MA thesis, University of Wales, Cardiff, unpaginated

Davis, R. 1964. *The Trade and Shipping of Hull, 1500–1700*, East Yorkshire Local History Society Publications, no. 17

Dobb, M. 1960. *Wages*, Cambridge

Dobson, C.R. 1980. *Masters and Journeymen: A Prehistory of Industrial Relations 1717–1800*, London

Dobson, R.B. 1973. 'Admissions to the Freedom of the City of York in the Later Middle Ages', *Economic History Review*, 2nd series, 26, 1–22

Drummond, J.C. & Wilbraham, A. 1964. *The Englishman's Food: Five Centuries of English Diet*, London

Dunlop, J. 1912. *English Apprenticeship and Child Labour: A History*, London

Dyer, A. 1973. *The City of Worcester in the Sixteenth Century*, Leicester
 1979. 'Growth and Decay in English Towns 1500–1700', *Urban History Yearbook*, Leicester, 60–72

Dyer, C. 1986. 'English Peasant Buildings in the Later Middle Ages', *Medieval Archaeology*, 30, 19–45
 1989. *Standards of Living in the Later Middle Ages: Social Change in England c. 1200–1520*, Cambridge

Earle, P. 1977. *The World of Defoe*, Newton Abbot

Eden, F.M. 1966 (1st edn 1797). *The State of the Poor*, 3 vols., London

Elliott, V.B. 1978. 'Mobility and Marriage in Pre-Industrial England', unpublished PhD thesis, University of Cambridge

Ellis, S. & Crowther, D.R. 1990. *Humber Perspectives: A Region Through the Ages*, Hull

Evans, J.T. 1979. *Seventeenth-Century Norwich: Politics, Religion and Government, 1620–1690*, Oxford

Falkus, M. 1976. 'Lighting in the Dark Ages of English Economic History', in D.C. Coleman & A.H. John, *Trade, Government and Economy in Pre-Industrial England*, London, 248–73

Farr, M.W. 1977. 'Nicholas Eyffeler of Warwick, Glazier', *Miscellany*, I, Dugdale Society Publications, 31, 29–110

Fisher, F.J. 1965. 'Influenza and Inflation in Tudor England', *Economic History Review*, 2nd series, 18, 120–9
 1990. *London and the English Economy 1500–1700*, London

Flinn, M.W. 1962. *Men of Iron: The Crowleys in the Early Iron Industry*, Edinburgh
 1984. *The History of the British Coal Industry*, II: *1700–1830*, Oxford

Foot, S. 1980. *The Effect of the Elizabethan Statute of Artificers on Wages in England*, Exeter Research Group, Discussion Paper 5

Freudenberger, H. & Cummins, G. 1976. 'Health, Work and Leisure before the Industrial Revolution', *Explorations in Economic History*, 13, 1–12

Gilboy, E.W. 1934. *Wages in Eighteenth Century England*, Cambridge, Mass

Gillett, E. 1970. *A History of Grimsby*, London

Gillett, E. & MacMahon, K.A. 1989. *A History of Hull*, Hull

Gittings, C. 1984. *Death, Burial and the Individual in Early Modern England*, London

Glassman, D. & Redish, A. 1988. 'Currency Depreciation in Early Modern England and France', *Explorations in Economic History*, 25, 75–97

Goldberg, P.J.P. 1986. 'Female Labour, Service and Marriage in Northern Towns during the Later Middle Ages', *Northern History*, 22, 18–38

Goldthwaite, R.A. 1980. *The Building of Renaissance Florence: An Economic and Social History*, Baltimore and London

Groombridge, M.J. 1952. 'The City Guilds of Chester', *Journal of the Chester and North Wales Architectural, Archaeological and Historic Society*, 39, 93–107

Guy, J. 1990. *Tudor England*, Oxford

Hatcher, J. 1977. *Plague, Population and the English Economy 1348–1530*, London
    1993. *The History of the British Coal Industry*, vol. I: *Before 1700: Towards the Age of Coal*, Oxford

Hey, D. 1972. *The Rural Metalworkers of the Sheffield Region*, University of Leicester, Dept. of English Local History, Occasional Papers, 2nd series, 5, Leicester

Hill, B. 1989. *Women, Work, and Sexual Politics in Eighteenth-Century England*, London

Hill, C. 1967. *Reformation to Industrial Revolution*, London

Hill, J.W.F. 1956. *Tudor and Stuart Lincoln*, Cambridge
    1966. *Georgian Lincoln*, Cambridge

Hilton, R.H. 1985. 'Women Traders in Medieval England', in his *Class, Conflict and the Crisis of Feudalism; Essays in Medieval Social History*, London

Hobsbawm, E.J. 1964. *Labouring Men: Studies in the History of Labour*, London

Holderness, B.A. 1976. *Pre-Industrial England: Economy and Society from 1500–1750*, London

Hopkins, E. 1982. 'Working Hours and Conditions during the Industrial Revolution: A Re-Appraisal', *Economic History Review*, 2nd series, 35, 53–66

Hoskins, W.G. 1953. 'The Rebuilding of Rural England, 1570–1640', *Past and Present*, 4, 44–59
    1963. *Provincial England*, London
    1964. 'Harvest Fluctuations and English Economic History, 1480–1619', *Agricultural History Review*, 12, 28–46
    1968. 'Harvest Fluctuations and English Economic History, 1620–1759', *Agricultural History Review*, 16, 15–31
    1976. *The Age of Plunder: The England of Henry VIII 1500–1547*, London and New York

Houston, R.A. 1982. 'The Development of Literacy in Northern England, 1640–1750', *Economic History Review*, 2nd series, 35, 199–216

Howell, R. 1967. *Newcastle upon Tyne and the Puritan Revolution: A Study of the Civil War in the North of England*, Oxford

Hughes, E. 1952. *North Country Life in the Eighteenth Century: The North East 1700–1750*, Oxford

Hughes, J. 1971. 'The Plague in Carlisle 1597/98', *Cumberland and Westmorland Antiquarian and Archaeological Society*, 71, 52–63

Hunt, E.H. & Botham, F.W. 1987. 'Wages in Britain during the Industrial Revolution', *Economic History Review*, 2nd series, 40, 380–99

Hutchins, B.L. 1900. 'The Regulation of Wages by Gilds and Town Authorities', *Economic Journal*, 10, 404–11

Hutton, D. 1985. 'Women in Fourteenth-Century Shrewsbury', in Charles & Duffin (1985), 83–99

Jackson, G. 1972. *Hull in the Eighteenth Century: A Study in Economic and Social History*, Oxford

James, F.G. 1951. 'The Population of the Diocese of Carlisle in 1676', *Cumberland and Westmorland Antiquarian and Archaeological Society*, 51, 137–41

Jones, B.C. 1960. 'Westmorland Pack-Horse Men in Southampton', *Cumberland and Westmorland Antiquarian and Archaeological Society*, 59, 65–84

1983. 'Carlisle Brickmakers and Bricklayers 1652–1752', *Cumberland and Westmorland Antiquarian and Archaeological Society*, 83, 125–9

1986. 'House Building in Carlisle in the Middle Ages', *Cumberland and Westmorland Antiquarian and Archaeological Society*, 86, 101–8

Jones, G.P. 1953. 'The Repairing of Crummock Bridge, Holm Cultram, 1554', *Cumberland and Westmorland Antiquarian and Archaeological Society*, 52, 85–100

Joyce, P. 1987. *The Historical Meanings of Work*, Cambridge

Kelsall, R.K. 1938. 'The General Trend of Real Wages in the North of England during the Eighteenth Century', *Yorkshire Archaeological Journal*, 33, 49–55

1939. 'Statute Wages during a Yorkshire Epidemic, 1679–81', *Yorkshire Archaeological Journal*, 34, 310–16

Keynes, J.M. 1960 (1st edn, 1936). *The General Theory of Employment, Interest and Money*, London

Kitching, C.J. 1981. 'Fire, Disasters and Fire Relief in Sixteenth Century England: The Nantwich Fire of 1583', *Bulletin of the Institute of Historical Research*, 54, 172–87

Knoop, D. & Jones, G.P. 1935. *The London Mason in the Seventeenth Century*, Manchester

1949. *The Medieval Mason: An Economic History of English Stone Building in the Later Middle Ages and Early Modern Times*, Manchester (1st edn, 1933)

Lacey, K.E. 1985. 'Women and Work in Fourteenth and Fifteenth Century London', in Charles and Duffin (1985), 24–82

Laslett, P. 1983. *The World We Have Lost – Further Explored*, London

Laughton, J.W. 1987–8. 'The House that John Built: A Study of the Building of a Seventeenth-Century House in Chester', *Journal of the Chester Archaeological Society*, 70, 99–132

Law, C.M. 1972. 'Some Notes on the Urban Population of England and Wales in the Eighteenth Century', *The Local Historian*, 10, 13–26

Levine, D. & Wrightson, K. 1991. *The Making of an Industrial Society: Whickham 1560–1765*, Oxford

Lewis, W.A. 1959. 'Economic Development with Unlimited Supplies of Labour', in A.N. Agarwala & S.P. Singh, *The Economics of Underdevelopment*, London, 400–49

Lilburn, A.J. 1986. 'Seventeenth-Century Accounts relating to Forts on Holy Island and at the Mouth of the Tyne, 1675–1681/2', *Archaeologia Aeliana*, 5th series, 14, 135–42

Lindert, P.H. & Williamson, J.G. 1983. 'English Workers' Living Standards during the Industrial Revolution: A New Look', *Economic History Review*, 2nd series, 36, 1–25

Linebaugh, P. 1982. 'Labour History without the Labour Process: A Note on John Gast and his Times', *Social History*, 7, 319–28

Lipson, E. 1934. *The Economic History of England*, 3 vols, London

Lis, C. & Soly, H. 1982. *Poverty and Capitalism in Pre-Industrial Europe*, Brighton

Lloyd, T.H. 1961. 'Some Aspects of the Building Industry in Medieval Stratford-upon-Avon', *Dugdale Society Occasional Papers*, no. 14, Oxford

Loschky, D. 1980. 'Seven Centuries of Real Income per Wage Earner Reconsidered', *Economica*, 47, 459–65

Louw, H. 1989. 'Of *Ancient Rights & Privileges*: Demarcation Disputes between the Companies of Joiners and Housecarpenters, Millwrights and Trunkmakers of Newcastle upon Tyne *c.* 1580–*c.* 1740', *Archaeologia Aeliana*, 5th series, 17, Newcastle

MacCaffrey, W.T. 1958. *Exeter 1540–1640*, Cambridge, Mass.

Machin, R. 1977. 'The Great Rebuilding: A Reassessment', *Past and Present*, 77, 33–56

Mantoux, P. 1961. *The Industrial Revolution in the Eighteenth Century*, London

Marshall, J.D. 1975. 'Kendal in the Late Seventeenth and Eighteenth Centuries', *Cumberland and Westmorland Antiquarian and Archaeological Society*, 75, 188–257

Minchinton, W.E. 1972. *Wage Regulation in Pre-Industrial England*, Newton Abbot

Moore, J.S. 1993. 'Jack Fisher's 'Flu: A Visitation Revisited', *Economic History Review*, 46, 280–307

Moorman, M.C. 1950. 'Ann Tyson's Ledger: An Eighteenth-Century Account Book', *Cumberland and Westmorland Antiquarian and Archaeological Society*, 50, 152–63

Morris, R.H. 1893. *Chester in the Plantagenet and Tudor Reigns*, Chester

Neave, D. 1983. 'William Catlyn (1628–1709), of Hull, the Architect of Wilberforce's Birthplace?', *East Yorkshire Local History Society Bulletin*, 28, 8–12

Neave, D. & Woodward, D. 1979. 'Memorials to a Yorkshire Family', *Country Life*, 166, no. 4292, 1230–5

Nef, J.U. 1966. 'Prices and Industrial Capitalism in France and England', in E. Carus-Wilson (ed.), *Essays in Economic History*, 1, 108–34

Oppenheim, M. 1926. 'The Royal Dockyards', in *VCH Kent*, II

Outhwaite, R.B. 1982. *Inflation in Tudor and Stuart England*, London

Palliser, D.M. 1972. 'The Trade Gilds of Tudor York', in Clark & Slack (1972), 86–116

1973a. 'Epidemics in Tudor York, *Northern History*, 8, 45–63

1973b. 'York under the Tudors: The Trading Life of the Northern Capital', in A. Everitt, *Perspectives in English Urban History*, London, 39–59

1979. *Tudor York*, Oxford

1982. 'Tawney's Century: Brave New World or Malthusian Trap?', *Economic History Review*, 2nd series, 35, 339–53

1983. *The Age of Elizabeth: England under the later Tudors 1547–1603*, London

Penn, S.A.C. 1987. 'Female Wage-Earners in Late Fourteenth-Century England', *Agricultural History Review*, 35, 1–14

Penn, S.A.C. & Dyer, C. 1990 'Wages and Earnings in Late Medieval England: Evidence from the Enforcement of the Labour Laws', *Economic History Review*, 2nd series, 43, 356–76

Perriam, D.R. 1987. 'The Demolition of the Priory of St Mary, Carlisle', *Cumberland and Westmorland Antiquarian and Archaeological Society*, 87, 127–58

Phillips, C.B. 1981. 'The Population of Kendal in 1576', *Cumberland and Westmorland Antiquarian and Archaeological Society*, 81, 57–62

1984. 'Town and Country: Economic Change in Kendal *c*. 1550–1700', in P. Clark, *The Transformation of English Provincial Towns*, London

1985. 'The Kendal Shoemakers in the Seventeenth Century', in P. Riden, *Probate Records and the Local Community*, Gloucester, 29–51

Phythian-Adams, C. 1979. *Desolation of a City: Coventry and the Urban Crisis of the Later Middle Ages*, Cambridge

Pound, J.F. 1966. 'The Social and Trade Structure of Norwich 1525–1575', *Past and Present*, 34, 49–69

Power, M.J. 1972. 'East London Housing in the Seventeenth Century', in Clark & Slack (1972), 237–62

1978. 'The East and West in Early-Modern London', in E.W. Ives, R.J. Knecht, & J.J. Scarisbrick, *Wealth and Power in Tudor England*, London, 167–85

Prior, M. 1985. 'Women and the Urban Economy: Oxford 1500–1800', in her *Women in English Society 1500–1800*, London, 93–117

Purvis, J.S. 1947. 'Dilapidations in Parsonage Property', *Yorkshire Archaeological Journal*, 36, 316–37

Ramsey, P. 1963. *Tudor Economic Problems*, London

Rappaport, S. 1983, 1984. 'Social Structure and Mobility in Sixteenth-Century London', 2 parts, *The London Journal*, 9, 197–35, and 10, 108–34

1989. *Worlds Within Worlds: Structures of Life in Sixteenth-Century London*, Cambridge

Reed, M. 1981. 'Economic Structure and Change in Seventeenth-Century Ipswich', in P. Clark, *Country Towns in Pre-Industrial England*, Leicester

Reed, M. 1986. *English Towns in Decline 1350–1800*, Centre for Urban History, University of Leicester, Working Papers no. 1, Leicester

Riden, P. 1985. *Probate Records and the Local Community*, Gloucester

Roberts, M.F. 1981. 'Wages and Wage-Earners in England: The Evidence of the Wage Assessments, 1563–1725', unpublished University of Oxford DPhil dissertation

1985. '"Words They Are Women, And Deeds They Are Men": Images of Work and Gender in Early Modern England', in Charles & Duffin (1985), 122–80

Rogers, J.E.T. 1882 and 1887. *A History of Prices in England*, vols. III and IV, *1401–1582* (1882); vols. V and VI, *1583–1702* (1887); Oxford

1908. *Six Centuries of Work and Wages: The History of English Labour*, London

Rosen, A. 1981. 'Winchester in Transition, 1580–1700', in P. Clark, (1981), 143–95

Rule, J. 1981. *The Experience of Labour in Eighteenth-Century England*, London

1986. *The Labouring Classes in Early Industrial England, 1750–1850*, London

1987. 'The Property of Skill in the Period of Manufacture', in P. Joyce (1987), 99–118

Salzman, L.F. 1952. *Building in England down to 1540: A Documentary History*, Oxford

Scholliers, P. 1989. *Real Wages in Nineteenth and Twentieth Century Europe: Historical and Comparative Perspectives*, New York, Oxford and Munich

Schwarz, L.D. 1985. 'The Standard of Living in the Long Run: London, 1700–1860', *Economic History Review*, 2nd series, 38, 24–41

1989. 'The Formation of the Wage: Some Problems', in P. Scholliers (1989), 21–39

Shammas, C. 1990. *The Pre-industrial Consumer in England and America*, Oxford

Shrewsbury, J.F.D. 1971. *A History of Bubonic Plague in the British Isles*, Cambridge

Slack, P. 1985. *The Impact of Plague in Tudor and Stuart England*, London

1988. *Poverty and Policy in Tudor and Stuart England*, London and New York

Small, C.M. 1989. 'The Crown as an Employer of Wage Labour in Angevin Basilicata', *Social History*, 14, 323–41

Smith, A.H. 1989. 'Labourers in Late Sixteenth-Century England: A Case Study from North Norfolk', 2 parts, *Continuity and Change*, 4, 11–52, 367–94

Snell, K.D.M. 1985. *Annals of the Labouring Poor: Social Change and Agrarian England, 1660–1900*, Cambridge

Sonenscher, M. 1987. 'Mythical Work: Workshop Production and the *Compagnonnages* of Eighteenth-Century France', in P. Joyce (1987), 31–63

1989. *Work and Wages: Natural Law, Politics and the Eighteenth-Century French Trades*, Cambridge

Sowler, T. 1972. *A History of the Town and Borough of Stockton-on-Tees*, Teesside

Speck, W.A. 1989. 'The Revolution of 1688 in the North of England', *Northern History*, 25, 188–204

Spufford, M. 1990. 'The Limitations of the Probate Inventory', in J. Chartres and D. Hey (eds.), *English Rural Society, Essays in Honour of Joan Thirsk*, Cambridge, 139–74

Steinfeld, R.J. 1991. *The Invention of Free Labor: The Employment Relation in English and American Law and Culture, 1350–1870*, Chapel Hill and London

Stephens, W.B. 1969. 'The Overseas Trade of Chester in the early Seventeenth Century', *Transactions of the Historic Society of Lancashire and Cheshire*, 120, 23–34

Storey, A. 1967. *Trinity House of Kingston upon Hull*, Hull

Supple, B.E. 1964. *Commercial Crisis and Change in England 1600–1642*, Cambridge

Swanson, H. 1983. *Building Craftsmen in Late Medieval York*, Borthwick Papers, 63

1988. 'The Illusion of Economic Structure: Craft Guilds in Late Medieval English Towns', *Past and Present*, 121, 29–48

1989. *Medieval Artisans: An Urban Class in Late Medieval England*, London

Taylor, A.H. 1917. 'The Municipal Records of Tenterden', *Archaeologia Cantiana*, 32, 283–302

Taylor, N.J. 1987. *The Archaeology of the Beverley Gate, Hull: Interim Report*, Hull

Thirsk, J. 1967. *The Agrarian History of England and Wales, IV: 1500–1640*, Cambridge

1978. *Economic Policy and Projects: The Development of a Consumer Society in Early Modern England*, Oxford

1984. 'Stamford in the Sixteenth and Seventeenth Centuries', in J. Thirsk, *The Rural Economy of England: Collected Essays*, London

1985. *The Agrarian History of England and Wales, Vii: 1640–1750*, Cambridge

Thomas, J.H. 1933. *Town Government in the Sixteenth Century*, London

Thomas, K. 1964. 'Work and Leisure in Pre-Industrial Society', *Past and Present* 29, 50–66

Tomlinson, H. 1973. 'The Ordnance Office and the King's Forts, 1660–1714', *Architectural History*, 16, 5–25

Tyson, B. 1979. 'Low Park Barn, Rydale: The Reconstruction of a Farm Building in Westmorland in the Seventeenth Century', *Cumberland and Westmorland Antiquarian and Archaeological Society*, 79, 85–97

1980. 'Rydal Hall Farmyard: the Development of a Westmorland Farmstead before 1700', *Cumberland and Westmorland Antiquarian and Archaeological Society*, 80, 113–29

1982a. 'Some Traditional Buildings in the Troutbeck Valley: A Documentary Study', *Cumberland and Westmorland Antiquarian and Archaeological Society*, 82, 151–76

1982b. 'Unerigg (Ewanrigg) Hall, Maryport, Cumbria', *Transactions of the Ancient Monuments Society*, NS, 26, 68–93

1983a. 'Building Work at Stockbridge Hall, its Farmyard and Neighbourhood, 1660–1710', *Cumberland and Westmorland Antiquarian and Archaeological Society*, 83, 107–24

1983b. 'William Thackeray's Rebuilding of Rose Castle Chapel, Cumbria, 1673–75', *Transactions of the Ancient Monuments Society*, NS, 27, 61–76

1984. 'The Work of William Thackeray and James Swingler at Flatt Hall (Whitehaven Castle) and other Cumbrian Buildings, 1676–1684', *Transactions of the Ancient Monuments Society*, 28, 61–92

1988. 'Two Post-Mills at Whitehaven in the Seventeenth Century', *Cumberland and Westmorland Antiquarian and Archaeological Society*, 88, 177–91

Tzannatos, Z. 1986–7. 'Female Pay: Has the State Unshackled the Market', *Economic Affairs*, Dec./Jan. 1986/7

Unwin, G. 1904. *Industrial Organisation in the Sixteenth and Seventeenth Centuries*, London

1908. *The Gilds and Companies of London*, London

Unwin, R.W. 1971. 'Trade and Transport in the Humber, Ouse and Trent Basins, 1660–1770', unpublished PhD thesis, University of Hull

VCH Beverley: The Victoria History of the County of York East Riding, VI, Beverley, ed. K.J. Allison, Oxford, 1989

VCH Hull: The Victoria History of the County of York East Riding, I, The City of Kingston upon Hull, ed. K.J. Allison, Oxford, 1969

VCH York: The Victoria History of the County of York, The City of York, ed. P.M. Tillott, Oxford, 1961

Vries, J. de. 1978. 'An Inquiry into the Behaviour of Wages in the Dutch Republic and Southern Netherlands, 1580–1800', *Acta Historiae Neerlandicae*, 10, 79–97

1985. 'The Population and Economy of the Pre-Industrial Netherlands', *Journal of Interdisciplinary History*, 15, 661–82

Walker, M.J. 1981. 'The Guild Control of Trades in England, c. 1660–1820', unpublished paper, Economic History Society Conference, University of Loughborough

Walter, J. & Schofield, R. 1989. *Famine and Disease and the Social Order in Early Modern Society*, Cambridge

Weatherill, L. 1988. *Consumer Behaviour and Material Culture in Britain 1660–1760*, London

Webb, S. & B. 1904. 'The Assize of Bread', *Economic Journal*, 14, 196–218

Whipp, R. 1987. '"A Time to Every Purpose": An Essay on Time and Work', in P. Joyce (1987), 210–36

Wigfull, J.R. 1929. 'House Building in Queen Elizabeth's Days', *Transactions of the Hunter Archaeological Society*, 3, 66–73

Willan, T.S. 1980. *Elizabethan Manchester*, Chetham Society, 3rd series, 27
  1983. 'Plague in Perspective: The Case of Manchester in 1605', *Transactions of the Historic Society of Lancashire and Cheshire*, 132, 29–40
Willen, D. 1984. 'Guildswomen in the City of York, 1560–1700', *The Historian: A Journal of History*, 46, 204–18
Wilson, C. 1965. *England's Apprenticeship 1603–1763*, London
Winchester, A.J.L. 1986. 'Medieval Cockermouth', *Cumberland and Westmorland Antiquarian and Archaeological Society*, 86, 109–28
Wood, G.H. 1901. 'Statutory Wage Rates', *Economic Journal*, 11, 151–6
Woodward, D. 1968a. 'Robert Brerewood: An Elizabethan Master Craftsman', *The Cheshire Round*, 1, 311–16
  1968b. 'The Leather Industry of Chester 1558–1625', *Transactions of the Historic Society of Lancashire and Cheshire*, 119, 65–111
  1969. 'The Assessment of Wages by Justices of Peace', *The Local Historian*, 8, 293–9
  1970a. 'Sources for Urban History: 1. Freemen's Rolls', *The Locan Historian*, 9, 89–95
  1970b. *The Trade of Elizabethan Chester*, Hull
  1970c. 'The Overseas Trade of Chester 1600–1650', *Transactions of the Historic Society of Lancashire and Cheshire*, 122, 25–42
  1973. 'The Anglo-Irish Livestock Trade in the Seventeenth Century', *Irish Historical Studies*, 18, 489–523
  1977. 'Cattle Droving in the Seventeenth Century: A Yorkshire Example', in W.H. Chaloner & B.M. Ratcliffe, *Trade and Transport*, Manchester
  1979. 'Labour Regulation at Hull, 1560: Select Document', *The Yorkshire Archaeological Journal*, 51
  1980a. 'The Background to the Statute of Artificers: The Genesis of Labour Policy, 1558–1563', *Economic History Review*, 2nd series, 33, 32–44
  1980b. 'Wage Regulation in Mid-Tudor York', *The York Historian*, 3, 7–9
  1981. 'Wage Rates and Living Standards in Pre-Industrial England', *Past and Present*, 91, 28–46
  1985. '"Swords into Ploughshares": Recycling in Pre-Industrial England', *Economic History Review*, 2nd series, 38, 175–91
  1994. 'The Determination of Wage Rates in the Early Modern North of England', *Economic History Review*, 47, 22–43
Wootton, B. 1962. *The Social Foundations of Wage Policy: A Study of Contemporary British Wage and Salary Structure*, Cambridge
Wright, S. 1985. 'Churmaids, Huswyfes and Hucksters: The Employment of Women in Tudor and Stuart Salisbury', in L. Charles & L. Duffin (1985), 100–21
Wrightson, K. 1982. *English Society 1580–1680*, London
  1987. 'The Social Order of Early Modern England: Three Approaches', in R.M. Smith and K. Wrightson (eds.), *The World We Have Gained*, Cambridge, 177–202
Wrigley, E.A. 1985. 'Urban Growth and Agricultural Change: England and the Continent in the Early Modern Period', *Journal of Interdisciplinary History*, 15, 683–728
Wrigley, E.A. & Schofield, R.S. 1981. *The Population History of England 1541–1871: A Reconstruction*, London

Index

The place name attributed to particular individuals is usually the place where the person was working; in some cases it is the place of domicile; and, probably, in most cases it is both the place of work and the place of domicile (the text will make these things clear).

Millington, William, Chester, joiner,
80
Missell, Robert, Whitby, master mariner,
241
Mold, Henry, Hull, carpenter, 118
Monkhouse, Isaac, Carlisle, mason, 242
Moon, Richard, Chester, journeyman
joiner, 70
Moor, Thomas, Newcastle, joiner, 81
Morley, Henry, Hull, labourer, 101–2
Mosse, Widow, Chester, labourer, 110
Mounfort, Thomas, Chester, mason, 36

Nantwich, Cheshire, joiner of, 157
Nef, J.U., historian, 212
Neston, near Chester, 111
Newcastle, Northumberland, 7, 9
apprentices at; control of, 57; status of
fathers of, 54–5; fees of, 60; marriage
of, 59; origin of, 53–4; payments to,
62; probation of, 56; turnover of,
58–9; work of, 62
Civil War at, 204
coal from, 222–3, 225
council revenues of, 37
drink prices at, 286–7
food and drink at, 149, 150–1, 154, 155,
159
freemen's rolls of, 23, 24
gilds at, 18, 29, 30; bricklayers' gild, 31,
32, 48, 73; demarcation disputes
between, 34, 50; entry fees of, 74;
joiners' gild, 31, 48, 80, 119; records
of, 30; vigour of, 35; women's role in,
88
holidays at, 132
hours of work at, 125
intensity of work at, 128–9
journeymen at, 64, 71
labourers at, 95–6, 98, 105–6, 113
mobility of labour at, 162
night watching at, 126
overtime at, 126
parishes of, 15, 106
perquisites at, 145, 146
plague at, 196–7
population of, 8
poverty at, 192
property values at, 228
records of, 248
riverfront repairs at, 5
seasonality at, 136, 140–1
storehouse at, 122
Sunday working at, 131
trade of, 8, 10
Trinity House of, 6, 20

wages at, 12, 38, 171, 173–9, 195, 200–3,
270–1
wage regulation at, 185
welfare payments at, 160–1
workplace at, 121
Newlove, John, Hull, carpenter, 230–1
William, Hull, carpenter, 133
Newton, Matthew, Durham, waller, 113
Nicholson, Frances, Widow, Penrith, 233
John, Penrith, carpenter, 233
Martin, Hull, labourer, 104
Nixon, Thomas, Carlisle, bricklayer, 60
Norham Castle, Northumberland, 50
North Wales, coal from, 222
Northampton, building craftsmen in, 22n
Northamptonshire, wage regulation in,
184
northern England, definition of, 7
real wages of, 213–15
Norwich, building craftsmen in, 22n
labourers from, 98
Nottingham, bells from, 162
Nottinghamshire, timber from, 45
nutrition and work, 128

Offley, Robert, London, 74
William, London, 74
Oliver, Matthew, Newcastle, joiner, 34
Richard, Durham, labourer, 113
Robert, Hull, labourer, 104
Thomas, Newcastle, carpenter, 34
Oxford, apprentices of, 22
Bishop of, 35
wages at, 194

Pacocke, William, York, overseer, 166
Page, William, Beverley, 27–8
Paget, Robert, Hull, carpenter, 41, 143–4,
163
Pain, William, author, 21
Paley, Mr, York, tenant, 227
Palin, Richard, Chester, journeyman
joiner, 71
parishes, significance of, 116–18
Park, Robert, York, labourer, 107
Parsyvall, John, Beverley, plumber and
glazier, 37
Peach, Philip, Lincoln, plumber, 42, 43
Pears, Ellen, Chester, plumber, 88–9
Peter, Chester, plumber, 89
Pearson, John, Hull, labourer, 104
Penrith, Cumberland, 10
building craftsmen of, 238
wages at, 272
Penrose, William, Hull, carpenter, 26
perquisites, 142–59

Cambridge Studies in Population, Economy and Society in Past Time

Titles available in paperback are marked with an asterisk